The Elements of Computing Systems

Noam Nisan and Shimon Schocken

The Elements of Computing Systems
Building a Modern Computer from First Principles

Second Edition

The MIT Press
Cambridge, Massachusetts
London, England

This book was set in Times by Westchester Publishing Services. Printed and bound in the United States of America.

Library of Congress Cataloging-in-Publication Data

Names: Nisan, Noam, author. | Schocken, Shimon, author.
Title: The elements of computing systems : building a modern computer from first principles / Noam Nisan and Shimon Schocken.
Description: Second edition. | Cambridge, Massachusetts : The MIT Press, [2021] | Includes index.
Identifiers: LCCN 2020002671 | ISBN 9780262539807 (paperback)
Subjects: LCSH: Electronic digital computers.
Classification: LCC TK7888.3 .N57 2020 | DDC 004.16—dc23
LC record available at https://lccn.loc.gov/2020002671

10   9   8   7   6   5   4   3   2

To our parents,
for teaching us that less is more.

Contents

Preface

What I hear, I forget; What I see, I remember; What I do, I understand.

—Confucius (551–479 B.C.)

It is commonly argued that enlightened people of the twenty-first century ought to familiarize themselves with the key ideas underlying BANG: Bits, Atoms, Neurons, and Genes. Although science has been remarkably successful in uncovering their basic operating systems, it is quite possible that we will never fully grasp how atoms, neurons, and genes actually work. Bits, however, and computing systems at large, entail a consoling exception: in spite of their fantastic complexity, one can completely understand how modern computers work, and how they are built. So, as we gaze with awe at the BANG around us, it is a pleasing thought that at least one field in this quartet can be fully laid bare to human comprehension.

Indeed, in the early days of computers, any curious person who cared to do so could gain a gestalt understanding of how the machine works. The interactions between hardware and software were simple and transparent enough to produce a coherent picture of the computer's operations. Alas, as digital technologies have become increasingly more complex, this clarity is all but lost: the most fundamental ideas and techniques in computer science—the very essence of the field—are now hidden under many layers of obscure interfaces and proprietary implementations. An inevitable consequence of this complexity has been specialization: the study of applied computer science became a pursuit of many niche courses, each covering a single aspect of the field.

We wrote this book because we felt that many computer science students are missing the forest for the trees. The typical learner is marshaled through a series of courses in programming, theory, and engineering, without pausing to appreciate the beauty of the picture at large. And the picture at large is such that hardware, software, and application systems are tightly interrelated through a hidden web of abstractions, interfaces, and contract-based implementations.

Failure to see this intricate enterprise in the flesh leaves many learners and professionals with an uneasy feeling that, well, they don't fully understand what's going on inside computers. This is unfortunate, since computers are the most important machines in the twenty-first century.

We believe that the best way to understand how computers work is to build one from scratch. With that in mind, we came up with the following idea: Let's specify a simple but sufficiently powerful computer system, and invite learners to build its hardware platform and software hierarchy from the ground up. And while we are at it, let's do it right. We are saying this because building a general-purpose computer from first principles is a huge enterprise.

Therefore, we identified a unique educational opportunity to not only build the thing, but also illustrate, in a hands-on fashion, how to effectively plan and manage large-scale hardware and software development projects. In addition, we sought to demonstrate the thrill of constructing, through careful reasoning and modular planning, fantastically complex and useful systems from first principles.

The outcome of this effort became what is now known colloquially as *Nand to Tetris*: a hands-on journey that starts with the most elementary logic gate, called Nand, and ends up, twelve projects later, with a general-purpose computer system capable of running Tetris, as well as any other program that comes to your mind. After designing, building, redesigning, and rebuilding the computer system several times ourselves, we wrote this book, explaining how any learner can do the same. We also launched the www.nand2tetris.org website, making all our project materials and software tools freely available to anyone who wants to learn, or teach, Nand to Tetris courses.

We are gratified to say that the response has been overwhelming. Today, Nand to Tetris courses are taught in numerous universities, high schools, coding boot camps, online platforms, and hacker clubs around the world. The book and our online courses became highly popular, and thousands of learners—ranging from high school students to Google engineers—routinely post reviews describing Nand to Tetris as their best educational experience ever. As Richard Feynman famously said: "What I cannot create, I do not understand." Nand to Tetris is all about understanding through creation. Apparently, people connect passionately to this maker mentality.

Since the publication of the book's first edition, we received numerous questions, comments, and suggestions. As we addressed these issues by modifying our online materials, a gap developed between the web-based and the book-based versions of Nand to Tetris. In addition, we felt that many book sections could benefit from more clarity and a better organization. So, after delaying this surgery as much as we could, we decided to roll up our sleeves and write a second edition, leading to the present book. The remainder of this preface describes this new edition, ending with a section that compares it to the previous one.

Scope

The book exposes learners to a significant body of computer science knowledge, gained through a series of hardware and software construction tasks. In particular, the following topics are illustrated in the context of hands-on projects:

- *Hardware:* Boolean arithmetic, combinational logic, sequential logic, design and implementation of logic gates, multiplexers, flip-flops, registers, RAM units, counters, Hardware Description Language (HDL), chip simulation, verification and testing.

- *Architecture:* ALU/CPU design and implementation, clocks and cycles, addressing modes, fetch and execute logic, instruction set, memory-mapped input/output.

- *Low-level languages:* Design and implementation of a simple machine language (binary and symbolic), instruction sets, assembly programming, assemblers.

- *Virtual machines:* Stack-based automata, stack arithmetic, function call and return, handling recursion, design and implementation of a simple VM language.

- *High-level languages:* Design and implementation of a simple object-based, Java-like language: abstract data types, classes, constructors, methods, scoping rules, syntax and semantics, references.

- *Compilers:* Lexical analysis, parsing, symbol tables, code generation, implementation of arrays and objects, two-tier compilation.

- *Programming:* Implementation of an assembler, virtual machine, and compiler, following supplied APIs. Can be done in any programming language.

- *Operating systems:* Design and implementation of memory management, math library, input/ output drivers, string processing, textual output, graphical output, high-level language support.

- *Data structures and algorithms:* Stacks, hash tables, lists, trees, arithmetic algorithms, geometric algorithms, running time considerations.

- *Software engineering:* Modular design, the interface/implementation paradigm, API design and documentation, unit testing, proactive test planning, quality assurance, programming at the large.

A unique feature of Nand to Tetris is that all these topics are presented cohesively, with a clear, over-arching purpose: building a modern computer system from the ground up. In fact, this has been our topic selection criterion: the book focuses on the minimal set of topics necessary for building a general-purpose computer system, capable of running programs written in a high-level, object-based language. As it turns out, this critical set includes most of the fundamental concepts and techniques, as well as some of the most beautiful ideas, in applied computer science.

Courses

Nand to Tetris courses are typically cross-listed for both undergraduate and graduate students, and are highly popular among self-learners. Courses based on this book are "perpendicular" to the typical computer science curriculum and can be taken at almost any point during the program. Two natural slots are CS-2—an introductory yet post-programming course—and

CS-99—a synthesis course coming at the end of the program. The former course entails a forward-looking, systems-oriented introduction to applied computer science, while the latter is an integrative, project-based course that fills gaps left by previous courses.

Another increasingly popular slot is a course that combines, in one framework, key topics from traditional computer architecture courses and compilation courses. Whichever purpose they are made to serve, Nand to Tetris courses go by many names, including Elements of Computing Systems, Digital Systems Construction, Computer Organization, Let's Build a Computer, and, of course, Nand to Tetris.

The book and the projects are highly modular, starting from the top division into Part I: Hardware and Part II: Software, each comprising six chapters and six projects. Although we recommend going through the full experience, it is entirely possible to learn each of the two parts separately. The book and the projects can support two independent courses, each six to seven weeks long, a typical semester-long course, or two semester-long courses, depending on topic selection and pace of study.

The book is completely self-contained: all the necessary knowledge for building the hardware and software systems described in the book is given in its chapters and projects. Part I: Hardware requires no prerequisite knowledge, making projects 1–6 accessible to any student and self-learner. Part II: Software and projects 7–12 require programming (in any high-level language) as a prerequisite.

Nand to Tetris courses are not restricted to computer science majors. Rather, they lend themselves to learners from any discipline who seek to gain a hands-on understanding of hardware architectures, operating systems, compilation, and software engineering—all in one course. Once again, the only prerequisite (for part II) is programming. Indeed, many Nand to Tetris students are nonmajors who took an introduction to computer science course and now wish to learn more computer science without committing themselves to a multicourse program. Many other learners are software developers who wish to "go below," understand how the enabling technologies work, and become better high-level programmers.

Following the acute shortage of developers in the hardware and software industries, there is a growing demand for compact and focused programs in applied computer science. These often take the form of coding boot camps and clusters of online courses designed to prepare learners for the job market without going through the full gamut of an academic degree. Any such solid program must offer, at minimum, working knowledge of programming, algorithms, and systems. Nand to Tetris is uniquely positioned to cover the systems element of such programs, in the framework of one course. Further, the Nand to Tetris projects provide an attractive means for synthesizing, and putting to practice, much of the algorithmic and programmatic knowledge learned in other courses.

Resources

All the necessary tools for building the hardware and software systems described in the book are supplied freely in the Nand to Tetris software suite. These include a hardware simulator, a CPU emulator, a VM emulator (all in open source), tutorials, and executable versions of the assembler, virtual machine, compiler, and operating system described in the book. In addition, the www.nand2tetris.org website includes all the project materials—about two hundred test programs and test scripts—allowing incremental development and unit testing of each one of the twelve projects. The software tools and project materials can be used as is on any computer running Windows, Linux, or macOS.

Structure

Part I: Hardware consists of chapters 1–6. Following an introduction to Boolean algebra, chapter 1 starts with the elementary Nand gate and builds a set of elementary logic gates on top of it. Chapter 2 presents combinational logic and builds a set of adders, leading up to an ALU. Chapter 3 presents sequential logic and builds a set of registers and memory devices, leading up to a RAM. Chapter 4 discusses low-level programming and specifies a machine language in both its symbolic and binary forms. Chapter 5 integrates the chips built in chapters 1–3 into a hardware architecture capable of executing programs written in the machine language presented in chapter 4. Chapter 6 discusses low-level program translation, culminating in the construction of an assembler.

Part II: Software consists of chapters 7–12 and requires programming background (in any language) at the level of introduction to computer science courses. Chapters 7–8 present stack-based automata and describe the construction of a JVM-like virtual machine. Chapter 9 presents an object-based, Java-like high-level language. Chapters 10–11 discuss parsing and code generation algorithms and describe the construction of a two-tier compiler. Chapter 12 presents various memory management, algebraic, and geometric algorithms and describes the implementation of an operating system that puts them to practice. The OS is designed to close gaps between the high-level language implemented in part II and the hardware platform built in part I.

The book is based on an *abstraction-implementation* paradigm. Each chapter starts with an Introduction describing relevant concepts and a generic hardware or software system. The next section is always Specification, describing the system's abstraction, that is, the various services that it is expected to deliver, one way or another. Having presented the *what*, each chapter proceeds to discuss *how* the abstraction can be realized, leading to a proposed Implementation section. The next section is always Project, providing step-by-step guidelines, testing materials, and software tools for building and unit-testing the system described in the chapter. The closing Perspective section highlights noteworthy issues left out from the chapter.

Projects

The computer system described in the book is *for real*. It is designed to be built, and it works! The book is geared toward active readers who are willing to get their hands dirty and build the computer from the ground up. If you'll take the time and effort to do so, you will gain a depth of understanding and a sense of accomplishment unmatched by mere reading.

The hardware devices built in projects 1, 2, 3, and 5 are implemented using a simple Hardware Description Language (HDL) and simulated on a supplied software-based hardware simulator, which is exactly how hardware architects work in industry. Projects 6, 7, 8, 10, and 11 (assembler, virtual machine I + II, and compiler I + II) can be written in any programming language. Project 4 is written in the computer's assembly language, and projects 9 and 12 (a simple computer game and a basic operating system) are written in Jack—the Java-like high-level language for which we build a compiler in chapters 10 and 11.

There are twelve projects altogether. On average, each project entails a weekly homework load in a typical rigorous university-level course. The projects are self-contained and can be done (or skipped) in any desired order. The full Nand to Tetris experience entails doing all the projects in their order of appearance, but this is only one option.

Is it possible to cover so much ground in a one-semester course? The answer is yes, and the proof is in the pudding: more than 150 universities teach semester-long Nand to Tetris courses. The student satisfaction is exceptional, and Nand to Tetris MOOCs are routinely listed at the top of the top-rated lists of online course. One reason why learners respond to our methodology is *focus*. Except for obvious cases, we pay no attention to optimization, leaving this important subject to other, more specific courses. In addition, we allow students to assume error-free inputs. This eliminates the need to write code for handling exceptions, making the software projects significantly more focused and manageable. Dealing with incorrect input is of course critically important, but this skill can be honed elsewhere, for example, in project extensions and in dedicated programming and software design courses.

The Second Edition

Although Nand to Tetris was always structured around two themes, the second edition makes this structure explicit: The book is now divided into two distinct and standalone parts, Part I: Hardware and Part II: Software. Each part consists of six chapters and six projects and begins with a newly written introduction that sets the stage for the part's chapters. Importantly, the two parts are independent of each other. Thus, the new book structure lends itself well to quarter-long as well as semester-long courses.

In addition to the two new introduction chapters, the second edition features four new appendices. Following the requests of many learners, these new appendices give focused presentations of various technical topics that, in the first edition, were scattered across the chapters. Another new appendix provides a formal proof that any Boolean function can be built from Nand operators, adding a theoretical perspective to the applied hardware construction projects. Many new sections, figures, and examples were added.

All the chapters and project materials were rewritten with an emphasis on separating abstraction from implementation—a major theme in Nand to Tetris. We took special care to add examples and sections that address the thousands of questions that were posted over the years in Nand to Tetris Q&A forums.

Acknowledgments

The software tools that accompany the book were developed by our students at IDC Herzliya and at the Hebrew University. The two chief software architects were Yaron Ukrainitz and Yannai Gonczarowski, and the developers included Iftach Ian Amit, Assaf Gad, Gal Katzhendler, Hadar Rosen-Sior, and Nir Rozen. Oren Baranes, Oren Cohen, Jonathan Gross, Golan Parashi, and Uri Zeira worked on other aspects of the tools. Working with these student-developers has been a great pleasure, and we are proud to have had the opportunity to play a role in their education.

We also thank our teaching assistants, Muawyah Akash, Philip Hendrix, Eytan Lifshitz, Ran Navok, and David Rabinowitz, who helped run early versions of the course that led to this book. Tal Achituv, William Bahn, Yong Bakos, Tali Gutman and Michael Schröder provided great help with various aspects of the course materials, and Aryeh Schnall, Tomasz Różański and Rudolf Adamkovič gave meticulous editing suggestions. Rudolf's comments were particularly enlightening, for which we are very grateful.

Many people around the world got involved in Nand to Tetris, and we cannot possibly thank them individually. We do take one exception. Mark Armbrust, a software and firmware engineer from Colorado, became the guarding angel of Nand to Tetris learners. Volunteering to manage our global Q&A forum, Mark answered numerous questions with great patience and graceful style. His answers never gave away the solutions; rather, he guided learners how to apply themselves and see the light on their own. In doing so, Mark has gained the respect and admiration of numerous learners around the world. Serving at the forefront of Nand to Tetris for more than ten years, Mark wrote 2,607 posts, discovered dozens of bugs, and wrote corrective scripts and fixes. Doing all this in addition to his regular day job, Mark became a pillar of the Nand to Tetris community, and the community became his second home. Mark died in March 2019, following a struggle with heart disease that lasted several months. During his hospitalization, Mark received a daily stream of hundreds of emails from Nand to Tetris students. Young men and women from all over the world thanked Mark for his boundless generosity and shared the impact that he has had on their lives.

In recent years, computer science education became a powerful driver of personal growth and economic mobility. Looking back, we feel fortunate that we decided, early on, to make all our teaching resources freely available, in open source. Quite simply, any person who wants to do so can not only learn but also teach Nand to Tetris courses, without any restrictions. All you have to do is go to our website and take what you need, so long as you operate in a nonprofit setting. This turned Nand to Tetris into a readily available vehicle for disseminating high-quality computer science education, freely and equitably. The result became a vast educational ecosystem, fueled by endless supplies of good will. We thank the many people around the world who helped us make it happen.

I   Hardware

The true voyage of discovery consists not of going to new places, but of having a new pair of eyes.

—Marcel Proust (1871–1922)

This book is a voyage of discovery. You are about to learn three things: how computer systems work, how to break complex problems into manageable modules, and how to build large-scale hardware and software systems. This will be a hands-on journey, as you create a complete and working computer system from the ground up. The lessons you will learn, which are far more important than the computer itself, will be gained as side effects of these constructions. According to the psychologist Carl Rogers, "The only kind of learning which significantly influences behavior is self-discovered or self-appropriated—truth that has been assimilated in experience." This introduction chapter sketches some of the discoveries, truths, and experiences that lie ahead.

Hello, World Below

If you have some programming experience, you've probably encountered something like the program below early in your training. And if you haven't, you can still guess what the program is doing: it displays the text Hello World and terminates. This particular program is written in Jack—a simple, Java-like high-level language:

```
// First example in Programming 101
class Main {
   function void main() {
      do Output.printString("Hello World");
      return;
   }
}
```

Trivial programs like `Hello World` are deceptively simple. Did you ever stop to think about what it takes to *actually run* such a program on a computer? Let's look under the hood. For starters, note that the program is nothing more than a sequence of plain characters, stored in a text file. This abstraction is a complete mystery for the computer, which understands only instructions written in machine language. Thus, if we want to execute this program, the first thing we must do is parse the string of characters of which the high-level code is made, uncover its semantics—figure out what the program seeks to do—and then generate low-level code that reexpresses this semantics using the machine language of the target computer. The result of this elaborate translation process, known as *compilation*, will be an executable sequence of machine language instructions.

Of course, machine language is also an abstraction—an agreed upon set of binary codes. To make this abstraction concrete, it must be realized by some *hardware architecture*. And this architecture, in turn, is implemented by a certain set of chips—registers, memory units, adders, and so on. Now, every one of these hardware devices is constructed from lower-level, *elementary logic gates*. And these gates, in turn, can be built from primitive gates like *Nand* and *Nor*. These primitive gates are very low in the hierarchy, but they, too, are made of several *switching devices*, typically implemented by transistors. And each transistor is made of—Well, we won't go further than that, because that's where computer science ends and physics starts.

You may be thinking: "On *my* computer, compiling and running programs is much easier—all I have to do is click this icon or write that command!" Indeed, a modern computer system is like a submerged iceberg: most people get to see only the top, and their knowledge of computing systems is sketchy and superficial. If, however, you wish to explore beneath the surface, then Lucky You! There's a fascinating world down there, made of some of the most beautiful stuff in computer science. An intimate understanding of this underworld is what separates naïve programmers from sophisticated developers—people who can create complex hardware and software technologies. And the best way to understand how these technologies work—and we mean understand them in the marrow of your bones—is to build a complete computer system from the ground up.

Nand to Tetris

Assuming that we want to build a computer system from the ground up, which specific computer should we build? As it turns out, every general-purpose computer—every PC, smartphone, or server—is a Nand to Tetris machine. First, all computers are based, at bottom, on elementary logic gates, of which Nand is the most widely used in industry (we'll explain what exactly is a Nand gate in chapter 1). Second, every general-purpose computer can be programmed to run a Tetris game, as well as any other program that tickles your fancy. Thus, there is nothing unique about either Nand or Tetris. It is the word *to* in *Nand to Tetris* that turns this book into the magical journey that you are about to undertake: going all the way from a heap of barebone switching devices to a machine that engages the mind with text, graphics, animation, music, video, analysis, simulation, artificial intelligence, and all the capabilities that we came to expect from general-purpose computers. Therefore, it doesn't really matter which specific hardware platform and software hierarchy we will build, so long as they will be based on the same ideas and techniques that characterize *all* computing systems out there.

Figure I.1 describes the key milestones in the Nand to Tetris road map. Starting at the bottom tier of the figure, any general-purpose computer has an architecture that includes a ALU (Arithmetic Logic Unit) and a RAM (Random Access Memory). All ALU and RAM devices are made of elementary logic gates. And, surprisingly and fortunately, as we will soon see, all logic gates can be made from Nand gates alone. Focusing on the software hierarchy, all high-level languages rely on a suite of translators (compiler/interpreter, virtual machine, assembler) for reducing high-level code all the way down to machine-level instructions. Some high-level languages are interpreted rather than compiled, and some don't use a virtual machine, but the big picture is essentially the same. This observation is a manifestation of a fundamental computer science principle, known as the *Church-Turing conjecture*: at bottom, all computers are essentially equivalent.

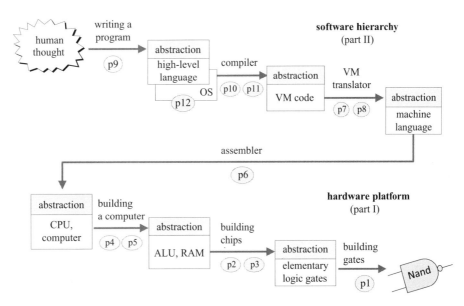

Figure I.1 Major modules of a typical computer system, consisting of a hardware platform and a software hierarchy. Each module has an *abstract view* (also called the module's *interface*) and an *implementation*. The right-pointing arrows signify that each module is implemented using abstract building blocks from the level below. Each circle represents a Nand to Tetris project and chapter—twelve projects and chapters altogether.

We make these observations in order to emphasize the generality of our approach: the challenges, insights, tips, tricks, techniques, and terminology that you will encounter in this book are exactly the same as those encountered by practicing hardware and software engineers. In that respect, Nand to Tetris is a form of initiation: if you'll manage to complete the journey, you will gain an excellent basis for becoming a hardcore computer professional yourself.

So, which specific hardware platform, and which specific high-level language, shall we build in Nand to Tetris? One possibility is building an industrial-strength, widely used computer model and writing a compiler for a popular high-level language. We opted against these choices, for three reasons. First, computer models come and go, and hot programming languages give way to new ones. Therefore, we didn't want to commit to any particular hardware/software configuration. Second, the computers and languages that are used in practice feature numerous details that have little instructive value, yet take ages to implement. Finally, we sought a hardware platform and a software hierarchy that could be easily controlled, understood, and extended. These considerations led to the creation of Hack, the computer platform built in part I of the book, and Jack, the high-level language implemented in part II.

Typically, computer systems are described *top-down*, showing how high-level abstractions can be reduced to, or realized by, simpler ones. For example, we can describe how binary machine instructions executing on the computer architecture are broken into microcodes that travel through the architecture's wires and end up manipulating the lower-level ALU and RAM chips. Alternatively, we can go *bottom-up*, describing how the ALU and RAM chips are judiciously designed to execute micro-codes that, taken together, form binary machine instructions. Both the top-down and the bottom-up approaches are enlightening, each giving a different perspective on the system that we are about to build.

In figure I.1, the direction of the arrows suggests a top-down orientation. For any given pair of modules, there is a right-pointing arrow connecting the higher module with the lower one. The meaning of this arrow is precise: it implies that the higher-level module is implemented using abstract building blocks from the level below. For example, a high-level program is implemented by translating each high-level statement into a set of abstract VM commands. And each VM command, in turn, is translated further into a set of abstract machine language instructions. And so it goes. The distinction between *abstraction* and *implementation* plays a major role in systems design, as we now turn to discuss.

Abstraction and Implementation

You may wonder how it is humanly possible to construct a complete computer system from the ground up, starting with nothing more than elementary logic gates. This must be a humongous enterprise! We deal with this complexity by breaking the system into *modules*. Each module is described separately, in a dedicated chapter, and built separately, in a standalone project. You might then wonder, how is it possible to describe and construct these modules in isolation? Surely they are interrelated! As we will demonstrate throughout the book, a good modular design implies just that: you can work on the individual modules independently, while completely ignoring the rest of the system. In fact, if the system is well designed, you can build these modules in any desired order, and even in parallel, if you work in a team.

The cognitive ability to "divide and conquer" a complex system into manageable modules is empowered by yet another cognitive gift: our ability to discern between the *abstraction* and the *implementation* of each module. In computer science, we take these words concretely: abstraction describes what the module does, and implementation describes how it does it. With this distinction in mind, here is the most important rule in system engineering: when using a module as a building block—*any module*—you are to focus exclusively on the module's abstraction, ignoring completely its implementation details.

For example, let's focus on the bottom tier of figure I.1, starting at the "computer architecture" level. As seen in the figure, the implementation of this architecture uses several building blocks from the level below, including a Random Access Memory. The RAM is a remarkable device. It may contain billions of registers, yet any one of them can be accessed directly, and almost instantaneously. Figure I.1 informs us that the computer architect should use this direct-access device abstractly, without paying any attention to how it is actually realized. All the work, cleverness, and drama that went into implementing the direct-access RAM magic—the *how*—should be completely ignored, since this information is irrelevant in the context of *using* the RAM for its effect.

Going one level downward in figure I.1, we now find ourselves in the position of having to build the RAM chip. How should we go about it? Following the right-pointing arrow, we see that the RAM implementation will be based on elementary logic gates and chips from the level below. In particular, the RAM storage and direct-access capabilities will be realized using *registers* and *multiplexers*, respectively. And once again, the same abstraction-implementation principle kicks in: we will use these chips as abstract building blocks, focusing on their interfaces, and caring naught about *their* implementations. And so it goes, all the way down to the Nand level.

To recap, whenever your implementation uses a lower-level hardware or software module, you are to treat this module as an off-the-shelf, black box abstraction: all you need is the documentation of the module's interface, describing *what* it can do, and off you go. You are to pay no attention whatsoever to *how* the module performs what its interface advertises. This abstraction-implementation paradigm helps developers manage complexity and maintain sanity: by dividing an overwhelming system into well-defined modules, we create manageable chunks of implementation work and localize error detection and correction. This is the most important design principle in hardware and software construction projects.

Needless to say, everything in this story hinges on the intricate art of *modular design*: the human ability to separate the problem at hand into an elegant collection of well-defined modules, each having a clear interface, each representing a reasonable chunk of standalone implementation work, each lending itself to an independent unit-testing program. Indeed, modular design is the bread and butter of applied computer science: every system architect routinely defines abstractions, sometimes referred to as *modules* or *interfaces*, and then implements them, or asks other people to implement them. The abstractions are often built layer upon layer, resulting in higher and higher levels of functionality. If the system architect designs a good set of modules, the implementation work will flow like clear water; if the design is slipshod, the implementation will be doomed.

Modular design is an acquired art, honed by seeing and implementing many well-designed abstractions. That's exactly what you are about to experience in Nand to Tetris: you will learn to appreciate the elegance and functionality of hundreds of hardware and software abstractions. You will then be guided how to implement each one of these abstractions, one step at a time, creating bigger and bigger chunks of functionality. As you push ahead in this journey, going from one chapter to the next, it will be thrilling to look back and appreciate the computer system that is gradually taking shape in the wake of your efforts.

Methodology

The Nand to Tetris journey entails building a hardware platform and a software hierarchy. The hardware platform is based on a set of about thirty logic gates and chips, built in part I of the book. Every one of these gates and chips, including the topmost computer architecture, will be built using a *Hardware Description Language*. The HDL that we will use is documented in appendix 2 and can be learned in about one hour. You will test the correctness of your HDL programs using a software-based hardware simulator running on your PC. This is exactly how hardware engineers work in practice: they build and test chips using software-based simulators. When they are satisfied with the simulated performance of the chips, they ship their specifications (HDL programs) to a fabrication company. Following optimization, the HDL programs become the input of robotic arms that build the hardware in silicon.

Moving up on the Nand to Tetris journey, in part II of the book we will build a software stack that includes an assembler, a virtual machine, and a compiler. These programs can be implemented in any high-level programming language. In addition, we will build a basic operating system, written in Jack.

You may wonder how it is possible to develop these ambitious projects in the scope of one course or one book. Well, in addition to modular design, our secret sauce is reducing design uncertainty to an absolute minimum. We'll provide elaborate scaffolding for each project, including detailed APIs, skeletal programs, test scripts, and staged implementation guidelines.

All the software tools that are necessary for completing projects 1–12 are available in the Nand to Tetris software suite, which can be downloaded freely from www.nand2tetris.org. These include a hardware simulator, a CPU emulator, a VM emulator, and executable versions of the hardware chips, assembler, compiler, and OS. Once you download the software suite to your PC, all these tools will be at your fingertips.

The Road Ahead

The Nand to Tetris journey entails twelve hardware and software construction projects. The general direction of development *across* these projects, as well as the book's table of contents, imply a bottom-up journey: we start with elementary logic gates and work our way upward, leading to a high-level, object-based programming language. At the same time, the direction of development *within* each project is top-down. In particular, whenever we present a hardware or software module, we will always start with an abstract description of *what* the module is designed to do and why it is needed. Once you understand the module's abstraction (a rich world in its own right), you'll proceed to implement it, using abstract building blocks from the level below.

So here, finally, is the grand plan of part I of our tour de force. In chapter 1 we start with a single logic gate—Nand—and build from it a set of elementary and commonly used logic gates like And, Or, Xor, and so on. In chapters 2 and 3 we use these building blocks for constructing an Arithmetic Logic Unit and memory devices, respectively. In chapter 4 we pause our hardware construction journey and introduce a low-level machine language in both its symbolic and binary forms. In chapter 5 we use the previously built ALU and memory units for building a Central Processing Unit (CPU) and a Random Access Memory (RAM). These devices will then be integrated into a hardware platform capable of running programs written in the machine language presented in chapter 4. In chapter 6 we describe and build an *assembler*, which is a program that translates low-level programs written in symbolic machine language into executable binary code. This will complete the construction of the hardware platform. This platform will then become the point of departure for part II of the book, in which we'll extend the barebone hardware with a modern software hierarchy consisting of a virtual machine, a compiler, and an operating system.

We hope that we managed to convey what lies ahead, and that you are eager to get started on this grand voyage of discovery. So, assuming that you are ready and set, let the countdown start: 1, 0, Go!

1   Boolean Logic

Such simple things, and we make of them something so complex it defeats us, Almost.

—John Ashbery (1927–2017)

Every digital device—be it a personal computer, a cell phone, or a network router—is based on a set of chips designed to store and process binary information. Although these chips come in different shapes and forms, they are all made of the same building blocks: elementary *logic gates*. The gates can be physically realized using many different hardware technologies, but their logical behavior, or *abstraction*, is consistent across all implementations.

In this chapter we start out with one primitive logic gate—Nand—and build all the other logic gates that we will need from it. In particular, we will build Not, And, Or, and Xor gates, as well as two gates named *multiplexer* and *demultiplexer* (the function of all these gates is described below). Since our target computer will be designed to operate on 16-bit values, we will also build 16-bit versions of the basic gates, like Not16, And16, and so on. The result will be a rather standard set of logic gates, which will be later used to construct our computer's processing and memory chips. This will be done in chapters 2 and 3, respectively.

The chapter starts with the minimal set of theoretical concepts and practical tools needed for designing and implementing logic gates. In particular, we introduce Boolean algebra and Boolean functions and show how Boolean functions can be realized by logic gates. We then describe how logic gates can be implemented using a Hardware Description Language (HDL) and how these designs can be tested using hardware simulators. This introduction will carry its weight throughout part I of the book, since Boolean algebra and HDL will come into play in every one of the forthcoming hardware chapters and projects.

1.1   Boolean Algebra

Boolean algebra manipulates two-state binary values that are typically labeled true/false, 1/0, yes/no, on/off, and so forth. We will use 1 and 0. A Boolean function is a function that operates on binary inputs and returns binary outputs. Since computer hardware is based on representing and manipulating binary values, Boolean functions play a central role in the specification, analysis, and optimization of hardware architectures.

Boolean operators: Figure 1.1 presents three commonly used Boolean functions, also known as *Boolean operators*. These functions are named And, Or, and Not, also written using the notation $x \cdot y$, $x + y$, and $\bar{x}$, or $x \wedge y$, $x \vee y$, and $\neg x$, respectively. Figure 1.2 gives the definition of *all* the possible Boolean functions that can be defined over two variables, along with their common names. These functions were constructed systematically by enumerating all the possible combinations of values spanned by two binary variables. Each operator has a conventional name that seeks to describe its underlying semantics. For example, the name of the Nand operator is shorthand for *Not-And*, coming from the observation that $\mathrm{Nand}\,(x, y)$ is equivalent to $\mathrm{Not}\,(\mathrm{And}\,(x, y))$. The Xor operator—shorthand for *exclusive or*—evaluates to 1 when exactly one of its two variables is 1. The Nor gate derives its name from *Not-Or*. All these gate names are not terribly important.

Figure 1.2 begs the question: What makes And, Or, and Not more interesting, or privileged, than any other subset of Boolean operators? The short answer is that indeed there is nothing special about And, Or, and Not. A deeper answer is that various subsets of logical operators can be used for expressing *any* Boolean function, and {And, Or, Not} is one such subset. If you find this claim impressive, consider this: any one of these three basic operators can be expressed using yet another operator—Nand. Now, *that's* impressive! It follows that any Boolean function can be realized using Nand gates only. Appendix 1, which is an optional reading, provides a proof of this remarkable claim.

Boolean Functions

Every Boolean function can be defined using two alternative representations. First, we can define the function using a *truth table*, as we do in figure 1.3. For each one of the 2^n possible tuples of variable values $v_1, \ldots, v_n$ (here $n = 3$), the table lists the value of $f(v_1, \ldots, v_n)$. In addition to this data-driven definition, we can also define Boolean functions using Boolean expressions, for example, $f(x, y, z) = (x \text{ Or } y) \text{ And Not}(z)$.

How can we verify that a given Boolean expression is equivalent to a given truth table? Let's use figure 1.3 as an example. Starting with the first row, we compute $f(0, 0, 0)$, which

x	y	x And y		x	y	x Or y		x	Not x
0	0	0		0	0	0		0	1
0	1	0		0	1	1		1	0
1	0	0		1	0	1			
1	1	1		1	1	1			

Figure 1.1 Three elementary Boolean functions.

| | | x | 0 | 0 | 1 | 1 |
		y	0	1	0	1
Constant 0	0		0	0	0	0
And	$x \cdot y$		0	0	0	1
x And Not y	$x \cdot \bar{y}$		0	0	1	0
x	x		0	0	1	1
Not x And y	$\bar{x} \cdot y$		0	1	0	0
y	y		0	1	0	1
Xor	$x \cdot \bar{y} + \bar{x} \cdot y$		0	1	1	0
Or	$x + y$		0	1	1	1
Nor	$\overline{x + y}$		1	0	0	0
Equivalence	$x \cdot y + \bar{x} \cdot \bar{y}$		1	0	0	1
Not y	$\bar{y}$		1	0	1	0
If y then x	$x + \bar{y}$		1	0	1	1
Not x	$\bar{x}$		1	1	0	0
If x then y	$\bar{x} + y$		1	1	0	1
Nand	$\overline{x \cdot y}$		1	1	1	0
Constant 1	1		1	1	1	1

Figure 1.2 All the Boolean functions of two binary variables. In general, the number of Boolean functions spanned by n binary variables (here $n = 2$) is 2^{2^n} (that's a lot of Boolean functions).

x	y	z	$f(x, y, z) = (x \text{ Or } y) \text{ And Not}(z)$
0	0	0	0
0	0	1	0
0	1	0	1
0	1	1	0
1	0	0	1
1	0	1	0
1	1	0	1
1	1	1	0

Figure 1.3 Truth table and functional definitions of a Boolean function (example).

is (0 Or 0) And Not (0). This expression evaluates to 0, the same value listed in the truth table. So far so good. A similar equivalence test can be applied to every row in the table—a rather tedious affair. Instead of using this laborious bottom-up proof technique, we can prove the equivalence top-down, by analyzing the Boolean expression $(x \text{ Or } y) \text{ And Not}(z)$. Focusing on the left-hand side of the And operator, we observe that the overall expression evaluates to 1 only when $((x \text{ is } 1) \text{ Or } (y \text{ is } 1))$. Turning to the right-hand side of the And operator, we observe that the overall expression evaluates to 1 only when $(z \text{ is } 0)$. Putting these two observations together, we conclude that the expression evaluates to 1 only when $(((x$ is 1) Or $(y$ is 1)) And $(z$ is 0)). This pattern of 0's and 1's occurs only in rows 3, 5, and 7 of the truth table, and indeed these are the only rows in which the table's rightmost column contains a 1.

Truth Tables and Boolean Expressions

Given a Boolean function of n variables represented by a Boolean expression, we can always construct from it the function's truth table. We simply compute the function for every set of values (row) in the table. This construction is laborious, and obvious. At the same time, the dual construction is not obvious at all: Given a truth table representation of a Boolean function, can we always synthesize from it a Boolean expression for the underlying function? The answer to this intriguing question is *yes*. A proof can be found in appendix 1.

When it comes to building computers, the truth table representation, the Boolean expression, and the ability to construct one from the other are all highly relevant. For example, suppose that we are called to build some hardware for sequencing DNA data and that our domain expert biologist wants to describe the sequencing logic using a truth table. Our job is to realize this logic in hardware. Taking the given truth table data as a point of departure, we can synthesize from it a Boolean expression that represents the underlying function. After simplifying the expression using Boolean algebra, we can proceed to implement it using logic gates, as we'll do later in the chapter. To sum up, a truth table is often a convenient means for describing some states of nature, whereas a Boolean expression is a convenient formalism for realizing this description in silicon. The ability to move from one representation to the other is one of the most important practices of hardware design.

We note in passing that although the truth table representation of a Boolean function is unique, every Boolean function can be represented by many different yet equivalent Boolean expressions, and some will be shorter and easier to work with. For example, the expression (Not $(x$ And $y)$ And (Not (x) Or $y)$ And (Not (y) Or $y))$ is equivalent to the expression Not (x). We see that the ability to simplify a Boolean expression is the first step toward hardware optimization. This is done using Boolean algebra and common sense, as illustrated in appendix 1.

1.2   Logic Gates

A *gate* is a physical device that implements a simple Boolean function. Although most digital computers today use electricity to realize gates and represent binary data, any alternative technology permitting switching and conducting capabilities can be employed. Indeed, over the years, many hardware implementations of Boolean functions were created, including magnetic, optical, biological, hydraulic, pneumatic, quantum-based, and even domino-based mechanisms (many of these implementations were proposed as whimsical "can do" feats). Today, gates are typically implemented as transistors etched in silicon, packaged as *chips.* In Nand to Tetris we use the words *chip* and *gate* interchangeably, tending to use the latter for simple instances of the former.

The availability of alternative switching technologies, on the one hand, and the observation that Boolean algebra can be used to abstract the behavior of logic gates, on the other, is extremely important. Basically, it implies that computer scientists don't have to worry about physical artifacts like electricity, circuits, switches, relays, and power sources. Instead, computer scientists are content with the abstract notions of Boolean algebra and gate logic, trusting blissfully that someone else—physicists and electrical engineers—will figure out how to actually realize them in hardware. Hence, primitive gates like those shown in figure 1.4 can be viewed as black box devices that implement elementary logical operations in one way or another—we don't care how. The use of Boolean algebra for analyzing the abstract behavior of logic gates was articulated in 1937 by Claude Shannon, leading to what is sometimes described as the most important M.Sc. thesis in computer science.

Primitive and Composite Gates

Since all logic gates have the same input and output data types (0's and 1's), they can be combined, creating *composite gates* of arbitrary complexity. For example, suppose we are asked to implement the three-way Boolean function And (a, b, c), which returns 1 when every one of its inputs is 1, and 0 otherwise. Using Boolean algebra, we can begin by observing that $a \cdot b \cdot c = (a \cdot b) \cdot c$, or, using prefix notation, And $(a, b, c) =$ And (And $(a, b), c$). Next, we can use this result to construct the composite gate depicted in figure 1.5.

We see that any given logic gate can be viewed from two different perspectives: internal and external. The right side of figure 1.5 gives the gate's internal architecture, or *implementation*, whereas the left side shows the gate *interface*, namely, its input and output pins and the behavior

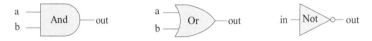

Figure 1.4   Standard gate diagrams of three elementary logic gates.

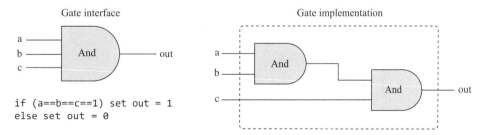

Figure 1.5   Composite implementation of a three-way And gate. The rectangular dashed outline defines the boundary of the gate interface.

that it exposes to the outside world. The internal view is relevant only to the gate builder, whereas the external view is the right level of detail for designers who wish to use the gate as an abstract, off-the-shelf component, without paying attention to its implementation.

Let us consider another logic design example: Xor. By definition, Xor (a, b) is 1 exactly when either a is 1 and b is 0 or a is 0 and b is 1. Said otherwise, Xor $(a, b) = $ Or $($And$(a,$ Not$(b))$, And $($Not $(a), b))$. This definition is implemented in the logic design shown in figure 1.6.

Note that the *interface* of any given gate is unique: there is only one way to specify it, and this is normally done using a truth table, a Boolean expression, or a verbal specification. This interface, however, can be realized in many different ways, and some will be more elegant and efficient than others. For example, the Xor implementation shown in figure 1.6 is one possibility; there are more efficient ways to realize Xor, using less logic gates and less inter-gate connections. Thus, from a functional standpoint, the fundamental requirement of logic design is that *the gate implementation will realize its stated interface, one way or another*. From an efficiency standpoint, the general rule is to try to use as few gates as possible, since fewer gates imply less cost, less energy, and faster computation.

To sum up, the art of logic design can be described as follows: Given a gate abstraction (also referred to as *specification*, or *interface*), find an efficient way to implement it using other gates that were already implemented.

1.3   Hardware Construction

We are now in a position to discuss how gates are actually built. Let us start with an intentionally naïve example. Suppose we open a chip fabrication shop in our home garage. Our first contract is to build a hundred Xor gates. Using the order's down payment, we purchase a soldering gun, a roll of copper wire, and three bins labeled "And gates," "Or gates," and "Not gates," each containing many identical copies of these elementary logic gates. Each of these gates is sealed in a plastic casing that exposes some input and output

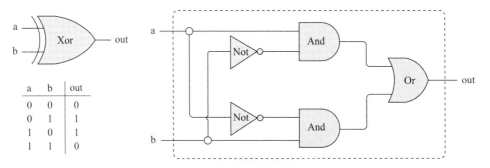

Figure 1.6   Xor gate interface (left) and a possible implementation (right).

pins, as well as a power supply port. Our goal is to realize the gate diagram shown in figure 1.6 using this hardware.

We begin by taking two And gates, two Not gates, and one Or gate and mounting them on a board, according to the figure's layout. Next, we connect the chips to one another by running wires among them and soldering the wire ends to the respective input/output pins.

Now, if we follow the gate diagram carefully, we will end up having three exposed wire ends. We then solder a pin to each one of these wire ends, seal the entire device (except for the three pins) in a plastic casing, and label it "Xor." We can repeat this assembly process many times over. At the end of the day, we can store all the chips that we've built in a new bin and label it "Xor gates." If we wish to construct some other chips in the future, we'll be able to use these Xor gates as black box building blocks, just as we used the And, Or, and Not gates before.

As you have probably sensed, the garage approach to chip production leaves much to be desired. For starters, there is no guarantee that the given chip diagram is correct. Although we can prove correctness in simple cases like Xor, we cannot do so in many realistically complex chips. Thus, we must settle for empirical testing: build the chip, connect it to a power supply, activate and deactivate the input pins in various configurations, and hope that the chip's input/output behavior delivers the desired specification. If the chip fails to do so, we will have to tinker with its physical structure—a rather messy affair. Further, even if we do come up with a correct and efficient design, replicating the chip assembly process many times over will be a time-consuming and error-prone affair. There must be a better way!

1.3.1   Hardware Description Language

Today, hardware designers no longer build anything with their bare hands. Instead, they design the chip architecture using a formalism called *Hardware Description Language*, or *HDL*. The designer specifies the chip logic by writing an *HDL program*, which is then subjected to a rigorous battery of tests. The tests are carried out virtually, using computer simulation: A special software tool, called a *hardware simulator*, takes the HDL program as input and creates a software representation of the chip logic. Next, the designer can instruct the simulator to test the virtual chip on various sets of inputs. The simulator computes the chip outputs, which are then compared to the desired outputs, as mandated by the client who ordered the chip built.

In addition to testing the chip's correctness, the hardware designer will typically be interested in a variety of parameters such as speed of computation, energy consumption, and the overall cost implied by the proposed chip implementation. All these parameters can be simulated and quantified by the hardware simulator, helping the designer optimize the design until the simulated chip delivers desired cost/performance levels.

Thus, using HDL, one can completely plan, debug, and optimize an entire chip before a single penny is spent on physical production. When the performance of the simulated chip satisfies the client who ordered it, an optimized version of the HDL program can become the blueprint from which many copies of the physical chip can be stamped in silicon. This final step in the chip design process—from an optimized HDL program to mass production—is typically outsourced to companies that specialize in robotic chip fabrication, using one switching technology or another.

Example: Building an Xor Gate: The remainder of this section gives a brief introduction to HDL, using an Xor gate example; a detailed HDL specification can be found in appendix 2.

Let us focus on the bottom left of figure 1.7. An HDL definition of a chip consists of a *header* section and a *parts* section. The header section specifies the chip *interface*, listing the chip name and the names of its input and output pins. The PARTS section describes the chip-parts from which the chip architecture is made. Each chip-part is represented by a single *statement* that specifies the part name, followed by a parenthetical expression that specifies how it is connected to other parts in the design. Note that in order to write such statements, the HDL programmer must have access to the interfaces of all the underlying

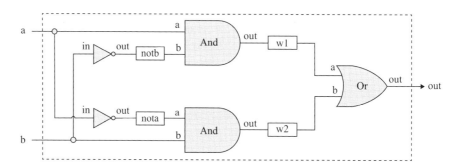

HDL program (Xor.hdl)	Test script (Xor.tst)	Output file (Xor.out)
``/* Xor (exclusive or) gate:
If a!=b out=1 else out=0. */
CHIP Xor {
IN a, b;
OUT out;
PARTS:
Not (in=a,   out=nota);
Not (in=b,   out=notb);
And (a=a,   b=notb, out=w1);
And (a=nota, b=b,   out=w2);
Or (a=w1,   b=w2,   out=out);
}```	```load Xor.hdl,
output-list a, b, out;
set a 0, set b 0,
eval, output;
set a 0, set b 1,
eval, output;
set a 1, set b 0,
eval, output;
set a 1, set b 1;
eval, output;```	```a	b	out

0	0	0
0	1	1
1	0	1
1	1	0```

Figure 1.7 Gate diagram and HDL implementation of the Boolean function Xor $(a, b) = $ Or (And $(a,$ Not $(b))$, And (Not (a), $b)$), used as an example. A test script and an output file generated by the test are also shown. Detailed descriptions of HDL and the testing language are given in appendices 2 and 3, respectively.

chip-parts: the names of their input and output pins, as well as their intended operation. For example, the programmer who wrote the HDL program listed in figure 1.7 must have known that the input and output pins of the Not gate are named in and out and that those of the And and Or gates are named a, b, and out. (The APIs of all the chips used in Nand to Tetris are listed in appendix 4).

Inter-part connections are specified by creating and connecting *internal pins*, as needed. For example, consider the bottom of the gate diagram, where the output of a Not gate is piped into the input of a subsequent And gate. The HDL code describes this connection by the pair of statements Not(..., out=nota) and And(a=nota, ...). The first statement creates an internal pin (outbound connection) named nota and pipes the value of the out pin into it. The second statement pipes the value of nota into the a input of an And gate. Two comments are in order here. First, internal pins are created "automatically" the first time they appear in an HDL program. Second, pins may have an unlimited fan-out. For example, in figure 1.7, each input is simultaneously fed into two gates. In gate diagrams, multiple connections are described by drawing them, creating forked patterns. In HDL programs, the existence of forks is inferred from the code.

The HDL that we use in Nand to Tetris has a similar look and feel to industrial strength HDLs but is much simpler. Our HDL syntax is mostly self-explanatory and can be learned by seeing a few examples and consulting appendix 2, as needed.

Testing

Rigorous quality assurance mandates that chips be tested in a specific, replicable, and well-documented fashion. With that in mind, hardware simulators are typically designed to run *test scripts*, written in a scripting language. The test script listed in figure 1.7 is written in the scripting language understood by the Nand to Tetris hardware simulator.

Let us give a brief overview of this test script. The first two lines instruct the simulator to load the Xor.hdl program and get ready to print the values of selected variables. Next, the script lists a series of testing scenarios. In each scenario, the script instructs the simulator to bind the chip inputs to selected data values, compute the resulting output, and record the test results in a designated output file. In the case of simple gates like Xor, one can write an exhaustive test script that enumerates all the input values that the gate can possibly get. In this case, the resulting output file (right side of figure 1.7) provides a complete empirical test that the chip is well behaving. The luxury of such certitude is not feasible in more complex chips, as we will see later.

Readers who plan to build the Hack computer will be pleased to know that all the chips that appear in the book are accompanied by skeletal HDL programs and supplied test scripts, available in the Nand to Tetris software suite. Unlike HDL, which must be learned in order to complete the chip specifications, there is no need to learn our testing language. At the same time, you have to be able to read and understand the supplied test scripts. The scripting language is described in appendix 3, which can be consulted on a need-to-know basis.

1.3.2 Hardware Simulation

Writing and debugging HDL programs is similar to conventional software development. The main difference is that instead of writing code in a high-level language, we write it in HDL, and instead of compiling and running the code, we use a *hardware simulator* to test it. The hardware simulator is a computer program that knows how to parse and interpret HDL code, turn it into an executable representation, and test it according to supplied test scripts. There exist many such commercial hardware simulators in the market. The Nand to Tetris software suite includes a simple hardware simulator that provides all the necessary tools for building, testing, and integrating all the chips presented in the book, leading up to the construction of a general-purpose computer. Figure 1.8 illustrates a typical chip simulation session.

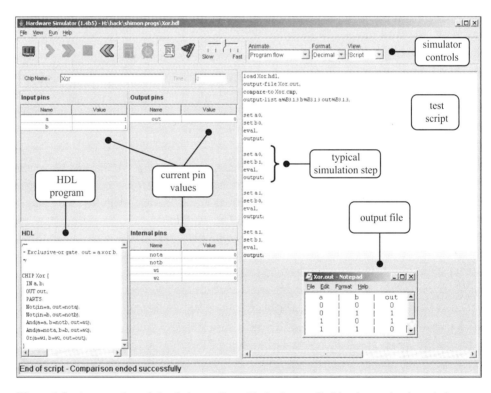

Figure 1.8 A screenshot of simulating an Xor chip in the supplied hardware simulator (other versions of this simulator may have a slightly different GUI). The simulator state is shown just after the test script has completed running. The pin values correspond to the last simulation step (a=b=1). Not shown in this screenshot is a *compare file* that lists the expected output of the simulation specified by this particular test script. Like the test script, the compare file is typically supplied by the client who wants the chip built. In this particular example, the output file generated by the simulation (bottom right of the figure) is identical to the supplied compare file.

1.4 Specification

We now turn to specify a set of logic gates that will be needed for building the chips of our computer system. These gates are ordinary, each designed to carry out a common Boolean operation. For each gate, we'll focus on the gate interface (*what* the gate is supposed to do), delaying implementation details (*how* to build the gate's functionality) to a later section.

1.4.1 Nand

The starting point of our computer architecture is the Nand gate, from which all other gates and chips will be built. The Nand gate realizes the following Boolean function:

a	b	Nand(a, b)
0	0	1
0	1	1
1	0	1
1	1	0

Or, using API style:

```
Chip name: Nand
Input:     a, b
Output:    out
Function:  if ((a==1) and (b==1)) then out = 0, else out = 1
```

Throughout the book, chips are specified using the API style shown above. For each chip, the API specifies the chip name, the names of its input and output pins, the chip's intended function or operation, and optional comments.

1.4.2 Basic Logic Gates

The logic gates that we present here are typically referred to as *basic*, since they come into play in the construction of more complex chips. The Not, And, Or, and Xor gates implement classical logical operators, and the multiplexer and demultiplexer gates provide means for controlling flows of information.

Not: Also known as *inverter*, this gate outputs the opposite value of its input's value. Here is the API:

```
Chip name: Not
Input:     in
Output:    out
Function:  if (in==0) then out = 1, else out = 0
```

And: Returns 1 when both its inputs are 1, and 0 otherwise:

```
Chip name: And
Input:     a, b
Output:    out
Function:  if ((a==1) and (b==1)) then out = 1, else out = 0
```

Or: Returns 1 when at least one of its inputs is 1, and 0 otherwise:

```
Chip name: Or
Input:     a, b
Output:    out
Function:  if ((a==0) and (b==0)) then out = 0, else out = 1
```

Xor: Also known as *exclusive or*, this gate returns 1 when exactly one of its inputs is 1, and 0 otherwise:

```
Chip name: Xor
Input:     a, b
Output:    out
Function:  if (a!=b) then out = 1, else out = 0
```

Multiplexer: A multiplexer is a three-input gate (see figure 1.9). Two input bits, named a and b, are interpreted as *data bits*, and a third input bit, named sel, is interpreted as a *selection bit*. The multiplexer uses sel to select and output the value of either a or b. Thus, a sensible name for this device could have been *selector*. The name *multiplexer* was adopted from communications systems, where extended versions of this device are used for serializing (multiplexing) several input signals over a single communications channel.

Demultiplexer: A demultiplexer performs the opposite function of a multiplexer: it takes a single input value and routes it to one of two possible outputs, according to a selector bit that selects the destination output. The other output is set to 0. Figure 1.10 gives the API.

1.4.3   Multi-Bit Versions of Basic Gates

Computer hardware is often designed to process multi-bit values—for example, computing a bitwise And function on two given 16-bit inputs. This section describes several 16-bit logic gates that will be needed for constructing our target computer platform. We note in passing that the logical architecture of these *n*-bit gates is the same, irrespective of *n*'s value (e.g., 16, 32, or 64 bits). HDL programs treat multi-bit values like single-bit values, except that the values can be indexed in order to access individual bits. For example, if in and out represent 16-bit values, then out[3]=in[5] sets the 3rd bit of out to the value

a	b	sel	out
0	0	0	0
0	1	0	0
1	0	0	1
1	1	0	1
0	0	1	0
0	1	1	1
1	0	1	0
1	1	1	1

sel	out
0	a
1	b

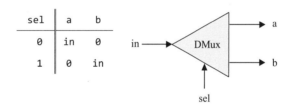

```
Chip name: Mux
Input:     a, b, sel
Output:    out
Function:  if (sel==0) then out = a, else out = b
```

Figure 1.9   Multiplexer. The table at the top right is an abbreviated version of the truth table.

sel	a	b
0	in	0
1	0	in

```
Chip name: DMux
Input:     in, sel
Output:    a, b
Function:  if (sel==0) then {a, b} = {in, 0},
           else              {a, b} = {0, in}
```

Figure 1.10   Demultiplexer.

of the 5th bit of in. The bits are indexed from right to left, the rightmost bit being the 0'th bit and the leftmost bit being the 15'th bit (in a 16-bit setting).

Multi-bit Not: An *n*-bit Not gate applies the Boolean operation Not to every one of the bits in its *n*-bit input:

```
Chip name: Not16
Input:     in[16]
Output:    out[16]
Function:  for i = 0..15 out[i] = Not(in[i])
```

Multi-bit And: An *n*-bit And gate applies the Boolean operation And to every respective pair in its two *n*-bit inputs:

```
Chip name: And16
Input:     a[16], b[16]
Output:    out[16]
Function:  for i = 0..15 out[i] = And(a[i], b[i])
```

Multi-bit Or: An *n*-bit Or gate applies the Boolean operation Or to every respective pair in its two *n*-bit inputs:

```
Chip name: Or16
Input:     a[16], b[16]
Output:    out[16]
Function:  for i = 0..15 out[i] = Or(a[i], b[i])
```

Multi-bit multiplexer: An *n*-bit multiplexer operates exactly the same as a basic multiplexer, except that its inputs and output are *n*-bits wide:

```
Chip name: Mux16
Input:     a[16], b[16], sel
Output:    out[16]
Function:  if (sel==0) then for i = 0..15 out[i] = a[i],
           else for i = 0..15 out[i] = b[i]
```

1.4.4   Multi-Way Versions of Basic Gates

Logic gates that operate on one or two inputs have natural generalization to multi-way variants that operate on more than two inputs. This section describes a set of multi-way gates that will be used subsequently in various chips in our computer architecture.

Multi-way Or: An *m*-way Or gate outputs 1 when at least one of its *m* input bits is 1, and 0 otherwise. We will need an 8-way variant of this gate:

```
Chip name: Or8Way
Input:     in[8]
Output:    out
Function:  out = Or(in[0], in[1],…,in[7])
```

Multi-way/Multi-bit multiplexer: An *m*-way *n*-bit multiplexer selects one of its *m* *n*-bit inputs, and outputs it to its *n*-bit output. The selection is specified by a set of *k* selection bits, where $k = log_2 m$. Here is the API of a 4-way multiplexer:

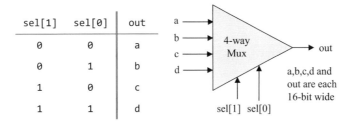

sel[1]	sel[0]	out
0	0	a
0	1	b
1	0	c
1	1	d

Our target computer platform requires two variants of this chip: a 4-way 16-bit multiplexer and an 8-way 16-bit multiplexer:

```
Chip name: Mux4Way16
Input:     a[16],b[16],c[16],d[16],sel[2]
Output:    out[16]
Function:  if (sel==00,01,10, or 11) then out = a,b,c, or d
Comment:   The assignment is a 16-bit operation.
           For example, "out = a" means "for i = 0..15 out[i] = a[i]".

Chip name: Mux8Way16
Input:     a[16],b[16],c[16],d[16],e[16],f[16],g[16],h[16], sel[3]
Output:    out[16]
Function:  if (sel==000,001,010, ..., or 111)
           then out = a,b,c,d, ..., or h
Comment:   The assignment is a 16-bit operation.
           For example, "out = a" means "for i = 0..15 out[i] = a[i]".
```

Multi-way/Multi-bit demultiplexer: An *m*-way *n*-bit demultiplexer routes its single *n*-bit input to one of its *m n*-bit outputs. The other outputs are set to 0. The selection is specified by a set of *k* selection bits, where $k = log_2 m$. Here is the API of a 4-way demultiplexer:

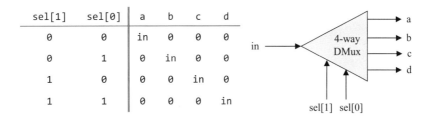

sel[1]	sel[0]	a	b	c	d
0	0	in	0	0	0
0	1	0	in	0	0
1	0	0	0	in	0
1	1	0	0	0	in

Our target computer platform requires two variants of this chip: a 4-way 1-bit demultiplexer and an 8-way 1-bit demultiplexer:

```
Chip name: DMux4Way
Input:     in, sel[2]
Output:    a, b, c, d
Function:  if (sel==00)     then {a,b,c,d} = {1,0,0,0},
           else if (sel==01) then {a,b,c,d} = {0,1,0,0},
           else if (sel==10) then {a,b,c,d} = {0,0,1,0},
           else if (sel==11) then {a,b,c,d} = {0,0,0,1}

Chip name: Dmux8Way
Input:     in, sel[3]
Output:    a, b, c, d, e, f, g, h
Function:  if (sel==000)     then {a,b,c,…, h} = {1,0,0,0,0,0,0,0},
           else if (sel==001) then {a,b,c,…, h} = {0,1,0,0,0,0,0,0},
           else if (sel==010) then {a,b,c,…, h} = {0,0,1,0,0,0,0,0},
           …
           else if (sel==111) then {a,b,c,…, h} = {0,0,0,0,0,0,0,1}
```

1.5   Implementation

The previous section described the specifications, or interfaces, of a family of basic logic gates. Having described the *what*, we now turn to discuss the *how*. In particular, we'll focus on two general approaches to implementing logic gates: *behavioral simulation* and *hardware implementation*. Both approaches play important roles in all our hardware construction projects.

1.5.1   Behavioral Simulation

The chip descriptions presented thus far are strictly abstract. It would have been nice if we could experiment with these abstractions hands-on, before setting out to build them in HDL. How can we possibly do so?

Well, if all we want to do is interact with the chips' behavior, we don't have to go through the trouble of building them in HDL. Instead, we can opt for a much simpler implementation, using conventional programming. For example, we can use some object-oriented language to create a set of classes, each implementing a generic chip. We can write class constructors for creating chip instances and *eval* methods for evaluating their logic, and we can have the classes interact with each other so that high-level chips can be defined in terms of lower-level ones. We could then add a nice graphical user interface that enables putting different values in the chip inputs, evaluating their logic, and observing the chip outputs. This software-based technique, called *behavioral simulation*, makes a lot of sense. It enables experimenting with chip interfaces before starting the laborious process of building them in HDL.

The Nand to Tetris *hardware simulator* provides exactly such a service. In addition to simulating the behavior of HDL programs, which is its main purpose, the simulator features built-in software implementations of all the chips built in the Nand to Tetris hardware projects. The built-in version of each chip is implemented as an executable software module, invoked by a skeletal HDL program that provides the chip interface. For example, here is the HDL program that implements the built-in version of the Xor chip:

```
/* Xor (exclusive or) gate:
   If a!=b out=1 else out=0. */
CHIP Xor {
    IN  a, b;
    OUT out;
    BUILTIN Xor;
}
```

Compare this to the HDL program listed in figure 1.7. First, note that regular chips and built-in chips have precisely the same interface. Thus, they provide exactly the same functionality. In the built-in implementation though, the PARTS section is replaced with the single statement BUILTIN Xor. This statement informs the simulator that the chip is implemented by Xor.class. This class file, like all the Java class files that implement built-in chips, is located in the folder nand2tetris/tools/builtIn.

We note in passing that realizing logic gates using high-level programming is not difficult, and that's another virtue of behavioral simulation: it's inexpensive and quick. At some point, of course, hardware engineers must do the real thing, which is implementing the chips not as software artifacts but rather as HDL programs that can be committed to silicon. That's what we'll do next.

1.5.2   Hardware Implementation

This section gives guidelines on how to implement the fifteen logic gates described in this chapter. As a rule in this book, our implementation guidelines are intentionally brief. We give just enough insights to get started, leaving you the pleasure of discovering the rest of the gate implementations yourself.

Nand: Since we decided to base our hardware on elementary Nand gates, we treat Nand as a primitive gate whose functionality is given externally. The supplied hardware simulator features a built-in implementation of Nand, and thus there is no need to implement it.

Not: Can be implemented using a single Nand gate. *Tip:* Inspect the Nand truth table, and ask yourself how the Nand inputs can be arranged so that a single input signal, 0, will cause the Nand gate to output 1, and a single input signal, 1, will cause it to output 0.

And: Can be implemented from the two previously discussed gates.

Or / Xor: The Boolean function Or can be defined using the Boolean functions And and Not. The Boolean function Xor can be defined using And, Not, and Or.

Multiplexer / Demultiplexer: Can be implemented using previously built gates.

Multi-bit Not / And / Or gates: Assuming that you've already built the basic versions of these gates, the implementation of their n-ary versions is a matter of arranging arrays of n basic gates and having each gate operate separately on its single-bit inputs. The resulting HDL code will be somewhat boring and repetitive (using copy-paste), but it will carry its weight when these multi-bit gates are used in the construction of more complex chips, later in the book.

Multi-bit multiplexer: The implementation of an n-ary multiplexer is a matter of feeding the same selection bit to every one of n binary multiplexers. Again, a boring construction task resulting in a very useful chip.

Multi-way gates: Implementation tip: Think forks.

1.5.3   Built-In Chips

As we pointed out when we discussed behavioral simulation, our hardware simulator provides software-based, built-in implementations of most of the chips described in the book. In Nand to Tetris, the most celebrated built-in chip is of course Nand: whenever you use a Nand chip-part in an HDL program, the hardware simulator invokes the built-in `tools/builtIn/Nand.hdl` implementation. This convention is a special case of a more general chip invocation strategy: whenever the hardware simulator encounters a chip-part, say, *Xxx*, in an HDL program, it looks up the file *Xxx*`.hdl` in the current folder; if the file is found, the simulator evaluates its underlying HDL code. If the file is not found, the simulator looks it up in the `tools/builtIn` folder. If the file is found there, the simulator executes the chip's built-in implementation; otherwise, the simulator issues an error message and terminates the simulation.

This convention comes in handy. For example, suppose you began implementing a `Mux.hdl` program, but, for some reason, you did not complete it. This could be an annoying setback, since, in theory, you cannot continue building chips that use Mux as a chip-part. Fortunately, and actually by design, this is where built-in chips come to the rescue. All you have to do is rename your partial implementation `Mux1.hdl`, for example. Each time the hardware simulator is called to simulate the functionality of a Mux chip-part, it will fail to find a `Mux.hdl` file in the current folder. This will cause behavioral simulation to kick in, forcing the simulator to use the built-in Mux version instead. Exactly what we want! At a later stage you may want to go back to Mux1.hdl and resume working on its implementation. At this point you can restore its original file name, Mux.hdl, and continue from where you left off.

1.6   Project

This section describes the tools and resources needed for completing project 1 and gives recommended implementation steps and tips.

Objective: Implement all the logic gates presented in the chapter. The only building blocks that you can use are primitive Nand gates and the composite gates that you will gradually build on top of them.

Resources: We assume that you've already downloaded the Nand to Tetris zip file, containing the book's software suite, and that you've extracted it into a folder named nand2tetris on your computer. If that is the case, then the nand2tetris/tools folder on your computer contains the hardware simulator discussed in this chapter. This program, along with a plain text editor, are the only tools needed for completing project 1 as well as all the other hardware projects described in the book.

The fifteen chips mentioned in this chapter, except for Nand, should be implemented in the HDL language described in appendix 2. For each chip *Xxx*, we provide a skeletal *Xxx.* hdl program (sometimes called a *stub file*) with a missing implementation part. In addition, for each chip we provide an *Xxx*.tst script that tells the hardware simulator how to test it, along with an *Xxx*.cmp compare file that lists the correct output that the supplied test is expected to generate. All these files are available in your nand2tetris/projects/01 folder. Your job is to complete and test all the *Xxx*.hdl files in this folder. These files can be written and edited using any plain text editor.

Contract: When loaded into the hardware simulator, your chip design (modified .hdl program), tested on the supplied .tst file, should produce the outputs listed in the supplied .cmp file. If the actual outputs generated by the simulator disagree with the desired outputs, the simulator will stop the simulation and produce an error message.

Steps: We recommend proceeding in the following order:

0. The *hardware simulator* needed for this project is available in nand2tetris/tools.

1. Consult appendix 2 (HDL), as needed.

2. Consult the Hardware Simulator Tutorial (available at www.nand2tetris.org), as needed.

3. Build and simulate all the chips listed in nand2tetris/projects/01.

General Implementation Tips

(We use the terms *gate* and *chip* interchangeably.)

· Each gate can be implemented in more than one way. The simpler the implementation, the better. As a general rule, strive to use as few chip-parts as possible.

· Although each chip can be implemented directly from Nand gates only, we recommend always using composite gates that were already implemented. See the previous tip.

· There is no need to build "helper chips" of your own design. Your HDL programs should use only the chips mentioned in this chapter.

· Implement the chips in the order in which they appear in the chapter. If, for some reason, you don't complete the HDL implementation of some chip, you can still use it as a chip-part in other HDL programs. Simply rename the chip file, or remove it from the folder, causing the simulator to use its built-in version instead.

A web-based version of project 1 is available at www.nand2tetris.org.

1.7   Perspective

This chapter specified a set of basic logic gates that are widely used in computer architectures. In chapters 2 and 3 we will use these gates for building our processing and storage chips, respectively. These chips, in turn, will be later used for constructing the central processing unit and the memory devices of our computer.

Although we have chosen to use Nand as our basic building block, other logic gates can be used as possible points of departure. For example, you can build a complete computer platform using Nor gates only or, alternatively, a combination of And, Or, and Not gates. These constructive approaches to logic design are theoretically equivalent, just like the same geometry can be founded on alternative sets of agreed-upon axioms. In principle, if electrical engineers or physicists can come up with efficient and low-cost implementations of logic gates using any technology that they see fit, we will happily use them as primitive building blocks. The reality, though, is that most computers are built from either Nand or Nor gates.

Throughout the chapter, we paid no attention to efficiency and cost considerations, such as energy consumption or the number of wire crossovers implied by our HDL programs. Such considerations are critically important in practice, and a great deal of computer science and technology expertise focuses on optimizing them. Another issue we did not address is physical aspects, for example, how primitive logic gates can be built from transistors embedded in silicon or from other switching technologies. There are of course several such implementation options, each having its own characteristics (speed, energy consumption, production cost, and so on). Any nontrivial coverage of these issues requires venturing into areas outside computer science, like electrical engineering and solid-state physics.

The next chapter describes how bits can be used to represent binary numbers and how logic gates can be used to realize arithmetic operations. These capabilities will be based on the elementary logic gates built in this chapter.

2 Boolean Arithmetic

Counting is the religion of this generation, its hope and salvation.

—Gertrude Stein (1874–1946)

In this chapter we build a family of chips designed to represent numbers and perform arithmetic operations. Our starting point is the set of logic gates built in chapter 1, and our ending point is a fully functional *Arithmetic Logic Unit*. The ALU will later become the computational centerpiece of the *Central Processing Unit* (CPU)—the chip that executes all the instructions handled by the computer. Hence, building the ALU is an important milestone in our Nand to Tetris journey.

As usual, we approach this task gradually, starting with a background section that describes how binary codes and Boolean arithmetic can be used, respectively, to represent and add signed integers. The Specification section presents a succession of *adder chips* designed to add two bits, three bits, and pairs of n-bit binary numbers. This sets the stage for the ALU specification, which is based on a surprisingly simple logic design. The Implementation and Project sections provide tips and guidelines on how to build the adder chips and the ALU using HDL and the supplied hardware simulator.

2.1 Arithmetic Operations

General-purpose computer systems are required to perform at least the following arithmetic operations on signed integers:

- addition
- sign conversion
- subtraction
- comparison
- multiplication
- division

We'll start by developing gate logic that carries out addition and sign conversion. Later, we will show how the other arithmetic operations can be implemented from these two building blocks.

In mathematics as well as in computer science, *addition* is a simple operation that runs deep. Remarkably, all the functions performed by digital computers—not only arithmetic operations—can be reduced to adding binary numbers. Therefore, constructive understanding of binary addition holds the key to understanding many fundamental operations performed by the computer's hardware.

2.2   Binary Numbers

When we are told that a certain code, say, 6083, represents a number using the *decimal system*, then, by convention, we take this number to be:

$$(6083)_{10} = 6 \cdot 10^3 + 0 \cdot 10^2 + 8 \cdot 10^1 + 3 \cdot 10^0 = 6083$$

Each digit in the decimal code contributes a value that depends on the *base* 10 and on the digit's position in the code. Suppose now that we are told that the code 10011 represents a number using base 2, or *binary* representation. To compute the value of this number, we follow exactly the same procedure, using base 2 instead of base 10:

$$(10011)_2 = 1 \cdot 2^4 + 0 \cdot 2^3 + 0 \cdot 2^2 + 1 \cdot 2^1 + 1 \cdot 2^0 = 19$$

Inside computers, *everything* is represented using binary codes. For example, when we press the keyboard keys labeled 1, 9, and Enter in response to "Give an example of a prime number," what ends up stored in the computer's memory is the binary code 10011. When we ask the computer to display this value on the screen, the following process ensues. First, the computer's operating system calculates the decimal value that 10011 represents, which happens to be 19. After converting this integer value to the two characters 1 and 9, the OS looks up the current font and gets the two bitmap images used for rendering these characters on the screen. The OS then causes the screen driver to turn on and off the relevant pixels, and, don't hold your breath—the whole thing lasts a tiny fraction of a second—we finally see the image 19 appear on the screen.

In chapter 12 we'll develop an operating system that carries out such rendering operations, among many other low-level services. For now, suffice it to observe that the decimal representation of numbers is a human indulgence explained by the obscure fact that, at some point in ancient history, humans decided to represent quantities using their ten fingers, and the habit stuck. From a mathematical perspective, the number ten is utterly uninteresting, and, as far as computers go, is a complete nuisance. Computers handle *everything* in binary and care naught about decimal. Yet since humans insist on dealing with numbers using decimal codes, computers have to work hard behind the scenes to carry out binary-to-decimal and decimal-to-binary conversions whenever humans want to see, or supply, numeric information. At all other times, computers stick to binary.

Fixed word size: Integer numbers are of course unbounded: for any given number x there are integers that are less than x and integers that are greater than x. Yet computers are finite machines that use a fixed word size for representing numbers. *Word size* is a common hardware term used for specifying the number of bits that computers use for representing a basic chunk of information—in this case, integer values. Typically, 8-, 16-, 32-, or 64-bit registers are used for representing integers.[1] The fixed word size implies that there is a limit on the number of values that these registers can represent.

For example, suppose we use 8-bit registers for representing integers. This representation can code $2^8 = 256$ different things. If we wish to represent only nonnegative integers, we can assign `00000000` for representing 0, `00000001` for representing 1, `00000010` for representing 2, `00000011` for representing 3, all the way up to assigning `11111111` for representing 255. In general, using n bits we can represent all the nonnegative integers ranging from 0 to $2^n - 1$.

What about representing negative numbers using binary codes? Later in the chapter we'll present a technique that meets this challenge in a most elegant and satisfying way.

And what about representing numbers that are greater than, or less than, the maximal and minimal values permitted by the fixed register size? Every high-level language provides abstractions for handling numbers that are as large or as small as we can practically want. These abstractions are typically implemented by lashing together as many n-bit registers as necessary for representing the numbers. Since executing arithmetic and logical operations on multi-word numbers is a slow affair, it is recommended to use this practice only when the application requires processing extremely large or extremely small numbers.

2.3   Binary Addition

A pair of binary numbers can be added bitwise from right to left, using the same decimal addition algorithm learned in elementary school. First, we add the two rightmost bits, also called the *least significant bits* (LSB) of the two binary numbers. Next, we add the resulting carry bit to the sum of the next pair of bits. We continue this lockstep process until the two left *most significant bits* (MSB) are added. Here is an example of this algorithm in action, assuming that we use a fixed word size of 4 bits:

```
  0   0   0   1      (carry)      1   1   1   1
      1   0   0   1      x            1   0   1   1
 +    0   1   0   1      y        +   0   1   1   1
  0   1   1   1   0    x + y      1   0   0   1   0
       no overflow                     overflow
```

1. Which correspond, respectively, to the typical high-level data types *byte*, *short*, *int*, and *long*. For example, when reduced to machine-level instructions, *short* variables can be handled by 16-bit registers. Since 16-bit arithmetic is four times faster than 64-bit arithmetic, programmers are advised to always use the most compact data type that satisfies the application's requirements.

If the most significant bitwise addition generates a carry of 1, we have what is known as *overflow*. What to do with overflow is a matter of decision, and ours is to ignore it. Basically, we are content to guarantee that the result of adding any two *n*-bit numbers will be correct up to *n* bits. We note in passing that ignoring things is perfectly acceptable as long as one is clear and forthcoming about it.

2.4   Signed Binary Numbers

An *n*-bit binary system can code 2^n different things. If we have to represent signed (positive and negative) numbers in binary code, a natural solution is to split the available code space into two subsets: one for representing nonnegative numbers, and the other for representing negative numbers. Ideally, the coding scheme should be chosen such that the introduction of signed numbers would complicate the hardware implementation of arithmetic operations as little as possible.

Over the years, this challenge has led to the development of several coding schemes for representing signed numbers in binary code. The solution used today in almost all computers is called the *two's complement* method, also known as *radix complement*. In a binary system that uses a word size of *n* bits, the two's complement binary code that represents negative *x* is taken to be the code that represents $2^n - x$. For example, in a 4-bit binary system, −7 is represented using the binary code associated with $2^4 - 7 = 9$, which happens to be `1001`. Recalling that +7 is represented by `0111`, we see that `1001 + 0111 = 0000` (ignoring the overflow bit). Figure 2.1 lists all the signed numbers represented by a 4-bit system using the two's complement method.

An inspection of figure 2.1 suggests that an *n*-bit binary system with two's complement representation has the following attractive properties:

- The system codes 2^n signed numbers, ranging from $-(2^{n-1})$ to $2^{n-1} - 1$.
- The code of any nonnegative number begins with a `0`.
- The code of any negative number begins with a `1`.
- To obtain the binary code of −*x* from the binary code of *x*, leave all the least significant `0`-bits and the first least significant `1`-bit of *x* intact, and flip all the remaining bits (convert `0`'s to `1`'s and vice versa). Alternatively, flip all the bits of *x* and add 1 to the result.

A particularly attractive feature of the two's complement representation is that *subtraction* is handled as a special case of addition. To illustrate, consider $5 - 7$. Noting that this is equivalent to $5 + (-7)$, and following figure 2.1, we proceed to compute `0101 + 1001`. The result is `1110`, which indeed is the binary code of −2. Here is another example: To compute $(-2) + (-3)$, we add `1110 + 1101`, obtaining the sum `11011`. Ignoring the overflow bit, we get `1011`, which is the binary code of −5.

We see that the two's complement method enables adding and subtracting signed numbers using nothing more than the hardware required for adding nonnegative numbers.

```
0000:   0
0001:   1
0010:   2
0011:   3
0100:   4
0101:   5
0110:   6
0111:   7
1000:  -8      (16 - 8)
1001:  -7      (16 - 7)
1010:  -6      (16 - 6)
1011:  -5      (16 - 5)
1100:  -4      (16 - 4)
1101:  -3      (16 - 3)
1110:  -2      (16 - 2)
1111:  -1      (16 - 1)
```

Figure 2.1   Two's complement representation of signed numbers, in a 4-bit binary system.

As we will see later in the book, every arithmetic operation, from multiplication to division to square root, can be implemented reductively using binary addition. So, on the one hand, we observe that a huge range of computer capabilities rides on top of binary addition, and on the other hand, we observe that the two's complement method obviates the need for special hardware for adding and subtracting signed numbers. Taking these two observations together, we are compelled to conclude that the two's complement method is one of the most remarkable and unsung heroes of applied computer science.

2.5   Specification

We now turn to specifying a hierarchy of chips, starting with simple adders and culminating with an Arithmetic Logic Unit (ALU). As usual in this book, we focus first on the abstract (*what* the chips are designed to), delaying implementation details (*how* they do it) to the next section. We cannot resist reiterating, with pleasure, that thanks to the two's complement method we don't have to say anything special about handling signed numbers. All the arithmetic chips that we'll present work equally well on nonnegative, negative, and mixed-sign numbers.

2.5.1   Adders

We'll focus on the following hierarchy of *adders*:

- *Half-adder*: designed to add two bits
- *Full-adder*: designed to add three bits
- *Adder*: designed to add two *n*-bit numbers

We'll also specify a special-purpose adder, called an *incrementer*, designed to add 1 to a given number. (The names *half-adder* and *full-adder* derive from the implementation detail that a full-adder chip can be realized from two half-adders, as we'll see later in the chapter.)

Half-adder: The first step on our road to adding binary numbers is adding two bits. Let us treat the result of this operation as a 2-bit number, and call its right and left bits `sum` and `carry`, respectively. Figure 2.2 presents a chip that carries out this addition operation.

Full-adder: Figure 2.3 presents a *full-adder* chip, designed to add three bits. Like the half-adder, the full-adder chip outputs two bits that, taken together, represent the addition of the three input bits.

Adder: Computers represent integer numbers using a fixed word size like 8, 16, 32, or 64 bits. The chip whose job is to add two such n-bit numbers is called *adder*. Figure 2.4 presents a 16-bit adder.

We note in passing that the logic design for adding 16-bit numbers can be easily extended to implement any n-bit adder chip, irrespective of n.

Incrementer: When we later design our computer architecture, we will need a chip that adds 1 to a given number (*Spoiler*: This will enable fetching the next instruction from memory, after executing the current one). Although the $x + 1$ operation can be realized by our general-propose `Adder` chip, a dedicated *incrementer* chip can do it more efficiently. Here is the chip interface:

```
Chip name: Inc16
Input:     in[16]
Output:    out[16]
Function:  out = in + 1
Comment:   The overflow bit is ignored.
```

2.5.2   The Arithmetic Logic Unit

All the adder chips presented so far are generic: any computer that performs arithmetic operations uses such chips, one way or another. Building on these chips, we now turn to describe an *Arithmetic Logic Unit*, a chip that will later become the computational center-piece of our CPU. Unlike the generic gates and chips discussed thus far, the ALU design is unique to the computer built in Nand to Tetris, named Hack. That said, the design principles underlying the Hack ALU are general and instructive. Further, our ALU architecture achieves a great deal of functionality using a minimal set of internal parts. In that respect, it provides a good example of an efficient and elegant logic design.

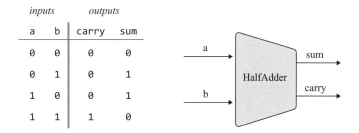

inputs		outputs	
a	b	carry	sum
0	0	0	0
0	1	0	1
1	0	0	1
1	1	1	0

```
Chip name: HalfAdder
Input:     a, b
Output:    sum, carry
Function:  sum   = LSB of a + b
           carry = MSB of a + b
```

Figure 2.2   Half-adder, designed to add 2 bits.

a	b	c	carry	sum
0	0	0	0	0
0	0	1	0	1
0	1	0	0	1
0	1	1	1	0
1	0	0	0	1
1	0	1	1	0
1	1	0	1	0
1	1	1	1	1

```
Chip name: FullAdder
Input:     a, b, c
Output:    sum, carry
Function:  sum   = LSB of a + b + c
           carry = MSB of a + b + c
```

Figure 2.3   Full-adder, designed to add 3 bits.

As its name implies, an Arithmetic Logic Unit is a chip designed to compute a set of arithmetic and logic operations. Exactly *which* operations an ALU should feature is a design decision derived from cost-effectiveness considerations. In the case of the Hack platform, we decided that (i) the ALU will perform only integer arithmetic (and not, for example, floating point arithmetic) and (ii) the ALU will compute the set of eighteen arithmetic-logical functions shown in figure 2.5a.

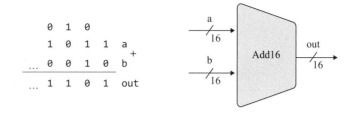

```
          0   1   0
          1   0   1   1    a
                               +
     ...  0   0   1   0    b
     _____
     ...  1   1   0   1    out
```

```
Chip name:  Add16
Input:      a[16], b[16]
Output:     out[16]
Function:   Adds two 16-bit numbers.
            The overflow bit is ignored.
```

Figure 2.4   16-bit adder, designed to add two 16-bit numbers, with an example of addition action (on the left).

As seen in figure 2.5a, the Hack ALU operates on two 16-bit two's complement integers, denoted x and y, and on six 1-bit inputs, called *control bits*. These control bits "tell" the ALU which function to compute. The exact specification is given in figure 2.5b.

To illustrate the ALU logic, suppose we wish to compute the function $x - 1$, for $x = 27$. To get started, we feed the 16-bit binary code of 27 into the x input. In this particular example we don't care about y's value, since it has no impact on the required calculation. Now, looking up x − 1 in figure 2.5b, we set the ALU's control bits to 001110. According to the specification, this setting should cause the ALU to output the binary code representing 26.

Is that so? To find out, let's delve deeper, and reckon how the Hack ALU performs its magic. Focusing on the top row of figure 2.5b, note that each one of the six control bits

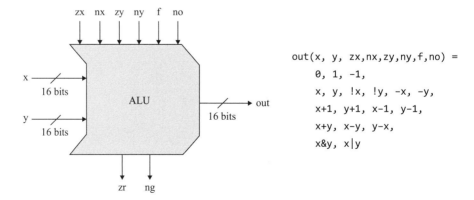

Figure 2.5a   The Hack ALU, designed to compute the eighteen arithmetic-logical functions shown on the right (the symbols !, &, and | represent, respectively, the 16-bit operations Not, And, and Or). For now, ignore the zr and ng output bits.

pre-setting the x input		pre-setting the y input		computing + or &	post-setting the output	resulting ALU output
if zx then x=0	if nx then x=!x	if zy then y=0	if ny then y=!y	if f then out=x+y else out=x&y	if no then out=!out	out(x,y) =
zx	**nx**	**zy**	**ny**	**f**	**no**	**out**
1	0	1	0	1	0	0
1	1	1	1	1	1	1
1	1	1	0	1	0	-1
0	0	1	1	0	0	x
1	1	0	0	0	0	y
0	0	1	1	0	1	!x
1	1	0	0	0	1	!y
0	0	1	1	1	1	-x
1	1	0	0	1	1	-y
0	1	1	1	1	1	x+1
1	1	0	1	1	1	y+1
0	0	1	1	1	0	x-1
1	1	0	0	1	0	y-1
0	0	0	0	1	0	x+y
0	1	0	0	1	1	x-y
0	0	0	1	1	1	y-x
0	0	0	0	0	0	x&y
0	1	0	1	0	1	x|y

Figure 2.5b   Taken together, the values of the six control bits zx, nx, zy, ny, f, and no cause the ALU to compute one of the functions listed in the rightmost column.

is associated with a standalone, conditional micro-action. For example, the zx bit is associated with "if (zx==1) then set x to 0". These six directives are to be performed in order: first, we either set the x and y inputs to 0, or not; next, we either negate the resulting values, or not; next, we compute either + or & on the preprocessed values; and finally, we either negate the resulting value, or not. All these settings, negations, additions, and conjunctions are 16-bit operations.

With this logic in mind, let us revisit the row associated with x-1 and verify that the micro-operations coded by the six control bits will indeed cause the ALU to compute $x - 1$. Going left to right, we see that the zx and nx bits are 0, so we neither zero nor negate the x input—we leave it as is. The zy and ny bits are 1, so we first zero the y input and then negate the result, yielding the 16-bit value 1111111111111111. Since this binary code happens to represent -1 in two's complement, we see that the two data inputs of the ALU are now x's value and −1. Since the f bit is 1, the selected operation is *addition*, causing the ALU to compute $x + (-1)$. Finally, since the no bit is 0, the output is not negated. To conclude, we've illustrated that if we feed the ALU with x and y values and set the six control bits to 001110, the ALU will compute $x - 1$, as specified.

What about the other seventeen functions listed in figure 2.5b? Does the ALU actually compute them as well? To verify that this is indeed the case, you are invited to focus on other rows in the table, go through the same process of carrying out the micro-actions coded by the six control bits, and figure out for yourself what the ALU will output. Or, you can believe us that the ALU works as advertised.

Note that the ALU actually computes a total of sixty-four functions, since six control bits code that many possibilities. We've decided to focus on, and document, only eighteen of these possibilities, since these will suffice for supporting the instruction set of our target computer system. The curious reader may be intrigued to know that some of the undocumented ALU operations are quite meaningful. However, we've opted not to exploit them in the Hack system.

The Hack ALU interface is given in figure 2.5c. Note that in addition to computing the specified function on its two inputs, the ALU also computes the two output bits zr and ng. These bits, which flag whether the ALU output is zero or negative, respectively, will be used by the future CPU of our computer system.

```
Chip name: ALU
Input:     x[16], y[16], // Two 16-bit data inputs
           zx,           // Zero the x input
           nx,           // Negate the x input
           zy,           // Zero the y input
           ny,           // Negate the y input
           f,            // if f==1 out=add(x,y) else out=and(x,y)
           no            // Negate the out output
Output:    out[16],      // 16-bit output
           zr,           // if out==0 zr=1 else zr=0
           ng            // if out<0  ng=1 else ng=0
Function:
           if zx x=0     // 16-bit zero constant
           if nx x=!x    // Bit-wise negation
           if zy y=0     // 16-bit zero constant
           if ny y=!y    // Bit-wise negation
           if f out=x+y  // Integer two's complement addition
           else out=x&y  // Bit-wise And
           if no out=!out // Bit-wise negation
           if out==0 zr=1 else zr=0  // 16-bit equality comparison
           if out<0 ng=1  else ng=0  // two's complement comparison
Comment:   The overflow bit is ignored.
```

Figure 2.5c The Hack ALU API.

It may be instructive to describe the thought process that led to the design of our ALU. First, we made a tentative list of the primitive operations that we wanted our computer to perform (right column of figure 2.5b). Next, we used backward reasoning to figure out how x, y, and out can be manipulated in binary fashion in order to carry out the desired operations. These processing requirements, along with our objective to keep the ALU logic as simple as possible, have led to the design decision to use six control bits, each associated with a straightforward operation that can be easily implemented with basic logic gates. The resulting ALU is simple and elegant. And in the hardware business, simplicity and elegance carry the day.

2.6   Implementation

Our implementation guidelines are intentionally minimal. We already gave many implementation tips along the way, and now it is your turn to discover the missing parts in the chip architectures.

Throughout this section, when we say "build/implement a logic design that...," we expect you to (i) figure out the logic design (e.g., by sketching a gate diagram), (ii) write the HDL code that realizes the design, and (iii) test and debug your design using the supplied test scripts and hardware simulator. More details are given in the next section, which describes project 2.

Half-adder: An inspection of the truth table in figure 2.2 reveals that the outputs sum(a,b) and carry(a,b) happen to be identical to those of two simple Boolean functions discussed and implemented in project 1. Therefore, the half-adder implementation is straightforward.

Full-adder: A full-adder chip can be implemented from two half-adders and one additional gate (and that's why these adders are called *half* and *full*). Other implementations are possible, including direct approaches that don't use half-adders.

Adder: The addition of two *n*-bit numbers can be done bitwise, from right to left. In step 0, the least significant pair of bits is added, and the resulting carry bit is fed into the addition of the next significant pair of bits. The process continues until the pair of the most significant bits is added. Note that each step involves the addition of three bits, one of which is propagated from the "previous" addition.

Readers may wonder how we can add pairs of bits "in parallel" before the carry bit has been computed by the previous pair of bits. The answer is that these computations are sufficiently fast as to complete and stabilize within one clock cycle. We'll discuss clock cycles and synchronization in the next chapter; for now, you can ignore the time element completely, and write HDL code that computes the addition operation by acting on all the bit-pairs simultaneously.

Incrementer: An *n*-bit incrementer can be implemented easily in a number of different ways.

ALU: Our ALU was carefully planned to effect all the desired ALU operations *logically*, using the simple Boolean operations implied by the six control bits. Therefore, the *physical* implementation of the ALU can be reduced to implementing these simple operations, following the pseudocode specifications listed at the top of figure 2.5b. Your first step will likely be creating a logic design for zeroing and negating a 16-bit value. This logic can be used for handling the x and y inputs as well as the out output. Chips for bitwise And-ing and addition have already been built in projects 1 and 2, respectively. Thus, what remains is building logic that selects between these two operations, according to the f control bit (this selection logic was also implemented in project 1). Once this main ALU functionality works properly, you can proceed to implement the required functionality of the single-bit zr and ng outputs.

2.7   Project

Objective: Implement all the chips presented in this chapter. The only building blocks that you need are some of the gates described in chapter 1 and the chips that you will gradually build in this project.

Built-in chips: As was just said, the chips that you will build in this project use, as chip-parts, some of the chips described in chapter 1. Even if you've built these lower-level chips successfully in HDL, we recommend using their built-in versions instead. As best-practice advice pertaining to all the hardware projects in Nand to Tetris, always prefer using built-in chip-parts instead of their HDL implementations. The built-in chips are guaranteed to operate to specification and are designed to speed up the operation of the hardware simulator.

There is a simple way to follow this best-practice advice: Don't add to the project folder nand2tetris/projects/02 any .hdl file from project 1. Whenever the hardware simulator will encounter in your HDL code a reference to a chip-part from project 1, for example, And16, it will check whether there is an And16.hdl file in the current folder. Failing to find it, the hardware simulator will resort by default to using the built-in version of this chip, which is exactly what we want.

The remaining guidelines for this project are identical to those of project 1. In particular, remember that good HDL programs use as few chip-parts as possible, and there is no need to invent and implement any "helper chips"; your HDL programs should use only chips that were specified in chapters 1 and 2.

A web-based version of project 2 is available at www.nand2tetris.org.

2.8   Perspective

The construction of the multi-bit adder presented in this chapter was standard, although no attention was paid to efficiency. Indeed, our suggested adder implementation is inefficient, due to the delays incurred while the carry bits propagate throughout the n-bit addends. This computation can be accelerated by logic circuits that effect so-called *carry lookahead* heuristics. Since addition is the most prevalent operation in computer architectures, any such low-level improvement can result in dramatic performance gains throughout the system. Yet in this book we focus mostly on functionality, leaving chip optimization to more specialized hardware books and courses.[2]

The overall functionality of any hardware/software system is delivered jointly by the CPU and the operating system that runs on top of the hardware platform. Thus, when designing a new computer system, the question of how to allocate the desired functionality between the ALU and the OS is essentially a cost/performance dilemma. As a rule, direct hardware implementations of arithmetic and logical operations are more efficient than software implementations but make the hardware platform more expensive.

The trade-off that we have chosen in Nand to Tetris is to design a basic ALU with minimal functionality, and use system software to implement additional mathematical operations as needed. For example, our ALU features neither multiplication nor division. In part II of the book, when we discuss the operating system (chapter 12), we'll implement elegant and efficient bitwise algorithms for multiplication and division, along with other mathematical operations. These OS routines can then be used by compilers of high-level languages operating on top of the Hack platform. Thus, when a high-level programmer writes an expression like, say, x * 12 + sqrt(y), then, following compilation, some parts of the expression will be evaluated directly by the ALU and some by the OS, yet the high-level programmer will be completely oblivious to this low-level division of work. Indeed, one of the key roles of an operating system is closing gaps between the high-level language abstractions that programmers use and the barebone hardware on which they are realized.

---

2. A technical reason for not using carry look-ahead techniques in our adder chips is that their hardware implementation requires cyclical pin connections, which are not supported by the Nand to Tetris hardware simulator.

3 Memory

It's a poor sort of memory that only works backward.

—Lewis Carroll (1832–1898)

Consider the high-level operation $x = y + 17$. In chapter 2 we showed how logic gates can be utilized for representing numbers and for computing simple arithmetic expressions like $y + 17$. We now turn to discuss how logic gates can be used to *store values over time*—in particular, how a variable like x can be set to "contain" a value and persist it until we set it to another value. To do so, we'll develop a new family of *memory chips*.

So far, all the chips that we built in chapters 1 and 2, culminating with the ALU, were time independent. Such chips are sometimes called *combinational*: they respond to different combinations of their inputs without delay, except for the time it takes their inner chip-parts to complete the computation. In this chapter we introduce and build *sequential* chips. Unlike combinational chips, which are oblivious to time, the outputs of sequential chips depend not only on the inputs in the current time but also on inputs and outputs that have been processed previously.

Needless to say, the notions of *current* and *previous* go hand in hand with the notion of *time*: you remember now what was committed to memory before. Thus, before we start talking about memory, we must first figure out how to use logic to model the progression of time. This can be done using a *clock* that generates an ongoing train of binary signals that we call *tick* and *tock*. The time between the beginning of a tick and the end of the subsequent tock is called a *cycle*, and these cycles will be used to regulate the operations of all the memory chips used by the computer.

Following a brief, user-oriented introduction to memory devices, we will present the art of sequential logic, which we will use for building time-dependent chips. We will then set out to build registers, RAM devices, and counters. These memory devices, along with the arithmetic devices built in chapter 2, comprise all the chips needed for building a complete, general-purpose computer system—a challenge that we will take up in chapter 5.

3.1   Memory Devices

Computer programs use variables, arrays, and objects—abstractions that persist data over time. Hardware platforms support this ability by offering memory devices that know how to *maintain state*. Because evolution gave humans a phenomenal electro-chemical memory system, we tend to take for granted the ability to remember things over time. However, this ability is hard to implement in classical logic, which is aware of neither time nor state. Thus, to get started, we must first find a way to model the progression of time and endow logic gates with the ability to maintain state and respond to time changes.

We will approach this challenge by introducing a clock and an elementary, time-dependent logic gate that can flip and flop between two stable states: representing 0 and representing 1. This gate, called *data flip-flop* (DFF), is the fundamental building block from which all memory devices will be built. In spite of its central role, though, the DFF is a low-profile, inconspicuous gate: unlike registers, RAM devices, and counters, which play prominent roles in computer architectures, DFFs are used implicitly, as low-level chip-parts embedded deep within other memory devices.

The fundamental role of the DFF is seen clearly in figure 3.1, where it serves as the foundation of the memory hierarchy that we are about to build. We will show how DFFs can be used to create 1-bit registers and how *n* such registers can be lashed together to create an *n*-bit register. Next, we'll construct a RAM device containing an arbitrary number of such registers. Among other things, we'll develop a means for *addressing*, that is, accessing by address, any randomly chosen register from the RAM directly and instantaneously.

Before setting out to build these chips, though, we'll present a methodology and tools that enable modeling the progression of time and maintaining state over time.

3.2   Sequential Logic

All the chips discussed in chapters 1 and 2 were based on classical logic, which is time independent. In order to develop memory devices, we need to extend our gate logic with the ability to respond not only to input changes but also to the ticking of a clock: we remember the meaning of the word *dog* in time t since we remembered it in time $t-1$, all the way back to the point of time when we first committed it to memory. In order to develop this temporal ability to *maintain state*, we must extend our computer architecture with a time dimension and build tools that handle time using Boolean functions.

3.2.1   Time Matters

So far in our Nand to Tetris journey, we have assumed that chips respond to their inputs instantaneously: you input 7, 2, and "subtract" into the ALU, and…*poof!* the ALU output

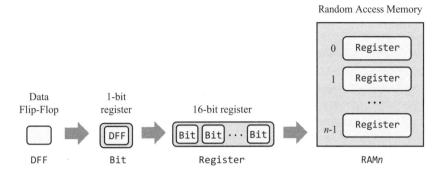

Figure 3.1 The memory hierarchy built in this chapter.

becomes 5. In reality, outputs are always delayed, due to at least two reasons. First, the inputs of the chips don't appear out of thin air; rather, the signals that represent them travel from the outputs of other chips, and this travel takes time. Second, the computations that chips perform also take time; the more chip-parts the chip has—the more elaborate its logic—the more time it will take for the chip's outputs to emerge fully formed from the chip's circuitry.

Thus *time* is an issue that must be dealt with. As seen at the top of figure 3.2, time is typically viewed as a metaphorical arrow that progresses relentlessly forward. This progression is taken to be continuous: between every two time-points there is another time-point, and changes in the world can be infinitesimally small. This notion of time, which is popular among philosophers and physicists, is too deep and mysterious for computer scientists. Thus, instead of viewing time as a continuous progression, we prefer to break it into fixed-length intervals, called *cycles*. This representation is discrete, resulting in cycle 1, cycle 2, cycle 3, and so on. Unlike the continuous arrow of time, which has an infinite granularity, the cycles are atomic and indivisible: changes in the world occur only during cycle transitions; within cycles, the world stands still.

Of course the world never stands still. However, by treating time discretely, we make a conscious decision to ignore continuous change. We are content to know the state of the world in cycle n, and then in cycle $n + 1$, but *during* each cycle the state is assumed to be—well, we don't care. When it comes to building computer architectures, this discrete view of time serves two important design objectives. First, it can be used for neutralizing the randomness associated with communications and computation time delays. Second, it can be used for synchronizing the operations of different chips across the system, as we'll see later.

To illustrate, let's focus on the bottom part of figure 3.2, which tracks how a Not gate (used as an example) responds to arbitrarily chosen inputs. When we feed the gate with 1, it takes a while before the gate's output stabilizes on 0. However, since the cycle duration is—*by design*—longer than the time delay, when we reach the cycle's end, the gate

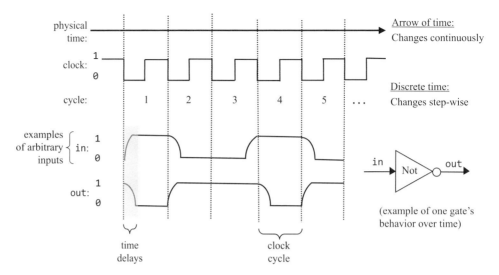

Figure 3.2   Discrete time representation: State changes (input and output values) are observed only during cycle transitions. Within cycles, changes are ignored.

output has already stabilized on 0. Since we probe the state of the world only at cycle ends, we don't get to see the interim time delays; rather, it appears as if we fed the gate with 0, and *poof!* the gate responded with 1. If we make the same observations at the end of each cycle, we can generalize that when a Not gate is fed with some binary input x, it instantaneously outputs Not (x).

Thoughtful readers have probably noticed that for this scheme to work, the *cycle's length* must be longer than the maximal time delays that can occur in the system. Indeed, cycle length is one of the most important design parameters of any hardware platform: When planning a computer, the hardware engineer chooses a cycle length that meets two design objectives. On the one hand, the cycle should be sufficiently long to contain, and neutralize, any possible time delay; on the other hand, the shorter the cycle, the faster the computer: if things happen only during cycle transitions, then obviously things happen faster when the cycles are shorter. To sum up, the cycle length is chosen to be slightly longer than the maximal time delay in any chip in the system. Following the tremendous progress in switching technologies, we are now able to create cycles as tiny as a billionth of a second, achieving remarkable computer speed.

Typically, the cycles are realized by an oscillator that alternates continuously between two phases labeled 0–1, *low-high*, or *ticktock* (as seen in figure 3.2). The elapsed time between the beginning of a tick and the end of the subsequent tock is called a *cycle*, and each cycle is taken to model one discrete time unit. The current clock phase (*tick* or *tock*) is represented by a binary signal. Using the hardware's circuitry, the same master clock signal is simultaneously broadcast to every memory chip in the system. In every such chip, the clock input is funneled to the lower-level DFF gates, where it serves to ensure that the chip will commit to a new state, and output it, only at the end of the clock cycle.

3.2.2 Flip-Flops

Memory chips are designed to "remember", or store, information over time. The low-level devices that facilitate this storage abstraction are named *flip-flop* gates, of which there are several variants. In Nand to Tetris we use a variant named *data flip-flop*, or DFF, whose interface includes a single-bit data input and a single-bit data output (see top of figure 3.3). In addition, the DFF has a clock input that feeds from the master clock's signal. Taken together, the data input and the clock input enable the DFF to implement the simple time-based behavior $out(t)=in(t-1)$, where in and out are the gate's input and output values, and t is the current time unit (from now on, we'll use the terms "time unit" and "cycle" interchangeably). Let us not worry how this behavior is actually implemented. For now, we simply observe that at the end of each time unit, the DFF outputs the input value from the previous time unit.

Like Nand gates, DFF gates lie deep in the hardware hierarchy. As shown in figure 3.1, all the memory chips in the computer—registers, RAM units, and counters—are based, at bottom, on DFF gates. All these DFFs are connected to the same master clock, forming a huge distributed "chorus line." At the end of each clock cycle, the outputs of *all* the DFFs in the computer commit to their inputs from the previous cycle. At all other times, the DFFs are *latched*, meaning that changes in their inputs have no immediate effect on their

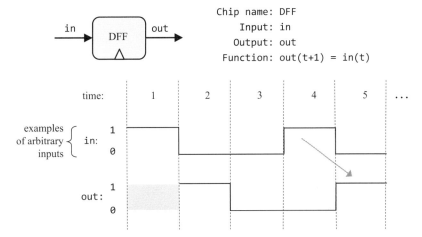

Figure 3.3 The data flip-flop (top) and behavioral example (bottom). In the first cycle the previous input is unknown, so the DFF's output is undefined. In every subsequent time unit, the DFF outputs the input from the previous time unit. Following gate diagramming conventions, the clock input is marked by a small triangle, drawn at the bottom of the gate icon.

outputs. This conduction operation effects any one of the system's numerous DFF gates many times per second (depending on the computer's clock frequency).

Hardware implementations realize the time dependency using a dedicated clock bus that feeds the master clock signal simultaneously to all the DFF gates in the system. Hardware simulators emulate the same effect in software. In particular, the Nand to Tetris hardware simulator features a clock icon, enabling the user to advance the clock interactively, as well as `tick` and `tock` commands that can be used programmatically, in test scripts.

3.2.3   Combinational and Sequential Logic

All the chips that were developed in chapters 1 and 2, starting with the elementary logic gates and culminating with the ALU, were designed to respond only to changes that occur during the current clock cycle. Such chips are called *time-independent* chips, or *combinational* chips. The latter name alludes to the fact that these chips respond only to different combinations of their input values, while paying no attention to the progression of time.

In contrast, chips that are designed to respond to changes that occurred during previous time units (and possibly during the current time unit as well) are called *sequential*, or *clocked*. The most fundamental sequential gate is the DFF, and any chip that includes it, either directly or indirectly, is also said to be sequential. Figure 3.4 depicts a typical sequential logic configuration. The main element in this configuration is a set of one or more chips that include DFF chip-parts, either directly or indirectly. As shown in the figure, these sequential chips may also interact with combinational chips. The feedback loop enables the sequential chip to respond to inputs and outputs from the previous time unit. In combi-

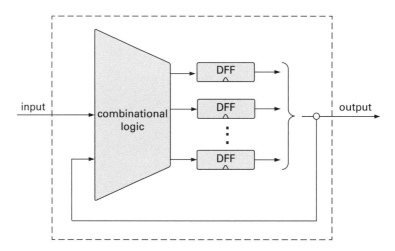

Figure 3.4   Sequential logic design typically involves DFF gates that feed from, and connect to, combinational chips. This gives sequential chips the ability to respond to current as well as to previous inputs and outputs.

national chips, where time is neither modeled nor recognized, the introduction of feedback loops is problematic: the output of the chip would depend on its input, which itself would depend on the output, and thus the output would depend on itself. Note, however, that there is no difficulty in feeding outputs back into inputs, as long as the feedback loop goes through a DFF gate: the DFF introduces an inherent time delay so that the output at time t does not depend on itself but rather on the output at time $t-1$.

The time dependency of sequential chips has an important side effect that serves to synchronize the overall computer architecture. To illustrate, suppose we instruct the ALU to compute $x + y$, where x is the output of a nearby register, and y is the output of a remote RAM register. Because of physical constraints like distance, resistance, and interference, the electric signals representing x and y will likely arrive at the ALU at different times. However, being a combinational chip, the ALU is insensitive to the concept of time—it continuously and happily adds up whichever data values happen to lodge at its inputs. Thus, it will take some time before the ALU's output stabilizes to the correct $x + y$ result. Until then, the ALU will generate garbage.

How can we overcome this difficulty? Well, if we use a discrete representation of time, *we simply don't care*. All we have to do is ensure, when we build the computer's clock, that the duration of the clock cycle will be slightly longer than the time it takes a bit to travel the longest distance from one chip to another, plus the time it takes to complete the most time-consuming within-chip calculation. This way, we are guaranteed that by the end of the clock cycle, the ALU's output will be valid. This, in a nutshell, is the trick that turns a set of standalone hardware components into a well-synchronized system. We will have more to say about this master orchestration when we build the computer architecture in chapter 5.

3.3   Specification

We now turn to specify the memory chips that are typically used in computer architectures:

- data flip-flops (DFFs)
- registers (based on DFFs)
- RAM devices (based on registers)
- counters (based on registers)

As usual, we describe these chips *abstractly*. In particular, we focus on each chip's interface: inputs, outputs, and function. How the chips deliver this functionality will be discussed in the Implementation section.

3.3.1   Data Flip-Flop

The most elementary sequential device that we will use—the basic component from which all other memory chips will be constructed—is the *data flip-flop*. A DFF gate has a single-bit data input, a single-bit data output, a clock input, and a simple time-dependent behavior: $\text{out}(t) = \text{in}(t-1)$.

Usage: If we put a one-bit value in the DFF's input, the DFF's state will be set to this value, and the DFF's output will emit it in the next time unit (see figure 3.3). This humble operation will prove most useful in the implementation of registers, which is described next.

3.3.2   Registers

We present a single-bit register, named `Bit`, and a 16-bit register, named `Register`. The `Bit` chip is designed to store a single bit of information—0 or 1—over time. The chip interface consists of an `in` input that carries a data bit, a `load` input that enables the register for writes, and an `out` output that emits the current state of the register. The `Bit` API and input/output behavior are described in figure 3.5.

Figure 3.5 illustrates how the single-bit register behaves over time, responding to arbitrary examples of `in` and `load` inputs. Note that irrespective of the input value, as long as the `load` bit is not asserted, the register is latched, maintaining its current state.

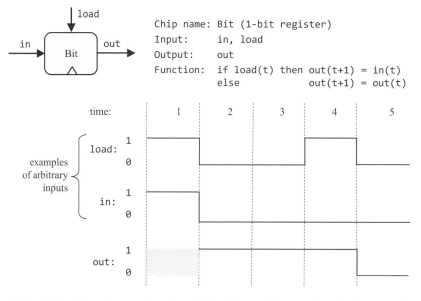

Figure 3.5   1-bit register. Stores and emits a 1-bit value until instructed to load a new value.

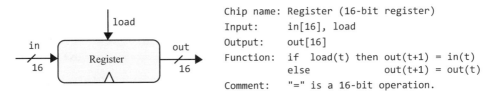

Chip name: Register (16-bit register)
Input: in[16], load
Output: out[16]
Function: if load(t) then out(t+1) = in(t)
          else   out(t+1) = out(t)
Comment: "=" is a 16-bit operation.

Figure 3.6   16-bit Register. Stores and emits a 16-bit value until instructed to load a new value.

The 16-bit `Register` chip behaves exactly the same as the `Bit` chip, except that it is designed to handle 16-bit values. Figure 3.6 gives the details.

Usage: The `Bit` register and the 16-bit `Register` are used identically. To read the state of the register, probe the value of `out`. To set the register's state to *v*, put *v* in the `in` input, and assert (put 1 into) the `load` bit. This will set the register's state to *v*, and, from the next time unit onward, the register will commit to the new value, and its `out` output will start emitting it. We see that the `Register` chip fulfills the classical function of a memory device: it remembers and emits the last value that was written into it, until we set it to another value.

3.3.3   Random Access Memory

A direct-access memory unit, also called *Random Access Memory*, or RAM, is an aggregate of *n* `Register` chips. By specifying a particular address (a number between 0 to *n*−1), each register in the RAM can be selected and made available for read/write operations. Importantly, the access time to any randomly selected memory register is instantaneous and independent of the register's address and the size of the RAM. That's what makes RAM devices so remarkably useful: even if they contain billions of registers, we can still access and manipulate each selected register directly, in the same instantaneous access time. The RAM API is given in figure 3.7.

Usage: To read the contents of register number *m*, set the `address` input to *m*. This action will select register number *m*, and the RAM's output will emit its value. To write a new value *v* into register number *m*, set the `address` input to *m*, set the `in` input to *v*, and assert the `load` bit (set it to 1). This action will select register number *m*, enable it for writing, and set its value to *v*. In the next time unit, the RAM's output will start emitting *v*.

The net result is that the RAM device behaves exactly as required: a bank of addressable registers, each of which can be accessed, and operated upon, independently. In the case of a read operation (`load==0`), the RAM's output immediately emits the value of the selected register. In the case of a write operation (`load==1`), the selected memory register is set to the input value, and the RAM's output will start emitting it from the next time unit onward.

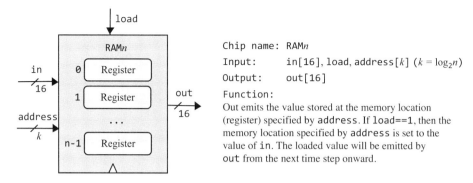

Figure 3.7   A RAM chip, consisting of n 16-bit `Register` chips that can be selected and manipulated separately. The register addresses (0 to $n-1$) are not part of the chip hardware. Rather, they are realized by a gate logic implementation that will be discussed in the next section.

Importantly, the RAM implementation must ensure that the access time to *any* register in the RAM will be nearly instantaneous. If this were not the case, we would not be able to fetch instructions and manipulate variables in a reasonable time, making computers impractically slow. The magic of instantaneous access time will be unfolded shortly, in the Implementation section.

3.3.4   Counter

The Counter is a chip that knows how to increment its value by 1 each time unit. When we build our computer architecture in chapter 5, we will call this chip `Program Counter`, or `PC`, so that's the name that we will use here also.

The interface of our `PC` chip is identical to that of a register, except that it also has control bits labeled `inc` and `reset`. When `inc==1`, the counter increments its state in every clock cycle, effecting the operation `PC++`. If we want to reset the counter to 0, we assert the `reset` bit; if we want to set the counter to the value v, we put v in the `in` input and assert the `load` bit, as we normally do with registers. The details are given in figure 3.8.

Usage: To read the current contents of the `PC`, probe the `out` pin. To reset the `PC`, assert the `reset` bit and set the other control bits to 0. To have the `PC` increment by 1 in each time unit until further notice, assert the `inc` bit and set the other control bits to 0. To set the `PC` to the value v, set the `in` input to v, assert the `load` bit, and set the other control bits to 0.

3.4   Implementation

The previous section presented a family of memory chip abstractions, focusing on their interface and functionality. This section focuses on how these chips can be realized, using

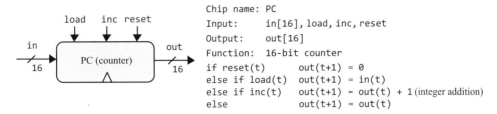

```
Chip name: PC
Input:      in[16], load, inc, reset
Output:     out[16]
Function:   16-bit counter
if reset(t)        out(t+1) = 0
else if load(t)    out(t+1) = in(t)
else if inc(t)     out(t+1) = out(t) + 1 (integer addition)
else               out(t+1) = out(t)
```

Figure 3.8 Program Counter (PC): To use it properly, at most one of the `load`, `inc`, or `reset` bits should be asserted.

simpler chips that were already built. As usual, our implementation guidelines are intentionally suggestive; we want to give you enough hints to complete the implementation yourself, using HDL and the supplied hardware simulator.

3.4.1   Data Flip-Flop

A DFF gate is designed to be able to "flip-flop" between two stable states, representing 0 and representing 1. This functionality can be implemented in several different ways, including ones that use Nand gates only. The Nand-based DFF implementations are elegant, yet intricate and impossible to model in our hardware simulator since they require feedback loops among combinational gates. Wishing to abstract away this complexity, we will treat the DFF as a primitive building block. In particular, the Nand to Tetris hardware simulator provides a built-in DFF implementation that can be readily used by other chips, as we now turn to describe.

3.4.2   Registers

Register chips are memory devices: they are expected to implement the basic behavior $out(t+1) = out(t)$, remembering and emitting their state over time. This looks similar to the DFF behavior, which is $out(t+1) = in(t)$. If we could only feed the DFF output back into its input, this could be a good starting point for implementing the one-bit `Bit` register. This solution is shown on the left of figure 3.9.

It turns out that the implementation shown on the left of figure 3.9 is invalid, for several related reasons. First, the implementation does not expose a `load` bit, as required by the register's interface. Second, there is no way to tell the `DFF` chip-part when to draw its input from the `in` wire and when from the incoming `out` value. Indeed, HDL programming rules forbid feeding a pin from more than one source.

The good thing about this invalid design is that it leads us to the correct implementation, shown on the right of figure 3.9. As the chip diagram shows, a natural way to resolve the input ambiguity is introducing a multiplexer into the design. The *load bit* of the overall register chip can then be funneled to the *select bit* of the inner multiplexer: If we set this bit to 1, the multiplexer will feed the `in` value into the `DFF`; if we set the load bit to 0, the

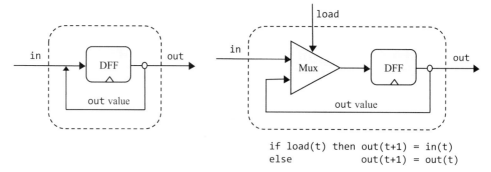

Figure 3.9 The Bit (1-bit register) implementation: invalid (left) and correct (right) solutions.

multiplexer will feed the DFF's previous output. This will yield the behavior "if load, set the register to a new value, else set it to the previously stored value"—exactly how we want a register to behave.

Note that the feedback loop just described does not entail cyclical *data race* problems: the loop goes through a DFF gate, which introduces a time delay. In fact, the Bit design shown in figure 3.9 is a special case of the general sequential logic design shown in figure 3.4.

Once we've completed the implementation of the single-bit Bit register, we can move on to constructing a w-bit register. This can be achieved by forming an array of w Bit chips (see figure 3.1). The basic design parameter of such a register is w—the number of bits that it is supposed to hold—for example, 16, 32, or 64. Since the Hack computer will be based on a 16-bit hardware platform, our Register chip will be based on sixteen Bit chip-parts.

The Bit register is the only chip in the Hack architecture that uses a DFF gate directly; all the higher-level memory devices in the computer use DFF chips indirectly, by virtue of using Register chips made of Bit chips. Note that the inclusion of a DFF gate in the design of any chip—directly or indirectly—turns the latter chip, as well as all the higher-level chips that use it as a chip-part, into time-dependent chips.

3.4.3   RAM

The Hack hardware platform requires a RAM device of 16K (16384) 16-bit registers, so that's what we have to implement. We propose the following gradual implementation roadmap:

chip	n	k	built from:
RAM8	8	3	8 Register chips
RAM64	64	6	8 RAM8 chips
RAM512	512	9	8 RAM64 chips
RAM4K	4096	12	8 RAM512 chips
RAM16K	16384	14	4 RAM4K chips

All these memory chips have precisely the same RAM*n* API given in figure 3.7. Each RAM chip has *n* registers, and the width of its address input is $k = log_2n$ bits. We now describe how these chips can be implemented, starting with RAM8.

A RAM8 chip features 8 registers, as shown in figure 3.7, for $n = 8$. Each register can be selected by setting the RAM8's 3-bit address input to a value between 0 and 7. The act of *reading* the value of a selected register can be described as follows: Given some address (a value between 0 and 7), how can we "select" register number address and pipe its output to the RAM8's output? *Hint:* We can do it using one of the combinational chips built in project 1. That's why reading the value of a selected RAM register is achieved nearly instantaneously, independent of the clock and of the number of registers in the RAM. In a similar way, the act of *writing* a value into a selected register can be described as follows: Given an address value, a load value (1), and a 16-bit in value, how can we set the value of register number address to in? *Hint:* The 16-bit in data can be fed simultaneously to the in inputs of all eight Register chips. Using another combinational chip developed in project 1, along with the address and load inputs, you can ensure that only one of the registers will accept the incoming in value, while all the other seven registers will ignore it.

We note in passing that the RAM registers are not marked with addresses in any physical sense. Rather, the logic described above is capable of, and sufficient for, selecting individual registers according to their address, and this is done by virtue of using combinational chips. Now here is a crucially important observation: since combinational logic is time independent, the access time to any individual register will be nearly instantaneous.

Once we've implemented the RAM8 chip, we can move on to implementing a RAM64 chip. The implementation can be based on eight RAM8 chip-parts. To select a particular register from the RAM64 memory, we use a 6-bit address, say *xxxyyy*. The *xxx* bits can be used to select one of the RAM8 chips, and the *yyy* bits can be used to select one of the registers within the selected RAM8. This hierarchical addressing scheme can be effected by gate logic. The same implementation idea can guide the implementation of the remaining RAM512, RAM4K, and RAM16K chips.

To recap, we take an aggregate of an unlimited number of registers, and impose on it a combinational superstructure that permits direct access to any individual register. We hope that the beauty of this solution does not escape the reader's attention.

3.4.4   Counter

A counter is a memory device that can increment its value in every time unit. In addition, the counter can be set to 0 or some other value. The basic storage and counting functionalities of the counter can be implemented, respectively, by a Register chip and by the incrementer chip built in project 2. The logic that selects between the counter's inc, load, and reset modes can be implemented using some of the multiplexers built in project 1.

3.5   Project

Objective: Build all the chips described in the chapter. The building blocks that you can use are primitive DFF gates, chips that you will build on top of them, and the gates built in previous chapters.

Resources: The only tool that you need for this project is the Nand to Tetris hardware simulator. All the chips should be implemented in the HDL language specified in appendix 2. As usual, for each chip we supply a skeletal .hdl program with a missing implementation part, a .tst script file that tells the hardware simulator how to test it, and a .cmp compare file that defines the expected results. Your job is to complete the missing implementation parts of the supplied .hdl programs.

Contract: When loaded into the hardware simulator, your chip design (modified .hdl program), tested on the supplied .tst file, should produce the outputs listed in the supplied .cmp file. If that is not the case, the simulator will let you know.

Tip: The data flip-flop (DFF) gate is considered primitive; thus there is no need to build it. When the simulator encounters a DFF chip-part in an HDL program, it automatically invokes the tools/builtIn/DFF.hdl implementation.

Folders structure of this project: When constructing RAM chips from lower-level RAM chip-parts, we recommend using built-in versions of the latter. Otherwise, the simulator will recursively generate numerous memory-resident software objects, one for each of the many chip-parts that make up a typical RAM unit. This may cause the simulator to run slowly or, worse, run out of the memory of the host computer on which the simulator is running.

To avert this problem, we've partitioned the RAM chips built in this project into two subfolders. The RAM8.hdl and RAM64.hdl programs are stored in projects/03/a, and the other, higher-level RAM chips are stored in projects/03/b. This partitioning is done for one purpose only: when evaluating the RAM chips stored in the b folder, the simulator will be forced to use built-in implementations of the RAM64 chip-parts, because RAM64. hdl cannot be found in the b folder.

Steps: We recommend proceeding in the following order:

1. The hardware simulator needed for this project is available in nand2tetris/tools.
2. Consult appendix 2 and the Hardware Simulator Tutorial, as needed.
3. Build and simulate all the chips specified in the projects/03 folder.

A web-based version of project 3 is available at www.nand2tetris.org.

3.6   Perspective

The cornerstone of all the memory systems described in this chapter is the flip-flop, which we treated abstractly as a primitive, built-in gate. The usual approach is to construct flip-flops from elementary combinational gates (e.g., Nand gates) connected in feedback loops. The standard construction begins by building a non-clocked flip-flop which is bi-stable, that is, can be set to be in one of two states (storing 0, and storing 1). Then a clocked flip-flop is obtained by cascading two such non-clocked flip-flops, the first being set when the clock *ticks* and the second when the clock *tocks*. This master-slave design endows the overall flip-flop with the desired clocked synchronization functionality.

Such flip-flop implementations are both elegant and intricate. In this book we have chosen to abstract away these low-level considerations by treating the flip-flop as a primitive gate. Readers who wish to explore the internal structure of flip-flop gates can find detailed descriptions in most logic design and computer architecture textbooks.

One reason not to dwell on flip-flop esoterica is that the lowest level of the memory devices used in modern computers is not necessarily constructed from flip-flop gates. Instead, modern memory chips are carefully optimized, exploiting the unique physical properties of the underlying storage technology. Many such alternative technologies are available today to computer designers; as usual, which technology to use is a cost-performance issue. Likewise, the recursive ascent method that we used to build the RAM chips is elegant but not necessarily efficient. More efficient implementations are possible.

Aside from these physical considerations, all the chip constructions described in this chapter—the registers, the counter, and the RAM chips—are standard, and versions of them can be found in every computer system.

In chapter 5, we will use the register chips built in this chapter, along with the ALU built in chapter 2, to build a Central Processing Unit. The CPU will then be augmented with a RAM device, leading up to a general-purpose computer architecture capable of executing programs written in a machine language. This machine language is discussed in the next chapter.

4   Machine Language

Works of imagination should be written in very plain language; the more purely imaginative they are, the more necessary it is to be plain.

—Samuel Taylor Coleridge (1772–1834)

In chapters 1–3 we built processing and memory chips that can be integrated into the hardware platform of a general-purpose computer. Before we set out to complete this construction, let's pause and ask: What exactly is the *purpose* of this computer? As the architect Louis Sullivan famously observed, "Form follows function." If you wish to understand a system, or build one, start by studying the function that the system is supposed to serve. With that in mind, before we set out to complete the construction of our hardware platform, we'll devote this chapter to studying the *machine language* that this platform is designed to realize. After all, executing programs written in machine language efficiently is the ultimate function of any general-purpose computer.

A machine language is an agreed-upon formalism designed to code machine instructions. Using these instructions, we can instruct the computer's processor to perform arithmetic and logical operations, read and write values from and to the computer's memory, test Boolean conditions, and decide which instruction to fetch and execute next. Unlike high-level languages, whose design goals are cross-platform compatibility and power of expression, machine languages are designed to effect direct execution in, and total control of, a specific hardware platform. Of course, generality, elegance, and power of expression are still desired, but only to the extent that they support the basic requirement of direct and efficient execution in hardware.

Machine language is the most profound interface in the computer enterprise—the fine line where hardware meets software. This is the point where the abstract designs of humans, as manifested in high-level programs, are finally reduced to physical operations performed in silicon. Thus, a machine language can be construed as both a programming artifact and an integral part of the hardware platform. In fact, just as we say that the machine language is designed to control a particular hardware platform, we can say that the hardware platform is designed to execute instructions written in a particular machine language.

The chapter begins with a general introduction to low-level programming in machine language. Next, we give a detailed specification of the *Hack machine language*, covering both its binary and symbolic versions. The project that ends the chapter focuses on writing some machine language programs. This provides a hands-on appreciation of low-level programming and sets the stage for completing the construction of the computer hardware in the next chapter.

Although programmers rarely write programs directly in machine language, the study of low-level programming is a prerequisite to a complete and rigorous understanding of how computers work. Further, an intimate understanding of low-level programming helps the programmer write better and more efficient high-level programs. Finally, it is rather fascinating to observe, hands-on, how the most sophisticated software systems are, at bottom, streams of simple instructions, each specifying a primitive bitwise operation on the underlying hardware.

4.1   Machine Language: Overview

This chapter focuses not on the machine but rather on the *language* used to control the machine. Therefore, we will abstract away the hardware platform, focusing on the minimal subset of hardware elements that are mentioned explicitly in machine language instructions.

4.1.1   Hardware Elements

A machine language can be viewed as an agreed-upon formalism designed to manipulate a *memory* using a *processor* and a set of *registers*.

Memory: The term *memory* refers loosely to the collection of hardware devices that store data and instructions in a computer. Functionally speaking, a memory is a continuous sequence of cells, also referred to as *locations* or *memory registers*, each having a unique *address*. An individual memory register is accessed by supplying its address.

Processor: The processor, normally called the *Central Processing Unit*, or *CPU*, is a device capable of performing a fixed set of primitive operations. These include arithmetic and logical operations, memory access operations, and control (also called *branching*) operations. The processor draws its inputs from selected registers and memory locations and writes its outputs to selected registers and memory locations. It consists of an ALU, a set of registers, and gate logic that enables it to parse and execute binary instructions.

Registers: The processor and the memory are implemented as two separate, standalone chips, and moving data from one to the other is a relatively slow affair. For this reason, processors are normally equipped with several on-board registers, each capable of holding a single value. Located inside the processor's chip, the registers serve as a high-speed local memory, allowing the processor to manipulate data and instructions without having to venture outside the chip.

The CPU-resident registers fall into two categories: *data registers*, designed to hold data values, and *address registers*, designed to hold values that can be interpreted either as data values or as memory addresses. The computer architecture is configured in such a way that placing a particular value, say *n*, in an address register, causes the memory location whose address is *n* to become *selected* instantaneously.[1] This sets the stage for a subsequent operation on the selected memory location.

4.1.2 Languages

Machine language programs can be written in two alternative, but equivalent, ways: *binary* and *symbolic*. For example, consider the abstract operation "set R1 to the value of R1+R2". As language designers, we can decide to represent the addition operation using the 6-bit code `101011`, and registers R1 and R2 using the codes `00001` and `00010`, respectively. Assembling these codes left to right, we can decide to use the 16-bit instruction `1010110001000001` as the binary version of "set R1 to the value of R1+R2".

In the early days of computer systems, computers were programmed manually: When proto-programmers wanted to issue the instruction "set R1 to the value of R1+R2", they pushed up and down mechanical switches that stored a binary code like `1010110001000001` in the computer's instruction memory. And if the program was a hundred instructions long, they had to go through this ordeal a hundred times. Of course debugging such programs was a perfect nightmare. This led programmers to invent and use symbolic codes as a convenient way for documenting and debugging programs *on paper*, before entering them into the computer. For example, the symbolic format `add R2,R1` could be chosen for representing the semantics "set R1 to the value of R1+R2" and the binary instruction `1010110001000001`.

It didn't take long before several people hit on the same idea: Symbols like R, 1, 2, and + can also be represented using agreed-upon binary codes. Why not use symbolic instructions for writing programs, and then use another program—a *translator*—for translating the symbolic instructions into executable binary code? This innovation liberated programmers from the tedium of writing binary code, paving the way for the subsequent onslaught of high-level programming languages. For reasons that will become clear in chapter 6, symbolic machine languages are called *assembly languages*, and the programs that translate them into binary code are called *assemblers*.

Unlike the syntax of high-level languages, which is portable and hardware independent, the syntax of an assembly language is tightly related to the low-level details of the target hardware: the available ALU operations, number and type of registers, memory size, and

---

1. By *instantaneously* we mean within the same clock cycle, or time unit.

so on. Since different computers vary greatly in terms of any one of these parameters, there is a Tower of Babel of machine languages, each with its obscure syntax, each designed to control a particular family of CPUs. Irrespective of this variety, though, all machine languages are theoretically equivalent, and all of them support similar sets of generic tasks, as we now turn to describe.

4.1.3   Instructions

In what follows, we assume that the computer's processor is equipped with a set of registers denoted R0, R1, R2,... The exact number and type of these registers are irrelevant to our present discussion.

Arithmetic and logical operations: Every machine language features instructions for performing basic arithmetic operations like addition and subtraction, as well as basic logical operations like And, Or, Not. For example, consider the following code segments:

```
// Adds up two numbers:
load R1,17    // R1 ← 17
load R2,4     // R2 ← 4
add  R1,R1,R2 // R1 ← R1 + R2
```

```
// Computes a logical operation:
load R1,true   // R1 ← binary representation of true
load R2,false  // R2 ← binary representation of false
and  R1,R1,R2  // R1 ← R1 And R2 (bit-wise And)
```

For such symbolic instructions to execute on a computer, they must first be translated into binary code. The translation is done by a program named *assembler*, which we'll develop in chapter 6. For now, we assume that we have access to such an assembler and that we can use it as needed.

Memory access: Every machine language features means for accessing, and then manipulating, selected memory locations. This is typically done using an *address register*, let's call it A. For example, suppose we wish to set memory location 17 to the value 1. We can decide to do so using the two instructions load A,17 followed by load M,1, where, by convention, M stands for the memory register selected by A (namely, the memory register whose address is the current value of A). With that in mind, suppose we wish to set the fifty memory locations 200, 201, 202,..., 249 to 1. This can be done by executing the instruction load A,200 and then entering a loop that executes the instructions load M,1 and add A,A,1 fifty times.

Flow control: While computer programs execute by default sequentially, one instruction after another, they also include occasional *jumps* to locations other than the next instruction. To facilitate such branching actions, machine languages feature several variants of conditional and unconditional *goto* instructions, as well as label declaration statements that mark the goto destinations. Figure 4.1 illustrates a simple branching action using machine language.

Symbols: Both code versions in figure 4.1 are written in assembly language; thus, both must be translated into binary code before they can be executed. Also, both versions perform exactly the same logic. However, the code version that uses symbolic references is much easier to write, debug, and maintain.

Further, unlike the code that uses physical addresses, the translated binary version of the code that uses symbolic references can be loaded into, and executed from, any memory segment that happens to be available in the computer's memory. Therefore, low-level code that mentions no physical addresses is said to be *relocatable*. Clearly, relocatable code is essential in computer systems like PCs and cell phones, which routinely load and execute multiple apps dynamically and simultaneously. Thus, we see that symbolic references are not just a matter of cosmetics—they are used to liberate the code from unnecessary physical attachments to the host memory.

This ends our brief introduction to some machine language essentials. The next section gives a formal description of one specific machine language—the native code of the Hack computer.

4.2   The Hack Machine Language

Programmers who write low-level code (or programmers who write compilers and interpreters that generate low-level code) interact with the computer abstractly, through its *interface*, which is the computer's machine language. Although programmers don't have to be aware of all the details of the underlying computer architecture, they should be familiar with the hardware elements that come to play in their low-level programs.

With that in mind, we begin the discussion of the Hack machine language with a conceptual description of the Hack computer. Next, we give an example of a complete program

```
Using physical addresses

...
// Sets R1 to 0+1+2, ...
12: load R1,0
13: add R1,R1,1
...
27: goto 13
...
```

```
Using symbolic addresses

...
// Sets R1 to 0+1+2, ...
    load R1,0
(LOOP)
    add R1,R1,1
    ...
    goto LOOP
    ...
```

Figure 4.1   Two versions of the same low-level code (it is assumed that the code includes some loop termination logic, not shown here).

written in the Hack assembly language. This sets the stage for the remainder of this section, in which we give a formal specification of the Hack language instructions.

4.2.1   Background

The design of the Hack computer, which will be presented in the next chapter, follows a widely used hardware paradigm known as the *von Neumann architecture*, named after the computing pioneer John von Neumann. Hack is a 16-bit computer, meaning that the CPU and the memory units are designed to process, move, and store, chunks of 16-bit values.

Memory: As seen in figure 4.2, the Hack platform uses two distinct memory units: a *data memory* and an *instruction memory*. The data memory stores the binary values that programs manipulate. The instruction memory stores the program's instructions, also represented as binary values. Both memories are 16-bit wide, and each has a 15-bit address space. Thus the maximum addressable size of each memory unit is 2^{15} or 32K 16-bit words (the symbol *K*, abbreviated from *kilo*—the Greek word for *thousand*—is commonly used to stand for the number $2^{10} = 1024$). It is convenient to think about each memory unit as a linear sequence of addressable memory registers, with addresses ranging from 0 to 32K–1.

The *data memory* (which we also call RAM) is a read/write device. Hack instructions can read data from, and write data to, selected RAM registers. An individual register is selected by supplying its address. Since the memory's address input always contains some value, there is always one selected register, and this register is referred to in Hack instructions as M. For example, the Hack instruction M=0 sets the selected RAM register to 0.

The *instruction memory* (which we also call ROM) is a read-only device, and programs are loaded into it using some exogenous means (more about this in chapter 5). Just like

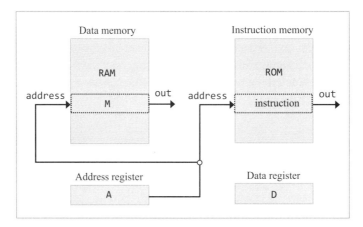

Figure 4.2   Conceptual model of the Hack memory system. Although the actual architecture is wired somewhat differently (as described in chapter 5), this model helps understand the semantics of Hack programs.

with the RAM, the instruction memory's `address` input always contains some value; thus, there is always one selected instruction memory register. The value of this register is referred to as the *current instruction*.

Registers: Hack instructions are designed to manipulate three 16-bit registers: a *data register*, denoted D, an *address register*, denoted A, and a selected data memory register, denoted M. Hack instructions have a self-explanatory syntax. For example: `D=M`, `M=D+1`, `D=0`, `D=M-1`, and so on.

The role of the data register D is straightforward: it serves to store a 16-bit value. The second register, A, serves as both an address register and a data register. If we wish to store the value 17 in the A register, we use the Hack instruction `@17` (the reason for this syntax will become clear soon). In fact, this is the only way to get a constant into the Hack computer. For example, if we wish to set the D register to 17, we use the two instructions `@17`, followed by `D=A`. In addition to serving as a second data register, the hard-working A register is also used for addressing the data memory and the instruction memory, as we now turn to discuss.

Addressing: The Hack instruction @*xxx* sets the A register to the value *xxx*. In addition, the @*xxx* instruction has two side effects. First, it makes the RAM register whose address is *xxx* the selected memory register, denoted M. Second, it makes the value of the ROM register whose address is *xxx* the selected instruction. Therefore, setting A to some value has the simultaneous effect of preparing the stage, potentially, for one of two very different subsequent actions: manipulating the selected data memory register or doing something with the selected instruction. Which action to pursue (and which to ignore) is determined by the subsequent Hack instruction.

To illustrate, suppose we wish to set the value of `RAM[100]` to 17. This can be done using the Hack instructions `@17`, `D=A`, `@100`, `M=D`. Note that in the first pair of instructions, A serves as a data register; in the second pair of instructions, it serves as an address register. Here is another example: To set `RAM[100]` to the value of `RAM[200]`, we can use the Hack instructions `@200`, `D=M`, `@100`, `M=D`.

In both of these scenarios, the A register also selected registers in the instruction memory—an action which the two scenarios ignored. The next section discusses the opposite scenario: using A for selecting instructions while ignoring its effect on the data memory.

Branching: The code examples thus far imply that a Hack program is a sequence of instructions, to be executed one after the other. This indeed is the default flow of control, but what happens if we wish to branch to executing not the next instruction but, say, instruction number 29 in the program? In the Hack language, this can be done using the Hack instruction `@29`, followed by the Hack instruction `0;JMP`. The first instruction selects the `ROM[29]` register (it also selects `RAM[29]`, but we don't care about it). The subsequent `0;JMP` instruction realizes the Hack version of *unconditional branching*: go to execute the instruction addressed by the A register (we'll explain the `;0` prefix later). Since the ROM is assumed to contain the program that we are presently executing, starting at address 0, the two instructions @29 and 0;JMP end up making the value of ROM[29] the next instruction to be executed.

The Hack language also features *conditional branching*. For example, the logic if D==0 goto 52 can be implemented using the instruction @52, followed by the instruction D;JEQ. The semantics of the second instruction is "evaluate D; if the value equals zero, jump to execute the instruction stored in the address selected by A". The Hack language features several such *conditional branching* commands, as we'll explain later in the chapter.

To recap: The A register serves two simultaneous, yet very different, addressing functions. Following an @*xxx* instruction, we either focus on the selected data memory register (M) and ignore the selected instruction, or we focus on the selected instruction and ignore the selected data memory register. This duality is a bit confusing, but note that we got away with using one address register to control two separate memory devices (see figure 4.2). The result is a simpler computer architecture and a compact machine language. As usual in our business, simplicity and thrift reign supreme.

Variables: The *xxx* in the Hack instruction @*xxx* can be either a constant or a symbol. If the instruction is @23, the A register is set to the value 23. If the instruction is @x, where x is a symbol that is bound to some value, say 513, the instruction sets the A register to 513. The use of symbols endows Hack assembly programs with the ability to use *variables* rather than physical memory addresses. For example, the typical high-level assignment statement let x=17 can be implemented in the Hack language as @17, D=A, @x, M=D. The semantics of this code is "select the RAM register whose address is the value that is bound to the symbol x, and set this register to 17". Here we assume that there is an agent who knows how to bind the symbols found in high-level languages, like x, to sensible and consistent addresses in the data memory. This agent is the assembler.

Thanks to the assembler, variables like x can be named and used in Hack programs at will, and as needed. For example, suppose we wish to write code that increments some counter. One option is to keep this counter in, say, RAM[30], and increment it using the instructions @30, M=M+1. A more sensible approach is to use @count, M=M+1, and let the assembler worry about where to put this variable in memory. We don't care about the specific address so long as the assembler will always resolve the symbol to that address. In chapter 6 we'll learn how to develop an assembler that implements this useful mapping operation.

In addition to the symbols that can be introduced into Hack assembly programs as needed, the Hack language features sixteen built-in symbols named R0, R1, R2,..., R15. These symbols are always bound by the assembler to the values 0, 1, 2,..., 15. Thus, for example, the two Hack instructions @R3, M=0 will end up setting RAM[3] to 0. In what follows, we sometimes refer to R0, R1, R2,..., R15 as *virtual registers*.

Before going on, we suggest you review, and make sure you fully understand, the code examples shown in figure 4.3 (some of which were already discussed).

Memory access examples   Branching examples   Variables use examples

```
// D = 17                   // goto 29                   // x = -1
@17                         @29                          @x
D=A                         0;JMP                        M=-1

// RAM[100] = 17            // if D>0 goto 63            // count = count - 1
@17                         @63                          @count
D=A                         D;JGT                        M=M-1
@100
M=D                                                      // sum = sum + x
                                                         @sum
// RAM[100] = RAM[200]                                   D=M
@200                                                     @x
D=M                                                      D=D+M
@100                                                     @sum
M=D                                                      M=D
```

Figure 4.3   Hack assembly code examples.

4.2.2   Program Example

Jumping into the cold water, let's review a complete Hack assembly program, deferring a formal description of the Hack language to the next section. Before we do so, a word of caution: Most readers will probably be mystified by the obscure style of this program. To which we say: Welcome to machine language programming. Unlike high-level languages, machine languages are not designed to please programmers. Rather, they are designed to control a hardware platform, efficiently and plainly.

Suppose we wish to compute the sum $1 + 2 + 3 + \cdots + n$, for a given value n. To operationalize things, we'll put the input n in RAM[0] and the output sum in RAM[1]. The program that computes this sum is listed in figure 4.4. Beginning with the pseudocode, note that instead of utilizing the well-known formula for computing the sum of an arithmetic series, we use brute-force addition. This is done for illustrating conditional and iterative processing in the Hack machine language.

Later in the chapter you will understand this program completely. For now, we suggest ignoring the details, and observing instead the following pattern: In the Hack language, every operation involving a memory location entails two instructions. The first instruction, @*addr*, is used to select a target memory address; the subsequent instruction specifies what to do at this address. To support this logic, the Hack language features two generic instructions, several examples of which we have already seen: an *address instruction*, also called *A*-instruction (the instructions that start with @), and a *compute instruction*, also called *C*-instruction (all the other instructions). Each instruction has a symbolic representation, a binary representation, and an effect on the computer, as we now turn to describe.

Pseudocode

```
// Program: Sum1ToN
// Computes RAM[1]=1+2+3+...+RAM[0]
// Usage: put a value>=1 in RAM[0]
   i = 1
   sum = 0
LOOP:
   if (i > R0) goto STOP
   sum = sum + i
   i = i + 1
   goto LOOP
STOP:
   R1 = sum
```

Hack assembly code

```
// File: Sum1ToN.asm
// Computes RAM[1]=1+2+3+...+RAM[0]
// Usage: put a value>=1 in RAM[0]
   // i = 1
   @i
   M=1
   // sum = 0
   @sum
   M=0
(LOOP)
   // if (i > R0) goto STOP
   @i
   D=M
   @R0
   D=D-M
   @STOP
   D;JGT
   // sum = sum + i
   @sum
   D=M
   @i
   D=D+M
   @sum
   M=D
   // i = i + 1
   @i
   M=M+1
   // goto LOOP
   @LOOP
   0;JMP
(STOP)
   // R1 = sum
   @sum
   D=M
   @R1
   M=D
(END)
   @END
   0;JMP
```

Figure 4.4 A Hack assembly program (example). Note that RAM[0] and RAM[1] can be referred to as R0 and R1.

4.2.3   The Hack Language Specification

The Hack machine language consists of two instructions, specified in figure 4.5.

The *A*-instruction

The *A*-instruction sets the A register to some 15-bit value. The binary version consists of two fields: an operation code, also known as *op-code*, which is 0 (the leftmost bit), followed by fifteen bits that code a nonnegative binary number. For example, the symbolic instruction @5, whose binary version is 0000000000000101, stores the binary representation of 5 in the A register.

The *A*-instruction is used for three different purposes. First, it provides the only way to enter a constant into the computer under program control. Second, it sets the stage for a subsequent *C*-instruction that manipulates a selected RAM register, referred to as M, by first setting A to the address of that register. Third, it sets the stage for a subsequent *C*-instruction that specifies a jump by first setting A to the address of the jump destination.

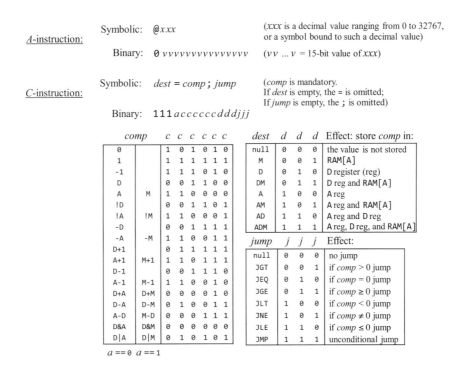

	Symbolic:	@*xxx*	(*xxx* is a decimal value ranging from 0 to 32767,
A-instruction:			or a symbol bound to such a decimal value)
	Binary:	0 *vvvvvvvvvvvvvvv*	(*vv ... v* = 15-bit value of *xxx*)

	Symbolic:	*dest* = *comp* ; *jump*	(*comp* is mandatory.
C-instruction:			If *dest* is empty, the = is omitted;
			If *jump* is empty, the ; is omitted)
	Binary:	111 *a c c c c c c d d d j j j*	

comp		c	c	c	c	c	c
0		1	0	1	0	1	0
1		1	1	1	1	1	1
-1		1	1	1	0	1	0
D		0	0	1	1	0	0
A	M	1	1	0	0	0	0
!D		0	0	1	1	0	1
!A	!M	1	1	0	0	0	1
-D		0	0	1	1	1	1
-A	-M	1	1	0	0	1	1
D+1		0	1	1	1	1	1
A+1	M+1	1	1	0	1	1	1
D-1		0	0	1	1	1	0
A-1	M-1	1	1	0	0	1	0
D+A	D+M	0	0	0	0	1	0
D-A	D-M	0	1	0	0	1	1
A-D	M-D	0	0	0	1	1	1
D&A	D&M	0	0	0	0	0	0
D|A	D|M	0	1	0	1	0	1

a == 0 a == 1

dest	d	d	d	Effect: store *comp* in:
null	0	0	0	the value is not stored
M	0	0	1	RAM[A]
D	0	1	0	D register (reg)
DM	0	1	1	D reg and RAM[A]
A	1	0	0	A reg
AM	1	0	1	A reg and RAM[A]
AD	1	1	0	A reg and D reg
ADM	1	1	1	A reg, D reg, and RAM[A]

jump	j	j	j	Effect:
null	0	0	0	no jump
JGT	0	0	1	if *comp* > 0 jump
JEQ	0	1	0	if *comp* = 0 jump
JGE	0	1	1	if *comp* ≥ 0 jump
JLT	1	0	0	if *comp* < 0 jump
JNE	1	0	1	if *comp* ≠ 0 jump
JLE	1	1	0	if *comp* ≤ 0 jump
JMP	1	1	1	unconditional jump

Figure 4.5   The Hack instruction set, showing symbolic mnemonics and their corresponding binary codes.

The *C*-instruction

The *C*-instruction answers three questions: what to compute (an ALU operation, denoted *comp*), where to store the computed value (*dest*), and what to do next (*jump*). Along with the *A*-instruction, the *C*-instruction specifies all the possible operations of the computer.

In the binary version, the leftmost bit is the *C*-instruction's op-code, which is 1. The next two bits are not used, and are set by convention to 1. The next seven bits are the binary representation of the *comp* field. The next three bits are the binary representation of the *dest* field. The rightmost three bits are the binary representation of the *jump* field. We now describe the syntax and semantics of these three fields.

Computation specification (*comp*): The Hack ALU is designed to compute one out of a fixed set of functions on two given 16-bit inputs. In the Hack computer, the two ALU data inputs are wired as follows. The first ALU input feeds from the D register. The second ALU input feeds either from the A register (when the a-bit is 0) or from M, the selected data memory register (when the a-bit is 1). Taken together, the computed function is specified by the a-bit and the six c-bits comprising the instruction's *comp* field. This 7-bit pattern can potentially code 128 different calculations, of which only the twenty-eight listed in figure 4.5 are documented in the language specification.

Recall that the format of the *C*-instruction is 111acccccdddjjj. Suppose we want to compute the value of the D register, minus 1. According to figure 4.5, this can be done using the symbolic instruction D-1, which is 111**0001110**000000 in binary (the relevant 7-bit *comp* field is underlined for emphasis). To compute a bitwise Or between the values of the D and M registers, we use the instruction D|M (in binary: 111**1010101**000000). To compute the constant -1, we use the instruction -1 (in binary: 111**0111010**000000), and so on.

Destination specification (*dest*): The ALU output can be stored in zero, one, two, or three possible destinations, simultaneously. The first and second d-bits code whether to store the computed value in the A register and in the D register, respectively. The third d-bit codes whether to store the computed value in M, the currently selected memory register. One, more than one, or none of these three bits may be asserted.

Recall that the format of the *C*-instruction is 111acccccdddjjj. Suppose we wish to increment the value of the memory register whose address is 7 and also to store the new value in the D register. According to figure 4.5, this can be accomplished using the two instructions:

```
0000000000000111 // @7
1111110111011000 // DM=M+1
```

Jump directive (*jump*): The *jump* field of the *C*-instruction specifies what to do next. There are two possibilities: fetch and execute the next instruction in the program, which is the default, or fetch and execute some other, designated instruction. In the latter case, we assume that the A register was already set to the address of the target instruction.

During run-time, whether or not to jump is determined jointly by the three j-bits of the instruction's *jump* field and by the ALU output. The first, second, and third j-bits specify whether to jump in case the ALU output is negative, zero, or positive, respectively. This gives eight possible jump conditions, listed at the bottom right of figure 4.5. The convention for specifying an unconditional goto instruction is 0;JMP (since the *comp* field is mandatory, the convention is to compute 0—an arbitrarily chosen ALU operation—which is ignored).

Preventing conflicting uses of the *A* register: The Hack computer uses one address register for addressing both the RAM and the ROM. Thus, when we execute the instruction @n, we select both RAM[n] and ROM[n]. This is done in order to set the stage for either a subsequent *C*-instruction that operates on the selected data memory register, M, or a subsequent *C*-instruction that specifies a jump. To make sure that we perform exactly one of these two operations, we issue the following best-practice advice: A *C*-instruction that contains a reference to M should specify no jump, and vice versa: a *C*-instruction that specifies a jump should make no reference to M.

4.2.4   Symbols

Assembly instructions can specify memory locations (addresses) using either constants or symbols. The symbols fall into three functional categories: *predefined symbols*, representing special memory addresses; *label symbols*, representing destinations of goto instructions; and *variable symbols*, representing variables.

Predefined symbols: There are several kinds of predefined symbols, designed to promote consistency and readability of low-level Hack programs.

R0, R1,..., R15: These symbols are bound to the values 0 to 15. This predefined binding helps make Hack programs more readable. To illustrate, consider the following code segment:

```
// Sets RAM[3] to 7:
@7
D=A
@R3
M=D
```

The instruction @7 sets the A register to 7, and @R3 sets the A register to 3. Why do we use R in the latter and not in the former? Because it makes the code more self-explanatory. In the instruction @7, the syntax hints that A is used as a *data register*, ignoring the side effect of also selecting RAM[7]. In the instruction @R3, the syntax hints that A is used *to select a data memory address.* In general, the predefined symbols R0, R1, ..., R15 can be viewed as ready-made working variables, sometimes referred to as *virtual registers*.

SP, LCL, ARG, THIS, THAT: These symbols are bound to the values 0, 1, 2, 3, and 4, respectively. For example, address 2 can be selected using either @2, @R2, or @ARG. The symbols SP, LCL, ARG, THIS, and THAT will be used in part II of the book, when we implement the compiler and the virtual machine that run on top of the Hack platform. These symbols can be completely ignored for now; we specify them for completeness.

SCREEN, KBD: Hack programs can read data from a keyboard and display data on a screen. The screen and the keyboard interface with the computer via two designated memory blocks known as *memory maps*. The symbols SCREEN and KBD are bound, respectively, to the values 16384 and 24576 (in hexadecimal: 4000 and 6000), which are the agreed-upon base addresses of the *screen memory map* and the *keyboard memory map*, respectively. These symbols are used by Hack programs that manipulate the screen and the keyboard, as we'll see in the next section.

Label symbols: Labels can appear anywhere in a Hack assembly program and are declared using the syntax (*xxx*). This directive binds the symbol *xxx* to the address of the next instruction in the program. Goto instructions that make use of label symbols can appear anywhere in the program, even before the label has been declared. By convention, label symbols are written using uppercase letters. The program listed in figure 4.4 uses three label symbols: LOOP, STOP and END.

Variable symbols: Any symbol *xxx* appearing in a Hack assembly program that is not predefined and is not declared elsewhere using (*xxx*) is treated as a variable and is bound to a unique running number starting at 16. By convention, variable symbols are written using lowercase letters. For example, the program listed in figure 4.4 uses two variables: i and sum. These symbols are bound by the assembler to 16 and 17, respectively. Therefore, following translation, instructions like @i and @sum end up selecting memory addresses 16 and 17, respectively. The beauty of this contract is that the assembly program is completely oblivious of the physical addresses. The assembly program uses symbols only, trusting that the assembler will know how to resolve them into actual addresses.

4.2.5   Input/Output Handling

The Hack hardware platform can be connected to two peripheral I/O devices: a screen and a keyboard. Both devices interact with the computer platform through *memory maps*.

Drawing pixels on the screen is done by writing binary values into a designated memory segment associated with the screen, and listening to the keyboard is done by reading a designated memory location associated with the keyboard. The physical I/O devices and their memory maps are synchronized via continuous refresh loops that are external to the main hardware platform.

Screen: The Hack computer interacts with a black-and-white screen organized as 256 rows of 512 pixels per row. The screen's contents are represented by a memory map, stored in an 8K memory block of 16-bit words, starting at RAM address 16384 (in hexadecimal: 4000), also referred to by the predefined symbol SCREEN. Each row in the physical screen, starting at the screen's top-left corner, is represented in the RAM by thirty-two consecutive 16-bit words. Following convention, the screen origin is the top-left corner, which is considered row 0 and column 0. With that in mind, the pixel at row *row* and column *col* is mapped onto the *col* % 16 bit (counting from LSB to MSB) of the word located at RAM[SCREEN + *row* · 32 + *col* / 16]. This pixel can be either read (probing whether it is black or white), made black by setting it to 1, or made white by setting it to 0. For example, consider the following code segment, which blackens the first 16 pixels at the top left of the screen:

```
// Sets the A register to the address of the RAM register that represents
// the 16 left-most pixels at the screen's top row:
@SCREEN
// Sets this RAM register to 1111111111111111:
M=-1
```

Note that Hack instructions cannot access individual pixels/bits directly. Instead, we must fetch a complete 16-bit word from the memory map, figure out which bit or bits we wish to manipulate, carry out the manipulation using arithmetic/logical operations (without touching the other bits), and then write the modified 16-bit word to the memory. In the example given above, we got away with not doing bit-specific manipulations since the task could be implemented using one bulk manipulation.

Keyboard: The Hack computer can interact with a standard physical keyboard via a single-word memory map located at RAM address 24576 (in hexadecimal: 6000), also referred to by the predefined symbol KBD. The contract is as follows: When a key is pressed on the physical keyboard, its 16-bit character code appears at RAM[KBD]. When no key is pressed, the code 0 appears. The Hack character set is listed in appendix 5.

By now, readers with programming experience have probably noticed that manipulating input/output devices using assembly language is a tedious affair. That's because they are accustomed to using high-level statements like write ("hello") or draw Circle (x,y, radius). As you can now appreciate, there is a considerable gap between these abstract, high-level I/O statements and the bit-by-bit machine instructions that end up realizing them in silicon. One of the agents that closes this gap is the *operating system*—a program that knows, among many other things, how to render text and draw graphics using pixel manipulations. We will discuss and write one such OS in part II of the book.

4.2.7   Syntax Conventions and File Formats

Binary code files: By convention, programs written in the binary Hack language are stored in text files with a `hack` extension, for example, `Prog.hack`. Each line in the file codes a single binary instruction, using a sequence of sixteen `0` and `1` characters. Taken together, all the lines in the file represent a machine language program. The contract is as follows: When a machine language program is loaded into the computer's instruction memory, the binary code appearing in the file's *n*th line is stored at address *n* of the instruction memory. The counts of program lines, instructions, and memory addresses start at 0.

Assembly language files: By convention, programs written in the symbolic Hack assembly language are stored in text files with an `asm` extension, for example, `Prog.asm`. An assembly language file is composed of text lines, each being an *A*-instruction, a *C*-instruction, a label declaration, or a comment.

A label declaration is a text line of the form (*symbol*). The assembler handles such a declaration by binding *symbol* to the address of the next instruction in the program. This is the only action that the assembler takes when handling a label declaration; no binary code is generated. That's why label declarations are sometimes referred to as *pseudo-instructions*: they exist only at the symbolic level, generating no code.

Constants and symbols: These are the *xxx*'s in *A*-instructions of the form @*xxx*. *Constants* are nonnegative values from 0 to $2^{15} - 1$, and are written in decimal notation. A *symbol* is any sequence of letters, digits, underscore (_), dot (.), dollar sign ($), and colon (:) that does not begin with a digit.

Comments: A text line beginning with two slashes (//) and ending at the end of the line is considered a comment and is ignored.

White space: Leading space characters and empty lines are ignored.

Case conventions: All the assembly mnemonics (figure 4.5) must be written in uppercase. By convention, label symbols are written in uppercase, and variable symbols in lowercase. See figure 4.4 for examples.

4.3   Hack Programming

We now turn to present three examples of low-level programming, using the Hack assembly language. Since project 4 focuses on writing Hack assembly programs, it will serve you well to carefully read and understand these examples.

Example 1: Figure 4.6 shows a program that adds up the values of the first two RAM registers, adds 17 to the sum, and stores the result in the third RAM register. Before running the program, the user (or a test script) is expected to put some values in RAM[0] and RAM[1].

Among other things, the program illustrates how the so-called virtual registers R0, R1, R2,... can be used as working variables. The program also illustrates the recommended way of terminating Hack programs, which is staging and entering an infinite loop. In the absence of this infinite loop, the CPU's fetch-execute logic (explained in the next chapter) will merrily glide forward, trying to execute whatever instructions are stored in the computer's memory following the last instruction in the current program. This may lead to unpredictable and potentially hazardous consequences. The deliberate infinite loop serves to control and contain the CPU's operation after completing the program's execution.

Example 2: The second example computes the sum $1 + 2 + 3 + \cdots + n$, where n is the value of the first RAM register, and puts the sum in the second RAM register. This program is shown in figure 4.4, and now we have what it takes to understand it fully.

Among other things, this program illustrates the use of symbolic variables—in this case i and sum. The example also illustrates our recommended practice for low-level program development: instead of writing assembly code directly, start by writing goto-oriented pseudocode. Next, test your pseudocode on paper, tracing the values of key variables. When convinced that the program's logic is correct, and that it does what it's supposed to do, proceed to express each pseudo-instruction as one or more assembly instructions.

```
// Program: Add.asm
// Computes: RAM[2] = RAM[0] + RAM[1] + 17
// Usage: put values in RAM[0] and in RAM[1]
    // D = RAM[0]
    @R0
    D=M
    // D = D + RAM[1]
    @R1
    D=D+M
    // D = D + 17
    @17
    D=D+A
    // RAM[2] = D
    @R2
    M=D
(END)
    @END
    0;JMP
```

Figure 4.6 A Hack assembly program that computes a simple arithmetic expression.

The virtues of writing and debugging symbolic (rather than physical) instructions were observed by the gifted mathematician and writer Augusta Ada King-Noel, Countess of Lovelace, back in 1843. This important insight has contributed to her lasting fame as history's first programmer. Before Ada Lovelace, proto-programmers who worked with early mechanical computers were reduced to tinkering with machine operations directly, and coding was hard and error prone. What was true in 1843 about symbolic and physical programming is equally true today about pseudo and assembly programming: When it comes to nontrivial programs, writing and testing pseudocode and then translating it into assembly instructions is easier and safer than writing assembly code directly.

Example 3: Consider the high-level array processing idiom for i = 0 ... n {do something with arr[i]}. If we wish to express this logic in assembly, then our first challenge is that the array abstraction does not exist in machine language. However, if we know the base address of the array in the RAM, we can readily implement this logic in assembly, using pointer-based access to the array elements.

To illustrate the notion of a pointer, suppose that variable x contains the value 523, and consider the two possible pseudo-instructions x=17 and *x=17 (of which we execute only one). The first instruction sets the value of x to 17. The second instruction informs that x is to be treated as a *pointer*, that is, a variable whose value is interpreted as a memory address. Hence, the instruction ends up setting RAM[523] to 17, leaving the value of x intact.

The program in figure 4.7 illustrates pointer-based array processing in the Hack machine language. The key instructions of interest are A=D+M, followed by M=−1. In the Hack language, the basic pointer-processing idiom is implemented by an instruction of the form A=..., followed by a C-instruction that operates on M (which stands for RAM[A], the memory location selected by A). As we will see when we write the compiler in the second part of the book, this humble low-level programming idiom enables implementing, in Hack assembly, any array access or object-based get/set operation expressed in any high-level language.

4.4   Project

Objective: Acquire a taste of low-level programming, and get acquainted with the Hack computer system. This will be done by writing and executing two low-level programs, written in the Hack assembly language.

Resources: The only resources required to complete the project are the Hack *CPU emulator*, available in nand2tetris/tools, and the test scripts described below, available in the projects/04 folder.

Contract: Write and test the two programs described below. When executed on the supplied CPU emulator, your programs should realize the described behaviors.

Multiplication (`Mult.asm`): The inputs of this program are the values stored in `R0` and `R1` (`RAM[0]` and `RAM[1]`). The program computes the product `R0 * R1` and stores the result in `R2`. Assume that $R0 \geq 0$, $R1 \geq 0$, and $R0 * R1 < 32768$ (your program need not test these assertions). The supplied `Mult.tst` and `Mult.cmp` scripts are designed to test your program on representative data values.

I/O handling (`Fill.asm`): This program runs an infinite loop that listens to the keyboard. When a key is pressed (any key), the program blackens the screen by writing *black* in every pixel. When no key is pressed, the program clears the screen by writing *white* in every pixel. You may choose to blacken and clear the screen in any spatial pattern, as long as pressing a key continuously for long enough will result in a fully blackened screen, and not pressing any key for long enough will result in a cleared screen. This program has a test script (`Fill.tst`) but no compare file—it should be checked by visibly inspecting the simulated screen in the CPU emulator.

Pseudocode

```
// Program: PointerDemo
// Starting at base address R0,
// sets the first R1 words to -1
  n = 0
LOOP:
  if (n == R1) goto END
  *(R0 + n) = -1
  n = n + 1
  goto LOOP
END:
```

Hack assembly code

```
// Program: PointerDemo.asm
// Starting at base address R0,
// sets the first R1 words to -1
  // n = 0
  @n
  M=0
(LOOP)
  // if (n == R1) goto END
  @n
  D=M
  @R1
  D=D-M
  @END
  D;JEQ
  // *(R0 + n) = -1
  @R0
  D=M
  @n
  A=D+M
  M=-1
  // n = n + 1
  @n
  M=M+1
  // goto LOOP
  @LOOP
  0;JMP
(END)
  @END
  0;JMP
```

Figure 4.7 Array processing example, using pointer-based access to array elements.

CPU emulator: This program, available in `nand2tetris/tools`, provides a visual simulation of the Hack computer (see figure 4.8). The program's GUI shows the current states of the computer's instruction memory (ROM), data memory (RAM), the two registers `A` and `D`, the program counter `PC`, and the `ALU`. It also displays the current state of the computer's screen and allows entering inputs through the keyboard.

The typical way to use the CPU emulator is to load a machine language program into the ROM, execute the code, and observe its impact on the simulated hardware elements. Importantly, the CPU emulator enables loading binary `.hack` files as well as symbolic `.asm` files, written in the Hack assembly language. In the latter case, the emulator translates the assembly program into binary code on the fly. Conveniently, the loaded code can be viewed in both its binary and symbolic representations.

Since the supplied CPU emulator features a built-in assembler, there is no need to use a standalone Hack assembler in this project.

Steps: We recommend proceeding as follows:

0. The supplied CPU emulator is available in the `nand2tetris/tools` folder. If you need help, consult the tutorial available at www.nand2tetris.org.

1. Write/edit the `Mult.asm` program using a plain text editor. Start with the skeletal program stored in `projects/04/mult/Mult.asm`.

2. Load `Mult.asm` into the CPU emulator. This can be done either interactively or by loading and executing the supplied `Mult.tst` script.

3. Run the script. If you get any translation or run-time errors, go to step 1.

Follow steps 1–3 for writing the second program, using the `projects/04/fill` folder.

Debugging tip: The Hack language is case-sensitive. A common assembly programming error occurs when one writes, say, `@foo` and `@Foo` in different parts of the program, thinking that both instructions refer to the same symbol. In fact, the assembler will generate and manage two variables that have nothing in common.

A web-based version of project 4 is available at www.nand2tetris.org.

4.5   Perspective

The Hack machine language is basic. Typical machine languages feature more operations, more data types, more registers, and more instruction formats. In terms of syntax, we have chosen to give Hack a lighter look and feel than that of conventional assembly languages. In particular, we have chosen a friendly syntax for the *C*-instruction, for example, `D=D+M`, instead of the more common prefix syntax `add M,D` used in many machine languages. The

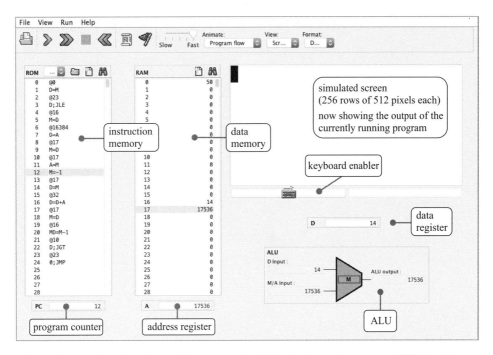

Figure 4.8   The CPU emulator, with a program loaded in the instruction memory (ROM) and some data in the data memory (RAM). The figure shows a snapshot taken during the program's execution.

reader should note, however, that this is just a syntax effect. For example, the + character in the operation code D+M plays no algebraic role whatsoever. Rather, the three-character string D+M, taken as a whole, is treated as a single assembly mnemonic, designed to code a single ALU operation.

One of the main characteristics that gives machine languages their particular flavor is the number of memory addresses that can be squeezed into a single instruction. In this respect, the austere Hack language may be described as a 1/2 *address* machine language: Since there is no room to pack both an instruction code and a 15-bit address in a single 16-bit instruction, operations involving memory access require two Hack instructions: one for specifying the address on which we wish to operate, and one for specifying the operation. In comparison, many machine languages can specify an operation and at least one address in every machine instruction.

Indeed, Hack assembly code typically ends up being mostly an alternating sequence of *A*- and *C*-instructions: @sum followed by M=0, @LOOP followed by 0;JMP, and so on. If you find this coding style tedious or peculiar, you should note that friendlier *macro-instructions* like sum=0 and goto LOOP can be easily introduced into the language, making Hack assembly code shorter and more readable. The trick is to extend the assembler to translate each macro-instruction into the two Hack instructions that it entails—a relatively simple tweak.

The *assembler*, mentioned many times in this chapter, is the program responsible for translating symbolic assembly programs into executable programs written in binary code. In addition, the assembler is responsible for managing all the system- and user-defined symbols found in the assembly program and for resolving them into physical memory addresses that are injected into the generated binary code. We will return to this translation task in chapter 6, which is dedicated to understanding and building assemblers.

5   Computer Architecture

Make everything as simple as possible, but not simpler.

—Albert Einstein (1879–1955)

This chapter is the pinnacle of the hardware part of our journey. We are now ready to take the chips that we built in chapters 1–3 and integrate them into a general-purpose computer system, capable of running programs written in the machine language presented in chapter 4. The specific computer that we will build, named Hack, has two important virtues. On the one hand, Hack is a simple machine that can be constructed in a few hours, using previously built chips and the supplied hardware simulator. On the other hand, Hack is sufficiently powerful to illustrate the key operating principles and hardware elements of any general-purpose computer. Therefore, building it will give you a hands-on understanding of how modern computers work, and how they are built.

Section 5.1 begins with an overview of the *von Neumann architecture*—a central dogma in computer science underlying the design of almost all modern computers. The Hack platform is a von Neumann machine variant, and section 5.2 gives its exact hardware specification. Section 5.3 describes how the Hack platform can be implemented from previously built chips, in particular the ALU built in project 2 and the registers and memory devices built in project 3. Section 5.4 describes the project in which you will build the computer. Section 5.5 provides perspective. In particular, we compare the Hack machine to industrial-strength computers and emphasize the critical role that optimization plays in the latter.

The computer that will emerge from this effort will be as simple as possible, but not simpler. On the one hand, the computer will be based on a minimal and elegant hardware configuration. On the other hand, the resulting configuration will be sufficiently powerful for executing programs written in a Java-like programming language, presented in part II of the book. This language will enable developing interactive computer games and applications involving graphics and animation, delivering a solid performance and a satisfying user experience. In order to realize these high-level applications on the barebone hardware platform, we will need to build a compiler, a virtual machine, and an operating system. This will be done in part II. For now, let's complete part I by integrating the chips that we've built so far into a complete, general-purpose hardware platform.

5.1   Computer Architecture Fundamentals

5.1.1   The Stored Program Concept

Compared to all the machines around us, the most remarkable feature of the digital computer is its amazing versatility. Here is a machine with a finite and fixed hardware that can perform an infinite number of tasks, from playing games to typesetting books to driving cars. This remarkable versatility—a boon that we have come to take for granted—is the fruit of a brilliant early idea called the *stored program* concept. Formulated independently by several scientists and engineers in the 1930s, the stored program concept is still considered the most profound invention in, if not the very foundation of, modern computer science.

Like many scientific breakthroughs, the basic idea is simple. The computer is based on a fixed hardware platform capable of executing a fixed repertoire of simple instructions. At the same time, these instructions can be combined like building blocks, yielding arbitrarily sophisticated programs. Moreover, the logic of these programs is not embedded in the hardware, as was customary in mechanical computers predating 1930. Instead, the program's code is temporarily stored in the computer's memory, *like data*, becoming what is known as *software*. Since the computer's operation manifests itself to the user through the currently executing software, the same hardware platform can be made to behave completely differently each time it is loaded with a different program.

5.1.2   The von Neumann Architecture

The stored program concept is the key element of both abstract and practical computer models, most notably the *Turing machine* (1936) and the *von Neumann machine* (1945). The Turing machine—an abstract artifact describing a deceptively simple computer—is used mainly in theoretical computer science for analyzing the logical foundations of computation. In contrast, the von Neumann machine is a practical model that informs the construction of almost all computer platforms today.

The von Neumann architecture, shown in figure 5.1, is based on a *Central Processing Unit* (CPU), interacting with a *memory* device, receiving data from some *input* device, and emitting data to some *output* device. At the heart of this architecture lies the *stored program* concept: the computer's memory stores not only the data that the computer manipulates but also the instructions that tell the computer what to do. Let us explore this architecture in some detail.

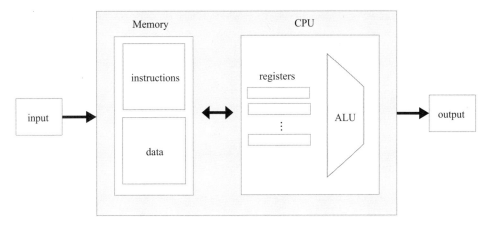

Figure 5.1   A generic von Neumann computer architecture.

5.1.3   Memory

The computer's *Memory* can be discussed from both physical and logical perspectives. Physically, the memory is a linear sequence of addressable, fixed-size *registers*, each having a unique address and a value. Logically, this address space serves two purposes: storing data and storing instructions. Both the "instruction words" and the "data words" are implemented exactly the same way—as sequences of bits.

All the memory registers—irrespective of their roles—are handled the same way: to access a particular memory register, we supply the register's address. This action, also referred to as *addressing*, provides an immediate access to the register's data. The term *Random Access Memory* derives from the important requirement that each randomly selected memory register can be reached instantaneously, that is, within the same cycle (or time step), irrespective of the memory size and the register's location. This requirement clearly carries its weight in memory units that have billions of registers. Readers who built the RAM devices in project 3 know that we've already satisfied this requirement.

In what follows, we'll refer to the memory area dedicated to data as *data memory* and to the memory area dedicated to instructions as *instruction memory*. In some variants of the von Neumann architecture, the data memory and the instruction memory are allocated and managed dynamically, as needed, within the same physical address space. In other variants, the data memory and the instruction memory are kept in two physically separate memory units, each having its own distinct address space. Both variants have pros and cons, as we'll discuss later.

Data memory: High-level programs are designed to manipulate abstract artifacts like variables, arrays, and objects. Yet at the hardware level, these data abstractions are realized by binary values stored in memory registers. In particular, following translation to machine language, abstract array processing and get/set operations on objects are reduced to *reading* and *writing* selected memory registers. To read a register, we supply an address and probe the value of the selected register. To write to a register, we supply an address and store a new value in the selected register, overriding its previous value.

Instruction memory: Before a high-level program can be executed on a target computer, it must first be translated into the machine language of the target computer. Each high-level statement is translated into one or more low-level instructions, which are then written as binary values to a file called the *binary*, or *executable*, version of the program. Before running a program, we must first load its binary version from a mass storage device, and serialize its instructions into the computer's *instruction memory*.

From the pure focus of computer architecture, *how* a program is loaded into the computer's memory is considered an external issue. What's important is that when the CPU is called upon to execute a program, the program's code will already reside in the computer's memory.

5.1.4   Central Processing Unit

The Central Processing Unit (CPU)—the centerpiece of the computer's architecture—is in charge of executing the instructions of the currently running program. Each instruction tells the CPU which computation to perform, which registers to access, and which instruction to fetch and execute next. The CPU executes these tasks using three main elements: An Arithmetic Logic Unit (ALU), a set of registers, and a control unit.

Arithmetic Logic Unit: The ALU chip is built to perform all the low-level arithmetic and logical operations featured by the computer. A typical ALU can add two given values, compute their bitwise And, compare them for equality, and so on. How much functionality the ALU should feature is a design decision. In general, any function not supported by the ALU can be realized later, using system software running on top of the hardware platform. The trade-off is simple: hardware implementations are typically more efficient but result in more expensive hardware, while software implementations are inexpensive and less efficient.

Registers: In the course of performing computations, the CPU is often required to store interim values temporarily. In theory, we could have stored these values in memory registers, but this would entail long-distance trips between the CPU and the RAM, which are two separate chips. These delays would frustrate the CPU-resident ALU, which is an ultra-fast combinational calculator. The result will be a condition known as *starvation*, which is what happens when a fast processor depends on a sluggish data store for supplying its inputs and consuming its outputs.

In order to avert starvation and boost performance, we normally equip the CPU with a small set of high-speed (and relatively expensive) *registers*, acting as the processor's immediate memory. These registers serve various purposes: *data registers* store interim values, *address registers* store values that are used to address the RAM, the *program counter* stores the address of the instruction that should be fetched and executed next, and the *instruction register* stores the current instruction. A typical CPU uses a few dozen such registers, but our frugal Hack computer will need only three.

Control: A computer instruction is a structured package of agreed-upon micro-codes, that is, sequences of one or more bits designed to signal different devices what to do. Thus, before an instruction can be executed, it must first be decoded into its micro-codes. Next, each micro-code is routed to its designated hardware device (ALU, registers, memory) within the CPU, where it tells the device how to partake in the overall execution of the instruction.

Fetch-Execute: In each step (cycle) of the program's execution, the CPU fetches a binary machine instruction from the instruction memory, decodes it, and executes it. As a side effect of the instruction's execution, the CPU also figures out which instruction to fetch and execute next. This repetitive process is sometimes referred to as the *fetch-execute cycle*.

5.1.5   Input and Output

Computers interact with their external environments using a great variety of input and output (I/O) devices: screens, keyboards, storage devices, printers, microphones, speakers, network interface cards, and so on, not to mention the bewildering array of sensors and activators embedded in automobiles, cameras, hearing aids, alarm systems, and all the gadgets around us. There are two reasons why we don't concern ourselves with these I/O devices. First, every one of them represents a unique piece of machinery, requiring a unique knowledge of engineering. Second, for that very same reason, computer scientists have devised clever schemes for abstracting away this complexity and making all I/O devices look exactly the same to the computer. The key element in this abstraction is called *memory-mapped* I/O.

The basic idea is to create a binary emulation of the I/O device, making it appear to the CPU as if it were a regular linear memory segment. This is done by allocating, for each I/O device, a designated area in the computer's memory that acts as its memory map. In the case of an input device like a keyboard, the memory map is made to continuously reflect the physical state of the device: when the user presses a key on the keyboard, a binary code representing that key appears in the keyboard's memory map. In the case of an output device like a screen, the screen is made to continuously reflect the state of its designated memory map: when we write a bit in the screen's memory map, a respective pixel is turned on or off on the screen.

The I/O devices and the memory maps are refreshed, or synchronized, many times per second, so the response time from the user's perspective appears to be instantaneous. Programmatically, the key implication is that low-level computer programs can access any I/O device by manipulating its designated memory map.

The memory map convention is based on several agreed-upon contracts. First, the data that drives each I/O device must be serialized, or mapped, onto the computer's memory, hence the name *memory map*. For example, the screen, which is a two-dimensional grid of pixels, is mapped on a one-dimensional block of fixed-size memory registers. Second, each I/O device is required to support an agreed-upon interaction protocol so that programs will be able to access it in a predictable manner. For example, it should be decided which binary codes should represent which keys on the keyboard. Given the multitude of computer platforms, I/O devices, and different hardware and software vendors, one can appreciate the crucial role that agreed-upon industry-wide *standards* play in realizing these low-level interaction contracts.

The practical implications of memory-mapped I/O are significant: The computer system is totally independent of the number, nature, or make of the I/O devices that interact, or may interact, with it. Whenever we want to connect a new I/O device to the computer, all we have to do is allocate to it a new memory map and take note of the map's base address (these onetime configurations are carried out by the so-called *installer* programs). Another necessary element is a *device driver* program, which is added to the computer's operating system. This program bridges the gap between the I/O device's memory map data and the way this data is actually rendered on, or generated by, the physical I/O device.

5.2   The Hack Hardware Platform: Specification

The architectural framework described thus far is characteristic of any general-purpose computer system. We now turn to describe one specific variant of this architecture: the Hack computer. As usual in Nand to Tetris, we start with the abstraction, focusing on *what* the computer is designed to do. The computer's implementation—*how* it does it—is described later.

5.2.1   Overview

The Hack platform is a 16-bit von Neumann machine designed to execute programs written in the Hack machine language. In order to do so, the Hack platform consists of a *CPU*, two separate memory modules serving as *instruction memory* and *data memory*, and two memory-mapped I/O devices: a *screen* and a *keyboard*.

The Hack computer executes programs that reside in an instruction memory. In physical implementations of the Hack platform, the instruction memory can be implemented as a ROM (Read-Only Memory) chip that is preloaded with the required program. Software-based emulators of the Hack computer support this functionality by providing means for loading the instruction memory from a text file containing a program written in the Hack machine language.

The Hack CPU consists of the ALU built in project 2 and three registers named *Data register* (D), *Address register* (A), and *Program Counter* (PC). The D register and the A register are identical to the `Register` chip built in project 3, and the program counter is identical to the `PC` chip built in project 3. While the D register is used solely for storing data values, the A register serves one of three different purposes, depending on the context in which it is used: storing a data value (like the D register), selecting an address in the instruction memory, or selecting an address in the data memory.

The Hack CPU is designed to execute instructions written in the Hack machine language. In case of an *A*-instruction, the 16 bits of the instruction are treated as a binary value which is loaded as is into the A register. In case of a *C*-instruction, the instruction is treated as a capsule of control bits that specify various micro-operations to be performed by various chip-parts within the CPU. We now turn to describe how the CPU materializes these micro-codes into concrete actions.

5.2.2   Central Processing Unit

The Hack CPU interface is shown in figure 5.2. The CPU is designed to execute 16-bit instructions according to the Hack machine language specification presented in chapter 4.

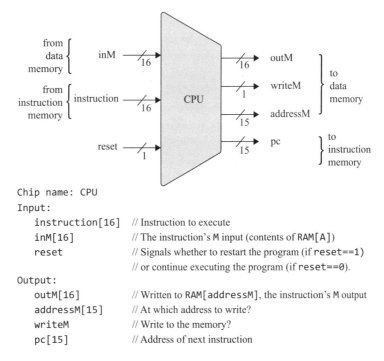

```
Chip name: CPU
Input:
    instruction[16]      // Instruction to execute
    inM[16]              // The instruction's M input (contents of RAM[A])
    reset                // Signals whether to restart the program (if reset==1)
                         // or continue executing the program (if reset==0).
Output:
    outM[16]             // Written to RAM[addressM], the instruction's M output
    addressM[15]         // At which address to write?
    writeM               // Write to the memory?
    pc[15]               // Address of next instruction
```

Figure 5.2   The Hack Central Processing Unit (CPU) interface.

The CPU consists of an ALU, two registers named A and D, and a program counter named PC (these internal chip-parts are not seen outside the CPU). The CPU expects to be connected to an instruction memory, from which it fetches instructions for execution, and to a data memory, from which it can read, and into which it can write, data values. The inM input and the outM output hold the values referred to as M in the *C*-instruction syntax. The addressM output holds the address at which outM should be written.

If the instruction input is an *A*-instruction, the CPU loads the 16-bit instruction value into the A register. If instruction is a *C*-instruction, then (i) the CPU causes the ALU to perform the computation specified by the instruction and (ii) the CPU causes this value to be stored in the subset of {A,D,M} destination registers specified by the instruction. If one of the destination registers is M, the CPU's outM output is set to the ALU output, and the CPU's writeM output is set to 1. Otherwise, writeM is set to 0, and any value may appear in outM.

As long as the reset input is 0, the CPU uses the ALU output and the jump bits of the current instruction to decide which instruction to fetch next. If reset is 1, the CPU sets pc to 0. Later in the chapter we'll connect the CPU's pc output to the address input of the instruction memory chip, causing the latter to emit the next instruction. This configuration will realize the fetch step of the fetch-execute cycle.

The CPU's outM and writeM outputs are realized by *combinational* logic; thus, they are affected instantaneously by the instruction's execution. The addressM and pc outputs are *clocked*: although they are affected by the instruction's execution, they commit to their new values only in the next time step.

5.2.3   Instruction Memory

The Hack *instruction memory*, called ROM32K, is specified in figure 5.3.

```
Chip name:  ROM32K
Input:      address[15]
Output:     out[16]
Function:   Emits the 16-bit value stored in the address selected by the
            address input. It is assumed that the chip is preloaded
            with a program written in the Hack machine language.
```

Figure 5.3   The Hack instruction memory interface.

5.2.4 Input/Output

Access to the input/output devices of the Hack computer is made possible by the computer's *data memory*, a read/write RAM device consisting of 32K addressable 16-bit registers. In addition to serving as the computer's general-purpose data store, the data memory also interfaces between the CPU and the computer's input/output devices, as we now turn to describe.

The Hack platform can be connected to two peripheral devices: a *screen* and a *keyboard*. Both devices interact with the computer platform through designated memory areas called *memory maps*. Specifically, images can be drawn on the screen by writing 16-bit values in a designated memory segment called a *screen memory map*. Similarly, which key is presently pressed on the keyboard can be determined by probing a designated 16-bit memory register called a *keyboard memory map*.

The screen memory map and the keyboard memory map are continuously updated, many times per second, by peripheral refresh logic that is external to the computer. Thus, when one or more bits are changed in the screen memory map, the change is immediately reflected on the physical screen. Likewise, when a key is pressed on the physical keyboard, the character code of the pressed key immediately appears in the keyboard memory map. With that in mind, when a low-level program wants to read something from the keyboard, or write something on the screen, the program manipulates the respective memory maps of these I/O devices.

In the Hack computer platform, the screen memory map and the keyboard memory map are realized by two built-in chips named `Screen` and `Keyboard`. These chips behave like standard memory devices, with the additional side effects of continuously synchronizing between the I/O devices and their respective memory maps. We now turn to specify these chips in detail.

Screen: The Hack computer can interact with a physical screen consisting of 256 rows of 512 black-and-white pixels each, spanning a grid of 131,072 pixels. The computer interfaces with the physical screen via a memory map, implemented by an 8K memory chip of 16-bit registers. This chip, named `Screen`, behaves like a regular memory chip, meaning that it can be read and written to using the regular RAM interface. In addition, the `Screen` chip features the side effect that the state of any one of its bits is continuously reflected by a respective pixel in the physical screen (1 = black, 0 = white).

The physical screen is a two-dimensional address space, where each pixel is identified by a row and a column. High-level programming languages typically feature a graphics library that allows accessing individual pixels by supplying (*row,column*) coordinates. However, the memory map that represents this two-dimensional screen at the low level is a one-dimensional sequence of 16-bit words, each identified by supplying an address. Therefore, individual pixels cannot be accessed directly. Rather, we have to figure out which word the target bit is located in and then access, and manipulate, the entire 16-bit word this pixel belongs to. The exact mapping between these two address spaces is specified in figure 5.4. This mapping will be realized by the screen driver of the operating system that we'll develop in part II of the book.

```
Chip name:  Screen       // Screen memory map
Input:      in[16]       // What to write
            address[13]  // Where to read/write
            load         // Write-enable bit
Output:     out[16]      // Screen value at the given address
Function:   Exactly like a 16-bit, 8K RAM, plus a screen refresh side effect.
```

Emits the value stored at the memory location specified by `address`.
If `load==1`, then the memory location specified by `address` is set to the value of `in`.

The loaded value will be emitted by `out` from the next time step onward.
In addition, the chip continuously refreshes a physical screen, consisting of 256 rows and 512 columns of black and white pixels.

The pixel at row r from the top and column c from the left ($0 \leq r \leq 255$, $0 \leq c \leq 511$) is mapped onto the $c\%16$ bit (counting from LSB to MSB) of the 16-bit word stored in `Screen[`$r * 32 + c / 16$`]`.

(Simulators of the Hack computer are expected to simulate the physical screen, the mapping, and the refresh contract).

Figure 5.4   The Hack `Screen` chip interface.

Keyboard: The Hack computer can interact with a physical keyboard, like that of a personal computer. The computer interfaces with the physical keyboard via a memory map, implemented by the `Keyboard` chip, whose interface is given in figure 5.5. The chip interface is identical to that of a read-only, 16-bit register. In addition, the `Keyboard` chip has the side effect of reflecting the state of the physical keyboard: When a key is pressed on the physical keyboard, the 16-bit code of the respective character is emitted by the `output` of the `Keyboard` chip. When no key is pressed, the chip outputs 0. The character set supported by the Hack computer is given in appendix 5, along with the code of each character.

5.2.5   Data Memory

The overall address space of the Hack *data memory* is realized by a chip named `Memory`. This chip is essentially a package of three 16-bit chip-parts: `RAM16K` (a RAM chip of 16K registers, serving as a general-purpose data store), `Screen` (a built-in RAM chip of 8K registers, acting as the screen memory map), and `Keyboard` (a built-in register chip, acting as the keyboard memory map). The complete specification is given in figure 5.6.

```
Chip name:  Keyboard     // Keyboard memory map
Output:     out[16]
Function:   Emits the 16-bit character code of the currently pressed
            key on the physical keyboard or 0 if no key is pressed.
```

(Simulators of the Hack computer are expected to simulate this refresh contract).

Figure 5.5   The Hack `Keyboard` chip interface.

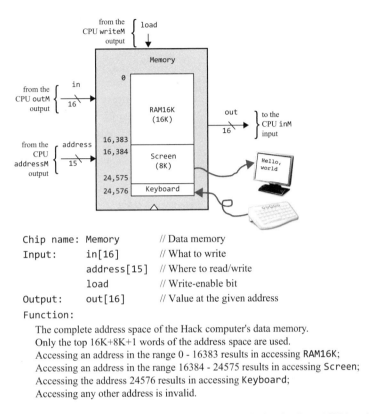

Chip name: Memory   // Data memory
Input: in[16]   // What to write
            address[15]   // Where to read/write
            load   // Write-enable bit
Output: out[16]   // Value at the given address
Function:
    The complete address space of the Hack computer's data memory.
    Only the top 16K+8K+1 words of the address space are used.
    Accessing an address in the range 0 - 16383 results in accessing RAM16K;
    Accessing an address in the range 16384 - 24575 results in accessing Screen;
    Accessing the address 24576 results in accessing Keyboard;
    Accessing any other address is invalid.

Figure 5.6   The Hack data memory interface. Note that the decimal values 16384 and 24576 are 4000 and 6000 in hexadecimal.

5.2.6   Computer

The topmost element in the Hack hardware hierarchy is a computer-on-a-chip named Computer (figure 5.7). The Computer chip can be connected to a screen and a keyboard. The user sees the screen, the keyboard, and a single bit input named reset. When the user sets this bit to 1 and then to 0, the computer starts executing the currently loaded program. From this point onward, the user is at the mercy of the software.

This startup logic realizes what is sometimes referred to as "*booting* the computer." For example, when you boot up a PC or a cell phone, the device is set up to run a ROM-resident program. This program, in turn, loads the operating system's kernel (also a program) into the RAM and starts executing it. The kernel then executes a process (yet another program) that listens to the computer's input devices, that is, keyboard, mouse, touch screen, microphone, and so on. At some point the user will do something, and the OS will respond by running another process or invoking some program.

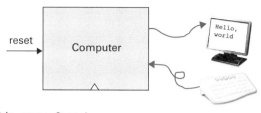

```
Chip name: Computer
Input:      reset
Function:
```

When reset==0, the program stored in the computer executes.
When reset==1, the execution of the program restarts.
To start the program's execution, set reset to 1, and then to 0.
(It is assumed that the computer's instruction memory is loaded
with a program written in the Hack machine language).

Figure 5.7   Interface of Computer, the topmost chip in the Hack hardware platform.

In the Hack computer, the software consists of a binary sequence of 16-bit instructions, written in the Hack machine language and stored in the computer's instruction memory. Typically, this binary code will be the low-level version of a program written in some high-level language and translated by a *compiler* into the Hack machine language. The compilation process will be discussed and implemented in part II of the book.

5.3   Implementation

This section describes a hardware implementation that realizes the Hack computer specified in the previous section. As usual, we don't give exact building instructions. Rather, we expect readers to discover and complete the implementation details on their own. All the chips described below can be built in HDL and simulated on a personal computer using the supplied hardware simulator.

5.3.1   The Central Processing Unit

The implementation of the Hack CPU entails building a logic gate architecture capable of (i) executing a given Hack instruction and (ii) determining which instruction should be fetched and executed next. In order to do so, we will use gate logic for decoding the current instruction, an Arithmetic Logic Unit (ALU) for computing the function specified by the instruction, a set of registers for storing the resulting value, as specified by the instruction, and a program counter for keeping track of which instruction should be fetched and executed next. Since all the underlying building blocks (ALU, registers, PC, and elementary logic gates) were already built in previous chapters, the key question that we now face is how to connect these chip-parts judiciously in a way that realizes the desired CPU operation. One possible configuration is illustrated in figure 5.8 and explained in the following pages.

Instruction decoding: Let's start by focusing on the CPU's instruction input. This 16-bit value represents either an *A*-instruction (when the leftmost bit is 0) or a *C*-instruction (when the leftmost bit is 1). In case of an *A*-instruction, the instruction bits are interpreted as a binary value that should be loaded into the A register. In case of a *C*-instruction, the instruction is treated as a capsule of control bits 1xxacccccccdddjjj, as follows. The a and ccccc bits code the *comp* part of the instruction; the ddd bits code the *dest* part of the instruction; the jjj bits code the *jump* part of the instruction. The xx bits are ignored.

Instruction execution: In case of an *A*-instruction, the 16 bits of the instruction are loaded as is into the A register (actually, this is a 15-bit value, since the MSB is the op-code 0). In case of a *C*-instruction, the a-bit determines whether the ALU input will be fed from the A register value or from the incoming M value. The ccccc bits determine which function

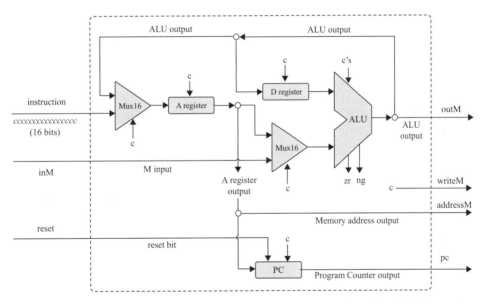

Figure 5.8 Proposed implementation of the Hack CPU, showing an incoming 16-bit instruction. We use the instruction notation *ccccccccccccccc* to emphasize that in the case of a *C*-instruction, the instruction is treated as a capsule of control bits, designed to control different CPU chip-parts. In this diagram, every *c* symbol entering a chip-part stands for some control bit extracted from the instruction (in the case of the ALU, the *c*'s input stands for the six control bits that instruct the ALU what to compute). Taken together, the distributed behavior induced by these control bits ends up executing the instruction. We don't specify which bits go where, since we want readers to answer these questions themselves.

the ALU will compute. The `ddd` bits determine which registers should accept the ALU output. The `jjj` bits are used for determining which instruction to fetch next.

The CPU architecture should extract the control bits described above from the `instruction` input and route them to their chip-part destinations, where they instruct the chip-parts what to do in order to partake in the instruction's execution. Note that every one of these chip-parts is already designed to carry out its intended function. Therefore, the CPU design is mostly a matter of connecting existing chips in a way that realizes this execution model.

Instruction fetching: As a side effect of executing the current instruction, the CPU determines, and outputs, the address of the instruction that should be fetched and executed next. The key element in this subtask is the *Program Counter*—a CPU chip-part whose role is to always store the address of the next instruction.

According to the Hack computer specification, the current program is stored in the instruction memory, starting at address 0. Hence, if we wish to start (or restart) a program's execution, we should set the Program Counter to 0. That's why in figure 5.8 the `reset` input of the CPU is fed directly into the `reset` input of the `PC` chip-part. If we assert this bit, we'll effect `PC=0`, causing the computer to fetch and execute the first instruction in the program.

What should we do next? Normally, we'd like to execute the next instruction in the program. Therefore, and assuming that the `reset` input had been set "back" to `0`, the default operation of the program counter is `PC++`.

But what if the current instruction includes a jump directive? According to the language specification, execution always branches to the instruction whose address is the current value of `A`. Thus, the CPU implementation must realize the following Program Counter behavior: if *jump* then `PC=A` else `PC++`.

How can we effect this behavior using gate logic? The answer is hinted in figure 5.8. Note that the output of the `A` register feeds into the input of the `PC` register. Thus, if we assert the `PC`'s load-bit, we'll enable the operation `PC=A` rather than the default operation `PC++`. We should do this only if we have to effect a jump. Which leads to the next question: How do we know if we have to effect a jump? The answer depends on the three j-bits of the current instruction and the two ALU output bits `zr` and `ng`. Taken together, these bits can be used to determine whether the jump condition is satisfied or not.

We'll stop here, lest we rob readers of the pleasure of completing the CPU implementation themselves. We hope that as they do so, they will savor the clockwork elegance of the Hack CPU.

5.3.2 Memory

The `Memory` chip of the Hack computer is an aggregate of three chip-parts: `RAM16K`, `Screen`, and `Keyboard`. This modularity, though, is implicit: Hack machine language programs see a *single address space*, ranging from address 0 to address 24576 (in hexadecimal: 6000).

The Memory chip interface is shown in figure 5.6. The implementation of this interface should realize the continuum effect just described. For example, if the address input of the Memory chip happens to be 16384, the implementation should access address 0 in the Screen chip, and so on. Once again, we prefer not to provide too many details and let you figure out the rest of the implementation yourself.

5.3.3   Computer

We have reached the end of our hardware journey. The topmost Computer chip can be realized using three chip-parts: the CPU, the data Memory chip, and the instruction memory chip, ROM32K. Figure 5.9 gives the details.

The Computer implementation is designed to realize the following fetch-execute cycle: When the user asserts the reset input, the CPU's pc output emits 0, causing the instruction memory (ROM32K) to emit the first instruction in the program. The instruction will be executed by the CPU, and this execution may involve reading or writing a data memory register. In the process of executing the instruction, the CPU figures out which instruction to fetch next, and emits this address through its pc output. The CPU's pc output feeds the address input of the instruction memory, causing the latter to output the instruction that ought to be executed next. This output, in turn, feeds the instruction input of the CPU, closing the fetch-execute cycle.

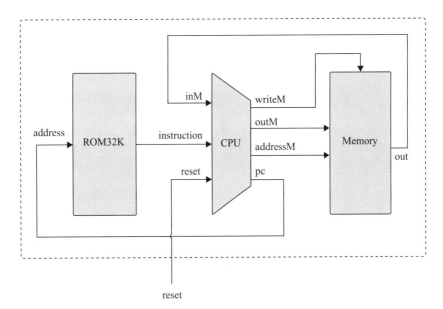

Figure 5.9   Proposed implementation of Computer, the topmost chip in the Hack platform.

5.4   Project

Objective: Build the Hack computer, culminating in the topmost `Computer` chip.

Resources: All the chips described in this chapter should be written in HDL and tested on the supplied hardware simulator, using the test programs described below.

Contract: Build a hardware platform capable of executing programs written in the Hack machine language. Demonstrate the platform's operations by having your `Computer` chip run the three supplied test programs.

Test programs: A natural way to test the overall `Computer` chip implementation is to have it execute sample programs written in the Hack machine language. In order to run such a test, one can write a test script that loads the `Computer` chip into the hardware simulator, loads a program from an external text file into the `ROM32K` chip-part (the instruction memory), and then runs the clock enough cycles to execute the program. We provide three such test programs, along with corresponding test scripts and compare files:

- `Add.hack`: Adds the two constants 2 and 3, and writes the result in `RAM[0]`.
- `Max.hack`: Computes the maximum of `RAM[0]` and `RAM[1]` and writes the result in `RAM[2]`.
- `Rect.hack`: Draws on the screen a rectangle of `RAM[0]` rows of 16 pixels each. The rectangle's top-left corner is located at the top-left corner of the screen.

Before testing your `Computer` chip on any one of these programs, review the test script associated with the program, and be sure to understand the instructions given to the simulator. If needed, consult appendix 3 ("Test Description Language").

Steps: Implement the computer in the following order:

`Memory`: This chip can be built along the general outline given in figure 5.6, using three chip-parts: `RAM16K`, `Screen`, and `Keyboard`. `Screen` and `Keyboard` are available as built-in chips; there is no need to build them. Although the `RAM16K` chip was built in project 3, we recommend using its built-in version instead.

`CPU`: The central processing unit can be built according to the proposed implementation given in figure 5.8. In principle, the CPU can use the ALU built in project 2, the `Register` and `PC` chips built in project 3, and logic gates from project 1, as needed. However, we recommend using the built-in versions of all these chips (in particular, use the built-in registers `ARegister`, `DRegister`, and `PC`). The built-in chips have exactly the same functionality as the memory chips built in previous projects, but they feature GUI side effects that make the testing and simulation of your work easier.

In the course of implementing the CPU, you may be tempted to specify and build internal ("helper") chips of your own. Be advised that there is no need to do so; the Hack CPU can be implemented elegantly and efficiently using only the chip-parts that appear in figure 5.8, plus some elementary logic gates built in project 1 (of which it is best to use their built-in versions).

Instruction memory: Use the built-in `ROM32K` chip.

`Computer`: The computer can be built according to the proposed implementation given in figure 5.9.

Hardware simulator: All the chips in this project, including the topmost `Computer` chip, can be implemented and tested using the supplied hardware simulator. Figure 5.10 is a screenshot of testing the `Rect.hack` program on a `Computer` chip implementation.

A web-based version of project 5 is available at www.nand2tetris.org.

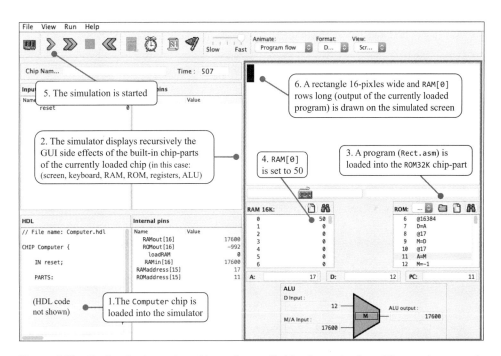

Figure 5.10   Testing the `Computer` chip on the supplied hardware simulator. The stored program is `Rect`, which draws a rectangle of `RAM[0]` rows of 16 pixels each, all black, at the top-left of the screen.

5.5   Perspective

Following the Nand to Tetris spirit, the architecture of the Hack computer is minimal. Typical computer platforms feature more registers, more data types, more powerful ALUs, and richer instruction sets. Most of these differences, though, are quantitative. From a qualitative standpoint, almost all digital computers, including Hack, are based on the same conceptual architecture: the von Neumann machine.

In terms of *purpose*, computer systems can be classified into two categories: *general-purpose computers* and *single-purpose computers*. General-purpose computers, like PCs and cell phones, typically interact with a user. They are designed to execute many programs and easily switch from one program to another. *Single-purpose computers* are usually embedded in other systems like automobiles, cameras, media streamers, medical devices, industrial controllers, and so on. For any particular application, a single program is burned into the dedicated computer's ROM (Read-Only Memory). For example, in some game consoles, the game software resides in an external cartridge, which is a replaceable ROM module encased in a fancy package. Although general-purpose computers are typically more complex and versatile than dedicated computers, they all share the same basic architectural ideas: stored programs, fetch-decode-execute logic, CPU, registers, and counters.

Most general-purpose computers use a single address space for storing both programs and data. Other computers, like Hack, use two separate address spaces. The latter configuration, which for historical reasons is called *Harvard architecture*, is less flexible in terms of ad hoc memory utilization but has distinct advantages. First, it is easier and cheaper to build. Second, it is often faster than the single address space configuration. Finally, if the size of the program that the computer has to run is known in advance, the size of the instruction memory can be optimized and fixed accordingly. For these reasons, the Harvard architecture is the architecture of choice in many dedicated, single-purpose, embedded computers.

Computers that use the same address space for storing instructions and data face the following challenge: How can we feed the address of the instruction, and the address of the data register on which the instruction has to operate, into the same address input of the shared memory device? Clearly, we cannot do it at the same time. The standard solution is to base the computer operation on a two-cycle logic. During the *fetch cycle*, the instruction address is fed to the address input of the memory, causing it to immediately emit the current instruction, which is then stored in an *instruction register*. In the subsequent *execute cycle*, the instruction is decoded, and the data address on which it has to operate is fed to the same address input. In contrast, computers that use separate instruction and data memories, like Hack, benefit from a single-cycle fetch-execute logic, which is faster and easier to handle. The price is having to use separate data and instruction memory units, although there is no need to use an instruction register.

The Hack computer interacts with a screen and a keyboard. General-purpose computers are typically connected to multiple I/O devices like printers, storage devices, network connections, and so on. Also, typical display devices are much fancier than the Hack screen, featuring more pixels, more colors, and faster rendering performance. Still, the basic principle that each pixel is driven by a memory-resident binary value is maintained: instead of a single bit controlling the pixel's black or white color, typically 8 bits are devoted to controlling the brightness level of each of several primary colors that, taken together, produce the pixel's ultimate color. The result is millions of possible colors, more than the human eye can discern.

The mapping of the Hack screen on the computer's main memory is simplistic. Instead of having memory bits drive pixels directly, many computers allow the CPU to send high-level graphic instructions like "draw a line" or "draw a circle" to a dedicated graphics chip or a standalone graphics processing unit, also known as GPU. The hardware and low-level software of these dedicated graphical processors are especially optimized for rendering graphics, animation, and video, offloading from the CPU and the main computer the burden of handling these voracious tasks directly.

Finally, it should be stressed that much of the effort and creativity in designing computer hardware is invested in achieving better performance. Many hardware architects devote their work to speeding up memory access, using clever caching algorithms and data structures, optimizing access to I/O devices, and applying pipelining, parallelism, instruction prefetching, and other optimization techniques that were completely sidestepped in this chapter.

Historically, attempts to accelerate processing performance have led to two main camps of CPU design. Advocates of the *Complex Instruction Set Computing* (CISC) approach argued for achieving better performance by building more powerful processors featuring more elaborate instruction sets. Conversely, the *Reduced Instruction Set Computing* (RISC) camp built simpler processors and tighter instruction sets, arguing that these actually deliver faster performance in benchmark tests. The Hack computer does not enter this debate, featuring neither a strong instruction set nor special hardware acceleration techniques.

6   Assembler

What's in a name? That which we call a rose by any other name would smell as sweet.
—Shakespeare, *Romeo and Juliet*

In the previous chapters, we completed the development of a hardware platform designed to run programs in the Hack machine language. We presented two versions of this language—symbolic and binary—and explained that symbolic programs can be translated into binary code using a program called an *assembler*. In this chapter we describe how assemblers work, and how they are built. This will lead to the construction of a *Hack assembler*—a program that translates programs written in the Hack symbolic language into binary code that can execute on the barebone Hack hardware.

Since the relationship between symbolic instructions and their corresponding binary codes is straightforward, implementing an assembler using a high-level programming language is not a difficult task. One complication arises from allowing assembly programs to use symbolic references to memory addresses. The assembler is expected to manage these symbols and resolve them to physical memory addresses. This task is normally done using a *symbol table*—a commonly used data structure.

Implementing the assembler is the first in a series of seven software development projects that accompany part II of the book. Developing the assembler will equip you with a basic set of general skills that will serve you well throughout all these projects and beyond: handling command-line arguments, handling input and output text files, parsing instructions, handling white space, handling symbols, generating code, and many other techniques that come into play in many software development projects.

If you have no programming experience, you can develop a paper-based assembler. This option is described in the web-based version of project 6, available at www.nand2tetris.org.

6.1   Background

Machine languages are typically specified in two flavors: *binary* and *symbolic*. A binary instruction, for example, 1100001000000110000000000000111, is an agreed-upon package of micro-codes designed to be decoded and executed by some target hardware platform. For example, the instruction's leftmost 8 bits, `11000010`, can represent an operation like "load." The next 8 bits, `00000011`, can represent a register, say `R3`. The remaining 16 bits, `0000000000000111`, can represent a value, say 7. When we set out to build a hardware architecture and a machine language, we can decide that this particular 32-bit instruction will cause the hardware to effect the operation "load the constant 7 into register `R3`." Modern computer platforms support hundreds of such possible operations. Thus, machine languages can be complex, involving many operation codes, memory addressing modes, and instruction formats.

Clearly, specifying these operations in binary code is a pain. A natural solution is using an agreed-upon equivalent symbolic syntax, say, "`load R3,7`". The `load` operation code is sometimes called a *mnemonic*, which in Latin means a pattern of letters designed to help with remembering something. Since the translation from mnemonics and symbols to binary code is straightforward, it makes sense to write low-level programs directly in symbolic notation and have a computer program translate them into binary code. The symbolic language is called *assembly*, and the translator program *assembler*. The assembler parses each assembly instruction into its underlying fields, for example, `load`, `R3`, and 7, translates each field into its equivalent binary code, and finally assembles the generated bits into a binary instruction that can be executed by the hardware. Hence the name *assembler*.

Symbols: Consider the symbolic instruction goto 312. Following translation, this instruction causes the computer to fetch and execute the instruction stored in address 312, which may be the beginning of some loop. Well, if it's the beginning of a loop, why not mark this point in the assembly program with a descriptive label, say LOOP, and use the command goto LOOP instead of goto 312? All we have to do is record somewhere that LOOP stands for 312. When we translate the program into binary code, we replace each occurrence of LOOP with 312. That's a small price to pay for the gain in program readability and portability.

In general, assembly languages use symbols for three purposes:

• *Labels*: Assembly programs can declare and use symbols that mark various locations in the code, for example, LOOP and END.

• *Variables*: Assembly programs can declare and use symbolic variables, for example, i and sum.

• *Predefined symbols*: Assembly programs can refer to special addresses in the computer's memory using agreed-upon symbols, for example, SCREEN and KBD.

Of course, there is no free lunch. Someone must be responsible for managing all these symbols. In particular, someone must remember that SCREEN stands for 16384, that LOOP stands for 312, that sum stands for some other address, and so on. This symbol-handling task is one of the most important functions of the assembler.

Example: Figure 6.1 lists two versions of the same program written in the Hack machine language. The symbolic version includes all sorts of things that humans are fond of seeing in computer programs: comments, white space, indentation, symbolic instructions, and symbolic references. None of these embellishments concern computers, which understand one thing only: bits. The agent that bridges the gap between the symbolic code convenient for humans and the binary code understood by the computer is the assembler.

Let us ignore for now all the details in figure 6.1, as well as the symbol table, and make some general observations. First, note that although the line numbers are not part of the code, they play an important, albeit implicit, role in the translation process. If the binary code will be loaded into the instruction memory starting at address 0, then the line number of each instruction will coincide with its memory address. Clearly, this observation should be of interest to the assembler. Second, note that comments and label declarations generate no code, and that's why the latter are sometimes called *pseudo-instructions*. Finally, and stating the obvious, note that in order to write an assembler for some machine language, the assembler's developer must get a complete specification of the language's symbolic and binary syntax.

With that in mind, we now turn to specify the Hack machine language.

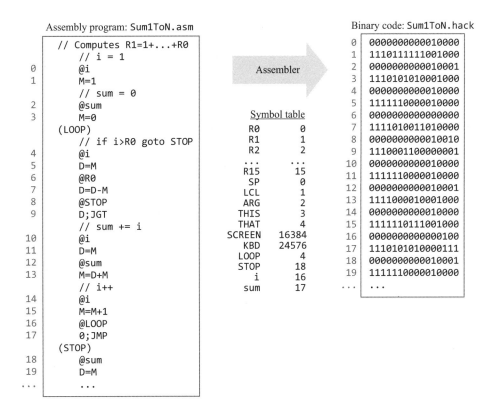

Figure 6.1 Assembly code, translated to binary code using a symbol table. The line numbers, which are not part of the code, are listed for reference.

6.2   The Hack Machine Language Specification

The Hack assembly language and its equivalent binary representation were described in chapter 4. The language specification is repeated here for ease of reference. This specification is the contract that Hack assemblers must implement, one way or another.

6.2.1   Programs

Binary Hack program: A binary Hack program is a sequence of text lines, each consisting of sixteen 0 and 1 characters. If the line starts with a 0, it represents a binary *A*-instruction. Otherwise, it represents a binary *C*-instruction.

Assembly Hack program: An assembly Hack program is a sequence of text lines, each being an *assembly instruction*, a *label declaration*, or a *comment*:

- *Assembly instruction*: A symbolic *A*-instruction or a symbolic *C*-instruction (see figure 6.2).
- *Label declaration*: A line of the form (*xxx*), where *xxx* is a symbol.
- *Comment*: A line beginning with two slashes (//) is considered a comment and is ignored.

6.2.2   Symbols

Symbols in Hack assembly programs fall into three categories: predefined symbols, label symbols, and variable symbols.

Predefined symbols: Any Hack assembly program is allowed to use predefined symbols, as follows. R0, R1, ..., R15 stand for 0, 1, ... 15, respectively. SP, LCL, ARG, THIS, THAT stand for 0, 1, 2, 3, 4, respectively. SCREEN and KBD stand for 16384 and 24576, respectively. The values of these symbols are interpreted as addresses in the Hack RAM.

Label symbols: The pseudo-instruction (*xxx*) defines the symbol *xxx* to refer to the location in the Hack ROM holding the next instruction in the program. A label symbol can be defined once and can be used anywhere in the assembly program, even before the line in which it is defined.

Variable symbols: Any symbol *xxx* appearing in an assembly program that is not predefined and is not defined elsewhere by a label declaration (*xxx*) is treated as a variable. Variables are mapped to consecutive RAM locations as they are first encountered, starting at RAM address 16. Thus, the first variable encountered in a program is mapped to RAM[16], the second to RAM[17], and so on.

A-instruction	(symbolic): @*x xx*	(*xxx* is a decimal value ranging from 0 to 32767, or a symbol bound to such a decimal value)
	(binary): 0 *v v v v v v v v v v v v v v v*	(*v v... v* = 15-bit value of *xxx*)

C-instruction	(symbolic): *dest* = *comp* ; *jump*	(*comp* is mandatory. If *dest* is empty, the = is omitted; If *jump* is empty, the ; is omitted)
	(binary): 111*acccccccdddjjj*	

comp		*c*	*c*	*c*	*c*	*c*	*c*
0		1	0	1	0	1	0
1		1	1	1	1	1	1
-1		1	1	1	0	1	0
D		0	0	1	1	0	0
A	M	1	1	0	0	0	0
!D		0	0	1	1	0	1
!A	!M	1	1	0	0	0	1
-D		0	0	1	1	1	1
-A	-M	1	1	0	0	1	1
D+1		0	1	1	1	1	1
A+1	M+1	1	1	0	1	1	1
D-1		0	0	1	1	1	0
A-1	M-1	1	1	0	0	1	0
D+A	D+M	0	0	0	0	1	0
D-A	D-M	0	1	0	0	1	1
A-D	M-D	0	0	0	1	1	1
D&A	D&M	0	0	0	0	0	0
D|A	D|M	0	1	0	1	0	1

a == 0   *a == 1*

dest	*d*	*d*	*d*	Effect: store *comp* in:
null	0	0	0	the value is not stored
M	0	0	1	RAM[A]
D	0	1	0	D register (reg)
DM	0	1	1	D reg and RAM[A]
A	1	0	0	A reg
AM	1	0	1	A reg and RAM[A]
AD	1	1	0	A reg and D reg
ADM	1	1	1	A reg, D reg, and RAM[A]

jump	*j*	*j*	*j*	Effect:
null	0	0	0	no jump
JGT	0	0	1	if *comp* > 0 jump
JEQ	0	1	0	if *comp* = 0 jump
JGE	0	1	1	if *comp* ≥ 0 jump
JLT	1	0	0	if *comp* < 0 jump
JNE	1	0	1	if *comp* ≠ 0 jump
JLE	1	1	0	if *comp* ≤ 0 jump
JMP	1	1	1	unconditional jump

Figure 6.2   The Hack instruction set, showing both symbolic mnemonics and their corresponding binary codes.

6.2.3   Syntax Conventions

Symbols: A *symbol* can be any sequence of letters, digits, underscore (_), dot (.), dollar sign ($), and colon (:) that does not begin with a digit.

Constants: May appear only in *A*-instructions of the form @*xxx*. The constant *xxx* is a value in the range 0–32767 and is written in decimal notation.

White space: Leading space characters and empty lines are ignored.

Case conventions: All the assembly mnemonics (like A+1, JEQ, and so on) must be written in uppercase. The remaining symbols—labels and variable names—are case-sensitive. The recommended convention is to use uppercase for labels and lowercase for variables.

This completes the Hack machine language specification.

6.3 Assembly-to-Binary Translation

This section describes how to translate Hack assembly programs into binary code. Although we focus on developing an assembler for the Hack language, the techniques that we present are applicable to any assembler.

The assembler takes as input a stream of assembly instructions and generates as output a stream of translated binary instructions. The resulting code can be loaded as is into the computer memory and executed. In order to carry out the translation process, the assembler must handle instructions and symbols.

6.3.1 Handling Instructions

For each assembly instruction, the assembler

- parses the instruction into its underlying fields;
- for each field, generates the corresponding bit-code, as specified in figure 6.2;
- if the instruction contains a symbolic reference, resolves the symbol into its numeric value;
- assembles the resulting binary codes into a string of sixteen 0 and 1 characters; and
- writes the assembled string to the output file.

6.3.2 Handling Symbols

Assembly programs are allowed to use symbolic labels (destinations of goto instructions) before the symbols are defined. This convention makes the life of assembly code writers easier and that of assembler developers harder. A common solution is to develop a *two-pass assembler* that reads the code twice, from start to end. In the first pass, the assembler builds a *symbol table*, adds all the label symbols to the table, and generates no code. In the second pass, the assembler handles the variable symbols and generates binary code, using the symbol table. Here are the details.

Initialization: The assembler creates a symbol table and initializes it with all the predefined symbols and their pre-allocated values. In figure 6.1, the result of the initialization stage is the symbol table with all the symbols up to, and including, KBD.

First pass: The assembler goes through the entire assembly program, line by line, keeping track of the line number. This number starts at 0 and is incremented by 1 whenever an *A*-instruction or a *C*-instruction is encountered, but does not change when a comment or a label declaration is encountered. Each time a label declaration (*xxx*) is encountered, the assembler adds a new entry to the symbol table, associating the symbol *xxx* with the current line number plus 1 (this will be the ROM address of the next instruction in the program).

This pass results in adding to the symbol table all the program's label symbols, along with their corresponding values. In figure 6.1, the first pass results in adding the symbols LOOP and STOP to the symbol table. No code is generated during the first pass.

Second pass: The assembler goes again through the entire program and parses each line as follows. Each time an *A*-instruction with a symbolic reference is encountered, namely, @*xxx*, where *xxx* is a symbol and not a number, the assembler looks up *xxx* in the symbol table. If the symbol is found, the assembler replaces it with its numeric value and completes the instruction's translation. If the symbol is not found, then it must represent a new variable. To handle it, the assembler (i) adds the entry <*xxx, value*> to the symbol table, where *value* is the next available address in the RAM space designated for variables, and (ii) completes the instruction's translation, using this address. In the Hack platform, the RAM space designated for storing variables starts at 16 and is incremented by 1 after each time a new variable is found in the code. In figure 6.1, the second pass results in adding the symbols i and sum to the symbol table.

6.4   Implementation

Usage: The Hack assembler accepts a single command-line argument, as follows,

```
prompt>HackAssembler Prog.asm
```

where the input file *Prog*.asm contains assembly instructions (the .asm extension is mandatory). The file name may contain a file path. If no path is specified, the assembler operates on the current folder. The assembler creates an output file named *Prog*.hack and writes the translated binary instructions into it. The output file is created in the same folder as the input file. If there is a file by this name in the folder, it will be overwritten.

We propose dividing the assembler implementation into two stages. In the first stage, develop a basic assembler for Hack programs that contain no symbolic references. In the second stage, extend the basic assembler to handle symbolic references.

6.4.1   Developing a Basic Assembler

The basic assembler assumes that the source code contains no symbolic references. Therefore, except for handling comments and white space, the assembler has to translate either *C*-instructions or *A*-instructions of the form @*xxx*, where *xxx* is a decimal value (and not a symbol). This translation task is straightforward: each mnemonic component (field) of a symbolic *C*-instruction is translated into its corresponding bit code, according to figure 6.2, and each decimal constant *xxx* in a symbolic *A*-instruction is translated into its equivalent binary code.

We propose basing the assembler on a software architecture consisting of a *Parser* module for parsing the input into instructions and instructions into fields, a *Code* module for translating the fields (symbolic mnemonics) into binary codes, and a *Hack assembler* program that drives the entire translation process. Before proceeding to specify the three modules, we wish to make a note about the style that we use to describe these specifications.

API documentation: The development of the Hack assembler is the first in a series of seven software construction projects that follow in part II of the book. Each one of these projects can be developed independently, using any high-level programming language. Therefore, our API documentation style makes no assumptions on the implementation language.

In each project, starting with this one, we propose an API consisting of several *modules*. Each module documents one or more *routines*. In a typical object-oriented language, a module corresponds to a *class*, and a routine corresponds to a *method*. In other languages, a module may correspond to a *file*, and a routine to a *function*. Whichever language you use for implementing the software projects, starting with the assembler, there should be no problem mapping the *modules* and *routines* of our proposed APIs on the programming elements of your implementation language.

The Parser

The Parser encapsulates access to the input assembly code. In particular, it provides a convenient means for advancing through the source code, skipping comments and white space, and breaking each symbolic instruction into its underlying components.

Although the basic version of the assembler is not required to handle symbolic references, the Parser that we specify below does. In other words, the Parser specified here serves both the basic assembler and the complete assembler.

The Parser ignores comments and white space in the input stream, enables accessing the input one line at a time, and parses symbolic instructions into their underlying components.

The Parser API is listed on the next page. Here are some examples of how the Parser services can be used. If the current instruction is @17 or @sum, a call to symbol() would return the string "17" or "sum", respectively. If the current instruction is (LOOP), a call to symbol() would return the string "LOOP". If the current instruction is D=D+1;JLE, a call to dest(), comp(), and jump() would return the strings "D", "D+1", and "JLE", respectively.

In project 6 you have to implement this API using some high-level programming language. In order to do so, you must be familiar with how this language handles text files, and strings.

Routine	Arguments	Returns	Function
Constructor / initializer	Input file / stream	—	Opens the input file / stream and gets ready to parse it.
`hasMoreLines`	—	boolean	Are there more lines in the input?
`advance`	—	—	Skips over white space and comments, if necessary. Reads the next instruction from the input, and makes it the current instruction. This routine should be called only if `hasMoreLines` is true. Initially there is no current instruction.
`instructionType`	—	`A_INSTRUCTION`, `C_INSTRUCTION`, `L_INSTRUCTION` (constants)	Returns the type of the current instruction: `A_INSTRUCTION` for @*xxx*, where *xxx* is either a decimal number or a symbol. `C_INSTRUCTION` for *dest=comp;jump* `L_INSTRUCTION` for (*xxx*), where *xxx* is a symbol.
`symbol`	—	string	If the current instruction is (*xxx*), returns the symbol *xxx*. If the current instruction is @*xxx*, returns the symbol or decimal *xxx* (as a string). Should be called only if `instructionType` is `A_INSTRUCTION` or `L_INSTRUCTION`.
`dest`	—	string	Returns the symbolic *dest* part of the current *C*-instruction (8 possibilities). Should be called only if `instructionType` is `C_INSTRUCTION`.
`comp`	—	string	Returns the symbolic *comp* part of the current *C*-instruction (28 possibilities). Should be called only if `instructionType` is `C_INSTRUCTION`.
`jump`	—	string	Returns the symbolic *jump* part of the current *C*-instruction (8 possibilities). Should be called only if `instructionType` is `C_INSTRUCTION`.

The Code Module

This module provides services for translating symbolic Hack mnemonics into their binary codes. Specifically, it translates symbolic Hack mnemonics into their binary codes according to the language specifications (see figure 6.2). Here is the API:

Routine	Arguments	Returns	Function
`dest`	string	3 bits, as a string	Returns the binary code of the *dest* mnemonic.
`comp`	string	7 bits, as a string	Returns the binary code of the *comp* mnemonic.
`jump`	string	3 bits, as a string	Returns the binary code of the *jump* mnemonic.

All the *n*-bit codes are returned as strings of `'0'` and `'1'` characters. For example, a call to `dest("DM")` returns the string `"011"`, a call to `comp("A+1")` returns the string `"0110111"`, a call to `comp("M+1")` returns the string `"1110111"`, a call to `jump("JNE")` returns the string `"101"`, and so on. All these mnemonic-binary mappings are specified in figure 6.2.

The Hack Assembler

This is the main program that drives the entire assembly process, using the services of the Parser and Code modules. The basic version of the assembler (which we describe now) assumes that the source assembly code contains no symbolic references. This means that (i) in all instructions of type @*xxx*, the *xxx* constants are decimal numbers and not symbols and (ii) the input file contains no label instructions, that is, no instructions of the form (*xxx*).

The basic assembler program can now be described as follows. The program gets the name of the input source file, say, *Prog*, from the command-line argument. It constructs a Parser for parsing the input file *Prog*`.asm` and creates an output file, *Prog*`.hack`, into which it will write the translated binary instructions. The program then enters a loop that iterates through the lines (assembly instructions) in the input file and processes them as follows.

For each *C*-instruction, the program uses the Parser and Code services for parsing the instruction into its fields and translating each field into its corresponding binary code. The program then assembles (concatenates) the translated binary codes into a string consisting of sixteen `'0'` and `'1'` characters and writes this string as the next line in the output `.hack` file.

For each *A*-instruction of type @*xxx*, the program translates *xxx* into its binary representation, creates a string of sixteen `'0'` and `'1'` characters, and writes it as the next line in the output `.hack` file.

We provide no API for this module, inviting you to implement it as you see fit.

6.4.2   Completing the Assembler

The Symbol Table

Since Hack instructions can contain symbolic references, the assembly process must resolve them into actual addresses. The assembler deals with this task using a *symbol table*, designed to create and maintain the correspondence between symbols and their meaning (in Hack's case, RAM and ROM addresses).

A natural means for representing this *<symbol, address>* mapping is any data structure designed to handle *<key, value>* pairs. Every modern high-level programming language features such a ready-made abstraction, typically called a *hash table*, *map*, *dictionary*, among other names. You can either implement the symbol table from scratch or customize one of these data structures. Here is the SymbolTable API:

Routine	Arguments	Returns	Function
Constructor / initializer	—	—	Creates a new empty symbol table.
addEntry	symbol (string), address (int)	—	Adds <symbol,address> to the table.
contains	symbol (string)	boolean	Does the symbol table contain the given symbol?
getAddress	symbol (string)	int	Returns the address associated with the symbol.

6.5   Project

Objective: Develop an assembler that translates programs written in Hack assembly language into Hack binary code.

This version of the assembler assumes that the source assembly code is error-free. Error checking, reporting, and handling can be added to later versions of the assembler but are not part of project 6.

Resources: The main tool you need for completing this project is the programming language in which you will implement your assembler. The assembler and CPU emulator supplied in nand2tetris/tools may also come in handy. These tools allow experimenting with a working assembler before setting out to build one yourself. Importantly, the supplied assembler allows comparing its output to the outputs generated by *your* assembler. For more information about these capabilities, refer to the assembler tutorial at www.nand2tetris.org.

Contract: When given to your assembler as a command line argument, a *Prog*.asm file containing a valid Hack assembly language program should be translated into the correct Hack binary code and stored in a file named *Prog*.hack, located in the same folder as the source file (if a file by this name exists, it is overwritten). The output produced by your assembler must be identical to the output produced by the supplied assembler.

Development plan: We suggest building and testing the assembler in two stages. First, write a basic assembler designed to translate programs that contain no symbolic references. Then extend your assembler with symbol-handling capabilities.

Test programs: The first test program has no symbolic references. The remaining test programs come in two versions: *Prog*.asm and *ProgL*.asm, which are with and without symbolic references, respectively.

Add.asm: Adds the constants 2 and 3 and puts the result in R0.

`Max.asm`: Computes max(R0, R1) and puts the result in R2.

`Rect.asm`: Draws a rectangle at the top-left corner of the screen. The rectangle is 16 pixels wide and R0 pixels high. Before running this program, put a nonnegative value in R0.

`Pong.asm`: A classical single-player arcade game. A ball bounces repeatedly off the screen's edges. The player attempts to hit the ball with a paddle, moving the paddle by pressing the left and right arrow keys. For every successful hit, the player gains a point and the paddle shrinks a little to make the game harder. If the player misses the ball, the game is over. To quit the game, press `ESC`.

The supplied Pong program was developed using tools that will be presented in part II of the book. In particular, the game software was written in the high-level Jack programming language and translated into the given `Pong.asm` file by the *Jack compiler*. Although the high-level `Pong.jack` program is only about three hundred lines of code, the executable Pong application is about twenty thousand lines of binary code, most of which is the Jack operating system. Running this interactive program in the supplied CPU emulator is a slow affair, so don't expect a high-powered Pong game. This slowness is actually a virtue, since it enables tracking the graphical behavior of the program. As you develop the software hierarchy in part II, this game will run much faster.

Testing: Let *Prog*`.asm` be an assembly Hack program, for example, one of the given test programs. There are essentially two ways to test whether your assembler translates *Prog*. `asm` correctly. First, you can load the *Prog*`.hack` file generated by your assembler into the supplied CPU emulator, execute it, and check that it's doing what it's supposed to be doing.

The second testing technique is to compare the code generated by your assembler to the code generated by the supplied assembler. To begin with, rename the file generated by your assembler to *Prog*1`.hack`. Next, load *Prog*`.asm` into the supplied assembler, and translate it. If your assembler is working correctly, it follows that *Prog*1`.hack` must be identical to the *Prog*`.hack` file produced by the supplied assembler. This comparison can be done by loading *Prog*1`.asm` as a compare file—see figure 6.3 for the details.

A web-based version of project 6 is available at www.nand2tetris.org.

6.6   Perspective

Like most assemblers, the Hack assembler is a relatively simple translator, dealing mainly with text processing. Naturally, assemblers for richer machine languages are more elaborate. Also, some assemblers feature more sophisticated symbol-handling capabilities not found in Hack. For example, some assemblers support *constant arithmetic* on symbols, like using `base+5` to refer to the fifth memory location after the address referred to by `base`.

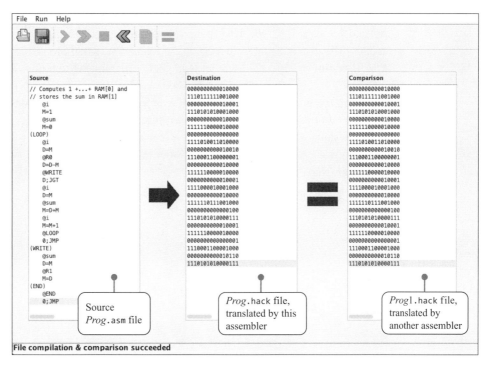

Figure 6.3   Testing the assembler's output using the supplied assembler.

Many assemblers are extended to handle *macro-instructions*. A macro-instruction is a sequence of machine instructions that has a name. For example, our assembler can be extended to translate agreed-upon macro-instructions, for example, D=M[*addr*], into the two primitive Hack instructions @*addr*, followed by D=M. Likewise, the macro-instruction goto *addr* can be translated into @*addr*, followed by 0;JMP, and so on. Such macro-instructions can considerably simplify the writing of assembly programs, at a low translation cost.

It should be noted that machine language programs are rarely written by humans. Rather, they are typically written by compilers. And a compiler—being an automaton—can optionally bypass the symbolic instructions and generate binary machine code directly. That said, an assembler is still a useful program, especially for developers of C/C++ programs who are concerned about efficiency and optimization. By inspecting the symbolic code generated by the compiler, the programmer can improve the high-level code to achieve better performance on the host hardware. When the generated assembly code is considered efficient, it can be translated further by the assembler into the final binary, executable code.

* * *

Congratulations! You've reached the end of part I of the Nand to Tetris journey. If you completed projects 1–6, you have built a general-purpose computer system from first principles. This is a fantastic achievement, and you should feel proud and accomplished.

Alas, the computer is capable of executing only programs written in machine language. In part II of the book we will use this barebone hardware platform as a point of departure and build on top of it a modern software hierarchy. The software will consist of a virtual machine, a compiler for a high-level, object-based programming language, and a basic operating system.

So, whenever you're ready for more adventures, let's move on to part II of our grand journey from Nand to Tetris.

II Software

Any sufficiently advanced technology is indistinguishable from magic.

—Arthur C. Clarke (1962)

To which we add: "and any sufficiently advanced magic is indistinguishable from hard work, behind the scenes." In part I of the book we built the hardware platform of a computer system named Hack, capable of running programs written in the Hack machine language. In part II we will transform this barebone machine into an advanced technology, indistinguishable from magic: a black box that can metamorphose into a chess player, a search engine, a flight simulator, a media streamer, or anything else that tickles your fancy. In order to do so, we'll unfold the elaborate behind-the-scenes software hierarchy that endows computers with the ability to execute programs written in high-level programming languages. In particular, we'll focus on Jack, a simple, Java-like, object-based programming language, described formally in chapter 9. Over the years, Nand to Tetris readers and students have used Jack to develop Tetris, Pong, Snake, Space Invaders, and numerous other games and interactive apps. Being a general-purpose computer, Hack can execute all these programs, and any other program that comes to your mind.

Clearly, the gap between the expressive syntax of high-level programming languages, on the one hand, and the clunky instructions of low-level machine language, on the other, is huge. If you are not convinced, try developing a Tetris game using instructions like @17 and M=M+1. Bridging this gap is what part II of this book is all about. We will build this bridge by developing gradually some of the most powerful and ambitious programs in applied computer science: a *compiler*, a *virtual machine*, and a basic *operating system*.

Our Jack compiler will be designed to take a Jack program, say Tetris, and produce from it a stream of machine language instructions that, when executed, makes the Hack platform deliver a Tetris game experience. Of course Tetris is just one example: the compiler that you build will be capable of translating *any* given Jack program into machine code that can be executed on the Hack computer. The compiler, whose main tasks consist of *syntax analysis* and *code generation*, will be built in chapters 10 and 11.

As with programming languages like Java and C#, the Jack compiler will be *two-tiered*: the compiler will generate interim *VM code*, designed to run on an abstract *virtual machine*. The VM code will then be compiled further by a separate translator into the Hack machine language. *Virtualization*—one of the most important ideas in applied computer science—comes into play in numerous settings including program compilation, cloud computing, distributed storage, distributed processing, and operating systems. We will devote chapters 7 and 8 to motivating, designing, and building our virtual machine.

Like many other high-level languages, the basic Jack language is surprisingly simple. What turns modern languages into powerful programming systems are *standard libraries* providing mathematical functions, string processing, memory management, graphics drawing, user interaction handling, and more. Taken together, these standard libraries form a basic *operating system* (OS) which, in the Jack framework, is packaged as Jack's *standard class library*. This basic OS, designed to bridge many gaps between the high-level Jack language and the low-level Hack platform, will be developed in Jack itself. You may be wondering how software that is supposed to enable a programming language can be developed in this very same language. We'll deal with this challenge by following a development strategy known as *bootstrapping*, similar to how the Unix OS was developed using the C language.

The construction of the OS will give us an opportunity to present elegant algorithms and classical data structures that are typically used to manage hardware resources and peripheral devices. We will then implement these algorithms in Jack, extending the language's capabilities one step at a time. As you go through the chapters of part II, you will deal with the OS from several different perspectives. In chapter 9, acting as an *application programmer*, you will develop a Jack app and use the OS services abstractly, from a high-level client perspective. In chapters 10 and 11, when building the Jack compiler, you will use the OS services as a low-level client, for example, for various memory management services required by the compiler. In chapter 12 you will finally don the hat of the OS developer and implement all these system services yourself.

II.1   A Taste of Jack Programming

Before delving into all these exciting projects, we'll give a brief and informal introduction of the Jack language. This will be done using two examples, starting with Hello World. We will use this example to demonstrate that even the most trivial high-level program has much more to it than meets the eye. We will then present a simple program that illustrates the object-based capabilities of the Jack language. Once we get a programmer-oriented taste of the high-level Jack language, we will be prepared to start the journey of realizing the language by building a virtual machine, a compiler, and an operating system.

Hello World, again: We began this book with the iconic Hello World program that learners often encounter as the first thing in introductory programming courses. Here is this trivial program once again, written in the Jack programming language:

```
// First example in Programming 101
class Main {
  function void main() {
    do Output.printString("Hello World");
    return;
  }
}
```

Let's discuss some of the implicit assumptions that we normally make when presented with such programs. The first magic that we take for granted is that a sequence characters, say, printString("Hello World"), can cause the computer to actually display something on the screen. How does the computer figure out *what* to do? And even if the computer knew what to do, *how* will it actually do it? As we saw in part I of the book, the screen is a grid of pixels. If we want to display H on the screen, we have to turn on and off a carefully selected subset of pixels that, taken together, render the desired letter's image on the screen. Of course this is just the beginning. What about displaying this H legibly on screens that have different sizes and resolutions? And what about dealing with *while* and *for* loops, *arrays*, *objects*, *methods*, *classes*, and all the other goodies that high-level programmers are trained to use without ever thinking about how they work?

Indeed, the beauty of high-level programming languages, and that of well-designed abstractions in general, is that they permit using them in a state of blissful ignorance. Application programmers are in fact encouraged to view the language as a black box abstraction, without paying any attention to how it is actually implemented. All you need is a good tutorial, a few code examples, and off you go.

Clearly though, at one point or another, *someone* must implement this language abstraction. Someone must develop, once and for all, the ability to efficiently compute square roots when the application programmer blissfully says sqrt(1764), to elicit a number from the user when the programmer happily says x=readInt(), to find and carve out an available memory block when the programmer nonchalantly creates an object using new, and to perform transparently all the other abstract services that programmers expect to get without ever thinking about them. So, who are the good souls who turn high-level programming into an advanced technology indistinguishable from magic? They are the software wizards who develop *compilers*, *virtual machines*, and *operating systems*. And that's precisely what *you* will do in the forthcoming chapters.

You may be wondering why you have to bother about this elusive behind-the-scenes scene. Didn't we just say that you can use high-level languages without worrying about how they work? There are at least two reasons why. First, the more you delve into low-level system internals, the more sophisticated high-level programmer you become. In particular, you learn how to write high-level code that exploits the hardware and the OS cleverly and efficiently and how to avoid baffling bugs like memory leaks.

Second, by getting your hands dirty and developing the system internals yourself, you will discover some of the most beautiful and powerful algorithms and data structures in applied computer science. Importantly, the ideas and techniques that will unfold in part II are not limited to compilers and operating systems. Rather, they are the building blocks of numerous software systems and applications that will accompany you throughout your career.

The PointDemo program: Suppose we want to represent and manipulate *points* on a plane. Figure II.1 shows two such points, p_1 and p_2, and a third point, p_3, resulting from the vector addition $p_3 = p_1 + p_2 = (1, 2) + (3, 4) = (4, 6)$. The figure also depicts the *Euclidean distance* between p_1 and p_3, which can be computed using the Pythagorean theorem. The code in the Main class illustrates how such algebraic manipulations can be done using the object-based Jack language.

You may wonder why Jack uses keywords like var, let, and do. For now, we advise you not to dwell on syntactic details. Instead, let's focus on the big picture and proceed to review how the Jack language can be used to implement the Point abstract data type (figure II.2).

The code shown in figure II.2 illustrates that a Jack class (of which Main and Point are two examples) is a collection of one or more *subroutines*, each being a *constructor*, *method*, or *function*. *Constructors* are subroutines that create new objects, *methods* are subroutines that operate on the current object, and *functions* are subroutines that operate on no particular object. (Object-oriented design purists may frown about mixing methods and functions in the same class; we are doing it here for illustrative purposes).

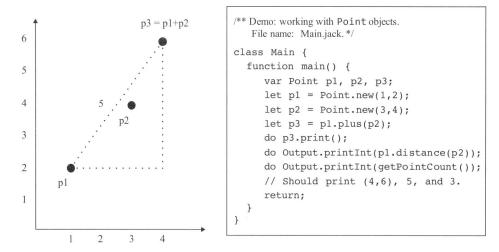

Figure II.1   Manipulating points on a plane: example and Jack code.

```
/** Represents a two-dimensional point.
    File name: Point.jack. */
class Point {

    // The coordinates of this point:
    field int x, y

    // The number of Point objects constructed so far:
    static int pointCount;

    /** Constructs a two-dimensional point and
        initializes it with the given coordinates. */
    constructor Point new(int ax, int ay) {
        let x = ax;
        let y = ay;
        let pointCount = pointCount + 1;
        return this;
    }
    /** Returns the x coordinate of this point. */
    method int getx() {return x;}

    /** Returns the y coordinate of this point. */
    method int gety() {return y;}

    /** Returns the number of Points constructed so far. */
    function int getPointCount() {
        return pointCount;
    }

    // Class declaration continues on top right.
```

```
    /** Returns a point which is this point plus
        the other point. */
    method Point plus(Point other) {
        return Point.new(x + other.getx(),
                         y + other.gety());
    }
    /** Returns the Euclidean distance between
        this and the other point. */
    method int distance(Point other) {
        var int dx, dy;
        let dx = x - other.getx();
        let dy = y - other.gety();
        return Math.sqrt((dx*dx) + (dy*dy));
    }
    /** Prints this point, as "(x,y)" */
    method void print() {
        do Output.printString("(");
        do Output.printInt(x);
        do Output.printString(",");
        do Output.printInt(y);
        do Output.printString(")");
        return;
    }
} // End of Point class declaration.
```

Figure II.2   Jack implementation of the Point abstraction.

The remainder of this section is an informal overview of the Main and the Point classes. Our goal is to give a taste of Jack programming, deferring a complete language description to chapter 9. So, allowing ourselves the luxury of focusing on essence only, let's get started. The Main.main function begins by declaring three *object variables* (also known as *references*, or *pointers*), designed to refer to instances of the Point class. It then goes on to construct two Point objects, and assigns the p1 and p2 variables to them. Next, it calls the plus method, and assigns p3 to the Point object returned by that method. The rest of the Main.main function prints some results.

The Point class begins by declaring that every Point object is characterized by two *field* variables (also known as *properties*, or *instance variables*). It then declares a *static variable*, that is, a class-level variable associated with no particular object. The class constructor sets up the field values of the newly created object and increments the number of instances derived from this class so far. Note that a Jack constructor must explicitly return the memory address of the newly created object, which, according to the language rules, is denoted this.

You may wonder why the result of the square root computed by the distance method is stored in an int variable—clearly a real-valued data type like float would make more sense. The reason for this peculiarity is simple: the Jack language features only three primitive data types: int, boolean, and char. Other data types can be implemented at will using classes, as we'll do in chapters 9 and 12.

The operating system: The `Main` and `Point` classes use three OS functions: `Output.printInt`, `Output.printString`, and `Math.sqrt`. Like other modern high-level languages, the Jack language is augmented by a set of *standard classes* that provide commonly used OS services (the complete OS API is given in appendix 6). We will have much more to say about the OS services in chapter 9, where we'll use them in the context of Jack programming, as well as in chapter 12, where we'll build the OS.

In addition to calling OS services for their effects directly from Jack programs, the OS comes to play in other, less obvious ways. For example, consider the `new` operation, used to construct objects in object-oriented languages. How does the compiler know where in the host RAM to put the newly constructed object? Well, it doesn't. An OS routine is called to figure it out. When we build the OS in chapter 12, you will implement, among many other things, a typical run-time memory management system. You will then learn, hands-on, how this system interacts with the hardware, from the one end, and with compilers, from the other, in order to allocate and reclaim RAM space cleverly and efficiently. This is just one example that illustrates how the OS bridges gaps between high-level applications and the host hardware platform.

II.2   Program Compilation

A high-level program is a symbolic abstraction that means nothing to the underlying hardware. Before executing a program, the high-level code must be translated into machine language. This translation process is called *compilation*, and the program that carries it out is called a *compiler*. Writing a compiler that translates high-level programs into low-level machine instructions is a worthy challenge. Some languages, for example, Java and C#, deal with this challenge by employing an elegant *two-tier* compilation model. First, the source program is translated into an interim, abstract VM code (called *bytecode* in Java and Python and *Intermediate Language* in C#/.NET). Next, using a completely separate and independent process, the VM code can be translated further into the machine language of any target hardware platform.

This modularity is at least one reason why Java became such a dominant programming language. Taking a historical perspective, Java can be viewed as a powerful object-oriented language whose two-tier compilation model was the right thing in the right time, just when computers began evolving from a few predictable processor/OS platforms into a bewildering hodgepodge of numerous PCs, cell phones, mobile devices, and Internet of Things devices, all connected by a global network. Writing high-level programs that can execute on any one of these host platforms is a daunting challenge. One way to streamline this distributed, multi-vendor ecosystem (from a compilation perspective) is to base it on some overarching, agreed-upon virtual machine architecture. Acting as a common, intermediate run-time environment, the VM approach allows developers to write high-level programs that run almost as is on many different hardware platforms, each equipped with its own VM implementation. We will have much more to say about the enabling power of this modularity as part II unfolds.

The road ahead: In the remainder of the book we'll apply ourselves to developing all the exciting software technologies mentioned above. Our ultimate goal is creating an infrastructure for turning high-level programs—*any* program—into executable code. The road map is shown in figure II.3.

Following the Nand to Tetris spirit, we'll pursue the part II road map from the bottom up. To get started, we assume that we have a hardware platform equipped with an assembly language. In chapters 7–8 we'll present a virtual machine architecture and a VM language, and we'll implement this abstraction by developing a *VM translator* that translates VM programs into Hack assembly programs. In chapter 9 we'll present the Jack high-level language and use it to develop a simple computer game. This way, you'll get acquainted with the Jack language and operating system before setting out to build them. In chapters 10–11 we'll develop the Jack compiler, and in chapter 12 we'll build the operating system.

So, let's roll up our sleeves and get to work!

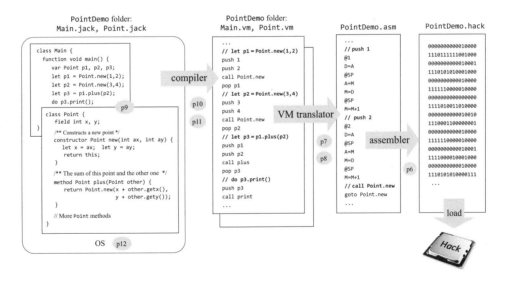

Figure II.3 Road map of part II (the assembler belongs to part I and is shown here for completeness). The road map describes a translation hierarchy, from a high-level, object-based, multi-class program to VM code, to assembly code, to executable binary code. The numbered circles stand for the projects that implement the compiler, the VM translator, the assembler, and the operating system. Project 9 focuses on writing a Jack application in order to get acquainted with the language.

7   Virtual Machine I: Processing

Programmers are creators of universes for which they alone are responsible. Universes of virtually unlimited complexity can be created in the form of computer programs.

—Joseph Weizenbaum, *Computer Power and Human Reason* (1974)

This chapter describes the first steps toward building a compiler for a typical object-based, high-level language. We approach this challenge in two major stages, each spanning two chapters. In chapters 10–11 we'll describe the construction of a *compiler*, designed to translate high-level programs into *intermediate code*; in chapters 7–8 we describe the construction of a follow-up *translator*, designed to translate the intermediate code into the machine language of a target hardware platform. As the chapter numbers suggest, we will pursue this substantial development from the bottom up, starting with the translator.

The intermediate code that lies at the core of this compilation model is designed to run on an abstract computer, called a *virtual machine*, or VM. There are several reasons why this two-tier compilation model makes sense, compared to traditional compilers that translate high-level programs directly to machine language. One benefit is cross-platform compatibility: since the virtual machine may be realized with relative ease on many hardware platforms, the same VM code can run as is on any device equipped with such a VM implementation. That's one reason Java became a dominant language for developing apps for mobile devices, which are characterized by many different processor/OS combinations. The VM can be implemented on the target devices by using software interpreters, or special-purpose hardware, or by translating the VM programs into the device's machine language. The latter implementation approach is taken by Java, Scala, C#, and Python, as well as by the Jack language developed in Nand to Tetris.

This chapter presents a typical VM architecture and VM language, conceptually similar to the Java Virtual Machine (JVM) and bytecode, respectively. As usual in Nand to Tetris, the virtual machine will be presented from two perspectives. First, we will motivate and specify the VM abstraction, describing what the VM is designed to do. Next, we will describe a proposed implementation of the VM over the Hack platform. Our implementation entails writing a program called a *VM translator* that translates VM code into Hack assembly code.

The VM language that we'll present consists of arithmetic-logical commands, memory access commands called *push* and *pop*, branching commands, and function call-and-return commands. We split the discussion and implementation of this language into two parts, each covered in a separate chapter and project. In this chapter we build a basic VM translator which implements the VM's arithmetic-logical and push/pop commands. In the next chapter we extend the basic translator to handle branching and function commands. The result will be a full-scale virtual machine implementation that will serve as the back end of the compiler that we will build in chapters 10–11.

The virtual machine that will emerge from this effort illustrates several important ideas and techniques. First, the notion of having one computing framework emulate another is a fundamental idea in computer science, tracing back to Alan Turing in the 1930s. Today, the virtual machine model is the centerpiece of several mainstream programming environments, including Java, .NET, and Python. The best way to gain an intimate inside view of how these programming environments work is to build a simple version of their VM cores, as we do here.

Another important theme in this chapter is *stack processing*. The *stack* is a fundamental and elegant data structure that comes to play in numerous computer systems, algorithms, and applications. Since the VM presented in this chapter is stack-based, it provides a working example of this remarkably versatile and powerful data structure.

7.1   The Virtual Machine Paradigm

Before a high-level program can run on a target computer, it must be translated into the computer's machine language. Traditionally, a separate compiler was developed specifically for any given pair of high-level language and low-level machine language. Over the years, the reality of many high-level languages, on the one hand, and many processors and instruction sets, on the other, has led to a proliferation of many different compilers, each depending on every detail of both its source and target languages. One way to decouple this dependency is to break the overall compilation process into two nearly separate stages. In the first stage, the high-level code is parsed and translated into intermediate and abstract processing steps—steps that are neither high nor low. In the second stage, the intermediate steps are translated further into the low-level machine language of the target hardware.

This decomposition is very appealing from a software engineering perspective. First, note that the first translation stage depends only on the specifics of the source high-level language, and the second stage only on the specifics of the target low-level machine language. Of course, the interface between the two translation stages—the exact definition of the intermediate processing steps—must be carefully designed and optimized. At some point in the evolution of program translation solutions, compiler developers concluded that this intermediate interface is sufficiently important to merit its own definition as a standalone language designed to run on an abstract machine. Specifically, one can describe a *virtual machine* whose commands realize the intermediate processing steps into which high-level commands are translated. The compiler that was formerly a single monolithic program is now split into two separate and much simpler programs. The first program, still termed *compiler*, translates the high-level code into intermediate VM commands; the second program, called *VM translator*, translates the VM commands further into the machine instructions of the target hardware platform. Figure 7.1 outlines how this two-tiered compilation framework has contributed to the cross-platform portability of Java programs.

The virtual machine framework entails many practical benefits. When a vendor introduces to the market a new digital device—say, a cell phone—it can develop for it a JVM

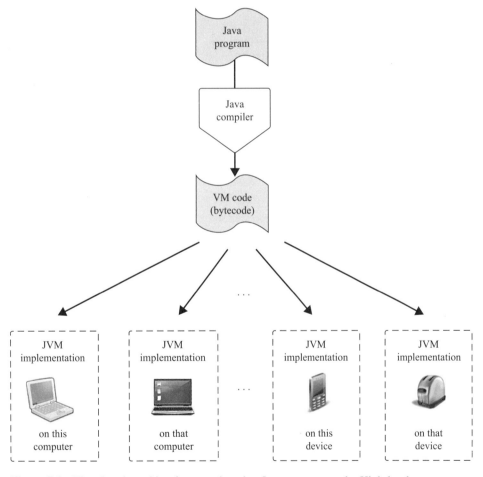

Figure 7.1   The virtual machine framework, using Java as an example. High-level programs are compiled into intermediate VM code. The same VM code can be shipped to, and executed on, any hardware platform equipped with a suitable *JVM implementation*. These VM implementations are typically realized as client-side programs that translate the VM code into the machine languages of the target devices.

implementation, known as JRE (Java Runtime Environment), with relative ease. This client-side enabling infrastrucutre immediately endows the device with a huge base of available Java software. And, in a world like .NET, in which several high-level languages are made to compile into the same intermediate VM language, compilers for different languages can share the same VM back end, allowing usage of common software libraries and language interoperability.

The price paid for the elegance and power of the VM framework is reduced efficiency. Naturally, a two-tier translation process results, ultimately, in generating machine code that is more verbose and cumbersome than the code produced by direct compilation. However, as processors become faster and VM implementations more optimized, the degraded efficiency is hardly noticeable in most applications. Of course, there will always be high-performance applications and embedded systems that will continue to demand the efficient code generated by single-tier compilers of language like C and C++. That said, modern versions of C++ feature both classical one-tier compilers and two-tier VM-based compilers.

7.2   Stack Machine

The design of an effective VM language seeks to strike a convenient balance between high-level programming languages, on the one hand, and a great variety of low-level machine languages, on the other. Thus, the desired VM language should satisfy several requirements coming both from above and from below. First, the language should have a reasonable expressive power. We achieve this by designing a VM language that features arithmetic-logical commands, push/pop commands, branching commands, and function commands. These VM commands should be sufficiently "high" so that the VM code generated by the compiler will be reasonably elegant and well structured. At the same time, the VM commands should be sufficiently "low" so that the machine code generated from them by VM translators will be tight and efficient. Said otherwise, we have to make sure that the translation gaps between the high-level and the VM level, on the one hand, and the VM level and the machine level, on the other, will not be wide. One way to satisfy these somewhat conflicting requirements is to base the interim VM language on an abstract architecture called a *stack machine*.

Before going on, we'd like to issue a plea for patience. The relationship between the stack machine that we now turn to describe and the compiler that we'll introduce later in the book is subtle. Therefore, we advise readers to allow themselves to savor the intrinsic beauty of the stack machine abstraction without worrying about its ultimate purpose in every step of the way. The full practical power of this remarkable abstraction will carry its weight only toward the end of the *next* chapter; for now, suffice it to say that any program, written in any high-level programming language, can be translated into a sequence of operations on a stack.

7.2.1   Push and Pop

The centerpiece of the stack machine model is an abstract data structure called a *stack*. A stack is a sequential storage space that grows and shrinks as needed. The stack supports various operations, the two key ones being `push` and `pop`. The `push` operation adds a value to the top of the stack, like adding a plate to the top of a stack of plates. The `pop` operation removes the stack's top value; the value that was just before it becomes the top stack element. See figure 7.2 for an example. Note that the push/pop logic results in a *last-in-first-out* (LIFO) access logic: the popped value is always the last one that was pushed onto the stack. As it turns out, this access logic lends itself perfectly to program translation and execution purposes, but this insight will take two chapters to unfold.

As figure 7.2 shows, our VM abstraction includes a *stack*, as well as a sequential, RAM-like memory segment. Observe that stack access is different from conventional memory access. First, the stack is accessible only from its top, whereas regular memory allows direct and indexed access to any value in the memory. Second, *reading* a value from the stack is a lossy operation: only the top value can be read, and the only way to access it entails

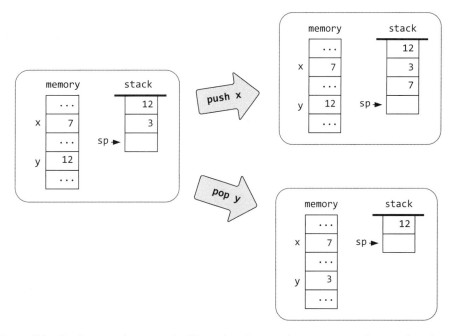

Figure 7.2 Stack processing example, illustrating the two elementary operations `push` and `pop`. The setting consists of two data structures: a RAM-like memory segment and a stack. Following convention, the stack is drawn as if it grows downward. The location just following the stack's top value is referred to by a pointer called *sp*, or *stack pointer*. The *x* and *y* symbols refer to two arbitrary memory locations.

removing it from the stack (although some stack models also provide a *peek* operation, which allows reading without removing). In contrast, the act of reading a value from a regular memory leaves no impact on the memory's state. Lastly, *writing* to the stack entails adding a value onto the stack's top without changing the other values in the stack. In contrast, writing an item into a regular memory location is a lossy operation, since it overrides the location's previous value.

7.2.2   Stack Arithmetic

Consider the generic operation *x op y*, where the operator *op* is applied to the operands *x* and *y*, for example, $7 + 5$, $3 - 8$, and so on. In a stack machine, each *x op y* operation is carried out as follows: first, the operands *x* and *y* are popped off the top of the stack; next, the value of *x op y* is computed; finally, the computed value is pushed onto the top of the stack. Likewise, the unary operation *op x* is realized by popping *x* off the top of the stack, computing the value of *op x*, and finally pushing this value onto the top of the stack. For example, here is how addition and negation are handled:

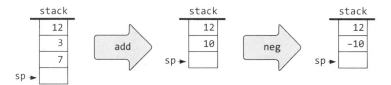

Stack-based evaluation of general arithmetic expressions is an extension of the same idea. For example, consider the expression $d = (2 - x) + (y + 9)$, taken from some high-level program. The stack-based evaluation of this expression is shown in figure 7.3a. Stack-based evaluation of logical expressions, shown in figure 7.3b, follows the same scheme.

Note that from the stack's perspective, each arithmetic or logical operation has the net impact of replacing the operation's operands with the operation's result, without affecting the rest of the stack. This is similar to how humans perform mental arithmetic, using our short-term memory. For example, how to compute the value of $3 \times (11 + 7) - 6$? We start by mentally popping 11 and 7 off the expression and calculating $11 + 7$. We then plug the resulting value back into the expression, yielding $3 \times 18 - 6$. The net effect is that $(11 + 7)$ has been replaced by 18, and the rest of the expression remains the same as before. We can now proceed to perform similar pop-compute-and-push mental operations until the expression is reduced to a single value.

These examples illustrate an important virtue of stack machines: any arithmetic and logical expression—no matter how complex—can be systematically converted into, and evaluated by, a sequence of simple operations on a stack. Therefore, one can write a *compiler* that translates high-level arithmetic and logical expressions into sequences of stack commands, as indeed we'll do in chapters 10–11. Once the high-level expressions have

```
// d = (2 - x) + (y + 9)
push 2
push x
sub
push y
push 9
add
add
pop d
```

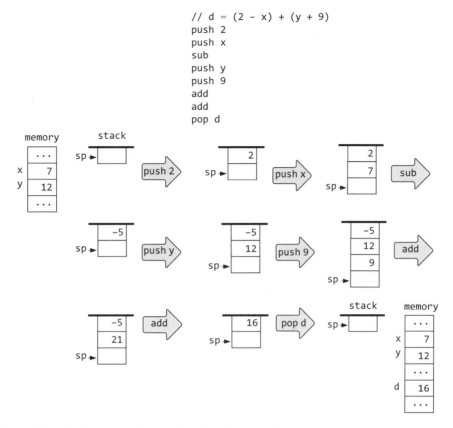

Figure 7.3a Stack-based evaluation of arithmetic expressions.

```
// (x < 7) or (y == 8)
push x
push 7
lt
push y
push 8
eq
or
```

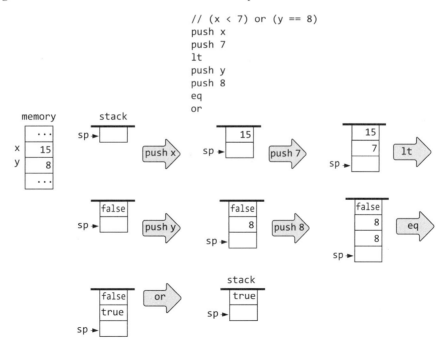

Figure 7.3b Stack-based evaluation of logical expressions.

been reduced into stack commands, we can proceed to evaluate them using a stack machine implementation.

7.2.3   Virtual Memory Segments

So far in our stack processing examples, the push/pop commands were illustrated conceptually, using the syntax push *x* and pop *y*, where *x* and *y* referred abstractly to arbitrary memory locations. We now turn to give a formal description of our push and pop commands.

High-level languages feature symbolic variables like x, y, sum, count, and so on. If the language is object-based, each such variable can be a class-level *static* variable, an instance-level *field* of an object, or a method-level *local* or *argument* variable. In virtual machines like Java's JVM and in our own VM model, there are no symbolic variables. Instead, variables are represented as entries in virtual memory segments that have names like static, this, local, and argument. In particular, as we'll see in later chapters, the compiler maps the first, second, third, ... static variable found in the high-level program onto static 0, static 1, static 2, and so on. The other variable kinds are mapped similarly on the segments this, local, and argument. For example, if the local variable x and the field y have been mapped on local 1 and this 3, respectively, then a high-level statement like let x = y will be translated by the compiler into push this 3 followed by pop local 1. Altogether, our VM model features eight memory segments, whose names and roles are listed in figure 7.4.

We note in passing that developers of VM implementations need not care about how the compiler maps symbolic variables on the virtual memory segments. We will deal with these issues at length when we develop the compiler in chapters 10–11. For now, we observe that VM commands access all the virtual memory segments in exactly the same way: by using the *segment name* followed by a nonnegative *index*.

Segment	*Role*
argument	Represents the function's arguments
local	Represents the function's local variables
static	Represents the static variables seen by the function
constant	Represents the constant values 0,1,2,3, ..., 32767
this	Described in later chapters
that	Described in later chapters
pointer	Described in later chapters
temp	Described in later chapters

Figure 7.4   Virtual memory segments.

7.3   VM Specification, Part I

Our VM model is *stack-based*: all the VM operations take their operands from, and store their results on, the *stack*. There is only one data type: a signed 16-bit integer. A VM *program* is a sequence of VM commands that fall into four categories:

· *Push / pop commands* transfer data between the stack and memory segments.
· *Arithmetic-logical commands* perform arithmetic and logical operations.
· *Branching commands* facilitate conditional and unconditional branching operations.
· *Function commands* facilitate function call-and-return operations.

 The specification and implementation of these commands span two chapters. In this chapter we focus on the *arithmetic-logical* and *push/pop* commands. In the next chapter we complete the specification of the remaining commands.

Comments and white space: Lines beginning with // are considered comments and are ignored. Blank lines are permitted and are ignored.

Push / Pop Commands

push *segment index*	Pushes the value of *segment*[*index*] onto the stack, where *segment* is argument, local, static, constant, this, that, pointer, or temp and *index* is a nonnegative integer.
pop *segment index*	Pops the top stack value and stores it in *segment*[*index*], where *segment* is argument, local, static, this, that, pointer, or temp and *index* is a nonnegative integer.

Arithmetic-Logical Commands

· *Arithmetic commands*: add, sub, neg
· *Comparison commands*: eq, gt, lt
· *Logical commands*: and, or, not

The commands add, sub, eq, gt, lt, and, and or have two implicit operands. To execute each one of them, the VM implementation pops two values off the stack's top, computes the stated function on them, and pushes the resulting value back onto the stack (by *implicit operand* we mean that the operand is not part of the command syntax: since the command is designed to always operate on the two top stack values, there is no need to specify them). The remaining neg and not commands have one implicit operand and work the same way. Figure 7.5 gives the details.

Command	Computes	Comment	
add	$x + y$	integer addition	(two's complement)
sub	$x - y$	integer subtraction	(two's complement)
neg	$-y$	arithmetic negation	(two's complement)
eq	$x == y$	equality	
gt	$x > y$	greater than	
lt	$x < y$	less than	
and	x And y	bit-wise And	
or	x Or y	bit-wise Or	
not	Not y	bit-wise Not	

Figure 7.5 The arithmetic-logical commands of the VM language.

7.4 Implementation

The virtual machine described up to this point is an abstraction. If we want to use this VM for real, it must be implemented on some real, host platform. There are several implementation options, of which we'll describe one: a VM *translator*. The VM translator is a program that translates VM commands into machine language instructions. Writing such a program entails two main tasks. First, we have to decide how to represent the stack and the virtual memory segments on the target platform. Second, we have to translate each VM command into a sequence of low-level instructions that can execute on the target platform.

For example, suppose that the target platform is a typical von Neumann machine. In this case, we can represent the VM's stack using a designated memory block in the host RAM. The lower end of this RAM block will be a fixed base address, and its higher end will change as the stack grows and shrinks. Thus, given a fixed stackBase address, we can manage the stack by keeping track of a single variable: a *stack pointer*, or SP, which holds the address of the RAM entry just following the stack's topmost value. To initialize the stack, we set SP to stackBase. From this point onward, each push x command can be implemented by the pseudocode operations RAM[SP] = x followed by SP++, and each pop x command can be implemented by SP-- followed by x = RAM[SP].

Let us assume that the host platform is the Hack computer and that we decide to anchor the stack base at address 256 in the Hack RAM. In that case, the VM translator can start by generating assembly code that realizes SP = 256, that is, @256, D = A, @SP, M = D. From this point onward, the VM translator can handle each push x and pop x command by generating assembly code that realizes the operations RAM[SP++] = x and x = RAM[--SP], respectively.

With that in mind, let us now consider the implementation of the VM arithmetic-logical commands add, sub, neg, and so on. Conveniently, all these commands share exactly the same access logic: popping the command's operands off the stack, carrying out a simple calculation, and pushing the result onto the stack. This means that once we figure out how to implement the VM's push and pop commands, the implementation of the VM's arithmetic-logical commands will follow straightforwardly.

7.4.1   Standard VM Mapping on the Hack Platform, Part I

So far in this chapter, we have made no assumption whatsoever about the target platform on which our virtual machine will be implemented: everything was described abstractly. When it comes to virtual machines, this platform independence is the whole point: you don't want to commit your abstract machine to any particular hardware platform, precisely because you want it to potentially run on *any* platform, including those that were not yet built or invented.

Of course, at some point we have to implement the VM abstraction on a particular hardware platform (for example, on one of the target platforms mentioned in figure 7.1). How should we go about it? In principle, we can do whatever we please, as long as we end up realizing the VM abstraction faithfully and efficiently. Nevertheless, VM architects normally publish basic implementation guidelines, known as *standard mappings*, for different hardware platforms. With that in mind, the remainder of this section specifies the standard mapping of our VM abstraction on the Hack computer. In what follows, we use the terms *VM implementation* and *VM translator* interchangeably.

VM program: The complete definition of a VM *program* will be presented in the next chapter. For now, we view a VM program as a sequence of VM commands stored in a text file named *FileName*.vm (the first character of the file name must be an uppercase letter, and the extension must be vm). The VM translator should read each line in the file, treat it as a VM command, and translate it into one or more instructions written in the Hack language. The resulting output—a sequence of Hack assembly instructions—should be stored in a text file named *FileName*.asm (the file name is identical to that of the source file; the extension must be asm). When translated by the Hack assembler into binary code or run as is on a Hack CPU emulator, this .asm file should perform the semantics mandated by the source VM program.

Data type: The VM abstraction has only one data type: a signed integer. This type is implemented on the Hack platform as a two's complement 16-bit value. The VM Boolean values *true* and *false* are represented as −1 and 0, respectively.

RAM usage: The host Hack RAM consists of 32K 16-bit words. VM implementations should use the top of this address space as follows:

RAM addresses	*Usage*
0 – 15	Sixteen virtual registers, usage described below
16 – 255	Static variables
256 – 2047	Stack

Recall that according to the *Hack machine language specification* (chapter 6), RAM addresses 0 to 4 can be referred to using the symbols SP, LCL, ARG, THIS, and THAT. This convention was introduced into the assembly language with foresight, to help developers of VM implementations write readable code. The expected use of these addresses in the VM implementation is as follows:

Name	*Location*	*Usage*
SP	RAM[0]	*Stack Pointer*: the memory address just following the memory address containing the topmost stack value
LCL	RAM[1]	Base address of the local segment
ARG	RAM[2]	Base address of the argument segment
THIS	RAM[3]	Base address of the this segment
THAT	RAM[4]	Base address of the that segment
TEMP	RAM[5–12]	Holds the temp segment
R13 R14 R15	RAM[13–15]	If the assembly code generated by the VM translator needs variables, it can use these registers.

When we say *base address* of a segment, we mean a physical address in the host RAM. For example, if we wish to map the local segment on the physical RAM segment starting at address 1017, we can write Hack code that sets LCL to 1017. We note in passing that deciding where to locate virtual memory segments in the host RAM is a delicate issue. For example, each time a function starts executing, we have to allocate RAM space to hold its local and argument memory segments. And when the function calls another function, we have to put these segments on hold and allocate additional RAM space for representing the segments of the called function, and so on and so forth. How can we ensure that these open-ended memory segments will not overflow into each other and into other reserved RAM areas? These memory management challenges will be addressed in the next chapter, when we'll implement the VM language's function-call-and-return commands.

For now though, none of these memory allocation issues should bother us. Instead, you are to assume that SP, ARG, LCL, THIS, and THAT have been already initialized to some sensible addresses in the host RAM. Note that VM implementations never see these addresses anyway. Rather, they manipulate them symbolically, using the pointer names.

For example, suppose we want to push the value of the D register onto the stack. This operation can be implemented using the logic `RAM[SP++] = D`, which can be expressed in Hack assembly as `@SP, A=M, M=D, @SP, M=M+1`. This code will execute the push operation perfectly, while knowing neither where the stack is located in the host RAM nor what is the current value of the stack pointer.

We suggest taking a few minutes to digest the assembly code just shown. If you don't understand it, you must refresh your knowledge of pointer manipulation in the Hack assembly language (section 4.3, example 3). This knowledge is a prerequisite for developing the VM translator, since the translation of each VM command entails generating code in the Hack assembly language.

Memory Segments Mapping

Local, argument, this, that: In the next chapter we discuss how the VM implementation maps these segments dynamically on the host RAM. For now, all we have to know is that the base addresses of these segments are stored in the registers LCL, ARG, THIS, and THAT, respectively. Therefore, any access to the i-th entry of a virtual segment (in the context of a VM "push / pop *segmentName i*" command) should be translated into assembly code that accesses address $(base + i)$ in the RAM, where *base* is one of the pointers LCL, ARG, THIS, or THAT.

Pointer: Unlike the virtual segments described above, the `pointer` segment contains exactly two values and is mapped directly onto RAM locations 3 and 4. Recall that these RAM locations are also called, respectively, THIS and THAT. Thus, the semantics of the `pointer` segment is as follows. Any access to `pointer 0` should result in accessing the THIS pointer, and any access to `pointer 1` should result in accessing the THAT pointer. For example, `pop pointer 0` should set THIS to the popped value, and `push pointer 1` should push onto the stack the current value of THAT. These peculiar semantics will make perfect sense when we write the compiler in chapters 10–11, so stay tuned.

Temp: This 8-word segment is also fixed and mapped directly on RAM locations 5 – 12. With that in mind, any access to `temp i`, where i varies from 0 to 7, should be translated into assembly code that accesses RAM location $5 + i$.

Constant: This virtual memory segment is truly virtual, as it does not occupy any physical RAM space. Instead, the VM implementation handles any access to `constant i` by simply supplying the constant i. For example, the command `push constant 17` should be translated into assembly code that pushes the value 17 onto the stack.

Static: Static variables are mapped on addresses 16 to 255 of the host RAM. The VM translator can realize this mapping automatically, as follows. Each reference to `static i` in a VM program stored in file Foo.vm can be translated to the assembly symbol Foo.*i*. According to the *Hack machine language specification* (chapter 6), the Hack assembler will map these symbolic variables on the host RAM, starting at address 16. This convention will cause the static variables that appear in a VM program to be mapped on addresses 16 and onward, *in the order in which they appear in the VM code*. For example, suppose that a VM program starts with the code push constant 100, push constant 200, pop static 5, pop static 2. The translation scheme described above will cause static 5 and static 2 to be mapped on RAM addresses 16 and 17, respectively.

This implementation of static variables is somewhat devious, but works well. It causes the static variables of different VM files to coexist without intermingling, since their generated *FileName.i* symbols have unique prefix file names. We note in closing that since the stack begins at address 256, the implementation limits the number of static variables in a Jack program to $255 - 16 + 1 = 240$.

Assembly language symbols: Let us summarize all the special symbols mentioned above. Suppose that the VM program that we have to translate is stored in a file named Foo.vm. VM translators conforming to the standard *VM mapping on the Hack platform* generate assembly code that uses the following symbols: SP, LCL, ARG, THIS, THAT, and Foo.*i*, where *i* is a nonnegative integer. If they need to generate code that uses variables for temporary storage, VM translators can use the symbols R13, R14, and R15.

7.4.2   The VM Emulator

One relatively simple way to implement a virtual machine is to write a high-level program that represents the stack and the memory segments and implements all the VM commands using high-level programming. For example, if we represent the stack using a sufficiently-large array named stack, then push and pop operations can be directly realized using high-level statements like stack[SP++] = x and x = stack[--SP], respectively. The virtual memory segments can also be handled using arrays.

If we want this VM emulation program to be fancy, we can augment it with a graphical interface, allowing users to experiment with VM commands and visually inspect their impact on images of the stack and the memory segments. The Nand to Tetris software suite includes one such emulator, written in Java (see figure 7.6). This handy program allows loading and executing VM code as is and observing visually, during simulated run-time, how the VM commands effect the states of the emulated stack and memory segments. In addition, the emulator shows how the stack and the memory segments are mapped on the host RAM and how the RAM state changes when VM commands execute. The supplied VM emulator is a cool program—try it!

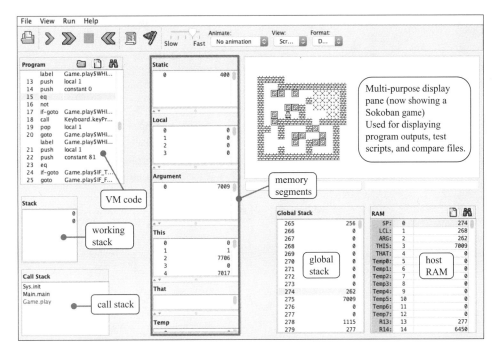

Figure 7.6   The VM emulator supplied with the Nand to Tetris software suite.

7.4.3   Design Suggestions for the VM Implementation

Usage: The VM translator accepts a single command-line argument, as follows:

```
prompt> VMTranslator source
```

where *source* is a file name of the form *ProgName*.vm. The file name may contain a file path. If no path is specified, the VM translator operates on the current folder. The first character in the file name must be an uppercase letter, and the vm extension is mandatory. The file contains a sequence of one or more VM commands. In response, the translator creates an output file, named *ProgName*.asm, containing the assembly instructions that realize the VM commands. The output file *ProgName*.asm is stored in the same folder as that of the input. If the file *ProgName*.asm already exists, it will be overwritten.

Program Structure

We propose implementing the VM translator using three modules: a main program called VMTranslator, a Parser, and a CodeWriter. The Parser's job is to make sense out of each VM command, that is, understand what the command seeks to do. The CodeWriter's job is to translate the understood VM command into assembly instructions that realize the desired operation on the Hack platform. The VMTranslator drives the translation process.

The Parser

This module handles the parsing of a single .vm file. The parser provides services for reading a VM command, unpacking the command into its various components, and providing convenient access to these components. In addition, the parser ignores all white space and comments. The parser is designed to handle all the VM commands, including the *branching* and *function* commands that will be implemented in chapter 8.

Routine	*Arguments*	*Returns*	*Function*
Constructor / initializer	Input file / stream	—	Opens the input file / stream, and gets ready to parse it.
hasMoreLines	—	boolean	Are there more lines in the input?
advance	—	—	Reads the next command from the input and makes it the current command. This routine should be called only if hasMoreLines is true. Initially there is no current command.
commandType	—	C_ARITHMETIC, C_PUSH, C_POP, C_LABEL, C_GOTO, C_IF, C_FUNCTION, C_RETURN, C_CALL (constant)	Returns a constant representing the type of the current command. If the current command is an arithmetic-logical command, returns C_ARITHMETIC.
arg1	—	string	Returns the first argument of the current command. In the case of C_ARITHMETIC, the command itself (add, sub, etc.) is returned. Should not be called if the current command is C_RETURN.
arg2	—	int	Returns the second argument of the current command. Should be called only if the current command is C_PUSH, C_POP, C_FUNCTION, or C_CALL.

For example, if the current command is push local 2, then calling arg1() and arg2() would return, respectively, "local" and 2. If the current command is add, then calling arg1() would return "add", and arg2() would not be called.

The CodeWriter

This module translates a parsed VM command into Hack assembly code.

Routine	Arguments	Returns	Function
Constructor / initializer	Output file / stream	—	Opens an output file / stream and gets ready to write into it.
writeArithmetic	command (string)	—	Writes to the output file the assembly code that implements the given arithmetic-logical command.
writePushPop	command (C_PUSH or C_POP), segment (string), index (int)	—	Writes to the output file the assembly code that implements the given push or pop command.
close	—	—	Closes the output file / stream.

More code writing routines will be added to this module in chapter 8.

For example, calling writePushPop (C_PUSH,"local",2) would result in generating assembly instructions that implement the VM command push local 2. Another example: Calling WriteArithmetic("add") would result in generating assembly instructions that pop the two topmost elements from the stack, add them up, and push the result onto the stack.

The VM Translator

This is the main program that drives the translation process, using the services of a Parser and a CodeWriter. The program gets the name of the input source file, say *Prog*.vm, from the command-line argument. It constructs a Parser for parsing the input file *Prog*.vm and creates an output file, *Prog*.asm, into which it will write the translated assembly instructions. The program then enters a loop that iterates through the VM commands in the input file. For each command, the program uses the Parser and the CodeWriter services for parsing the command into its fields and then generating from them a sequence of assembly instructions. The instructions are written into the output *Prog*.asm file.

We provide no API for this module, inviting you to implement it as you see fit.

Implementation Tips

1. When starting to translate a VM command, for example, push local 2, consider generating, and emitting to the output assembly code stream, a comment like // push local 2. These comments will help you read the generated code and debug your translator if needed.

2. Almost every VM command needs to push data onto and/or pop data off the stack. Therefore, your writeXxx routines will need to output similar assembly instructions over and

over. To avoid writing repetitive code, consider writing and using private routines (sometimes called *helper methods*) that generate these frequently used code snippets.

3. As was explained in chapter 6, it is recommended to end each machine language program with an infinite loop. Therefore, consider writing a private routine that writes the infinite loop code in assembly. Call this routine once, when you are done translating all the VM commands.

7.5   Project

Basically, you have to write a program that reads VM commands, one command at a time, and translates each command into Hack instructions. For example, how should we handle the VM command push local 2? *Tip:* We should write several Hack assembly instructions that, among other things, manipulate the SP and LCL pointers. Coming up with a sequence of Hack instructions that realizes each one of the VM arithmetic-logical and push/pop commands is the very essence of this project. That's what code generation is all about.

We recommend you start by writing and testing these assembly code snippets on paper. Draw a RAM segment, draw a trace table that records the values of, say, SP and LCL, and initialize these variables to arbitrary memory addresses. Now, track on paper the assembly code that you think realizes say, push local 2. Does the code impact the stack and the local segments correctly (RAM-wise)? Did you remember to update the stack pointer? And so on. Once you feel confident that your assembly code snippets do their jobs correctly, you can have your CodeWriter generate them, almost as is.

Since your VM translator has to write assembly code, you must flex your low-level Hack programming muscles. The best way to do it is by reviewing the assembly program examples in chapter 4 and the programs that you wrote in project 4. If you need to consult the Hack assembly language documentation, see section 4.2.

Objective: Build a basic VM translator designed to implement the *arithmetic-logical* and *push / pop* commands of the VM language.

This version of the VM translator assumes that the source VM code is error-free. Error checking, reporting, and handling can be added to later versions of the VM translator but are not part of project 7.

Resources: You will need two tools: the programming language in which you will implement the VM translator and the *CPU emulator* supplied in your nand2tetris/tools folder. The CPU emulator will allow you to execute and test the assembly code generated by your translator. If the generated code runs correctly in the CPU emulator, we will assume that your VM translator performs as expected. This is just a partial test of the translator, but it will suffice for our purposes.

Another tool that comes in handy in this project is the *VM emulator*, also supplied in your nand2tetris/tools folder. We encourage using this program for executing the supplied test programs and watching how the VM code effects the (simulated) states of the stack and the virtual memory segments. For example, suppose that a test program pushes a few constants onto the stack and then pops them into the local segment. You can run the test program on the VM emulator, inspect how the stack grows and shrinks, and see how the local segment becomes populated with values. This can help you understand which actions the VM translator is supposed to generate before setting out to implement it.

Contract: Write a VM-to-Hack translator conforming to the VM Specification given in section 7.3 and to the standard VM mapping on the Hack platform given in section 7.4.1. Use your translator to translate the supplied test VM programs, yielding corresponding programs written in the Hack assembly language. When executed on the supplied CPU emulator, the assembly programs generated by your translator should deliver the results mandated by the supplied test scripts and compare files.

Testing and Implementation Stages

We provide five test VM programs. We advise developing and testing your evolving translator on the test programs in the order in which they are given. This way, you will be implicitly guided to build the translator's code generation capabilities gradually, according to the demands presented by each test program.

SimpleAdd: This program pushes two constants onto the stack and adds them up. Tests how your implementation handles the commands push constant *i* and add.

StackTest: Pushes some constants onto the stack and tests how your implementation handles all the arithmetic-logical commands.

BasicTest: Executes push, pop, and arithmetic commands using the memory segments constant, local, argument, this, that, and temp. Tests how your implementation handles these memory segments (you've already handled constant).

PointerTest: Executes push, pop, and arithmetic commands using the memory segments pointer, this, and that. Tests how your implementation handles the pointer segment.

StaticTest: Executes push, pop, and arithmetic commands using constants and the memory segment static. Tests how your implementation handles the static segment.

Initialization: In order for any translated VM program to start running, it must include startup code that forces the generated assembly code to start executing on the host platform.

And, before this code starts running, the VM implementation must anchor the base addresses of the stack and the virtual memory segments in selected RAM locations. Both issues—startup code and segments initializations—are described and implemented in the next chapter. The difficulty here is that we need these initializations in place for executing the test programs in this project. The good news is that you need not worry about these details, since all the initializations necessary for this project are handled "manually" by the supplied test scripts.

Testing / Debugging: We supply five sets of test programs, test scripts, and compare files. For each test program *Xxx*.vm we recommend following these steps:

0. Use the *Xxx*VME.tst script to execute the test program *Xxx*.vm on the supplied VM emulator. This will familiarize you with the intended behavior of the test program. Inspect the simulated stack and virtual segments, and make sure that you understand what the test program is doing.

1. Use your partially implemented translator to translate the file *Xxx*.vm (test program). The result should be a text file named *Xxx*.asm, containing the Hack assembly code generated by your translator.

2. Inspect the generated *Xxx*.asm code produced by your translator. If there are visible errors, debug and fix your translator.

3. Use the supplied *Xxx*.tst and *Xxx*.cmp files to run and test your translated *Xxx*.asm program on the supplied *CPU emulator*. If there are any errors, debug and fix your translator.

When you are done with this project, be sure to save a copy of your VM translator. In the next chapter you will be asked to extend this program, adding the handling of more VM commands. If your project 8 modifications end up breaking the code developed in project 7, you'll be able to resort to your backup version.

A web-based version of project 7 is available at www.nand2tetris.org.

7.6   Perspective

In this chapter we began the process of developing a compiler for a high-level language. Following modern software engineering practices, we have chosen to base the compiler on a two-tier compilation model. In the *front-end* tier, covered in chapters 10 and 11, the high-level code is translated into an intermediate code designed to run on a virtual machine. In the *back-end* tier, covered in this and in the next chapter, the intermediate code is translated further into the machine language of a target hardware platform (see figure 7.1).

Over the years, this two-stage compilation model has been used—implicitly and explicitly—in many compiler construction projects. In the late 1970s, IBM and Apple corporations introduced two pioneering and phenomenally successful personal computers, known as the IBM PC and the Apple II. One high-level language that became popular on these early PCs was Pascal. Alas, different Pascal compilers had to be developed, since the IBM and Apple machines used different processors, different machine languages, and different operating systems. Also, IBM and Apple were rival companies and had no interest in helping developers port their software to the other machine. As a result, software developers who wanted their Pascal apps to run on both lines of computers had to use different compilers, each designed to generate machine-specific binary code. Could there not be a better way to handle cross-platform compilation, so that programs could be written once and run everywhere?

One solution to this challenge was an early virtual machine framework called *p-code*. The basic idea was to compile Pascal programs into intermediate p-code (similar to our VM language) and then use one implementation for translating the abstract p-code into Intel's x86 instruction set, used by IBM PCs, and another implementation for translating the same p-code into Motorola's 68000 instruction set, used by Apple computers. Meanwhile, other companies developed highly optimized Pascal compilers that generated efficient p-code. The net result was that the same Pascal program could run as is on practically every machine in this nascent PC market: no matter which computer your customers used, you could ship them exactly the same p-code files, obviating the need to use multiple compilers. Of course, the whole scheme was based on the assumption that the customer's computer was equipped with a client-side p-code implementation (equivalent to our VM translator). To make this happen, the p-code implementations were distributed freely over the Internet, and customers were invited to download them to their computers. Historically, this was perhaps the first time that the notion of a cross-platform high-level language began realizing its full potential.

Following the explosive growth of the Internet and mobile devices in the mid-1990s, cross-platform compatibility became a universally vexing issue. To address the problem, the Sun Microsystems company (later acquired by Oracle) sought to develop a new programming language whose compiled code could potentially run as is on any computer and digital device connected to the Internet. The language that emerged from this initiative—*Java*—was founded on an intermediate code execution model called the *Java Virtual Machine*, or JVM.

The JVM is a specification that describes an intermediate language called *bytecode*—the target VM language of Java compilers. Files written in bytecode are widely used for code distribution of Java programs over the Internet. In order to execute these portable programs, the client PCs, tablets, and cell phones that download them must be equipped with suitable JVM implementations, known as JREs (Java Runtime Environments). These programs are widely available for numerous processor and operating system combinations. Today, many personal computer and cell phone owners use these infrastructure programs (the JREs) routinely and implicitly, without ever noticing their existence on their devices.

The Python language, conceived in the late 1980s, is also based on a two-tier translation model, whose centerpiece is the PVM (Python Virtual Machine), which uses its own version of bytecode.

In the early 2000s, Microsoft launched its .NET Framework. The centerpiece of .NET is a virtual machine framework called *Common Language Runtime* (CLR). According to Microsoft's vision, many programming languages, like C# and C++, can be compiled into intermediate code running on the CLR. This enables code written in different languages to interoperate and share the software libraries of a common run-time environment. Of course, single-tier compilers for C and C++ are still widely used, especially in high-performance applications requiring tight and optimized code.

Indeed, one issue that was completely sidestepped in this chapter is *efficiency*. Our contract calls for developing a VM translator, without requiring that the generated assembly code be efficient. Clearly, this is a serious oversight. The VM translator is a mission-critical enabling technology, lying at the core of your PC, tablet, or cell phone: if it will generate tight and efficient low-level code, apps will run on your machine swiftly, using as little hardware resources as possible. Therefore, optimizing the VM translator is a top priority.

In general, there are numerous opportunities to optimize the VM translator. For example, assignments like `let x = y` are prevalent in high-level code; these statements are translated by the compiler into VM commands like, for example, `push local 3` followed by `pop static 1`. Clever implementations of such pairs of VM commands can generate assembly code that sidesteps the stack completely, resulting in dramatic performance gains. Of course, this is one out of many examples of possible VM optimizations. Indeed, over the years, the VM implementations of Java, Python, and C# became dramatically more powerful and sophisticated.

We note in closing that a crucial ingredient that must be added to the virtual machine model before its full potential is unleashed is a common software library. Indeed the Java Virtual Machine comes with the *standard Java class library*, and the Microsoft's .NET Framework comes with the *Framework Class Library*. These vast software libraries can be viewed as portable operating systems, providing numerous services like memory management, GUI toolkits, string functions, math functions, and so on. These extensions will be described and built in chapter 12.

8 Virtual Machine II: Control

If everything seems under control, you're just not going fast enough.
                                       —Mario Andretti (b. 1940), race car champion

Chapter 7 introduced the notion of a *virtual machine* (VM), and project 7 began implementing our abstract virtual machine and VM language over the Hack platform. The implementation entailed developing a program that translates VM commands into Hack assembly code. Specifically, in the previous chapter we learned how to use and implement the VM's arithmetic-logical commands and push/pop commands; in this chapter we'll learn how to use and implement the VM's branching commands and function commands. As the chapter progresses, we'll extend the basic translator developed in project 7, ending with a full-scale VM translator over the Hack platform. This translator will serve as the back-end module of the compiler that we will build in chapters 10 and 11.

In any Great Gems in Applied Computer Science contest, stack processing will be a strong finalist. The previous chapter showed how arithmetic and Boolean expressions can be represented and evaluated by elementary operations on a stack. This chapter goes on to show how this remarkably simple data structure can also support remarkably complex tasks like nested function calling, parameter passing, recursion, and the various memory allocation and recycling tasks required to support program execution during run-time. Most programmers tend to take these services for granted, expecting the compiler and the operating system to deliver them, one way or another. We are now in a position to open up this black box and see how these fundamental programming mechanisms are actually realized.

Run-time system: Every computer system must specify a run-time model. This model answers essential questions without which programs cannot run: how to start a program's execution, what the computer should do when a program terminates, how to pass arguments from one function to another, how to allocate memory resources to running functions, how to free memory resources when they are no longer needed, and so on.

In Nand to Tetris, these issues are addressed by the *VM language* specification, along with the *standard mapping on the Hack platform* specification. If a VM translator is developed according to these guidelines, it will end up realizing an executable run-time system. In particular, the VM translator will not only translate the VM commands (push, pop, add, and so on) into assembly instructions—it will also generate assembly code that realizes an envelope in which the program runs. All the questions mentioned above—how to start a program, how to manage the function call-and-return behavior, and so on—will be answered by generating enabling assembly code that wraps the code proper. Let's see an example.

8.1   High-Level Magic

High-level languages allow writing programs in high-level terms. For example, an expression like $x = -b + \sqrt{b^2 - 4 \cdot a \cdot c}$ can be written as x = -b + sqrt(power(b,2) - 4 * a * c), which is almost as descriptive as the real thing. Note the difference between primitive operations like + and – and functions like sqrt and power. The former are built into the basic syntax of the high-level language. The latter are extensions of the basic language.

The unlimited capacity to extend the language at will is one of the most important features of high-level programming languages. Of course, at some point, someone must implement functions like sqrt and power. However, the story of implementing these abstractions is completely separate from the story of using them. Therefore, application programmers can assume that each one of these functions will get executed—somehow—and that following its execution, control will return—somehow—to the next operation in one's code. Branching commands endow the language with additional expressive power, allowing writing conditional code like if !(a == 0) { x = (-b + sqrt(power(b,2) - 4 * a * c)) / (2 * a) } else { x = -c/b }. Once again, we see that high-level code enables the expression of high-level logic—in this case the algorithm for solving quadratic equations—almost directly.

Indeed, modern programming languages are programmer-friendly, offering useful and powerful abstractions. It is a sobering thought, though, that no matter how high we allow our high-level language to be, at the end of the day it must be realized on some hardware platform that can only execute primitive machine instructions. Thus, among other things, compiler and VM architects must find low-level solutions for realizing branching and function call-and-return commands.

Functions—the bread and butter of modular programming—are standalone programming units that are allowed to call each other for their effect. For example, solve can call sqrt, and sqrt, in turn, can call power. This calling sequence can be as deep as we please, as well as recursive. Typically, the calling function (the *caller*) passes arguments to the called function (the *callee*) and suspends its execution until the latter completes *its* execution. The callee uses the passed arguments to execute or compute something and then returns a value (which may be void) to the caller. The caller then snaps back into action, resuming its execution.

In general then, whenever one function (the *caller*) calls a function (the *callee*), someone must take care of the following overhead:

- Save the *return address*, which is the address within the caller's code to which execution must return after the callee completes its execution;
- Save the memory resources of the caller;
- Allocate the memory resources required by the callee;
- Make the arguments passed by the caller available to the callee's code;
- Start executing the callee's code.

When the callee terminates and returns a value, someone must take care of the following overhead:

- Make the callee's *return value* available to the caller's code;
- Recycle the memory resources used by the callee;
- Reinstate the previously saved memory resources of the caller;
- Retrieve the previously saved *return address*;
- Resume executing the caller's code, from the return address onward.

Blissfully, high-level programmers don't have to ever think about all these nitty-gritty chores: the assembly code generated by the compiler handles them, stealthily and efficiently. And, in a two-tier compilation model, this housekeeping responsibility falls on the compiler's back end, which is the VM translator that we are now developing. Thus, in this chapter, we will uncover, among other things, the run-time framework that enables what is probably the most important abstraction in the art of programming: *function call-and-return*. But first, let's start with the easier challenge of handling branching commands.

8.2   Branching

The default flow of computer programs is sequential, executing one command after the other. For various reasons like embarking on a new iteration in a loop, this sequential flow can be redirected by branching commands. In low-level programming, branching is accomplished by *goto destination* commands. The destination specification can take several forms, the most primitive being the physical memory address of the instruction that should be executed next. A slightly more abstract specification is established by specifying a symbolic label (bound to a physical memory address). This variation requires that the language be equipped with a labeling directive, designed to assign symbolic labels to selected locations in the code. In our VM language, this is done using a labeling command whose syntax is `label` *symbol*.

With that in mind, the VM language supports two forms of branching. *Unconditional branching* is effected using a `goto` *symbol* command, which means: jump to execute the command just after the `label` *symbol* command in the code. *Conditional branching* is effected using the `if-goto` *symbol* command, whose semantics is: Pop the topmost value off the stack; if it's not `false`, jump to execute the command just after the `label` *symbol* command; otherwise, execute the next command in the code. This contract implies that before specifying a conditional goto command, the VM code writer (for example, a compiler) must first specify a condition. In our VM language, this is done by pushing a Boolean expression onto the stack. For example, the compiler that we'll develop in chapters 10–11 will translate `if (n < 100) goto LOOP` into `push n`, `push 100`, `lt`, `if-goto LOOP`.

Example: Consider a function that receives two arguments, *x* and *y*, and returns the product $x \cdot y$. This can be done by adding *x* repetitively to a local variable, say `sum`, *y* times, and then returning `sum`'s value. A function that implements this naïve multiplication algorithm is listed in figure 8.1. This example illustrates how a typical looping logic can be expressed using the VM branching commands `goto`, `if-goto`, and `label`.

Notice how the Boolean condition `!(i < y)`, implemented as `push i`, `push y`, `lt`, `ng`, is pushed onto the stack just before the `if-goto WHILE_END` command. In chapter 7 we saw that VM commands can be used to express and evaluate any Boolean expression. As we see in figure 8.1, high-level control structures like `if` and `while` can be easily realized using nothing more than `goto` and `if-goto` commands. In general, any flow of control

High-level code	VM code
<pre>// Returns x * y
int mult(int x, int y) {
int sum = 0;
int i = 0;
while (i < y) {
sum += x;
i++;
}
return sum;
}</pre>	<pre>// Returns x * y
function mult(x,y)
push 0
pop sum
push 0
pop i
label WHILE_LOOP
push i
push y
lt
neg
if-goto WHILE_END
push sum
push x
add
pop sum
push i
push 1
add
pop i
goto WHILE_LOOP
label WHILE_END
push sum
return</pre>

Figure 8.1 Branching commands action. (The VM code on the right uses symbolic variable names instead of virtual memory segments, to make it more readable.)

structure found in high-level programming languages can be realized using our (rather minimal set of) VM logical and branching commands.

Implementation: Most low-level machine languages, including Hack, feature means for declaring symbolic labels and for effecting conditional and unconditional "goto label" actions. Therefore, if we base the VM implementation on a program that translates VM commands into assembly instructions, implementing the VM branching commands is a relatively simple matter.

Operating system: We end this section with two side comments. First, VM programs are not written by humans. Rather, they are written by compilers. Figure 8.1 illustrates source code on the left and VM code on the right. In chapters 10–11 we'll develop a *compiler* that translates the former into the latter. Second, note that the mult implementation shown in figure 8-1 is inefficient. Later in the book we'll present optimized multiplication and division algorithms that operate at the bit level. These algorithms will be used for realizing the Math.multiply and Math.divide functions, which are part of the operating system that we will build in chapter 12.

Our OS will be written in the Jack language, and translated by a Jack compiler into the VM language. The result will be a library of eight files named Math.vm, Memory.vm, String. vm, Array.vm, Output.vm, Screen.vm, Keyboard.vm, and Sys.vm (the OS API is given in appendix 6). Each OS file features a collection of useful functions that any VM function is welcome to call for their effect. For example, whenever a VM function needs multiplication or division services, it can call the Math.multiply or Math.divide function.

8.3   Functions

Every programming language is characterized by a fixed set of built-in operations. In addition, high-level and some low-level languages offer the great freedom of extending this fixed repertoire with an open-ended collection of programmer-defined operations. Depending on the language, these canned operations are typically called *subroutines*, *procedures*, *methods*, or *functions*. In our VM language, all these programming units are referred to as *functions*.

In well-designed languages, built-in commands and programmer-defined functions have the same look and feel. For example, to compute $x + y$ on our stack machine, we push x, push y, and add. In doing so, we expect the add implementation to pop the two top values off the stack, add them up, and push the result onto the stack. Suppose now that either we, or someone else, has written a *power* function designed to compute x^y. To use this function, we follow exactly the same routine: we push x, push y, and call power. This consistent calling protocol allows composing primitive commands and function calls seamlessly. For example, expressions like $(x + y)^3$ can be evaluated using push x, push y, add, push 3, call power.

We see that the only difference between applying a primitive operation and invoking a function is the keyword call preceding the latter. Everything else is exactly the same: both operations require the caller to set the stage by pushing arguments onto the stack, both operations are expected to consume their arguments, and both operations are expected to push return values onto the stack. This calling protocol has an elegant consistency which, we hope, is not lost on the reader.

Example: Figure 8.2 shows a VM program that computes the function $\sqrt{x^2 + y^2}$, also known as *hypot*. The program consists of three functions, with the following run-time behavior: main calls hypot, and then hypot calls mult, twice. There is also a call to a sqrt function, which we don't track, to reduce clutter.

The bottom part of figure 8.2 shows that during run-time, each function sees a private world, consisting of its own working stack and memory segments. These separate worlds are connected through two "wormholes": when a function says call mult, the arguments that it pushed onto its stack prior to the call are somehow passed to the argument segment of the callee. Likewise, when a function says return, the last value that it pushed onto its stack just before returning is somehow copied onto the stack of the caller, replacing the previously pushed arguments. These hand-shaking actions are carried out by the VM implementation, as we now turn to describe.

Implementation: A computer program consists of typically several and possibly many functions. Yet at any given point during run-time, only a few of these functions are actually doing something. We use the term *calling chain* to refer, conceptually, to all the functions that are currently involved in the program's execution. When a VM program starts running, the calling chain consists of one function only, say, main. At some point, main may call another function, say, foo, and that function may call yet another function, say, bar. At this point the calling chain is main→foo→bar. Each function in the calling chain waits for the function that it called to return. Thus, the only function that is truly active in the calling chain is the last one, which we call the *current function*, meaning the currently executing function.

In order to carry out their work, functions normally use *local* and *argument* variables. These variables are temporary: the memory segments that represent them must be allocated when the function starts executing and can be recycled when the function returns. This memory management task is complicated by the requirement that function calling is allowed to be arbitrarily nested, as well as recursive. During run-time, each function call must be executed independently of all the other calls and maintain its own stack, local variables, and argument variables. How can we implement this unlimited nesting mechanism and the memory management tasks associated with it?

```
0 function main()
// Computes hypot(3,4)
1     push 3
2     push 4
3     call hypot
4     return

5 function hypot(x,y)
// Computes sqrt(x*x + y*y)
6     push x
7     push x
8     call mult
9     push y
10    push y
11    call mult
12    add
13    call sqrt
14    return

15 function mult(x,y)
// Computes x * y (same as in figure 8.1)
16    push 0
17    pop sum
18    push 0
19    pop i
      ...
36    push sum
37    return
```

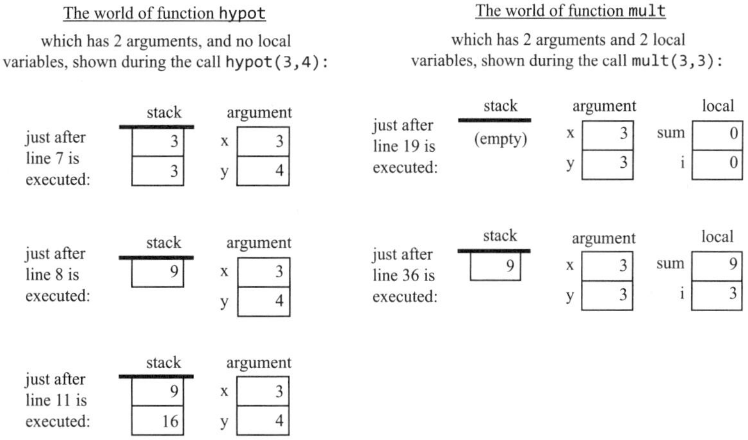

The world of function hypot
which has 2 arguments, and no local
variables, shown during the call hypot(3,4):

The world of function mult
which has 2 arguments and 2 local
variables, shown during the call mult(3,3):

Figure 8.2 Run-time snapshots of selected stack and segment states during the execution of a three-function program. The line numbers are not part of the code and are given for reference only.

The property that makes this housekeeping task tractable is the linear nature of the call-and-return logic. Although the function calling chain may be arbitrarily deep as well as recursive, at any given point in time only one function executes at the chain's end, while all the other functions up the calling chain are waiting for it to return. This *Last-In-First-Out* processing model lends itself perfectly to the stack data structure, which is also LIFO. Let's takes a closer look.

Assume that the current function is foo. Suppose that foo has already pushed some values onto its working stack and has modified some entries in its memory segments. Suppose that at some point foo wants to call another function, bar, for its effect. At this point we have to put foo's execution on hold until bar will terminate *its* execution. Now, putting foo's working stack on hold is not a problem: because the stack grows only in one direction, the working stack of bar will never override previously pushed values. Therefore, saving the working stack of the caller is easy—we get it "for free" thanks to the linear and uni-directional stack structure. But how can we save foo's memory segments? Recall that in chapter 7 we used the pointers LCL, ARG, THIS, and THAT to refer to the base RAM addresses of the local, argument, this, and that segments of the current function. If we wish to put these segments on hold, we can push their pointers onto the stack and pop them later, when we'll want to bring foo back to life. In what follows, we use the term *frame* to refer, collectively, to the set of pointer values needed for saving and reinstating the function's state.

We see that once we move from a single function setting to a multifunction setting, the humble stack begins to attain a rather formidable role in our story. Specifically, we now use the same data structure to hold both the working stacks as well as the frames of all the functions up the calling chain. To give it the respect that it deserves, from now on we'll refer to this hard-working data structure as the *global stack*. See figure 8.3 for the details.

As shown in figure 8.3, when handling the call *functionName* command, the VM implementation pushes the caller's frame onto the stack. At the end of this housekeeping, we are ready to jump to executing the callee's code. This mega jump is not hard to implement. As we'll see later, when handling a function *functionName* command, we use the function's name to create, and inject into the generated assembly code stream, a unique symbolic label that marks where the function starts. Thus, when handling a "function *functionName*" command, we can generate assembly code that effects a "goto *functionName*" operation. When executed, this command will effectively transfer control to the callee.

Returning from the callee to the caller when the former terminates is trickier, since the VM return command specifies no return address. Indeed, the caller's anonymity is inherent in the notion of a function call: functions like mult or sqrt are designed to serve any caller, implying that a return address cannot be specified a priori. Instead, a return command is interpreted as follows: redirect the program's execution to the memory location holding the command just following the call command that invoked the current function.

The VM implementation can realize this contract by (i) saving the return address just before control is transferred to executing the caller and (ii) retrieving the return address and jumping to it just after the callee returns. But where shall we save the return address? Once again, the resourceful stack comes to the rescue. To remind you, the VM translator advances

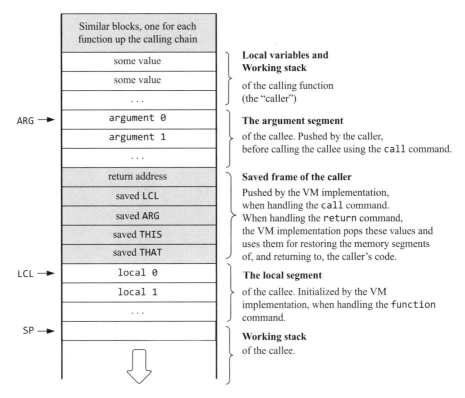

Figure 8.3   The global stack, shown when the callee is running. Before the callee terminates, it pushes a return value onto the stack (not shown). When the VM implementation handles the `return` command, it copies the return value onto `argument 0`, and sets SP to point to the address just following it. This effectively frees the global stack area below the new value of SP. Thus, when the caller resumes its execution, it sees the return value at the top of its working stack.

from one VM command to the next, generating assembly code as it goes along. When we encounter a `call foo` command in the VM code, we know exactly which command should be executed when `foo` terminates: it's the assembly command just after the assembly commands that realize the `call foo` command. Thus, we can have the VM translator plant a label right there, in the generated assembly code stream, and push this label onto the stack. When we later encounter a `return` command in the VM code, we can pop the previously saved return address off the stack—let's call it *returnAddress*—and effect the operation `goto` *returnAddress* in assembly. This is the low-level trick that enables the run-time magic of redirecting control back to the right place in the caller's code.

The VM implementation in action: We now turn to give a step-by-step illustration of how the VM implementation supports the function call-and-return action. We will do it in the context of executing a `factorial` function, designed to compute *n*! recursively. Figure 8.4 gives the program's code, along with selected snapshots of the global stack

<u>High-level code</u>   <u>VM code</u>

```
// Tests the factorial function        // Tests the factorial function
int main() {                           function main
    return factorial(3);                   push 3
}                                          call factorial
                                           return
// Computes n!                         // Computes n!
int factorial(int n) {                 function factorial(n)
    if (n==1)                              push n
        return 1;                          push 1
    else                                   eq
        return n * factorial(n-1);         if-goto BASE_CASE
}                                          push n
                                           push n
                                           push 1
                                           sub
                                           call factorial
                                           call mult
                                           return
                                       label BASE_CASE
                                           push 1
                                           return
```

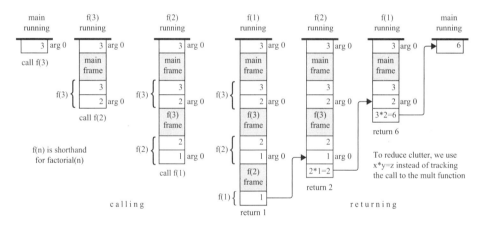

Figure 8.4   Several snapshots of the *global stack*, taken during the execution of the `main` function, which calls `factorial` to compute 3!. The running function sees only its working stack, which is the unshaded area at the tip of the global stack; the other unshaded areas in the global stack are the working stacks of functions up the calling chain, waiting for the currently running function to return. Note that the shaded areas are not "drawn to scale," since each frame consists of five words, as shown in figure 8.3.

during the execution of `factorial(3)`. A complete run-time simulation of this computation should also include the call-and-return action of the `mult` function, which, in this particular run-time example, is called twice: once before `factorial(2)` returns, and once before `factorial(3)` returns.

Focusing on the leftmost and rightmost parts of the bottom of figure 8.4, here is what transpired from `main`'s perspective: "To set the stage, I pushed the constant 3 onto the stack, and then called `factorial` for its effect (see the leftmost stack snapshot). At this point I was put to sleep; at some later point in time I was woken up to find out that the stack now contains 6 (see the final and rightmost stack snapshot); I have no idea how this magic happened, and I don't really care; all I know is that I set out to compute 3!, and I got exactly what I asked for." In other words, the caller is completely oblivious of the elaborate mini-drama that was unleashed by its `call` command.

As seen in figure 8.4, the back stage on which this drama plays out is the global stack, and the choreographer who runs the show is the VM implementation: Each `call` operation is implemented by saving the frame of the caller on the stack and jumping to execute the callee. Each `return` operation is implemented by (i) using the most recently stored frame for getting the return address within the caller's code and reinstating its memory segments, (ii) copying the topmost stack value (the return value) onto the stack location associated with `argument 0`, and (iii) jumping to execute the caller's code from the return address onward. All these operations must be realized by generated assembly code.

Some readers may wonder why we have to get into all these details. There are at least three reasons why. First, we need them in order to implement the VM translator. Second, the implementation of the function call-and-return protocol is a beautiful example of low-level software engineering, so we can simply enjoy seeing it in action. Third, an intimate understanding of the virtual machine internals helps us become better and more informed high-level programmers. For example, tinkering with the stack provides an in-depth understanding of the benefits and pitfalls associated with recursion. Note that during run-time, each recursive call causes the VM implementation to add to the stack a memory block consisting of arguments, function frames, local variables, and a working stack for the callee. Therefore, unchecked use of recursion may well lead to the infamous *stack overflow* run-time debacle. This, as well as efficiency considerations, leads compiler writers to try to reexpress recursive code as sequential code, where possible. But that's a different story that will be taken up in chapter 11.

8.4   VM Specification, Part II

So far in this chapter, we have presented general VM commands without committing to exact syntax and programming conventions. We now turn to specify formally the VM *branching* commands, the VM *function* commands, and the structure of VM *programs*. This completes the specification of the VM language that we began describing in VM Specification, Part I, in chapter 7.

It's important to reiterate that, normally, VM programs are not written by humans. Rather, they are generated by compilers. Therefore, the specifications described here are aimed at compiler developers. That is, if you write a compiler that is supposed to translate programs from some high-level language into VM code, the code that your compiler generates is expected to conform to the conventions described here.

Branching Commands

- `label` *label*: Labels the current location in the function's code. Only labeled locations can be jumped to. The scope of the label is the function in which it is defined. The *label* is a string composed of any sequence of letters, digits, underscore (_), dot (.), and colon (:) that does not begin with a digit. The `label` command can be located anywhere in the function, before or after the `goto` commands that refer to it.
- `goto` *label*: Effects an unconditional goto operation, causing execution to continue from the location marked by the label. The `goto` command and the labeled jump destination must be located in the same function.
- `if-goto` *label*: Effects a conditional goto operation. The stack's topmost value is popped; if the value is not zero, execution continues from the location marked by the label; otherwise, execution continues from the next command in the program. The `if-goto` command and the labeled jump destination must be located in the same function.

Function Commands

- `function` *functionName nVars*: Marks the beginning of a function named *functionName*. The command informs that the function has *nVars* local variables.
- `call` *functionName nArgs*: Calls the named function. The command informs that *nArgs* arguments have been pushed onto the stack before the call.
- `return`: Transfers execution to the command just following the `call` command in the code of the function that called the current function.

VM Program

VM programs are generated from high-level programs written in languages like Jack. As we'll see in the next chapter, a high-level Jack program is loosely defined as a collection of one or more `.jack` class files stored in the same folder. When applied to that folder, the Jack compiler translates each class file *FileName*.`jack` into a corresponding file named *FileName*.`vm`, containing VM commands.

Following compilation, each *constructor*, *function* (*static method*), and *method* named `bar` in a Jack file *FileName*.`jack` is translated into a corresponding VM function, uniquely identified by the VM function name *FileName*.`bar`. The scope of VM function names is global: all the VM functions in all the `.vm` files in the program folder see each other and may call each other using the unique and full function name *FileName.functionName*.

Program entry point: One file in any Jack program must be named `Main.jack`, and one function in this file must be named `main`. Thus, following compilation, one file in any VM program is expected to be named `Main.vm`, and one VM function in this file is expected to be named `Main.main`, which is the application's entry point. This run-time convention is implemented as follows. When we start running a VM program, the first function that always executes is an argument-less VM function named `Sys.init`, which is part of the operating system. This OS function is programmed to call the entry point function in the user's program. In the case of Jack programs, `Sys.init` is programmed to call `Main.main`.

Program execution: There are several ways to execute VM programs, one of which is using the supplied *VM emulator* introduced in chapter 7. When you load a program folder containing one or more `.vm` files into the VM emulator, the emulator loads all the VM functions in all these files, one after the other (the order of the loaded VM functions is insignificant). The resulting code base is a sequence of all the VM functions in all the `.vm` files in the program folder. The notion of VM files ceases to exist, although it is implicit in the names of the loaded VM functions (*FileName.functionName*).

The Nand to Tetris VM emulator, which is a Java program, features a built-in implementation of the Jack OS, also written in Java. When the emulator detects a call to an OS function, for example, `call Math.sqrt`, it proceeds as follows. If it finds a corresponding `function Math.sqrt` command in the loaded VM code, the emulator executes the function's VM code. Otherwise, the emulator reverts to using its built-in implementation of the `Math.sqrt` method. This implies that as long as you use the supplied VM emulator for executing VM programs, there is no need to include OS files in your code. The VM emulator will service all the OS calls found in your code, using its built-in OS implementation.

8.5   Implementation

The previous section completed the specification of our VM language and framework. In this section we focus on implementation issues, leading up to the construction of a full-scale, VM-to-Hack translator. Section 8.5.1 proposes how to implement the function call-and-return protocol. Section 8.5.2 completes the standard mapping of the VM implementation over the Hack platform. Section 8.5.3 gives a proposed design and API for completing the VM translator that we began building in project 7.

8.5.1   Function Call and Return

The events of calling a function and returning from a function call can be viewed from two perspectives: that of the *calling function*, also referred to as *caller*, and that of the *called function*, also referred to as *callee*. Both the caller and the callee have certain expectations, and certain responsibilities, regarding the handling of the `call`, `function`, and `return` commands. Fulfilling the expectations of one is the responsibility of the other. In addition, the VM implementation plays an important role in executing this contract. In what follows, the responsibilities of the VM implementation are marked by [†]:

The caller's view:	The callee's view:
• Before calling a function, I must push onto the stack as many arguments (*nArgs*) as the callee expects to get. • Next, I invoke the callee using the command `call` *fileName.functionName nArgs*. • After the callee returns, the argument values that I pushed before the call have disappeared from the stack, and a *return value* (that always exists) appears at the top of the stack. Except for this change, my working stack is exactly the same as it was before the call [†]. • After the callee returns, all my memory segments are exactly the same as they were before the call [†], except that the contents of my `static` segment may have changed, and the `temp` segment is undefined.	• Before I start executing, my `argument` segment has been initialized with the argument values passed by the caller, and my `local` variables segment has been allocated and initialized to zeros. My `static` segment has been set to the static segment of the VM file to which I belong, and my working stack is empty. The memory segments `this`, `that`, `pointer`, and `temp` are undefined upon entry [†]. • Before returning, I must push a return value onto the stack.

The VM implementation supports this contract by maintaining, and manipulating, the global stack structure described in figure 8.3. In particular, every `function`, `call`, and `return` command in the VM code is handled by generating assembly code that manipulates the global stack as follows: A `call` command generates code that saves the frame of the caller on the stack and jumps to execute the callee. A `function` command generates code that initializes the local variables of the callee. Finally, a `return` command generates code that copies the return value to the top of the caller's working stack, reinstates the segment pointers of the caller, and jumps to execute the latter from the return address onward. See figure 8.5 for the details.

8.5.2   Standard VM Mapping on the Hack Platform, Part II

Developers of the VM implementation on the Hack computer are advised to follow the conventions described here. These conventions complete the Standard VM Mapping on the Hack Platform, Part I, guidelines given in section 7.4.1.

The stack: On the Hack platform, RAM locations 0 to 15 are reserved for pointers and virtual registers, and RAM locations 16 to 255 are reserved for static variables. The stack

VM command	Assembly (pseudo) code, generated by the VM translator	

call *f* *nArgs*
 	
(calls a function *f*, informing that *nArgs* arguments were pushed to the stack before the call)
	push *returnAddress*
	push LCL
	push ARG
	push THIS
	push THAT
	ARG = SP-5-*nArgs*
	LCL = SP
	goto *f*
	(*returnAddress*)
		// generates a label and pushes it to the stack
		// saves LCL of the caller
		// saves ARG of the caller
		// saves THIS of the caller
		// saves THAT of the caller
		// repositions ARG
		// repositions LCL
		// transfers control to the callee
		// injects the return address label into the code

function *f* *nVars*
 	
(declares a function *f*, informing that the function has *nVars* local variables)
	(*f*)
	
	  repeat *nVars* times:
	  push 0
		// injects a function entry label into the code
		// *nVars* = number of local variables
		
		// initializes the local variables to 0

return
 	
(terminates the current function and returns control to the caller)
	frame = LCL
	retAddr = *(*frame*-5)
	*ARG = pop()
	SP = ARG+1
	THAT = *(*frame*-1)
	THIS = *(*frame*-2)
	ARG = *(*frame*-3)
	LCL = *(*frame*-4)
	goto *retAddr*
		// *frame* is a temporary variable
		// puts the return address in a temporary variable
		// repositions the return value for the caller
		// repositions SP for the caller
		// restores THAT for the caller
		// restores THIS for the caller
		// restores ARG for the caller
		// restores LCL for the caller
		// go to the return address

Figure 8.5 Implementation of the function commands of the VM language. All the actions described on the right are realized by generated Hack assembly instructions.

is mapped on address 256 onward. To realize this mapping, the VM translator should start by generating assembly code that sets SP to 256. From this point onward, when the VM translator encounters commands like pop, push, add, and so on in the source VM code, it generates assembly code that affects these operations by manipulating the address that SP points at, and modifying SP, as needed. These actions were explained in chapter 7 and implemented in project 7.

Special symbols: When translating VM commands into Hack assembly, the VM translator deals with two types of symbols. First, it manages predefined assembly-level symbols like SP, LCL, and ARG. Second, it generates and uses symbolic labels for marking return addresses and function entry points. To illustrate, let us revisit the PointDemo program presented in the introduction to part II. This program consists of two Jack class files, Main.jack (figure II.1) and Point.jack (figure II.2), stored in a folder named PointDemo. When applied to the PointDemo folder, the Jack compiler produces two VM files, named Main.vm and Point.vm. The first file contains a single VM function, Main.main, and the second file contains the VM functions Point.new, Point.getx, ..., Point.print.

When the VM translator is applied to this same folder, it produces a single assembly code file, named `PointDemo.asm`. At the assembly code level, the function abstractions no longer exist. Instead, for each `function` command, the VM translator generates an entry label in assembly; for each `call` command, the VM translator (i) generates an assembly `goto` instruction, (ii) creates a return address label and pushes it onto the stack, and (iii) injects the label into the generated code. For each `return` command, the VM translator pops the return address off the stack and generates a `goto` instruction. For example:

VM code	Generated assembly code
`function Main.main`	`(Main.main)`
...	...
`call Point.new`	`goto Point.new`
// Next VM command	`(Main.main$ret0)`
...	// Next VM command (in assembly)
	...
`function Point.new`	`(Point.new)`
...	...
`return`	`goto Main.main$ret0`

Figure 8.6 specifies all the symbols that the VM translator handles and generates.

Bootstrap code: The standard VM mapping on the Hack platform stipulates that the stack be mapped on the host RAM from address 256 onward, and that the first VM function that should start executing is the OS function `Sys.init`. How can we effect these conventions on the Hack platform? Recall that when we built the Hack computer in chapter 5, we wired it in such a way that upon reset, it will fetch and execute the instruction located in ROM address 0. Thus, if we want the computer to execute a predetermined code segment when it boots up, we can put this code in the Hack computer's instruction memory, starting at address 0. Here is the code:

```
// Bootstrap (pseudo) code, should be expressed in machine language
SP = 256
call Sys.init
```

The `Sys.init` function, which is part of the operating system, is then expected to call the main function of the application, and enter an infinite loop. This action will cause the translated VM program to start running. Note that the notions of *application* and *main function* vary from one high-level language to another. In the Jack language, the convention is that `Sys.init` should call the VM function `Main.main`. This is similar to the Java setting: when we instruct the JVM to execute a given Java class, say, `Foo`, it looks for, and executes, the `Foo.main` method. In general, we can effect language-specific startup routines by using different versions of the `Sys.init` function.

Symbol	Usage
SP	This predefined symbol points to the memory address within the host RAM just following the address containing the topmost stack value.
LCL, ARG, THIS, THAT	These predefined symbols point, respectively, to the base RAM addresses of the virtual segments local, argument, this, and that of the currently running VM function.
Xxx.i symbols (represent static variables)	Each reference to static *i* appearing in file *Xxx*.vm is translated to the assembly symbol *Xxx.i*. In the subsequent assembly process, the Hack assembler will allocate these symbolic variables to the RAM, starting at address 16.
functionName$*label* (destinations of goto commands)	Let foo be a function within the file *Xxx*.vm. The handling of each label bar command within foo generates, and injects into the assembly code stream, the symbol *Xxx*.foo$bar. When translating goto bar and if-goto bar commands (within foo) into assembly, the label *Xxx*.foo$bar must be used instead of bar.
functionName (function entry point symbols)	The handling of each function foo command within the file *Xxx*.vm generates, and injects into the assembly code stream, a symbol *Xxx*.foo that labels the entry-point to the function's code. In the subsequent assembly process, the assembler translates this symbol into the physical address where the function code starts.
functionName$ret.*i* (return address symbols)	Let foo be a function within the file *Xxx*.vm. The handling of each call command within foo's code generates, and injects into the assembly code stream, a symbol *Xxx*.foo$ret.*i*, where *i* is a running integer (one such symbol is generated for each call command within foo). This symbol is used to mark the return address within the caller's code. In the subsequent assembly process, the assembler translates this symbol into the physical memory address of the command immediately following the call command.
R13 - R15	These predefined symbols can be used for any purpose. For example, if the VM translator generates assembly code that needs to use low-level variables for temporary storage, R13 - R15 can come handy.

Figure 8.6 The naming conventions described above are designed to support the translation of multiple .vm files and functions into a single .asm file, ensuring that the generated assembly symbols will be unique within the file.

Usage: The translator accepts a single command-line argument, as follows,

```
prompt> VMTranslator source
```

where *source* is either a file name of the form *Xxx*.vm (the extension is mandatory) or the name of a folder (in which case there is no extension) containing one or more .vm files. The file/folder name may contain a file path. If no path is specified, the translator operates on the current folder. The output of the VM translator is a single assembly file, named *source*.asm.

If *source* is a folder name, the single `.asm` file contains the translation of all the functions in all the `.vm` files in the folder, one after the other. The output file is created in the same folder as the input file. If there is a file by this name in the folder, it will be overwritten.

8.5.3   Design Suggestions for the VM Implementation

In project 7 we proposed building the basic VM translator using three modules: `VMTrans-lator`, `Parser`, and `CodeWriter`. We now describe how to extend this basic implementation into a full-scale VM translator. This extension can be accomplished by adding the functionality described below to the three modules already built in project 7. There is no need to develop additional modules.

The VMTranslator

If the translator's input is a single file, say `Prog.vm`, the `VMTranslator` constructs a `Parser` for parsing `Prog.vm` and a `CodeWriter` that starts by creating an output file named `Prog. asm`. Next, the `VMTranslator` enters a loop that uses the `Parser` services for iterating through the input file and parsing each line as a VM command, barring white space. For each parsed command, the `VMTranslator` uses the `CodeWriter` for generating Hack assembly code and emitting the generated code into the output file. All this was already done in project 7.

   If the translator's input is a folder, named, say, `Prog`, the `VMTranslator` constructs a `Parser` for handling each `.vm` file in the folder, and a single `CodeWriter` for generating Hack assembly code into the single output file `Prog.asm`. Each time the `VMTranslator` starts translating a new `.vm` file in the folder, it must inform the `CodeWriter` that a new file is now being processed. This is done by calling a `CodeWriter` routine named `setFileName`, as we now turn to describe.

The Parser

This module is identical to the `Parser` developed in project 7.

The CodeWriter

The `CodeWriter` developed in project 7 was designed to handle the VM *arithmetic-logical* and *push / pop* commands. Here is the API of a complete `CodeWriter` that handles all the commands in the VM language:

Routine	Arguments	Returns	Function
Constructor / initializer	Output file / stream	—	Opens an output file / stream and gets ready to write into it.
			Writes the assembly instructions that effect the bootstrap code that starts the program's execution. This code must be placed at the beginning of the generated output file / stream.
			Comment: See the *Implementation Tips* at the end of section 8.6.
setFileName	fileName (string)	—	Informs that the translation of a new VM file has started (called by the VMTranslator).
writeArithmetic (developed in project 7)	command (string)	—	Writes to the output file the assembly code that implements the given arithmetic-logical command.
writePushPop (developed in project 7)	command (C_PUSH or C_POP), segment (string), index (int)	—	Writes to the output file the assembly code that implements the given push or pop command.
writeLabel	label (string)	—	Writes assembly code that effects the label command.
writeGoto	label (string)	—	Writes assembly code that effects the goto command.
writeIf	label (string)	—	Writes assembly code that effects the if-goto command.
writeFunction	functionName (string) nVars (int)	—	Writes assembly code that effects the function command.
writeCall	functionName (string) nArgs (int)	—	Writes assembly code that effects the call command.
writeReturn	—	—	Writes assembly code that effects the return command.
close (developed in project 7)	—	—	Closes the output file / stream.

8.6   Project

In a nutshell, we have to extend the basic translator developed in chapter 7 with the ability to handle multiple .vm files and the ability to translate VM *branching* commands and VM *function* commands into Hack assembly code. For each parsed VM command, the VM translator has to generate assembly code that implements the command's semantics on the host Hack platform. The translation of the three *branching* commands into assembly is not difficult. The translation of the three *function* commands is more challenging and entails implementing the pseudocode listed in figure 8.5, using the symbols described in figure 8.6. We repeat the suggestion given in the previous chapter: Start by writing the required assembly code on paper. Draw RAM and global stack images, keep track of the stack pointer and the relevant memory segment pointers, and make sure that your paper-based assembly code successfully implements all the low-level actions associated with handling the `call`, `function`, and `return` commands.

Objective: Extend the basic VM translator built in project 7 into a full-scale VM translator, designed to handle multi-file programs written in the VM language.

This version of the VM translator assumes that the source VM code is error-free. Error checking, reporting, and handling can be added to later versions of the VM translator but are not part of project 8.

Contract: Complete the construction of a VM-to-Hack translator, conforming to VM Specification, Part II (section 8.4) and to the Standard VM Mapping on the Hack Platform, Part II (section 8.5.2). Use your translator to translate the supplied VM test programs, yielding corresponding programs written in the Hack assembly language. When executed on the supplied CPU emulator along with the supplied test scripts, the assembly programs generated by your translator should deliver the results mandated by the supplied compare files.

Resources: You will need two tools: the programming language in which you will implement your VM translator and the *CPU emulator* supplied in the Nand to Tetris software suite. Use the CPU emulator to execute and test the assembly code generated by your translator. If the generated code runs correctly, we will assume that your VM translator performs as expected. This partial test of the translator will suffice for our purposes.

Another tool that comes in handy in this project is the supplied *VM emulator*. Use this program to execute the supplied test VM programs, and watch how the VM code effects the simulated states of the stack and the virtual memory segments. This can help understand the actions that the VM translator must eventually realize in assembly.

Since the full-scale VM translator is implemented by extending the VM translator built in project 7, you will also need the source code of the latter.

Testing and Implementation Stages

We recommend completing the implementation of the VM translator in two stages. First, implement the *branching* commands, and then the *function* commands. This will allow you to unit-test your implementation incrementally, using the supplied test programs.

Testing the Handling of the VM Commands `label`, `if`, `if-goto`:

- `BasicLoop`: Computes $1 + 2 + \cdots + \text{argument}[0]$, and pushes the result onto the stack. Tests how the VM translator handles the `label` and `if-goto` commands.

- `FibonacciSeries`: Computes and stores in memory the first n elements of the Fibonacci series. A more rigorous test of handling the `label`, `goto`, and `if-goto` commands.

Testing the Handling of the VM Commands `call`, `function`, `return`:

Unlike what we did in project 7, we now expect the VM translator to handle multi-file programs. We remind the reader that by convention, the first function that starts running in a VM program is `Sys.init`. Normally, `Sys.init` is programmed to call the program's `Main.main` function. For the purpose of this project, though, we use the supplied `Sys.init` functions for setting the stage for the various tests that we wish to perform.

- `SimpleFunction`: Performs a simple calculation and returns the result. Tests how the VM translator handles the `function` and `return` commands. Since this test entails the handling of a single file consisting of a single function, no `Sys.init` test function is needed.

- `FibonacciElement`: This test program consists of two files: `Main.vm` contains a single Fibonacci function that returns recursively the n-th element of the Fibonacci series; `Sys.vm` contains a single `Sys.init` function that calls `Main.fibonacci` with $n = 4$ and then enters an infinite loop (recall that the VM translator generates bootstrap code that calls `Sys.init`). The resulting setting provides a rigorous test of the VM translator's handling of multiple `.vm` files, the VM function-call-and-return commands, the bootstrap code, and most of the other VM commands. Since the test program consists of two `.vm` files, the entire folder must be translated, producing a single `FibonacciElement.asm` file.

- `StaticsTest`: This test program consists of three files: `Class1.vm` and `Class2.vm` contain functions that set and get the values of several static variables; `Sys.vm` contains a single `Sys.init` function that calls these functions. Since the program consists of several `.vm` files, the entire folder must be translated, producing a single `StaticsTest.asm` file.

Implementation Tips

Since project 8 is based on extending the basic VM translator developed in project 7, we advise making a backup copy of the source code of the latter (if you haven't done it already).

Start by figuring out the assembly code that is necessary to realize the logic of the VM commands `label`, `goto`, and `if-goto`. Next, proceed to implement the methods `writeLabel`, `writeGoto`, and `writeIf` of the `CodeWriter`. Test your evolving VM translator by having it translate the supplied `BasicLoop.vm` and `FibonacciSeries.vm` programs.

Bootstrapping code: In order for any translated VM program to start running, it must include startup code that forces the VM implementation to start executing the program on the host platform. Further, for any VM code to operate properly, the VM implementation must store the base addresses of the stack and the virtual segments in the correct locations in the host RAM. The first three test programs in this project (`BasicLoop`, `FibonaciiSeries`, `SimpleFunction`) assume that the startup code was not yet implemented, and include test scripts that effect the necessary initializations *manually*, meaning that at this development stage you don't have to worry about it. The last two test programs (`FibonaciiElement` and `StaticsTest`) assume that the startup code is already part of the VM implementation.

With that in mind, the constructor of the `CodeWriter` must be developed in two stages. The first version of your constructor must not generate any bootstrapping code (that is, ignore the constructor's API guideline beginning with the text "Writes the assembly instructions...". Use this version of your translator for unit-testing the programs `BasicLoop`, `FibonaciiSeries`, and `SimpleFunction`. The second and final version of your `CodeWriter` constructor must write the bootstrapping code, as specified in the constructor's API. This version should be used for unit-testing `FibonaciiElement` and `StaticsTest`.

The supplied test programs were carefully planned to test the specific features of each stage in your VM implementation. We recommend implementing your translator in the proposed order, and testing it using the appropriate test programs at each stage. Implementing a later stage before an early one may cause the test programs to fail.

A web-based version of project 8 is available at www.nand2tetris.org.

8.7   Perspective

The notions of *branching* and *function calling* are fundamental to all high-level languages. This means that somewhere down the translation path from a high-level language to binary code, someone must take care of handling the intricate housekeeping chores related to their implementation. In Java, C#, Python, and Jack, this burden falls on the virtual machine level. And if the VM architecture is *stack-based*, it lends itself nicely to the job, as we have seen throughout this chapter.

To appreciate the expressive power of our stack-based VM model, take a second look at the programs presented in this chapter. For example, figures 8.1 and 8.4 present high-level programs and their VM translations. If you do some line counting, you will note that each line of high-level code generates an average of about four lines of compiled VM code. As it turns out, this 1:4 translation ratio is quite consistent when compiling Jack programs into VM code. Even without knowing much about the art of compilation, one can appreciate the brevity and readability of the VM code generated by the compiler. For example, as we will see when we build the compiler, a high-level statement like `let y = Math.sqrt(x)` is translated into `push x`, `call Math.sqrt`, `pop y`. The two-tier compiler can get away with so little work since it counts on the VM implementation for handling the rest of the translation. If we had to translate high-level statements like `let y = Math.sqrt(x)` directly into Hack code, without having the benefit of an intermediate VM layer, the resulting code would be far less elegant, and more cryptic.

That said, it would also be more efficient. Let us not forget that the VM code must be realized in machine language—that's what projects 7 and 8 are all about. Typically, the final machine code resulting from a two-tier translation process is longer and less efficient than that generated from direct translation. So, which is more desirable: a two-tier Java program that eventually generates one thousand machine instructions or an equivalent one-tier C++ program that generates seven hundred instructions? The pragmatic answer is that each programming language has its pros and cons, and each application has different operational requirements.

One of the great virtues of the two-tier model is that the intermediate VM code (e.g., Java's bytecode) can be *managed*, for example, by programs that test whether it contains malicious code, programs that monitor the code for business process modeling, and so on. In general, for most applications, the benefits of managed code justify the performance degradation caused by the VM level. Yet for high-performance programs like operating systems and embedded applications, the need to generate tight and efficient code typically mandates using C/C++, compiled directly to machine language.

For compiler writers, an obvious advantage of using an explicit interim VM language is that it simplifies the tasks of writing and maintaining compilers. For example, the VM implementation developed in this chapter frees the compiler from the significant tasks of handling the low-level implementation of the function call-and-return protocol. In general, the intermediate VM layer decouples the daunting challenge of building a high-level-to-low-level compiler into two far simpler challenges: building a high-level-to-VM compiler and building a VM-to-low-level translator. Since the latter translator, also called the compiler's *back end*, was already developed in projects 7 and 8, we can be content that about half of the overall compilation challenge has already been accomplished. The other half—developing the compiler's *front end*—will be taken up in chapters 10 and 11.

We end this chapter with a general observation about the virtue of separating abstraction from implementation—an ongoing theme in Nand to Tetris and a crucial systems-building principle that goes far beyond the context of program compilation. Recall that VM functions can access their memory segments using commands like push argument 2, pop local 1, and so on while having no idea *how* these values are represented, saved, and reinstated during run-time. The VM implementation takes care of all the gory details. This complete separation of abstraction and implementation implies that developers of compilers that generate VM code don't have to worry about how the code they generate will end up running; they have enough problems of their own, as you will soon realize.

So cheer up! You are halfway through writing a two-tier compiler for a high-level, object-based, Java-like programming language. The next chapter is devoted to describing this language. This will set the stage for chapters 10 and 11, in which we'll complete the compiler's development. We begin seeing Tetris bricks falling at the end of the tunnel.

9   High-Level Language

High thoughts need a high language.

—Aristophanes (427–386 B.C.)

The assembly and VM languages presented so far in this book are low-level, meaning that they are intended for controlling machines, not for developing applications. In this chapter we present a high-level language, called Jack, designed to enable programmers to write high-level programs. Jack is a simple object-based language. It has the basic features and flavor of mainstream languages like Java and C++, with a simpler syntax and no support for inheritance. Despite this simplicity, Jack is a general-purpose language that can be used to create numerous applications. In particular, it lends itself nicely to interactive games like Tetris, Snake, Pong, Space Invaders, and similar classics.

The introduction of Jack marks the beginning of the end of our journey. In chapters 10 and 11 we will write a compiler that translates Jack programs into VM code, and in chapter 12 we will develop a simple operating system for the Jack/Hack platform. This will complete the computer's construction. With that in mind, it's important to say at the outset that the goal of this chapter is not to turn you into a Jack programmer. Neither do we claim that Jack is an important language outside the Nand to Tetris context. Rather, we view Jack as a necessary scaffold for chapters 10–12, in which we will build a compiler and an operating system that make Jack possible.

If you have any experience with a modern object-oriented programming language, you will immediately feel at home with Jack. Therefore, we begin the chapter with a few representative examples of Jack programs. All these programs can be compiled by the Jack compiler supplied in nand2tetris/tools. The VM code produced by the compiler can then be executed as is on any VM implementation, including the supplied VM emulator. Alternatively, you can translate the compiled VM code further into machine language, using the VM translator built in chapters 7–8. The resulting assembly code can then be executed on the supplied CPU emulator or translated further into binary code and executed on the hardware platform built in chapters 1–5.

Jack is a simple language, and this simplicity has a purpose. First, you can learn (and unlearn) Jack in about one hour. Second, the Jack language was carefully designed to lend itself nicely to common compilation techniques. As a result, you can write an elegant *Jack compiler* with relative ease, as we will do in chapters 10 and 11. In other words, the deliberately simple structure of Jack is designed to help uncover the software infrastructure of modern languages like Java and C#. Rather than taking the compilers and run-time environments of these languages apart, we find it more instructive to build a compiler and a run-time environment ourselves, focusing on the most important ideas underlying their construction. This will be done later, in the last three chapters of the book. Presently, let's take Jack out of the box.

9.1   Examples

Jack is mostly self-explanatory. Therefore, we defer the language specification to the next section and start with examples. The first example is the inevitable *Hello World* program. The second example illustrates procedural programming and array processing. The third example illustrates how abstract data types can be implemented in the Jack language. The fourth example illustrates a linked list implementation using the language's object-handling capabilities.

Throughout the examples, we discuss briefly various object-oriented idioms and commonly used data structures. We assume that the reader has a basic familiarity with these subjects. If not, read on—you'll manage.

Example 1: Hello World: The program shown in figure 9.1 illustrates several basic Jack features. By convention, when we execute a compiled Jack program, execution always starts with the `Main.main` function. Thus, each Jack program must include at least one class, named `Main`, and this class must include at least one function, named `Main.main`. This convention is illustrated in figure 9.1.

```
/** Prints "Hello World". File name: Main.jack */
class Main {
    function void main() {
        do Output.printString("Hello World");
        do Output.println();       // New line
        return;                    // The return statement is mandatory
    }
}
```

Figure 9.1 *Hello World*, written in the Jack language.

Jack comes with a *standard class library* whose complete API is given in appendix 6. This software library, also known as the *Jack OS*, extends the basic language with various abstractions and services such as mathematical functions, string processing, memory management, graphics, and input/output functions. Two such OS functions are invoked by the Hello World program, affecting the program's output. The program also illustrates the comment formats supported by Jack.

Example 2: Procedural programming and array handling: Jack features typical statements for handling assignment and iteration. The program shown in figure 9.2 illustrates these capabilities in the context of array processing.

Most high-level programming languages feature array declaration as part of the basic syntax of the language. In Jack, we have opted for treating arrays as instances of an `Array` class, which is part of the OS that extends the basic language. This was done for pragmatic reasons, as it simplifies the construction of Jack compilers.

Example 3: Abstract data types: Every programming language features a fixed set of primitive data types, of which Jack has three: `int`, `char`, and `boolean`. In object-based languages, programmers can introduce new types by creating classes that represent abstract

```
/** Inputs a sequence of integers, and computes their average. */
class Main {
    function void main() {
        var Array a;        // Jack arrays are not typed
        var int length;
        var int i, sum;
        let i = 0;
        let sum = 0;
        let length = Keyboard.readInt("How many numbers? ");
        let a = Array.new(length); // Constructs the array
        while (i < length) {
            let a[i] = Keyboard.readInt("Enter a number: ");
            let sum = sum + a[i];
            let i = i + 1;
        }
        do Output.printString("The average is: ");
        do Output.printInt(sum / length);
        do Output.println();
        return;
    }
}
```

Figure 9.2 Typical procedural programming and simple array handling. Uses the services of the OS classes `Array`, `Keyboard`, and `Output`.

data types as needed. For example, suppose we wish to endow Jack with the ability to handle rational numbers like 2/3 and 314159/100000 without loss of precision. This can be done by developing a standalone Jack class designed to create and manipulate fraction objects of the form *x*/*y*, where *x* and *y* are integers. This class can then provide a fraction abstraction to any Jack program that needs to represent and manipulate rational numbers. We now turn to describe how a `Fraction` class can be used and developed. This example illustrates typical multi-class, object-based programming in Jack.

Using classes: Figure 9.3a lists a class skeleton (a set of method signatures) that specifies some of the services that one can reasonably expect to get from a fraction abstraction. Such a specification is often called an *Application Program Interface*. The client code at the bottom of the figure illustrates how this API can be used for creating and manipulating fraction objects.

Figure 9.3a illustrates an important software engineering principle: users of an abstraction (like `Fraction`) don't have to know anything about its implementation. All they need is the class *interface*, also known as API. The API informs what functionality the class offers and how to use this functionality. That's all the client needs to know.

```
/** Represents the Fraction type and related operations (class skeleton) */
class Fraction {

    /** Constructs a (reduced) fraction from x and y */
    constructor Fraction new(int x, int y)

    /** Returns the numerator of this fraction */
    method int getNumerator()

    /** Returns the denominator of this fraction */
    method int getDenominator()

    /** Returns the sum of this fraction and the other one */
    method Fraction plus(Fraction other)

    /** Prints this fraction in the format x/y */
    method void print()

    /** Disposes this fraction */
    method void dispose() {

    // More fraction-related methods:
    // minus, times, div, invert, etc.
}
```

```
// Computes and prints the sum of 2/3 and 1/5
class Main {
    function void main() {
        // Creates 3 fraction variables (pointers to Fraction objects)
        var Fraction a, b, c;
        let a = Fraction.new(4,6); // a = 2/3
        let b = Fraction.new(1,5); // b = 1/5

        // Adds up the two fractions, and prints the result
        let c = a.plus(b);   // c = a + b
        do c.print();        // Should print "13/15"
        return;
    }
}
```

Figure 9.3a `Fraction` API (top) and sample Jack class that uses it for creating and manipulating `Fraction` objects.

Implementing classes: So far, we have seen only the client perspective of the `Fraction` class—the view from which `Fraction` is used as a black box abstraction. Figure 9.3b lists one possible implementation of this abstraction.

The `Fraction` class illustrates several key features of object-based programming in Jack. *Fields* specify object properties (also called *member variables*). *Constructors* are subroutines that create new objects, and *methods* are subroutines that operate on the current object (referred to using the keyword `this`). *Functions* are class-level subroutines (also called *static methods*) that operate on no particular object. The `Fraction` class also demonstrates all the statement types available in the Jack language: `let`, `do`, `if`, `while`, and `return`. The `Fraction` class is of course just one example of the unlimited number of classes that can be created in Jack to support any conceivable programming objective.

Example 4: Linked list implementation: The data structure *list* is defined recursively as a value, followed by a list. The value `null`—the definition's base case—is also considered a list. Figure 9.4 shows a possible Jack implementation of a list of integers. This example illustrates how Jack can be used for realizing a major data structure, widely used in computer science.

The operating system: Jack programs make extensive use of the Jack operating system, which will be discussed and developed in chapter 12. For now, suffice it to say that Jack

```
/** Represents the Fraction type and related operations. */
class Fraction {
    // Each Fraction object has a numerator and a denominator
    field int numerator, denominator;
    /** Constructs a (reduced) fraction from x and y */
    constructor Fraction new(int x, int y) {
        let numerator = x;
        let denominator = y;
        do reduce();      // Reduces this fraction
        return this;      // Returns a reference to the new object
    }
    // Reduces this fraction
    method void reduce() {
        var int g;
        let g = Fraction.gcd(numerator, denominator);
        if (g > 1) {
            let numerator = numerator / g;
            let denominator = denominator / g;
        }
        return;
    }
    // Computes the greatest common divisor of two given integers
    function int gcd(int a, int b) {
        // Applies Euclid's algorithm
        var int r;
        while (~(b = 0)) {
            let r = a - (b * (a / b));   // r = remainder
            let a = b;
            let b = r;
        }
        return a;
    }
    // The Fraction class declaration continues on the top right
```

```
    /** Accessors */
    method int getNumerator() {
        return numerator;
    }
    method int getDenominator() {
        return denominator;
    }
    /** Returns the sum of this fraction and the other one */
    method Fraction plus(Fraction other) {
        var int sum;
        let sum = (numerator * other.getDenominator())+
                (other.getNumerator() * denominator);
        return Fraction.new(sum, denominator *
                other.getDenominator());
    }
    /** Prints this fraction in the format x/y */
    method void print() {
        do Output.printInt(numerator);
        do Output.printString("/");
        do Output.printInt(denominator);
        return;
    }
    /** Disposes this fraction */
    method void dispose() {
        // Frees the memory held by this object
        do Memory.deAlloc(this);
        return;
    }
    // More fraction-related methods can come here:
    // minus, times, div, invert, etc.
}   // End of the Fraction class declaration.
```

Figure 9.3b A Jack implementation of the `Fraction` abstraction.

```
/** Represents a list of integers. */
class List {

    field int data;        // A list consists of an int value,
    field List next;       // followed by a List

    /* Creates a list whose head is car and whose tail is cdr */
    // These identifiers are used in memory of the Lisp programming language
    constructor List new(int car, List cdr) {
        let data = car;
        let next = cdr;
        return this;
    }

    /* Accessors */
    method int getData() { return data; }
    method List getNext() { return next; }

    /* Prints the elements of this list */
    method void print() {
        // Initializes a pointer to the first element of this list
        var List current;
        let current = this;
        // Iterates through the list
        while (~(current = null)) {
            do Output.printInt(current.getData());
            do Output.printChar(32);  // Prints a space
            let current = current.getNext();
        }
        return;
    }

    // The List class declaration continues on the top right
```

```
/* Disposes this List */
    method void dispose() {
        // Disposes the tail of this list, recursively
        if (~(next = null)) {
            do next.dispose();
        }
        // Uses an OS routine to free the memory
        // held by this object.
        do Memory.deAlloc(this);
        return;
    }

    // More list-related methods can come here

} // End of the List class declaration.
```

```
// Client code example:

// Creates, prints, and disposes the list (2,3,5),
// which is shorthand for the list (2,(3,(5,null))).

// (This code can appear in any Jack class):
...
var List v;
let v = List.new(5,null);
let v = List.new(2,List.new(3,v));
do v.print();      // Prints 2 3 5
do v.dispose();    // Disposes the list
...
```

Figure 9.4   Linked list implementation in Jack (left and top right) and sample usage (bottom right).

OS class	Services
Math	Common mathematical operations: `max(int,int)`, `sqrt(int)`, ...
String	Represents strings and related operations: `length()`, `charAt(int)`, ...
Array	Represents arrays and related operations: `new(int)`, `dispose()`
Output	Facilitates text output to the screen: `printString(String)`, `printInt(int)`, `println()`, ...
Screen	Facilitates graphics output to the screen : `setColor(boolean)`, `drawPixel(int,int)`, `drawLine(int,int,int,int)`, ...
Keyboard	Facilitates input from the keyboard: `readLine(String)`, `readInt(String)`, ...
Memory	Facilitates access to the host RAM: `peek(int)`, `poke(int,int)`, `alloc(int)`, `deAlloc(Array)`
Sys	Facilitates execution-related services: `halt()`, `wait(int)`, ...

Figure 9.5   Operating system services (summary). The complete OS API is given in appendix 6.

programs use the OS services abstractly, without paying attention to their underlying implementation. Jack programs can use the OS services directly—there is no need to include or import any external code.

The OS consists of eight classes, summarized in figure 9.5 and documented in appendix 6.

9.2   The Jack Language Specification

This section can be read once and then used as a technical reference, to be consulted as needed.

9.2.1   Syntactic Elements

A Jack program is a sequence of tokens, separated by an arbitrary amount of white space and comments. Tokens can be symbols, reserved words, constants, and identifiers, as listed in figure 9.6.

9.2.2   Program Structure

A Jack program is a collection of one or more classes stored in the same folder. One class must be named Main, and this class must have a function named main. The execution of a compiled Jack program always starts with the Main.main function.

The basic programming unit in Jack is a *class*. Each class *Xxx* resides in a separate file named *Xxx*.jack and is compiled separately. By convention, class names begin with an uppercase letter. The file name must be identical to the class name, including capitalization. The class declaration has the following structure:

```
class name {
     field variable declarations     // Must precede the subroutine declarations
     static variable declarations    // Must precede the subroutine declarations
     subroutine declarations         // Constructor, method and function declarations, in any order
}
```

Each class declaration specifies a name through which the class services can be globally accessed. Next comes a sequence of zero or more field declarations and zero or more static variable declarations. Next comes a sequence of one or more subroutine declarations, each defining a *method*, a *function*, or a *constructor*.

Methods are designed to operate on the current object. *Functions* are class-level *static methods* that are not associated with any particular object. *Constructors* create and return new objects of the class type. A subroutine declaration has the following structure:

subroutine type name (*parameter-list*) {
    local variable declarations
    statements
}

where *subroutine* is either `constructor`, `method`, or `function`. Each subroutine has a *name* through which it can be accessed and a *type* specifying the data type of the value returned by the subroutine. If the subroutine is designed to return no value, its type is declared `void`. The *parameter-list* is a comma-separated list of <*type identifier*> pairs, for example, (`int x, boolean sign, Fraction g`).

White space and comments	Space characters, newline characters, and comments are ignored. The following comment formats are supported:
	  `//` Comment to end of line
	  `/*` Comment until closing `*/`
	  `/**` Aimed at software tools that extract API documentation. `*/`

Symbols	`()` Used for grouping arithmetic expressions and for enclosing argument-lists (in subroutine calls) and parameter-lists (in subroutine declarations) `[]` Used for array indexing `{}` Used for grouping program units and statements `,` Variable-list separator `;` Statement terminator `=` Assignment and comparison operator `.` Class membership `+ - * / &	~ < >` Operators
Reserved words	`class, constructor, method, function` Program components `int, boolean, char, void` Primitive types `var, static, field` Variable declarations `let, do, if, else, while, return` Statements `true, false, null` Constant values `this` Object reference
Constants	• *Integer constants* are values in the range 0 to 32767. Negative integers are not constants but rather expressions consisting of a unary minus operator applied to an integer constant. The resulting valid range of values is −32768 to 32767 (the former can be obtained using the expression −32767−1). • *String constants* are enclosed within double quote (`"`) characters and may contain any character except newline or double quote. These characters are supplied by the OS functions `String.newLine()` and `String.doubleQuote()`. • *Boolean constants* are `true` and `false`. • The `null` constant signifies a null reference.
Identifiers	Identifiers are composed from arbitrarily long sequences of letters (`A-Z`, `a-z`), digits (`0-9`), and "`_`". The first character must be a letter or "`_`". The language is case sensitive: `x` and `X` are treated as different identifiers.

Figure 9.6   The syntax elements of the Jack language.

If the subroutine is a *method* or a *function*, its return type can be any of the primitive data types supported by the language (int, char, or boolean), any of the class types supplied by the standard class library (String or Array), or any of the types realized by other classes in the program (e.g., Fraction or List). If the subroutine is a *constructor*, it may have an arbitrary name, but its type must be the name of the class to which it belongs. A class can have 0, 1, or more constructors. By convention, one of the constructors is named new.

Following its interface specification, the subroutine declaration contains a sequence of zero or more local variable declarations (var statements) and then a sequence of one or more statements. Each subroutine must end with the statement return *expression*. In the case of a void subroutine, when there is nothing to return, the subroutine must end with the statement return (which can be viewed as a shorthand of return void, where void is a constant representing "nothing"). Constructors must terminate with the statement return this. This action returns the memory address of the newly constructed object, denoted this (Java constructors do the same, implicitly).

9.2.3 Data Types

The data type of a variable is either *primitive* (int, char, or boolean), or *ClassName*, where *ClassName* is either String, Array, or the name of a class residing in the program folder.

Primitive types: Jack features three primitive data types:

int: two's-complement 16-bit integer

char: nonnegative, 16-bit integer

boolean: true or false

Each one of the three primitive data types int, char, and boolean is represented internally as a 16-bit value. The language is weakly typed: a value of any type can be assigned to a variable of any type without casting.

Arrays: Arrays are declared using the OS class Array. Array elements are accessed using the typical arr[*i*] notation, where the index of the first element is 0. A multidimensional array may be obtained by creating an array of arrays. The array elements are not typed, and different elements in the same array may have different types. The declaration of an array creates a reference, while the array proper is constructed by executing the constructor call Array.new (*arrayLength*). For an example of working with arrays, see figure 9.2.

Object types: A Jack class that contains at least one method defines an object type. As typical in object-oriented programming, object creation is a two-step affair. Here is an example:

```
// This client code example uses the Car and Employee classes, whose code is not shown here.
// The Car class has two fields: model (a String) and licensePlate (a String).
// The Employee class has two fields: name (a String) and car (a Car).
...
// Declares a Car object and two Employee objects (three pointer variables):
var Car c;
var Employee emp1, emp2;
...
// Constructs a new car:
let c = Car.new("Aston Martin","007");  // Sets c to the base address of a memory block
                                         // containing the new car's data.
// Constructs a new employee, and assigns a car to it:
let emp1 = Employee.new("Bond",c);
...
// Creates an alias of Bond:
let emp2 = emp1;  // Only the reference (address) is copied, no new object is constructed.
```

// We now have two Employee pointers referring to the same object.

Strings: Strings are instances of the OS class `String`, which implements strings as arrays of `char` values. The Jack compiler recognizes the syntax `"foo"` and treats it as a `String` object. The contents of a `String` object can be accessed using charAt(*index*) and other methods documented in the `String` class API (see appendix 6). Here is an example:

```
var String s;   // An object variable
var char c;     // A primitive variable
...
let s = "Hello World";  // Sets s to the String object "Hello World"
let c = s.charAt(6);    // Sets c to 87, the integer character code of 'W'
```

The statement `let s = "Hello World"` is equivalent to the statement `let s = String.new(11)`, followed by the eleven method calls `do s.appendChar(72)`,..., `do s.appendChar(100)`, where the argument of `appendChar` is the character's integer code. In fact, that's exactly how the compiler handles the translation of `let s = "Hello World"`. Note that the single character idiom, for example, `'H'`, is not supported by the Jack language. The only way to represent a character is to use its integer character code or a `charAt` method call. The Hack character set is documented in appendix 5.

Type conversions: Jack is weakly typed: the language specification does not define what happens when a value of one type is assigned to a variable of a different type. The decisions of whether to allow such casting operations, and how to handle them, are left to specific Jack compilers. This under-specification is intentional, allowing the construction of minimal compilers that ignore typing issues. Having said that, all Jack compilers are expected to support, and automatically perform, the following assignments.

- A character value can be assigned to an integer variable, and vice versa, according to the Jack character set specification (appendix 5). Example:

```
var char c;
let c = 33; // 'A'

// Equivalently:
var String s;
let s = "A";
let c = s.charAt(0);
```

- An integer can be assigned to a reference variable (of any object type), in which case it is interpreted as a memory address. Example:

```
var Array arr;        // Creates a pointer variable
let arr = 5000;       // Sets arr to 5000
let arr[100] = 17;    // Sets the contents of memory address 5100 to 17
```

- An object variable may be assigned to an Array variable, and vice versa. This allows accessing the object fields as array elements, and vice versa. Example:

```
// Creates the array [2,5]:
var Array arr;
let arr = Array.new(2);
let arr[0] = 2;
let arr[1] = 5;

// Creates the Fraction 2/5:
var Fraction x;
let x = arr;   // sets x to the base address of the memory block
               // representing the array [2,5]

do Output.printInt(x.getNumerator())  // prints "2"
do x.print()                          // prints "2/5"
```

9.2.4 Variables

Jack features four kinds of variables. *Static variables* are defined at the class level and can be accessed by all the class subroutines. *Field variables*, also defined at the class level, are used to represent the properties of individual objects and can be accessed by all the class constructors and methods. *Local variables* are used by subroutines for local computations, and *parameter variables* represent the arguments that were passed to the subroutine by the caller. Local and parameter values are created just before the subroutine starts executing and are recycled when the subroutine returns. Figure 9.7 gives the details. The *scope* of a variable is the region in the program in which the variable is recognized.

Variable initialization: Static variables are not initialized, and it is up to the programmer to write code that initializes them before using them. Field variables are not initialized; it

Kind	Description	Declared in	Scope
Class variables	`static` *type varName*1, *varName*2, ... ; One copy of each `static` variable exists, and this copy is shared by all the class subroutines (like *private static variables* in Java)	Class declaration	The class in which they are declared
Field variables	`field` *type varName*1, *varName*2, ... ; Every object (instance of the class) has a private copy of the field variables (like *member variables* in Java)	Class declaration	The class in which they are declared
Local variables	`var` *type varName*1, *varName*2, ... ; Created when the subroutine starts running and disposed when the subroutine returns.	Subroutine declaration	The subroutine in which they are declared
Parameter variables	Represent the arguments passed to the subroutine. Treated like local variables whose values are initialized by the subroutine caller.	Subroutine declaration	The subroutine in which they are declared

Figure 9.7 Variable kinds in the Jack language. Throughout the table, *subroutine* refers to either a *function*, a *method*, or a *constructor*.

is expected that they will be initialized by the class constructor, or constructors. Local variables are not initialized, and it is up to the programmer to initialize them. Parameter variables are initialized to the values of the arguments passed by the caller.

Variable visibility: Static and field variables cannot be accessed directly from outside the class in which they are defined. They can be accessed only through accessor and mutator methods, as facilitated by the class designer.

9.2.5   Statements

The Jack language features five statements, as seen in figure 9.8.

9.2.6   Expressions

A Jack expression is one of the following:

- A *constant*
- A *variable name* in scope. The variable may be *static*, *field*, *local*, or *parameter*
- The `this` keyword, denoting the current object (cannot be used in functions)
- An *array element* using the syntax *arr*[*expression*], where *arr* is a variable name of type `Array` in scope
- A *subroutine call* that returns a non-void type
- An expression prefixed by one of the unary operators - or ~:

- *expression*: arithmetic negation

~ *expression*: Boolean negation (bitwise for integers)

- An expression of the form *expression op expression* where *op* is one of the following binary operators:

  + - * /:   integer arithmetic operators

  & |:   Boolean And and Boolean Or (bitwise for integers) operators

  < > =:   comparison operators

- (*expression*): an expression in parentheses

Operator priority and order of evaluation: Operator priority is *not* defined by the language, except that expressions in parentheses are evaluated first. Thus the value of the expression $2 + 3 * 4$ is unpredictable, whereas $2 + (3 * 4)$ is guaranteed to evaluate to 14. The Jack compiler supplied in Nand to Tetris (as well as the compiler that we'll develop in chapters 10–11) evaluates expressions left to right, so the expression $2 + 3 * 4$ evaluates to 20. Once again, if you wish to get the algebraically correct result, use $2 + (3 * 4)$.

The need to use parentheses for enforcing operator priority makes Jack expressions a bit cumbersome. This lack of formal operator priority is intentional, though, as it simplifies the implementation of Jack compilers. Different Jack compilers are welcome to specify an operator priority and add it to the language documentation, if so desired.

Statement	*Syntax*	*Description*
let	let *varName* = *expression*; or: let *varName*[*expression1*] = *expression2*;	An assignment operation. The variable kind may be *static*, *local*, *field*, or *parameter*.

if	if (*expression*) {
	   statements1;
	} else {
	   statements2;
	}
		Typical *if* statement, with an optional *else* clause.
		The curly brackets are mandatory, even if *statements* is a single statement.

while	while (*expression*) {
	   statements;
	}
		Typical *while* statement.
		The curly brackets are mandatory, even if *statements* is a single statement.

do	do *function-or-method-call*;	Used to call a function or a method for its effect, ignoring the returned value, if any.
return	return *expression*; or return;	Used to return a value from a subroutine. The second form must be used by void subroutines. Constructors must return the value this.

Figure 9.8   Statements in the Jack language.

9.2.7   Subroutine Calls

A subroutine call invokes a function, a constructor, or a method for its effect, using the general syntax *subroutineName* (*exp₁*, *exp₂*, ..., *expₙ*), where each argument *exp* is an expression. The number and type of the arguments must match those of the subroutine's parameters, as specified in the subroutine's declaration. The parentheses must appear even if the argument list is empty.

Subroutines can be called from the class in which they are defined, or from other classes, according to the following syntax rules:

Function calls / Constructor calls:

· *className.functionName* (*exp₁*, *exp₂*, ..., *expₙ*)

· *className.constructorName* (*exp₁*, *exp₂*, ..., *expₙ*)

The *className* must always be specified, even if the function/constructor is in the same class as the caller.

Method calls:

· *varName.methodName* (*exp₁*, *exp₂*, ..., *expₙ*)

  Applies the method to the object referred to by *varName*.

· *methodName* (*exp₁*, *exp₂*, ..., *expₙ*)

  Applies the method to the *current object*.
  Same as this.*methodName* (*exp₁*, *exp₂*, ..., *expₙ*).

Here are subroutine call examples:

```
class Foo {
    ...
    method void f() {
        var Bar b;          // Declares a local variable of class type Bar
        var int i;          // Declares a local variable of primitive type int
        ...
        do Foo.g()          // Calls function g of the current class
        do Bar.h()          // Calls function h of class Bar
        do m()              // Calls method m of the current class, on the this object
        do b.q()            // Calls method q of class Bar, on object b
        let i = w(b.s(), Foo.t())  // Calls method w on the this object,
                                   // Calls method s of class Bar on object b,
                                   // Calls function or constructor t of class Foo.
    }
}
```

9.2.8 Object Construction and Disposal

Object construction is done in two stages. First, a reference variable (pointer to an object) is declared. To complete the object's construction (if so desired), the program must call a constructor from the object's class. Thus, a class that implements a type (e.g., `Fraction`) must feature at least one constructor. Jack constructors may have arbitrary names; by convention, one of them is named `new`.

Objects are constructed and assigned to variables using the idiom `let` *varName* = *className.constructorName* (exp_1, exp_2, ..., exp_n), for example, `let c = Circle.new` `(x,y,50)`. Constructors typically include code that initializes the fields of the new object to the argument values passed by the caller.

When an object is no longer needed, it can be disposed, to free the memory that it occupies. For example, suppose that the object that `c` points at is no longer needed. The object can be deallocated from memory by calling the OS function `Memory.deAlloc(c)`. Since Jack has no garbage collection, the best-practice advice is that every class that represents an object must feature a `dispose()` method that properly encapsulates this deallocation. Figures 9.3 and 9.4 give examples. To avoid memory leaks, Jack programmers are advised to dispose objects when they are no longer needed.

9.3   Writing Jack Applications

Jack is a general-purpose language that can be implemented over different hardware platforms. In Nand to Tetris we develop a *Jack compiler over the Hack platform*, and thus it is natural to discuss Jack applications in the Hack context.

Examples: Figure 9.9 shows screenshots of four sample Jack programs. Generally speaking, the Jack/Hack platform lends itself nicely to simple interactive games like Pong, Snake, Tetris, and similar classics. Your `projects/09/Square` folder includes the full Jack code of a simple interactive program that allows the user to move a square image on the screen using the four keyboard arrow keys.

Executing this program while reviewing its Jack source code is a good way for learning how to use Jack to write interactive graphical applications. Later in the chapter we describe how to compile and execute Jack programs using the supplied tools.

Application design and implementation: Software development should always rest on careful planning, especially when done over a spartan hardware platform like the Hack computer. First, the program designer must consider the physical limitations of the hardware and plan accordingly. To start with, the dimensions of the computer's screen limit the size of the graphical images that the program can handle. Likewise, one must consider

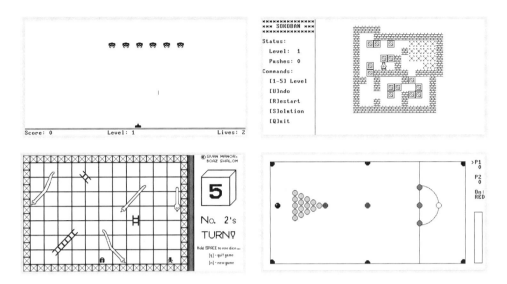

Figure 9.9   Screenshots of Jack applications running on the Hack computer.

the language's range of input/output commands and the platform's execution speed to gain a realistic expectation of what can and cannot be done.

The design process normally starts with a conceptual description of the desired program's behavior. In the case of graphical and interactive programs, this may take the form of hand-written drawings of typical screens. Next, one normally designs an object-based architecture of the program. This entails the identification of *classes*, *fields*, and *subroutines*. For example, if the program is supposed to allow the user to create square objects and move them around the screen using the keyboard's arrow keys, it will make sense to design a Square class that encapsulates these operations using methods like moveRight, moveLeft, moveUp, and move-Down, as well as a constructor subroutine for creating squares and a disposer subroutine for disposing them. In addition, it will make sense to create a SquareGame class that carries out the user interaction and a Main class that gets things started. Once the APIs of these classes are carefully specified, one can proceed to implement, compile, and test them.

Compiling and executing Jack programs: All the .jack files comprising the program must reside in the same folder. When you apply the Jack compiler to the program folder, each source .jack file will be translated into a corresponding .vm file, stored in the same program folder.

The simplest way to execute or debug a compiled Jack program is to load the program folder into the VM emulator. The emulator will load all the VM functions in all the .vm files in the folder, one after the other. The result will be a (possibly long) stream of VM functions, listed in the VM emulator's code pane using their full *fileName.functionName* names. When you instruct the emulator to execute the program, the emulator will start executing the OS Sys.init function, which will then call the Main.main function in your Jack program.

Alternatively, you can use a VM translator (like the one built in projects 7–8) for translating the compiled VM code, as well as the eight supplied tools/OS/*.vm OS files, into a single .asm file written in the Hack machine language. The assembly code can then be executed on the supplied CPU emulator. Or, you can use an assembler (like the one built in project 6) for translating the .asm file further into a binary code .hack file. Next, you can load a Hack computer chip (like the one built in projects 1–5) into the hardware simulator or use the built-in Computer chip, load the binary code into the ROM chip, and execute it.

The operating system: Jack programs make extensive use of the language's *standard class library*, which we also refer to as the *Operating System*. In project 12 you will develop the OS class library in Jack (like Unix is written in C) and compile it using a Jack compiler. The compilation will yield eight .vm files, comprising the OS implementation. If you put these eight .vm files in your program folder, all the OS functions will become accessible to the compiled VM code, since they belong to the same code base (by virtue of belonging to the same folder).

Presently, though, there is no need to worry about the OS implementation. The supplied VM emulator, which is a Java program, features a built-in Java implementation of the Jack OS. When the VM code loaded into the emulator calls an OS function, say Math.sqrt, one of two things happens. If the OS function is found in the loaded code base, the VM emulator executes it, just like executing any other VM function. If the OS function is not found in the loaded code base, the emulator executes its built-in implementation.

9.4   Project

Unlike the other projects in this book, this one does not require building a hardware of software module. Rather, you have to pick some application of your choice and build it in Jack over the Hack platform.

Objective: The "hidden agenda" of this project is to get acquainted with the Jack language, for two purposes: writing the Jack compiler in projects 10 and 11, and writing the Jack operating system in project 12.

Contract: Adopt or invent an application idea like a simple computer game or some interactive program. Then design and build the application.

Resources: You will need the supplied tools/JackCompiler for translating your program into a set of .vm files, and the supplied tools/VMEmulator for running and testing the compiled code.

Compiling and Running a Jack Program

0. Create a folder for your program. Let's call it the *program folder*.

1. Write your Jack program—a set of one or more Jack classes—each stored in a separate *ClassName*.jack text file. Put all these .jack files in the program folder.

2. Compile the program folder using the supplied Jack compiler. This will cause the compiler to translate all the .jack classes found in the folder into corresponding .vm files. If a compilation error is reported, debug the program and recompile until no error messages are issued.

3. At this point the program folder should contain your source .jack files along with the compiled .vm files. To test the compiled program, load the program folder into the supplied VM emulator, and run the loaded code. In case of run-time errors or undesired program behavior, fix the relevant file and go back to step 2.

Program examples: Your nand2tetris/project/09 folder includes the source code of a complete, three-class interactive Jack program (Square). It also includes the source code of the Jack programs discussed in this chapter.

Bitmap editor: If you develop a program that needs high-speed graphics, it is best to design *sprites* for rendering the key graphical elements of the program. For example, the output of the Sokoban application depicted in figure 9.9 consists of several repeating sprites. If you wish to design such sprites and write them directly into the screen memory map (bypassing the services of the OS Screen class, which may be too slow), you will find the projects/09/BitmapEditor tool useful.

A web-based version of project 9 is available at www.nand2tetris.org.

9.5   Perspective

Jack is an *object-based* language, meaning that it supports objects and classes but not inheritance. In this respect it is positioned somewhere between procedural languages like Pascal or C and object-oriented languages like Java or C++. Jack is certainly more simple-minded than any of these industrial strength programming languages. However, its basic syntax and semantics are similar to those of modern languages.

Some features of the Jack language leave much to be desired. For example, its primitive type system is, well, rather primitive. Moreover, it is a weakly typed language, meaning that type conformity in assignments and operations is not strictly enforced. Also, you may wonder why the Jack syntax includes clunky keywords like do and let, why every subroutine must end with a `return` statement, why the language does not enforce operator priority, and so on—you may add your favorite complaint to the list.

All these somewhat tedious idiosyncrasies were introduced into Jack with one purpose: allowing the development of simple and minimal Jack compilers, as we will do in the next two chapters. For example, the parsing of a statement (in any language) is significantly easier if the first token of the statement reveals which statement we're in. That's why Jack uses a `let` keyword for prefixing assignment statements. Thus, although Jack's simplicity may be a nuisance when writing Jack *applications*, you'll be grateful for this simplicity when writing the Jack *compiler*, as we'll do in the next two chapters.

Most modern languages are deployed with a set of *standard classes*, and so is Jack. Taken together, these classes can be viewed as a portable, language-oriented operating system. Yet unlike the standard libraries of industrial-strength languages, which feature numerous classes, the Jack OS provides a minimal set of services, which is nonetheless sufficient for developing simple interactive applications.

Clearly, it would be nice to extend the Jack OS to provide concurrency for supporting multi-threading, a file system for permanent storage, sockets for communications, and so on. Although all these services can be added to the OS, readers will perhaps want to hone their programming skills elsewhere. After all, we don't expect Jack to be part of your life beyond Nand to Tetris. Therefore, it is best to view the Jack/Hack platform as a given environment and make the best out of it. That's precisely what programmers do when they write software for embedded devices and dedicated processors that operate in restricted environments. Instead of viewing the constraints imposed by the host platform as a problem, professionals view it as an opportunity to display their resourcefulness and ingenuity. That's what you are expected to do in project 9.

10   Compiler I: Syntax Analysis

Neither can embellishments of language be found without arrangement and expression of thoughts, nor can thoughts be made to shine without the light of language.
—Cicero (106–43 B.C.)

The previous chapter introduced Jack—a simple, object-based programming language with a Java-like syntax. In this chapter we start building a compiler for the Jack language. A *compiler* is a program that translates programs from a source language into a target language. The translation process, known as *compilation*, is conceptually based on two distinct tasks. First, we have to understand the syntax of the source program and, from it, uncover the program's semantics. For example, the parsing of the code can reveal that the program seeks to declare an array or manipulate an object. Once we know the semantics, we can reexpress it using the syntax of the target language. The first task, typically called *syntax analysis*, is described in this chapter; the second task—*code generation*—is taken up in the next chapter.

How can we tell that a compiler is capable of "understanding" programs? Well, as long as the code generated by the compiler is doing what it's supposed to be doing, we can optimistically assume that the compiler is operating properly. Yet in this chapter we build only the syntax analyzer module of the compiler, with no code generation capabilities. If we wish to unit-test the syntax analyzer in isolation, we have to contrive a way to demonstrate that it understands the source program. Our solution is to have the syntax analyzer output an XML file whose marked-up content reflects the syntactic structure of the source code. By inspecting the generated XML output, we'll be able to ascertain that the analyzer is parsing input programs correctly.

Writing a compiler from the ground up is an exploit that brings to bear several fundamental topics in computer science. It requires the use of parsing and language translation techniques, application of classical data structures like trees and hash tables, and use of recursive compilation algorithms. For all these reasons, writing a compiler is also a challenging feat. However, by splitting the compiler's construction into two separate projects (actually *four*, counting chapters 7 and 8 as well) and by allowing the modular development and unit-testing of each part in isolation, we turn the compiler's development into a manageable and self-contained activity.

Why should you go through the trouble of building a compiler? Aside from the benefits of feeling competent and accomplished, a hands-on grasp of compilation internals will turn you into a better high-level programmer. Further, the same rules and grammars used for describing programming languages are also used in diverse fields like computer graphics, communications and networks, bioinformatics, machine learning, data science, and block-chain technology. And, the vibrant area of *natural language processing*—the enabling science and practice behind intelligent chatbots, robotic personal assistants, language trans-lators, and many artificial intelligence applications—requires abilities for analyzing texts and synthesizing semantics. Thus, while most programmers don't develop compilers in their regular jobs, many programmers have to parse and manipulate texts and data sets of complex and varying structures. These tasks can be done efficiently and elegantly using the algorithms and techniques described in this chapter.

We start with a Background section that surveys the minimal set of concepts necessary for building a syntax analyzer: lexical analysis, context-free grammars, parse trees, and recursive descent parsing algorithms. This sets the stage for a Specification section that presents the Jack language grammar and the output that a Jack analyzer is expected to generate. The Implementation section proposes a software architecture for constructing a Jack analyzer, along with a suggested API. As usual, the Project section gives step-by-step instructions and test programs for building a syntax analyzer. In the next chapter, this analyzer will be extended into a full-scale compiler.

10.1   Background

Compilation consists of two main stages: *syntax analysis* and *code generation*. The syntax analysis stage is usually divided further into two substages: *tokenizing*, the grouping of input characters into language atoms called *tokens*, and *parsing*, the grouping of tokens into structured statements that have a meaning.

The tokenizing and parsing tasks are completely independent of the target language into which we seek to translate the source input. Since in this chapter we don't deal with code generation, we have chosen to have the syntax analyzer output the parsed structure of the input program as an XML file. This decision has two benefits. First, the output file can be readily inspected, demonstrating that the syntax analyzer is parsing source programs cor-rectly. Second, the requirement to output this file explicitly forces us to write the syntax analyzer in an architecture that can be later morphed into a full-scale compiler. Indeed, as figure 10.1 shows, in the next chapter we will extend the syntax analyzer developed in this chapter into a full-scale compilation engine capable of generating executable VM code rather than passive XML code.

In this chapter we focus only on the syntax analyzer module of the compiler, whose job is *understanding the structure of a program*. This notion needs explanation. When humans read the source code of a computer program, they can immediately relate to the program's structure.

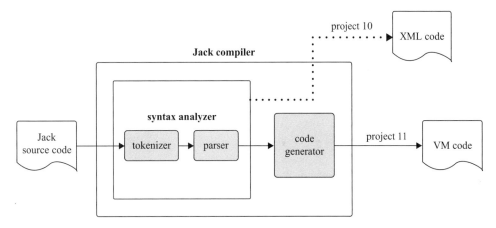

Figure 10.1   Staged development plan of the Jack compiler.

They can do so since they have a mental image of the language's *grammar*. In particular, they sense which program constructs are valid, and which are not. Using this grammatical insight, humans can identify where classes and methods begin and end, what are declarations, what are statements, what are expressions and how they are built, and so on. In order to recognize these language constructs, which may well be nested, humans recursively map them on the range of textual patterns accepted by the language grammar.

Syntax analyzers can be developed to perform similarly by building them according to a given *grammar*—the set of rules that define the syntax of a programming language. To understand—*parse*—a given program means to determine the exact correspondence between the program's text and the grammar's rules. To do so, we must first transform the program's text into a list of *tokens*, as we now turn to describe.

10.1.1   Lexical Analysis

Each programming language specification includes the types of *tokens*, or words, that the language recognizes. In the Jack language, tokens fall into five categories: *keywords* (like `class` and `while`), *symbols* (like + and <), *integer constants* (like 17 and 314), *string constants* (like `"FAQ"` and `"Frequently Asked Questions"`), and *identifiers*, which are the textual labels used for naming variables, classes, and subroutines. Taken together, the tokens defined by these lexical categories can be referred to as the language *lexicon*.

In its plainest form, a computer program is a stream of characters stored in a text file. The first step in analyzing the program's syntax is grouping the characters into tokens, as defined by the language lexicon, while ignoring white space and comments. This task is called *lexical analysis*, *scanning*, or *tokenizing*—all meaning exactly the same thing.

Once a program has been tokenized, the tokens, rather than the characters, are viewed as its basic atoms. Thus, the token stream becomes the compiler's main input.

Figure 10.2 presents the Jack language lexicon and illustrates the tokenization of a typical code segment. This version of the tokenizer outputs the tokens as well as their lexical classifications.

Tokenizing is a simple and important task. Given a language lexicon, it is not difficult to write a program that turns any given character stream into a stream of tokens. This capability provides the first stepping stone toward developing a syntax analyzer.

10.1.2 Grammars

Once we develop the ability to access a given text as a stream of tokens, or words, we can proceed to attempt grouping the words into valid sentences. For example, when we hear that "Bob got the job" we nod approvingly, while inputs like "Got job the Bob" or "Job Bob the got" sound weird. We perform these parsing tasks without thinking about them, since our brains have been trained to map sequences of words on patterns that are either accepted or rejected by the English grammar. The grammars of programming languages are much simpler than those of natural languages. See figure 10.3 for an example.

A grammar is written in a *meta-language*: a language describing a language. Compilation theory is rife with formalisms for specifying, and reasoning about, grammars, languages, and meta-languages. Some of these formalisms are, well, painfully formal. Trying to keep things simple, in Nand to Tetris we view a grammar as a set of rules. Each rule consists of

```
Prog.jack (character stream)                    Output (token stream)

...                                             ...
if (x < 0) {                                    <keyword>     if        </keyword>
    // handles the sign                         <symbol>      (         </symbol>
    let sign = "negative";                      <identifier>  x         </identifier>
}                           Tokenizing          <symbol>      <         </symbol>
...                            ⟹               <intConst>    0         </intConst>
                                                <symbol>      )         </symbol>
                                                <symbol>      {         </symbol>
                                                <keyword>     let       </keyword>
                                                <identifier>  sign      </identifier>
   keyword:   'class'|'constructor'|'function'| <symbol>      =         </symbol>
              'method'|'field'|'static'|'var'|  <stringConst> negative  </stringConst>
              'int'|'char'|'boolean'|'void'|    <symbol>      ;         </symbol>
              'true'|false'|'null'|'this'|'let'|<symbol>      }         </symbol>
              'do'|'if'|'else'|'while'|'return' ...

   symbol:    '{'|'}'|'('|')'|'['|']'|'.'|','|';'|
              '+'|'-'|'*'|'/'|'&'|'|'|'<'|'>'|'='|'~'
```

integerConstant: a decimal integer in the range 0 ... 32767

stringConstant: '"' a sequence of characters, not including double quote or newline '"'

identifier: a sequence of letters, digits, and underscore ('_'), not starting with a digit.

Figure 10.2 Definition of the Jack lexicon, and lexical analysis of a sample input.

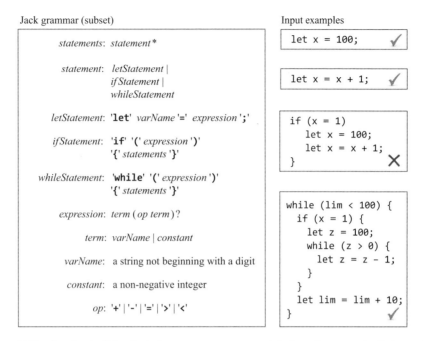

Figure 10.3 A subset of the Jack language grammar, and Jack code segments that are either accepted or rejected by the grammar.

a left side and a right side. The left side specifies the rule's name, which is not part of the language. Rather, it is made up by the person who describes the grammar, and thus it is not terribly important. For example, if we replace a rule's name with another name throughout the grammar, the grammar will be just as valid (though it may be less readable).

The rule's right side describes the lingual pattern that the rule specifies. This pattern is a left-to-right sequence consisting of three building blocks: *terminals*, *nonterminals*, and *qualifiers*. Terminals are tokens, nonterminals are names of other rules, and qualifiers are represented by the five symbols |, *, ?, (, and). Terminal elements, like `'if'`, are specified in bold font and enclosed within single quotation marks; nonterminal elements, like *expression*, are specified using italic font; qualifiers are specified using regular font. For example, the rule *ifStatement*: `'if'` `'('` *expression* `')'` `'{'` *statements* `'}'` stipulates that every valid instance of an *ifStatement* must begin with the token **if**, followed by the token (, followed by a valid instance of an *expression* (defined elsewhere in the grammar), followed by the token), followed by the token {, followed by a valid instance of *statements* (defined elsewhere in the grammar), followed by the token }.

When there is more than one way to parse a pattern, we use the qualifier | to list the alternatives. For example, the rule *statement*: *letStatement* | *ifStatement* | *whileStatement* stipulates that a *statement* can be either a *letStatement*, an *ifStatement*, or a *whileStatement*.

The qualifier * is used to denote "0, 1, or more times." For example, the rule *statements*: *statement** stipulates that *statements* stands for 0, 1, or more instances of *statement*. In a similar vein, the qualifier ? is used to denote "0 or 1 times." For example, the rule *expression*: *term (op term)?* stipulates that *expression* is a *term* that may or may not be followed by the sequence *op term*. This implies that, for example, x is an *expression*, and so are x+17,5 * 7, and x<y The qualifiers (and) are used for grouping grammar elements. For example, (*op term*) stipulates that, in the context of this rule, *op* followed by *term* should be treated as one grammatical element.

10.1.3   Parsing

Grammars are inherently recursive. Just like the sentence "Bob got the job that Alice offered" is considered valid, so is the statement if (x<0){if (y>0){...}}. How can we tell that this input is accepted by the grammar? After getting the first token and realizing that we have an if pattern, we focus on the rule *ifStatement*: 'if' '(' *expression* ')' '{' *statements* '}'. The rule informs that following the token if there ought to be the token (, followed by an *expression*, followed by the token). And indeed, these requirements are satisfied by the input element (x<0). Back to the rule, we see that we now have to anticipate the token {, followed by *statements*, followed by the token }. Now, *statements* is defined as 0 or more instances of *statement*, and *statement*, in turn, is either a *letStatement*, an *ifStatement*, or a *whileStatement*. This expectation is met by the inner input element if (y>0){...}, which is an *ifStatement*.

We see that the grammar of a programming language can be used to ascertain, without ambiguity, whether given inputs are accepted or rejected.[1] As a side effect of this parsing act, the parser produces an exact correspondence between the given input, on the one hand, and the syntactic patterns admitted by the grammar rules, on the other. The correspondence can be represented by a data structure called a *parse tree*, also called a *derivation tree*, like the one shown in figure 10.4a. If such a tree can be constructed, the parser renders the input valid; otherwise, it can report that the input contains syntax errors.

How can we represent parse trees textually? In Nand to Tetris, we decided to have the parser output an XML file whose marked-up format reflects the tree structure. By inspecting this XML output file, we can ascertain that the parser is parsing the input correctly. See figure 10.4b for an example.

---

1. And here lies a crucial difference between programming languages and natural languages. In natural languages, we can say things like "Whoever saves one life, saves the world entire." In the English language, putting the adjective after the noun is grammatically incorrect. Yet, in this particular case, it sounds perfectly acceptable. Unlike programming languages, natural languages mandate a poetic license to break grammar rules, so long as the writer knows what he or she is doing. This freedom of expression makes natural languages infinitely rich.

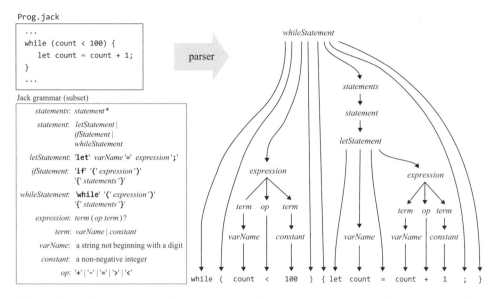

```
Prog.jack

...
while (count < 100) {
    let count = count + 1;
}
...
```

Jack grammar (subset)

statements: statement *

statement: letStatement |
           ifStatement |
           whileStatement

letStatement: 'let' varName '=' expression ';'

ifStatement: 'if' '(' expression ')'
             '{' statements '}'

whileStatement: 'while' '(' expression ')'
                '{' statements '}'

expression: term (op term)?

term: varName | constant

varName: a string not beginning with a digit

constant: a non-negative integer

op: '+' | '-' | '=' | '>' | '<'

Figure 10.4a   Parse tree of a typical code segment. The parsing process is driven by the grammar rules.

```
Prog.xml

    ...
    <whileStatement>
        <keyword> while </keyword>
        <symbol> ( </symbol>
        <expression>
            <term> <varName> count </varName> </term>
            <op> <symbol> < </symbol> </op>
            <term> <constant> 100 </constant> </term>
        </expression>
        <symbol> ) </symbol>
        <symbol> { </symbol>
        <statements>
            <statement> <letStatement>
                <keyword> let </keyword>
                <varName> count </varName>
                <symbol> = </symbol>
                <expression>
                    <term> <varName> count </varName> </term>
                    <op> <symbol> + </symbol> </op>
                    <term> <constant> 1 </constant> </term>
                </expression>
                <symbol> ; </symbol>
            </letStatement> </statement>
        </statements>
        <symbol> } </symbol>
    </whileStatement>
    ...
```

Figure 10.4b   Same parse tree, in XML.

10.1.4   Parser

A parser is an agent that operates according to a given grammar. The parser accepts as input a stream of tokens and attempts to produce as output the parse tree associated with the given input. In our case, the input is expected to be structured according to the Jack grammar, and the output is written in XML. Note, though, that the parsing techniques that we now turn to describe are applicable to handling any programming language and structured file format.

There are several algorithms for constructing parse trees. The top-down approach, also known as *recursive descent parsing*, attempts to parse the tokenized input recursively, using the nested structures admitted by the language grammar. Such an algorithm can be implemented as follows. For every nontrivial rule in the grammar, we equip the parser program with a routine designed to parse the input according to that rule. For example, the grammar listed in figure 10.3 can be implemented using a set of routines named compileStatement, compileStatements, compileLet, compileIf,..., compileExpression, and so on. We use the action verb *compile* rather than *parse*, since in the next chapter we will extend this logic into a full-scale compilation engine.

The parsing logic of each compile*xxx* routine should follow the syntactic pattern specified by the right side of the *xxx* rule. For example, let us focus on the rule *whileStatement*: `'while'` `'('` *expression* `')'` `'{'` *statements* `'}'`. According to our scheme, this rule will be implemented by a parsing routine named compileWhile. This routine should realize the left-to-right derivation logic specified by the pattern `'while'` `'('` *expression* `')'` `'{'` *statements* `'}'`. Here is one way to implement this logic, using pseudocode:

```
// This routine implements the rule whileStatement:
// 'while' '('expression ')' '{' statements '}'
// Should be called if the current token is 'while'.
compileWhile():
    print("<whileStatement>")
    process("while")
    process("(")
    compileExpression()
    process(")")
    process("{")
    compileStatements()
    process("}")
    print("</whileStatement>")
```

```
// A helper routine that handles
// the current token, and advances
// to get the next token.
process(str):
    if (currentToken == str)
        printXMLToken(str)
    else
        print("syntax error")
    // Gets the next token
    currentToken =
        tokenizer.advance()
```

This parsing process will continue until the *expression* and *statements* parts of the while statement have been fully parsed. Of course the *statements* part may well contain a lower-level while statement, in which case the parsing will continue recursively.

The example just shown illustrates the implementation of a relatively simple rule, whose derivation logic entails a simple case of straight-line parsing. In general, grammar rules can be more complex. For example, consider the following rule, which specifies the definition of class-level `static` and instance-level `field` variables in the Jack language:

classVarDec: ('**static**' | '**field**') *type varName* (',' *varName*)* ';'

> (where *type* and *varName* are defined elsewhere in the full Jack grammar)

Examples: `static int count;`

                `static char a, b, c;`

                `field boolean sign;`

                `field int up, down, left, right;`

This rule presents two parsing challenges that go beyond straight-line parsing. First, the rule admits either `static` or `field` as its first token. Second, the rule admits multiple variable declarations. To address both issues, the implementation of the corresponding `compileClassVarDec` routine can (i) handle the processing of the first token (`static` or `field`) directly, without calling a helper routine, and (ii) use a loop for handling all the variable declarations that the input contains. Generally speaking, different grammar rules entail slightly different parsing implementations. At the same time, they all follow the same contract: each `compile`*xxx* routine should get from the input, and handle, all the tokens that make up *xxx*, advance the tokenizer exactly beyond these tokens, and output the parse tree of *xxx*.

Recursive parsing algorithms are simple and elegant. If the language is simple, a single token lookahead is all that it takes to know which parsing rule to invoke next. For example, if the current token is `let`, we know that we have a *letStatement*; if the current token is `while`, we know that we have a *whileStatement*, and so on. Indeed, in the simple grammar shown in figure 10.3, looking ahead one token suffices to resolve, without ambiguity, which rule to use next. Grammars that have this lingual property are called *LL*(1). These grammars can be handled simply and elegantly by recursive descent algorithms, without backtracking.

The term *LL* comes from the observation that the grammar parses the input from *left* to right, performing *leftmost* derivation of the input. The (1) parameter informs that looking ahead 1 token is all that it takes to know which parsing rule to invoke next. If that token does not suffice to resolve which rule to use, we can look ahead one more token. If this lookahead settles the ambiguity, the parser is said to be *LL*(2). And if not, we can look ahead yet another token, and so on. Clearly, as we need to look ahead further and further down the token stream, things become complicated, requiring a sophisticated parser.

The complete Jack language grammar, which we now turn to present, is *LL*(1), barring one exception that can be easily handled. Thus, Jack lends itself nicely to a recursive descent parser, which is the centerpiece of project 10.

10.2   Specification

This section consists of two parts. First, we specify the Jack language's grammar. Next, we specify a syntax analyzer designed to parse programs according to this grammar.

10.2.1   The Jack Language Grammar

The functional specification of the Jack language presented in chapter 9 was aimed at Jack programmers; we now give a formal specification of the Jack language, aimed at developers of Jack compilers. The language specification, or *grammar*, uses the following notation:

'**xxx**'	:	Represents language tokens that appear verbatim
xxx	:	Represents names of terminal and nonterminal elements
( )	:	Used for grouping
x | *y*	:	Either *x* or *y*
x *y*	:	*x* is followed by *y*
x ?	:	*x* appears 0 or 1 times
x *	:	*x* appears 0 or more times

With this notation in mind, the complete Jack grammar is specified in figure 10.5.

10.2.2   A Syntax Analyzer for the Jack Language

A syntax analyzer is a program that performs both tokenizing and parsing. In Nand to Tetris, the main purpose of the syntax analyzer is to process a Jack program and understand its syntactic structure according to the Jack grammar. By *understanding* we mean that the syntax analyzer must know, at each point in the parsing process, the structural identity of the program element that it is currently handling, that is, whether it is an expression, a statement, a variable name, and so on. The syntax analyzer must possess this syntactic knowledge in a complete recursive sense. Without it, it will be impossible to move on to code generation—the ultimate goal of the compilation process.

Usage: The syntax analyzer accepts a single command-line argument, as follows,

```
prompt> JackAnalyzer source
```

where *source* is either a file name of the form *Xxx*.jack (the extension is mandatory) or the name of a folder (in which case there is no extension) containing one or more .jack files. The file/folder name may contain a file path. If no path is specified, the analyzer operates on the current folder. For each *Xxx*.jack file, the parser creates an output file

Lexical elements:	The Jack language includes five types of terminal elements (tokens):
keyword:	`'class'` | `'constructor'` | `'function'` | `'method'` | `'field'` | `'static'` | `'var'` | `'int'` | `'char'` | `'boolean'` | `'void'` | `'true'` | `'false'` | `'null'` | `'this'` | `'let'` | `'do'` | `'if'` | `'else'` | `'while'` | `'return'`
symbol:	`'{'` | `'}'` | `'('` | `')'` | `'['` | `']'` | `'.'` | `','` | `';'` | `'+'` | `'-'` | `'*'` | `'/'` | `'&'` | `'|'` | `'<'` | `'>'` | `'='` | `'~'`
integerConstant:	A decimal integer in the range 0...32767
StringConstant:	`'"'` A sequence of characters not including double quote or newline `'"'`
identifier:	A sequence of letters, digits, and underscore (`'_'`), not starting with a digit
Program structure:	A Jack program is a collection of classes, each appearing in a separate file. The compilation unit is a class. A *class* is a sequence of tokens, as follows:
class:	`'class'` *className* `'{'` *classVarDec* * *subroutineDec* * `'}'`
classVarDec:	(`'static'` | `'field'`) *type* *varName* (`','` *varName*)* `';'`
type:	`'int'` | `'char'` | `'boolean'` | *className*
subroutineDec:	(`'constructor'` | `'function'` | `'method'`) (`'void'` | *type*) *subroutineName* `'('` *parameterList* `')'` *subroutineBody*
parameterList:	((*type* *varName*) (`','` *type* *varName*)*)?
subroutineBody:	`'{'` *varDec** *statements* `'}'`
varDec:	`'var'` *type* *varName* (`','` *varName*)* `';'`
className:	*identifier*
subroutineName:	*identifier*
varName:	*identifier*
Statements:	
statements:	*statement* *
statement:	*letStatement* | *ifStatement* | *whileStatement* | *doStatement* | *returnStatement*
letStatement:	`'let'` *varName* (`'['` *expression* `']'`)? `'='` *expression* `';'`
ifStatement:	`'if'` `'('` expression `')'` `'{'` statements `'}'` (`'else'` `'{'` statements `'}'`)?
whileStatement:	`'while'` `'('` *expression* `')'` `'{'` *statements* `'}'`
doStatement:	`'do'` *subroutineCall* `';'`
returnStatement:	`'return'` *expression*? `';'`
Expressions:	
expression:	*term* (*op term*) *
term:	*integerConstant* | *stringConstant* | *keywordConstant* | *varName* | *varName* `'['` *expression* `']'` | `'('` *expression* `')'` | (*unaryOp term*) | *subroutineCall*
subroutineCall:	*subroutineName* `'('` *expressionList* `')'` | (*className* | *varName*) `'.'` *subroutineName* `'('` *expressionList* `')'`
expressionList:	(*expression* (`','` *expression*) *)?
op:	`'+'` | `'-'` | `'*'` | `'/'` | `'&'` | `'|'` | `'<'` | `'>'` | `'='`
unaryOp:	`'-'` | `'~'`
keywordConstant:	`'true'` | `'false'` | `'null'` | `'this'`

Figure 10.5 The Jack grammar.

Xxx.xml and writes the parsed output into it. The output file is created in the same folder as that of the input. If there is a file by this name in the folder, it will be overwritten.

Input: An *Xxx*.jack file is a stream of characters. If the file represents a valid program, it can be tokenized into a stream of valid tokens, as specified by the Jack lexicon. The tokens may be separated by an arbitrary number of space characters, newline characters, and comments, which are ignored. There are three possible comment formats: /* comment until closing */, /** API comment until closing */, and // comment until the line's end.

Output: The syntax analyzer emits an XML description of the input file, as follows. For each terminal element (*token*) of type *xxx* appearing in the input, the syntax analyzer prints the marked-up output <*xxx*> *token* </*xxx*>, where *xxx* is one of the tags keyword, symbol, integerConstant, stringConstant, or identifier, representing one of the five token types recognized by the Jack language. Whenever a nonterminal language element *xxx* is detected, the syntax analyzer handles it using the following pseudocode:

```
print("<xxx>")
    Recursive code for handling the body of the xxx element
print("</xxx>")
```

where *xxx* is one of the following (and only the following) tags: class, classVarDec, subroutineDec, parameterList, subroutineBody, varDec, statements, letStatement, ifStatement, whileStatement, doStatement, returnStatement, expression, term, expressionList.

To simplify things, the following Jack grammar rules are not accounted for explicitly in the XML output: *type, className, subroutineName, varName, statement, subroutineCall*. We will explain this further in the next section, when we discuss the architecture of our compilation engine.

10.3   Implementation

The previous section specified *what* a syntax analyzer should do, with few implementation insights. This section describes *how* to build such an analyzer. Our proposed implementation is based on three modules:

- JackAnalyzer: main program that sets up and invokes the other modules
- JackTokenizer: tokenizer
- CompilationEngine: recursive top-down parser

In the next chapter we will extend this software architecture with two additional modules that handle the language's semantics: a *symbol table* and a *VM code writer*. This will complete the construction of a full-scale compiler for the Jack language. Since the main module that drives the parsing process in this project will end up driving the overall compilation process as well, we name it `CompilationEngine`.

The JackTokenizer

This module ignores all comments and white space in the input stream and enables accessing the input one token at a time. Also, it parses and provides the *type* of each token, as defined by the Jack grammar.

Routine	*Arguments*	*Returns*	*Function*
Constructor / initializer	Input file / stream	–	Opens the input `.jack` file / stream and gets ready to tokenize it.
`hasMoreTokens`	–	boolean	Are there more tokens in the input?
`advance`	–	–	Gets the next token from the input, and makes it the current token. This method should be called only if `hasMoreTokens` is true. Initially there is no current token.
`tokenType`	–	`KEYWORD, SYMBOL,` `IDENTIFIER, INT_CONST,` `STRING_CONST`	Returns the type of the current token, as a constant.
`keyWord`	–	`CLASS, METHOD, FUNCTION,` `CONSTRUCTOR, INT,` `BOOLEAN, CHAR, VOID, VAR,` `STATIC, FIELD, LET, DO, IF,` `ELSE, WHILE, RETURN, TRUE,` `FALSE, NULL, THIS`	Returns the keyword which is the current token, as a constant. This method should be called only if `tokenType` is `KEYWORD`.
`symbol`	–	char	Returns the character which is the current token. Should be called only if `tokenType` is `SYMBOL`.
`identifier`	–	string	Returns the string which is the current token. Should be called only if `tokenType` is `IDENTIFIER`.
`intVal`	–	int	Returns the integer value of the current token. Should be called only if `tokenType` is `INT_CONST`.
`stringVal`	–	string	Returns the string value of the current token, without the opening and closing double quotes. Should be called only if `tokenType` is `STRING_CONST`.

The CompilationEngine

The `CompilationEngine` is the backbone module of both the syntax analyzer described in this chapter and the full-scale compiler described in the next chapter. In the syntax analyzer, the compilation engine emits a structured representation of the input source code wrapped in XML tags. In the compiler, the compilation engine will instead emit executable VM code. In both versions, the parsing logic and API presented below are exactly the same.

The compilation engine gets its input from a `JackTokenizer` and emits its output to an output file. The output is generated by a series of compile*xxx* routines, each designed to handle the compilation of a specific Jack language construct *xxx*. The contract between these routines is that each compile*xxx* routine should get from the input, and handle, all the tokens that make up *xxx*, advance the tokenizer exactly beyond these tokens, and output the parsing of *xxx*. As a rule, each compile*xxx* routine is called only if the current token is *xxx*.

Grammar rules that have no corresponding compile*xxx* routines: *type*, *className*, *subroutineName*, *varName*, *statement*, *subroutineCall*. We introduced these rules to make the Jack grammar more structured. As it turns out, the parsing logic of these rules is better handled by the routines that implement the rules that refer to them. For example, instead of writing a `compileType` routine, whenever *type* is mentioned in some rule *xxx*, the parsing of the possible types should be done directly by the compile*xxx* routine.

Token lookahead: Jack is almost an *LL*(1) language: the current token is sufficient for determining which `CompilationEngine` routine to call next. The only exception occurs when parsing a *term*, which occurs only when parsing an *expression*. To illustrate, consider the contrived yet valid expression `y+arr[5]-p.get(row)*count()-Math.sqrt(dist)/2`. This expression is made up of six terms: the variable `y`, the array element `arr[5]`, the method call on the `p` object `p.get(row)`, the method call on the `this` object `count()`, the call to the function (static method) `Math.sqrt(dist)`, and the constant 2.

Suppose that we are parsing this expression and the current token is one of the identifiers `y`, `arr`, `p`, `count`, or `Math`. In each one of these cases, we know that we have a *term* that begins with an *identifier*, but we don't know which parsing possibility to follow next. That's the bad news; the good news is that a single lookahead to the next token is all that we need to settle the dilemma.

The need for this irregular lookahead operation occurs in the `CompilationEngine` twice: when parsing a *term*, which happens only when parsing an *expression*, and when parsing a *subroutineCall*. Now, an inspection of the Jack grammar shows that *subroutineCall* appears in two places only: either in a `do` *subroutineCall* statement or in a *term*.

With that in mind, we propose parsing `do` *subroutineCall* statements as if their syntax were `do` *expression*. This pragmatic recommendation obviates the need to write the irregular lookahead code twice. It also implies that the parsing of *subroutineCall* can now be handled directly by the `compileTerm` routine. In short, we've localized the need to write

Routine	Arguments	Returns	Function
Constructor / initializer	Input file / stream	–	Creates a new compilation engine with the given input and output.
	Output file / stream		The next routine called (by the `JackAnalyzer` module) must be `compileClass`
`compileClass`	–	–	Compiles a complete class.
`compileClassVarDec`	–	–	Compiles a static variable declaration, or a field declaration.
`compileSubroutine`	–	–	Compiles a complete method, function, or constructor.
`compileParameterList`	–	–	Compiles a (possibly empty) parameter list. Does not handle the enclosing parentheses tokens (and).
`compileSubroutineBody`	–	–	Compiles a subroutine's body.
`compileVarDec`	–	–	Compiles a `var` declaration.
`compileStatements`	–	–	Compiles a sequence of statements. Does not handle the enclosing curly bracket tokens { and }.
`compileLet`	–	–	Compiles a `let` statement.
`compileIf`	–	–	Compiles an `if` statement, possibly with a trailing `else` clause.
`compileWhile`	–	–	Compiles a `while` statement.
`compileDo`	–	–	Compiles a `do` statement.
`compileReturn`	–	–	Compiles a `return` statement.
`compileExpression`	–	–	Compiles an expression.
`compileTerm`	–	–	Compiles a *term*. If the current token is an *identifier*, the routine must resolve it into a *variable*, an *array element*, or a *subroutine call*. A single lookahead token, which may be [, (, or ., suffices to distinguish between the possibilities. Any other token is not part of this term and should not be advanced over.
`compileExpressionList`	–	int	Compiles a (possibly empty) comma-separated list of expressions. Returns the number of expressions in the list.

the irregular token lookahead code to one routine only, compileTerm, and we've eliminated the need for a compileSubroutineCall routine.

The compileExpressionList routine: returns the number of expressions in the list. The return value is necessary for generating VM code, as we'll see when we'll complete the compiler's development in project 11. In this project we generate no VM code; therefore the returned value is not used and can be ignored by routines that call compileExpressionList.

The JackAnalyzer

This is the main program that drives the overall syntax analysis process, using the services of a JackTokenizer and a CompilationEngine. For each source *Xxx*.jack file, the analyzer

1. creates a JackTokenizer from the *Xxx*.jack input file;

2. creates an output file named *Xxx*.xml; and

3. uses the JackTokenizer and the CompilationEngine to parse the input file and write the parsed code to the output file.

We provide no API for this module, inviting you to implement it as you see fit. Remember that the first routine that must be called when compiling a .jack file is compileClass.

10.4   Project

Objective: Build a syntax analyzer that parses Jack programs according to the Jack grammar. The analyzer's output should be written in XML, as specified in section 10.2.2.

This version of the syntax analyzer assumes that the source Jack code is error-free. Error checking, reporting, and handling can be added to later versions of the analyzer but are not part of project 10.

Resources: The main tool in this project is the programming language that you will use for implementing the syntax analyzer. You will also need the supplied TextComparer utility. This program allows comparing files while ignoring white space. This will help you compare the output files generated by your analyzer with the supplied compare files. You may also want to inspect these files using an XML viewer. Any standard web browser should do the job—just use your browser's "open file" option to open the XML file that you wish to inspect.

Contract: Write a syntax analyzer for the Jack language, and test it on the supplied test files. The XML files produced by your analyzer should be identical to the supplied compare files, ignoring white space.

Test files: We provide several `.jack` files for testing purposes. The `projects/10/Square` program is a three-class app that enables moving a black square around the screen using the keyboard's arrow keys. The `projects/10/ArrayTest` program is a single-class app that computes the average of a user-supplied sequence of integers using array processing. Both programs were discussed in chapter 9, so they should be familiar. Note, though, that we made some harmless changes to the original code to make sure that the syntax analyzer will be fully tested on all aspects of the Jack language. For example, we've added a static variable to `projects/10/Square/Main.jack`, as well as a function named `more`, which are never used or called. These changes allow testing how the analyzer handles language elements that don't appear in the original `Square` and `ArrayTest` files, like static variables, `else`, and unary operators.

Development plan: We suggest developing and unit-testing the analyzer in four stages:

- First, write and test a Jack tokenizer.
- Next, write and test a basic compilation engine that handles all the features of the Jack language, except for expressions and array-oriented statements.
- Next, extend your compilation engine to handle expressions.
- Finally, extend your compilation engine to handle array-oriented statements.

We provide input `.jack` files and compare `.xml` files for unit-testing each one of the four stages, as we now turn to describe.

10.4.1 Tokenizer

Implement the `JackTokenizer` module specified in section 10.3. Test your implementation by writing a basic version of the `JackAnalyzer`, defined as follows. The analyzer, which is the main program, is invoked using the command `JackAnalyzer` *source*, where *source* is either a file name of the form *Xxx*`.jack` (the extension is mandatory) or a folder name (in which case there is no extension). In the latter case, the folder contains one or more `.jack` files and, possibly, other files as well. The file/folder name may include a file path. If no path is specified, the analyzer operates on the current folder.

The analyzer handles each file separately. In particular, for each *Xxx*`.jack` file, the analyzer constructs a `JackTokenizer` for handling the input and an output file for writing the output. In this first version of the analyzer, the output file is named *Xxx*`T.xml` (where `T` stands for *tokenized output*). The analyzer then enters a loop to `advance` and handle all the tokens in the input file, one token at a time, using the `JackTokenizer` methods. Each token should be printed in a separate line, as *<tokenType> token </tokenType>*, where *tokenType* is one of five possible XML tags coding the token's type. Here is an example:

Input (e.g. Prog.jack)	**JackAnalyzer** *Output* (e.g. ProgT.xml)

```
...
// Comments and white space
// are ignored.
if (x < 0) {
   let quit = "yes";
}
...
```

```
<tokens>
   ...
   <keyword> if </keyword>
   <symbol> ( </symbol>
   <identifier> x </identifier>
   <symbol> &lt; </symbol>
   <integerConstant> 0 </integerConstant>
   <symbol> ) </symbol>
   <symbol> { </symbol>
   <keyword> let </keyword>
   <identifier> quit </identifier>
   <symbol> = </symbol>
   <stringConstant> yes </stringConstant>
   <symbol> ; </symbol>
   <symbol> } </symbol>
   ...
</tokens>
```

Note that in the case of *string constants*, the program ignores the double quotation marks. This requirement is by design.

The generated output has two trivial technicalities dictated by XML conventions. First, an XML file must be enclosed within some begin and end tags; this convention is satisfied by the <tokens> and </tokens> tags. Second, four of the symbols used in the Jack language (<, >, ", &) are also used for XML markup; thus they cannot appear as data in XML files. Following convention, the analyzer represents these symbols as <, >, ", and &, respectively. For example, when the parser encounters the < symbol in the input file, it outputs the line <symbol> < </symbol>. This so-called *escape sequence* is rendered by XML viewers as <symbol> < </symbol>, which is what we want.

Testing Guidelines

- Start by applying your JackAnalyzer to one of the supplied .jack files, and verify that it operates correctly on a single input file.

- Next, apply your JackAnalyzer to the Square folder, containing the files Main.jack, Square.jack, and SquareGame.jack, and to the TestArray folder, containing the file Main.jack.

- Use the supplied TextComparer utility to compare the output files generated by your JackAnalyzer to the supplied .xml compare files. For example, compare the generated file SquareT.xml to the supplied compare file SquareT.xml.

- Since the generated and compare files have the same names, we suggest putting them in separate folders.

10.4.2   Compilation Engine

The next version of your syntax analyzer should be capable of parsing every element of the Jack language, except for expressions and array-oriented commands. To that end, implement the `CompilationEngine` module specified in section 10.3, except for the routines that handle expressions and arrays. Test the implementation by using your Jack analyzer, as follows.

For each *Xxx*.`jack` file, the analyzer constructs a `JackTokenizer` for handling the input and an output file for writing the output, named *Xxx*.`xml`. The analyzer then calls the `compileClass` routine of the `CompilationEngine`. From this point onward, the `CompilationEngine` routines should call each other recursively, emitting XML output similar to the one shown in figure 10.4b.

Unit-test this version of your `JackAnalyzer` by applying it to the folder `ExpressionlessSquare`. This folder contains versions of the files `Square.jack`, `SquareGame.jack`, and `Main.jack`, in which each expression in the original code has been replaced with a single identifier (a variable name in scope). For example:

<table>
<tr><td>

Square folder:
```
// Square.jack
...
method void incSize() {
   if (((y + size) < 254) & ((x + size) <510)
      do erase();
      let size = size + 2;
      do draw();
   }
   return;
}
...
```

</td><td>

ExpressionlessSquare folder:
```
// Square.jack
...
method void incSize() {
    if (x) {
         do erase();
         let size = size;
         do draw();
   }
   return;
}
...
```

</td></tr>
</table>

Note that the replacement of expressions with variables results in nonsensical code. This is fine, since the program semantics is irrelevant to project 10. The nonsensical code is syntactically correct, and that's all that matters for testing the parser. Note also that the original and expressionless files have the same names but are located in separate folders.

Use the supplied `TextComparer` utility to compare the output files generated by your `JackAnalyzer` with the supplied `.xml` compare files.

Next, complete the `CompilationEngine` routines that handle expressions, and test them by applying your `JackAnalyzer` to the `Square` folder. Finally, complete the routines that handle arrays, and test them by applying your `JackAnalyzer` to the `ArrayTest` folder.

A web-based version of project 10 is available at www.nand2tetris.org.

10.5   Perspective

Although it is convenient to describe the structure of computer programs using parse trees and XML files, it's important to understand that compilers don't necessarily have to maintain such data structures explicitly. For example, the parsing algorithm described in this chapter parses the input as it reads it and does not keep the entire input program in memory. There are essentially two types of strategies for doing such parsing. The simpler strategy works top-down, and that is the one presented in this chapter. The more advanced parsing algorithms, which work bottom-up, were not described here since they require elaboration of more compilation theory.

Indeed, in this chapter we have sidestepped the formal language theory studied in typical compilation courses. Also, we have chosen a simple syntax for the Jack language—a syntax that can be easily compiled using recursive descent techniques. For example, the Jack grammar does not mandate the usual operator precedence in algebraic expressions evaluation, like multiplication before addition. This enabled us to avoid parsing algorithms that are more powerful, but also more intricate, than the elegant top-down parsing techniques presented in this chapter.

Every programmer experiences the disgraceful handling of compilation errors, which is typical of many compilers. As it turns out, error diagnostics and reporting are a challenging problem. In many cases, the impact of an error is detected several or many lines of code after the error was made. Therefore, error reporting is sometimes cryptic and unfriendly. Indeed, one aspect in which compilers vary greatly is their ability to diagnose, and help debug, errors. To do so, compilers persist parts of the parse tree in memory and extend the tree with annotations that help pinpoint the source of errors and backtrack the diagnostic process, as needed. In Nand to Tetris we bypass all these extensions, assuming that the source files that the compiler handles are error-free.

Another topic that we hardly mentioned is how the syntax and semantics of programming languages are studied in computer and cognitive science. There is a rich theory of formal and natural languages that discusses properties of classes of languages, as well as meta-languages and formalisms for specifying them. This is also the place where computer science meets the study of human languages, leading to the vibrant areas of research and practice known as computational linguistics and natural language processing.

Finally, it is worth mentioning that syntax analyzers are typically not standalone programs and are rarely written from scratch. Instead, programmers usually build tokenizers and parsers using a variety of *compiler generator* tools like LEX (for *LEXical analysis*) and YACC (for *Yet Another Compiler Compiler*). These utilities receive as input a context-free grammar and produce as output syntax analysis code capable of tokenizing and parsing programs written in that grammar. The generated code can then be customized to fit the specific needs of the compiler writer. Following the "show me" spirit of Nand to Tetris, though, we have chosen not to use such black boxes in the implementation of our compiler, but rather build everything from the ground up.

11   Compiler II: Code Generation

When I am working on a problem, I never think about beauty. But when I have finished, if the solution is not beautiful, I know it is wrong.

—R. Buckminster Fuller (1895–1993)

Most programmers take compilers for granted. But if you stop to think about it, the ability to translate a high-level program into binary code is almost like magic. In Nand to Tetris we devote four chapters (7–11) for demystifying this magic. Our hands-on methodology is based on developing a compiler for Jack—a simple, modern object-based language. As with Java and C#, the overall Jack compiler is based on two tiers: a virtual machine (VM) *back end* that translates VM commands into machine language and a *front end* compiler that translates Jack programs into VM code. Building a compiler is a challenging undertaking, so we divide it further into two conceptual modules: a *syntax analyzer*, developed in chapter 10, and a *code generator*—the subject of this chapter.

The syntax analyzer was built in order to develop, and demonstrate, a capability for parsing high-level programs into their underlying syntactical elements. In this chapter we'll morph the analyzer into a full-scale compiler: a program that converts the parsed elements into VM commands designed to execute on the abstract virtual machine described in chapters 7–8. This approach follows the modular analysis-synthesis paradigm that informs the construction of well-designed compilers. It also captures the very essence of translating text from one language to another: first, one uses the source language's *syntax* for analyzing the source text and figuring out its underlying *semantics*, that is, what the text seeks to say; next, one reexpresses the parsed semantics using the syntax of the target language. In the context of this chapter, the source and the target are Jack and the VM language, respectively.

Modern high-level programming languages are rich and powerful. They allow defining and using elaborate abstractions like functions and objects, expressing algorithms using elegant statements, and building data structures of unlimited complexity. In contrast, the hardware platforms on which these programs ultimately run are spartan and minimal. Typically, they offer little more than a set of registers for storage and a set of primitive instructions for processing. Thus, the translation of programs from high level to low level is a challenging feat. If the target platform is a virtual machine and not the barebone hardware, life is somewhat easier since abstract VM commands are not as primitive as concrete machine instructions. Still, the gap between the expressiveness of a high-level language and that of a VM language is wide and challenging.

The chapter begins with a general discussion of *code generation*, divided into six sections. First, we describe how compilers use *symbol tables* for mapping symbolic variables onto virtual memory segments. Next, we present algorithms for compiling *expressions* and *strings* of characters. We then present techniques for compiling *statements* like `let`, `if`, `while`, `do`, and `return`. Taken together, the ability to compile *variables*, *expressions*, and *statements* forms a foundation for building compilers for simple, procedural, C-like languages. This sets the stage for the remainder of section 11.1, in which we discuss the compilation of *objects* and *arrays*.

Section 11.2 (Specification) provides guidelines for mapping Jack programs on the VM platform and language, and section 11.3 (Implementation) proposes a software architecture and an API for completing the compiler's development. As usual, the chapter ends with a Project section, providing step-by-step guidelines and test programs for completing the compiler's construction, and a Perspective section that comments on various things that were left out from the chapter.

So what's in it for you? Although many professionals are eager to understand how compilers work, few end up getting their hands dirty and building a compiler from the ground up. That's because the cost of this experience—at least in academia—is typically a daunting, full-semester elective course. Nand to Tetris packs the key elements of this experience into four chapters and projects, culminating in the present chapter. In the process, we discuss and illustrate the key algorithms, data structures, and programming tricks underlying the construction of typical compilers. Seeing these clever ideas and techniques in action leads one to marvel, once again, at how human ingenuity can dress up a primitive switching machine to look like something approaching magic.

11.1   Code Generation

High-level programmers work with abstract building blocks like *variables*, *expressions*, *statements*, *subroutines*, *objects* and *arrays*. Programmers use these abstract building blocks for describing what they want the program to do. The job of the compiler is to translate this semantics into a language that a target computer understands.

In our case, the target computer is the virtual machine described in chapters 7–8. Thus, we have to figure out how to systematically translate *expressions*, *statements*, *subroutines*, and the handling of *variables*, *objects*, and *arrays* into sequences of stack-based VM commands that execute the desired semantics on the target virtual machine. We don't have to worry about the subsequent translation of VM programs into machine language, since we already took care of this royal headache in projects 7–8. Thank goodness for two-tier compilation, and for modular design.

Throughout the chapter, we present compilation examples of various parts of the `Point` class presented previously in the book. We repeat the class declaration in figure 11.1, which illustrates most of the features of the Jack language. We advise taking a quick look at this Jack code now to refresh your memory about the `Point` class functionality. You will then be ready to delve into the illuminating journey of systematically reducing this high-level functionality—and any other similar object-based program—into VM code.

11.1.1   Handling Variables

One of the basic tasks of compilers is mapping the variables declared in the source high-level program onto the host RAM of the target platform. For example, consider Java: `int` variables are designed to represent 32-bit values; `long` variables, 64-bit values; and so on. If the host RAM happens to be 32-bit wide, the compiler will map `int` and `long` variables on one memory word and on two consecutive memory words, respectively. In Nand to Tetris there are no mapping complications: all the primitive types in Jack (`int`, `char`, and `boolean`) are 16-bit wide, and so are the addresses and words of the Hack RAM. Thus, every Jack variable, including pointer variables holding 16-bit address values, can be mapped on exactly one word in memory.

```
/** Represents a two-dimensional point.
    File name: Point.jack. */
class Point {

    // The coordinates of this point:
    field int x, y

    // The number of Point objects constructed so far:
    static int pointCount;

    /** Constructs a two-dimensional point and
        initializes it with the given coordinates. */
    constructor Point new(int ax, int ay) {
        let x = ax;
        let y = ay;
        let pointCount = pointCount + 1;
        return this;
    }

    /** Returns the x coordinate of this point. */
    method int getx() { return x; }

    /** Returns the y coordinate of this point. */
    method int gety() { return y; }

    /** Returns the number of Point  constructed so far. */
    function int getPointCount() {
        return pointCount;
    }

    // Class declaration continues on top right.
```

```
    /** Returns a point which is this point plus
        the other point. */
    method Point plus(Point other) {
        return Point.new(x + other.getx(),
                         y + other.gety());
    }

    /** Returns the Euclidean distance between
        this and the other point. */
    method int distance(Point other) {
        var int dx, dy;
        let dx = x - other.getx();
        let dy = y - other.gety();
        return Math.sqrt((dx*dx) + (dy*dy));
    }

    /** Prints this point, as "(x,y)" */
    method void print() {
        do Output.printString("(");
        do Output.printInt(x);
        do Output.printString(",");
        do Output.printInt(y);
        do Output.printString(")");
        return;
    }

} // End of Point class declaration.
```

Figure 11.1   The `Point` class. This class features all the possible variable kinds (`field`, `static`, `local`, and `argument`) and subroutine kinds (`constructor`, `method`, and `function`), as well as subroutines that return primitive types, object types, and void subroutines. It also illustrates function calls, constructor calls, and method calls on the current object (`this`) and on other objects.

The second challenge faced by compilers is that variables of different *kinds* have different life cycles. Class-level static variables are shared globally by all the subroutines in the class. Therefore, a single copy of each static variable should be kept alive during the complete duration of the program's execution. Instance-level field variables are treated differently: each object (instance of the class) must have a private set of its field variables, and, when the object is no longer needed, this memory must be freed. Subroutine-level local and argument variables are created each time a subroutine starts running and must be freed when the subroutine terminates.

That's the bad news. The good news is that we've already handled all these difficulties. In our two-tier compiler architecture, memory allocation and deallocation are delegated to the VM level. All we have to do now is map Jack *static* variables on `static 0`, `static 1`, `static 2`,...; *field* variables on `this 0`, `this 1`,...; *local* variables on `local 0`, `local 1`,...; and *argument* variables on `argument 0`, `argument 1`,.... The subsequent mapping of the virtual memory segments on the host RAM, as well as the intricate management of their run-time life cycles, are completely taken care of by the VM implementation.

Recall that this implementation was not achieved easily: we had to work hard to generate assembly code that dynamically maps the virtual memory segments on the host RAM as a side effect of realizing the function call-and-return protocol. Now we can reap the benefits of this effort: the only thing required from the compiler is mapping the high-level variables onto the virtual memory segments. All the subsequent gory details associated with managing these segments on the RAM will be handled by the VM implementation. That's why we sometimes refer to the latter as the compiler's *back end*.

To recap, in a two-tier compilation model, the handling of variables can be reduced to mapping high-level variables on virtual memory segments and using this mapping, as needed, throughout code generation. These tasks can be readily managed using a classical abstraction known as a *symbol table*.

Symbol table: Whenever the compiler encounters variables in a high-level statement, for example, `let y = foo(x)`, it needs to know what the variables stand for. Is `x` a static variable, a field of an object, a local variable, or an argument of a subroutine? Does it represent an `integer`, a `boolean`, a `char`, or some class type? All these questions must be answered— for code generation—each time the variable `x` comes up in the source code. Of course, the variable `y` should be treated exactly the same way.

The variable properties can be managed conveniently using a *symbol table*. When a static, field, local, or argument variable is declared in the source code, the compiler allocates it to the next available entry in the corresponding `static`, `this`, `local`, or `argument` VM segment and records the mapping in the symbol table. Whenever a variable is encountered elsewhere in the code, the compiler looks up its name in the symbol table, retrieves its properties, and uses them, as needed, for code generation.

An important feature of high-level languages is *separate namespaces*: the same identifier can represent different things in different regions of the program. To enable separate namespaces, each identifier is implicitly associated with a *scope*, which is the region of the program in which it is recognized. In Jack, the scope of static and field variables is the class in which they are declared, and the scope of local and argument variables is the subroutine in which they are declared. Jack compilers can realize the scope abstractions by managing two separate symbol tables, as seen in figure 11.2.

The scopes are nested, with inner scopes hiding outer ones. For example, when the Jack compiler encounters the expression x + 17 it first checks whether x is a subroutine-level variable (local or argument). Failing that, the compiler checks whether x is a static variable or a field. Some languages feature nested scoping of unlimited depth, allowing variables to be local in any block of code in which they are declared. To support unlimited nesting, the compiler can use a linked list of symbol tables, each reflecting a single scope nested within the next one in the list. When the compiler fails to find the variable in the table associated with the current scope, it looks it up in the next table in the list, from inner scopes outward. If the variable is not found in the list, the compiler can throw an "undeclared variable" error.

In the Jack language there are only two scoping levels: the subroutine that is presently being compiled, and the class in which the subroutine is declared. Therefore, the compiler can get away with managing two symbol tables only.

Handling variable declarations: When the Jack compiler starts compiling a class declaration, it creates a class-level symbol table and a subroutine-level symbol table. When the compiler parses a static or a field variable declaration, it adds a new row to the class-level symbol table. The row records the variable's *name*, *type* (integer, boolean, char, or class name), *kind* (static or field), and *index* within the kind.

High-level (Jack) code

```
class Point {
    field int x, y;
    static int pointCount;
    ...
    method int distance(Point other) {
        var int dx, dy;
        let dx = x - other.getx();
        let dy = y - other.gety();
        return Math.sqrt((dx*dx) + (dy*dy));
    }
    ...
}
```

name	type	kind	#
x	int	field	0
y	int	field	1
pointCount	int	static	0

Class-level symbol table

name	type	kind	#
this	Point	arg	0
other	Point	arg	1
dx	int	var	0
dy	int	var	1

Subroutine-level symbol table

Figure 11.2   Symbol table examples. The this row in the subroutine-level table is discussed later in the chapter.

When the Jack compiler starts compiling a subroutine (constructor, method, or function) declaration, it resets the subroutine-level symbol table. If the subroutine is a method, the compiler adds the row <this, *className*, arg, 0> to the subroutine-level symbol table (this initialization detail is explained in section 11.1.5.2 and can be ignored till then). When the compiler parses a local or an argument variable declaration, it adds a new row to the subroutine-level symbol table, recording the variable's name, type (integer, boolean, char, or class name), kind (var or arg), and index within the kind. The index of each kind (var or arg) starts at 0 and is incremented by 1 after each time a new variable of that kind is added to the table.

Handling variables in statements: When the compiler encounters a variable in a statement, it looks up the variable name in the subroutine-level symbol table. If the variable is not found, the compiler looks it up in the class-level symbol table. Once the variable has been found, the compiler can complete the statement's translation. For example, consider the symbol tables shown in figure 11.2, and suppose we are compiling the high-level statement let y = y + dy. The compiler will translate this statement into the VM commands push this 1, push local 1, add, pop this 1. Here we assume that the compiler knows how to handle expressions and let statements, subjects which are taken up in the next two sections.

11.1.2   Compiling Expressions

Let's start by considering the compilation of simple expressions like $x + y - 7$. By "simple expression" we mean a sequence of *term operator term operator term* . . . , where each *term* is either a variable or a constant, and each *operator* is either +, −, *, or /.

In Jack, as in most high-level languages, expressions are written using *infix* notation: To add x and y, one writes $x + y$. In contrast, our compilation's target language is *postfix*: The same addition semantics is expressed in the stack-oriented VM code as push x, push y, add. In chapter 10 we introduced an algorithm that emits the parsed source code in infix using XML tags. Although the parsing logic of this algorithm can remain the same, the output part of the algorithm must now be modified for generating postfix commands. Figure 11.3 illustrates this dichotomy.

To recap, we need an algorithm that knows how to parse an infix expression and generate from it as output postfix code that realizes the same semantics on a stack machine. Figure 11.4 presents one such algorithm. The algorithm processes the input expression from left to right, generating VM code as it goes along. Conveniently, this algorithm also handles unary operators and function calls.

If we execute the stack-based VM code generated by the codeWrite algorithm (right side of figure 11.4), the execution will end up consuming all the expression's terms and putting the expression's value at the stack's top. That's exactly what's expected from the compiled code of an expression.

XML code (infix)

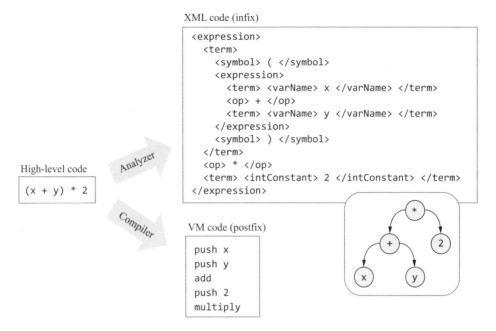

Figure 11.3   Infix and postfix renditions of the same semantics.

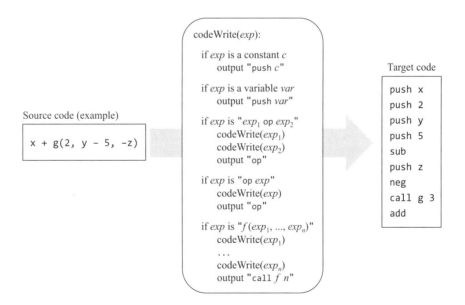

Figure 11.4   A VM code generation algorithm for expressions, and a compilation example. The algorithm assumes that the input expression is valid. The final implementation of this algorithm should replace the emitted symbolic variables with their corresponding symbol table mappings.

<u>Definition</u> (from the Jack grammar):

expression: *term* (*op term*) *

term: *integerConstant* | *stringConstant* | *keywordConstant* | *varName* |
varName '[' *expression* ']' | ' (' *expression* ')' | (*unaryOp term*) | *subroutineCall*

subroutineCall: *subroutineName* '(' *expressionList* ')' |
(*className* | *varName*) '.' *subroutineName* '(' *expressionList* ')'

expressionList: (*expression* (',' *expression*) *) ?

op: '+' | '-' | '*' | '/' | '&' | '|' | '<' | '>' | '='

unaryOp: '-' | '~'

keywordConstant: '**true**' | '**false**' | '**null**' | '**this**'

The definitions of *integerConstant*, *stringConstant*, *keywordConstant*, and other elements are given in the complete Jack grammar (figure 10.6), and are self-explanatory.

<u>Examples</u>:
```
5
x
x + 5
(-b + Math.sqrt(b*b - (4 * a * c))) / (2 * a)
arr[i] + foo(x)
foo(Math.abs(arr[x + foo(5)]))
```

Figure 11.5   Expressions in the Jack language.

So far we have dealt with relatively simple expressions. Figure 11.5 gives the complete grammatical definition of Jack expressions, along with several examples of actual expressions consistent with this definition.

The compilation of Jack expressions will be handled by a routine named `compileExpression`. The developer of this routine should start with the algorithm presented in figure 11.4 and extend it to handle the various possibilities specified in figure 11.5. We will have more to say about this implementation later in the chapter.

11.1.3   Compiling Strings

Strings—sequences of characters—are widely used in computer programs. Object-oriented languages typically handle strings as instances of a class named `String` (Jack's `String` class, which is part of the Jack OS, is documented in appendix 6). Each time a string constant comes up in a high-level statement or expression, the compiler generates code that calls the `String` constructor, which creates and returns a new `String` object. Next, the compiler initializes the new object with the string characters. This is done by generating a sequence of calls to the `String` method `appendChar`, one for each character listed in the high-level string constant.

This implementation of string constants can be wasteful, leading to potential memory leaks. To illustrate, consider the statement `Output.printString("Loading...please wait")`. Presumably, all the high-level programmer wants is to display a message; she certainly doesn't care if the compiler creates a new object, and she may be surprised to know that the object will persist in memory until the program terminates. But that's exactly what actually happens: a new `String` object will be created, and this object will keep lurking in the background, doing nothing.

Java, C#, and Python use a run-time *garbage collection* process that reclaims the memory used by objects that are no longer in play (technically, objects that have no variable referring to them). In general, modern languages use a variety of optimizations and specialized string classes for promoting the efficient use of string objects. The Jack OS features only one `String` class and no string-related optimizations.

Operating system services: In the handling of strings, we mentioned for the first time that the compiler can use OS services as needed. Indeed, developers of Jack compilers can assume that every constructor, method, and function listed in the OS API (appendix 6) is available *as a compiled VM function*. Technically speaking, any one of these VM functions can be called by the code generated by the compiler. This configuration will be fully realized in chapter 12, in which we will implement the OS in Jack and compile it into VM code.

11.1.4   Compiling Statements

The Jack programming language features five statements: `let`, `do`, `return`, `if`, and `while`. We now turn to discuss how the Jack compiler generates VM code that handles the semantics of these statements.

Compiling `return` statements: Now that we know how to compile expressions, the compilation of `return` *expression* is simple. First, we call the `compileExpression` routine, which generates VM code designed to evaluate and put the expression's value on the stack. Next, we generate the VM command `return`.

Compiling `let` statements: Here we discuss the handling of statements of the form `let` *varName = expression*. Since parsing is a left-to-right process, we begin by remembering the *varName*. Next, we call `compileExpression`, which puts the expression's value on the stack. Finally, we generate the VM command pop *varName*, where *varName* is actually the symbol table mapping of *varName* (for example, `local 3`, `static 1`, and so on).

We'll discuss the compilation of statements of the form `let` *varName*[*expression*1] = *expression*2 later in the chapter, in a section dedicated to handling arrays.

Compiling do statements: Here we discuss the compilation of *function calls* of the form do *className.functionName* (*exp₁, exp₂, … , exp*n). The do abstraction is designed to call a subroutine for its effect, ignoring the return value. In chapter 10 we recommended compiling such statements as if their syntax were do *expression*. We repeat this recommendation here: to compile a do *className.functionName* (…) statement, we call compileExpression and then get rid of the topmost stack element (the expression's value) by generating a command like pop temp 0.

We'll discuss the compilation of *method calls* of the form do *varName.methodName* (…) and do *methodName* (…) later in the chapter, in a section dedicated to compiling method calls.

Compiling if and while statements: High-level programming languages feature a variety of *control flow statements* like if, while, for, and switch, of which Jack features if and while. In contrast, low-level assembly and VM languages control the flow of execution using two branching primitives: *conditional goto*, and *unconditional goto*. Therefore, one of the challenges faced by compiler developers is expressing the semantics of high-level control flow statements using nothing more than goto primitives. Figure 11.6 shows how this gap can be bridged systematically.

When the compiler detects an if keyword, it knows that it has to parse a pattern of the form if (*expression*) {*statements*} else {*statements*}. Hence, the compiler starts by calling

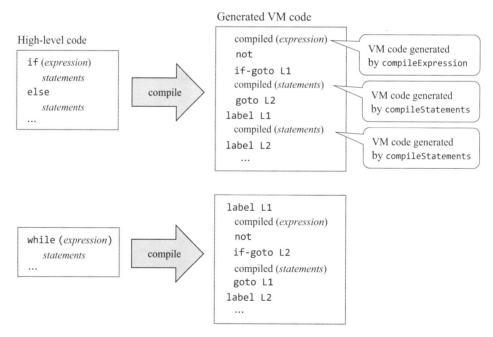

Figure 11.6 Compiling if and while statements. The L1 and L2 labels are generated by the compiler.

compileExpression, which generates VM commands designed to compute and push the expression's value onto the stack. The compiler then generates the VM command not, designed to negate the expression's value. Next, the compiler creates a label, say L1, and uses it for generating the VM command if-goto L1. Next, the compiler calls compileStatements. This routine is designed to compile a sequence of the form *statement*; *statement*; ... *statement*;, where each *statement* is either a let, a do, a return, an if, or a while. The resulting VM code is referred to conceptually in figure 11.6 as "compiled (*statements*)." The rest of the compilation strategy is self-explanatory.

A high-level program normally contains multiple instances of if and while. To handle this complexity, the compiler can generate labels that are globally unique, for example, labels whose suffix is the value of a running counter. Also, control flow statements are often nested—for example, an if within a while within another while, and so on. Such nestings are taken care of implicitly since the compileStatements routine is inherently recursive.

11.1.5 Handling Objects

So far in this chapter, we described techniques for compiling *variables*, *expressions*, *strings*, and *statements*. This forms most of the know-how necessary for building a compiler for a procedural, C-like language. In Nand to Tetris, though, we aim higher: building a compiler for an object-based, Java-like language. With that in mind, we now turn to discuss the handling of *objects*.

Object-oriented languages feature means for declaring and manipulating aggregate abstractions known as *objects*. Each object is implemented physically as a memory block which can be referenced by a static, field, local, or argument variable. The reference variable, also known as an *object variable*, or *pointer*, contains the memory block's base address. The operating system realizes this model by managing a logical area in the RAM named *heap*. The *heap* is used as a memory pool from which memory blocks are carved, as needed, for representing new objects. When an object is no longer needed, its memory block can be freed and recycled back to the heap. The compiler stages these memory management actions by calling OS functions, as we'll see later.

At any given point during a program's execution, the heap can contain numerous objects. Suppose we want to apply a method, say foo, to one of these objects, say p. In an object-oriented language, this is done through the method call idiom p.foo(). Shifting our attention from the caller to the callee, we note that foo—like any other method—is designed to operate on a placeholder known as the *current object*, or this. In particular, when VM commands in foo's code make references to this 0, this 1, this 2, and so on, they should effect the fields of p, the object on which foo was called. Which begs the question: How do we align the this segment with p?

The virtual machine built in chapters 7–8 has a mechanism for realizing this alignment: the two-valued pointer segment, mapped directly onto RAM locations 3–4, also known as THIS and THAT. According to the VM specification, the pointer THIS (referred to as pointer 0) is designed to hold the base address of the memory segment `this`. Thus, to align the `this` segment with the object p, we can push p's value (which is an address) onto the stack and then pop it into `pointer 0`. Versions of this initialization technique are used conspicuously in the compilation of *constructors* and *methods*, as we now turn to describe.

11.1.5.1 Compiling Constructors

In object-oriented languages, objects are created by subroutines known as *constructors*. In this section we describe how to compile a constructor call (e.g., Java's `new` operator) from the *caller*'s perspective and how to compile the code of the constructor itself—the *callee*.

Compiling constructor calls: Object construction is normally a two-stage affair. First, one declares a variable of some class type, for example, `var Point p`. At a later stage, one can instantiate the object by calling a class constructor, for example, `let p = Point.new(2,3)`. Or, depending on the language used, one can declare *and* construct objects using a single high-level statement. Behind the scenes, though, this action is always broken into two separate stages: declaration followed by construction.

Let's take a close look at the statement `let p = Point.new(2,3)`. This abstraction can be described as "have the `Point.new` constructor allocate a two-word memory block for representing a new `Point` instance, initialize the two words of this block to 2 and 3, and have p refer to the base address of this block." Implicit in this semantics are two assumptions: First, the constructor knows how to allocate a memory block of the required size. Second, when the constructor—being a subroutine—terminates its execution, it returns to the caller the base address of the allocated memory block. Figure 11.7 shows how this abstraction can be realized.

Three observations about figure 11.7 are in order. First, note that there is nothing special about compiling statements like `let p = Point.new(2,3)` and `let p = Point.new(5,7)`. We already discussed how to compile `let` statements and subroutine calls. The only thing that makes these calls special is the hocus-pocus assumption that—somehow—two objects will be constructed. The implementation of this magic is entirely delegated to the compilation of the *callee*—the constructor. As a result of this magic, the constructor creates the two objects seen in the RAM diagram in figure 11.7. This leads to the second observation: The physical addresses 6012 and 9543 are irrelevant; the high-level code as well as the compiled VM code have no idea where the objects are stored in memory; the references to these objects are strictly symbolic, via p1 and p2 in the high-level code and `local 0` and `local 1` in the compiled code. (As a side comment, this makes the program relocatable and safer.) Third, and stating the obvious, nothing of substance actually happens until the generated VM code is executed. In particular, during *compile-time*, the symbol table is updated, low-level code is generated, and that's it. The objects will be constructed and bound to the variables only during *run-time*, that is, if and when the compiled code will be executed.

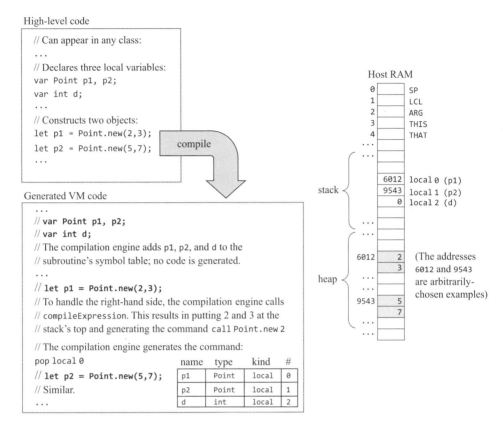

Figure 11.7   Object construction from the caller's perspective. In this example, the caller declares two object variables and then calls a class constructor for constructing the two objects. The constructor works its magic, allocating memory blocks for representing the two objects. The calling code then makes the two object variables refer to these memory blocks.

Compiling constructors: So far, we have treated constructors as black box abstractions: we assume that they create objects, *somehow*. Figure 11.8 unravels this magic. Before inspecting the figure, note that a constructor is, first and foremost, a *subroutine*. It can have arguments, local variables, and a body of statements; thus the compiler treats it as such. What makes the compilation of a constructor special is that in addition to treating it as a regular subroutine, the compiler must also generate code that (i) creates a new object and (ii) makes the new object the *current object* (also known as `this`), that is, the object on which the constructor's code is to operate.

The creation of a new object requires finding a free RAM block sufficiently large to accommodate the new object's data and marking the block as used. These tasks are delegated to the host operating system. According to the OS API listed in appendix 6, the OS function `Memory.alloc` (*size*) knows how to find an available RAM block of a given *size* (number of 16-bit words) and return the block's base address.

High-level code

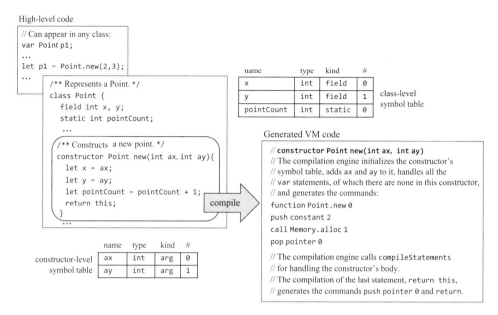

Figure 11.8   Object construction: the constructor's perspective.

Memory.alloc and its sister function Memory.deAlloc use clever algorithms for allocating and freeing RAM resources efficiently. These algorithms will be presented and implemented in chapter 12, when we'll build the operating system. For now, suffice it to say that compilers generate low-level code that uses alloc (in constructors) and deAlloc (in destructors), abstractly.

Before calling Memory.alloc, the compiler determines the size of the required memory block. This can be readily computed from the class-level symbol table. For example, the symbol table of the Point class specifies that each Point object is characterized by two int values (the point's *x* and *y* coordinates). Thus, the compiler generates the commands push constant 2 and call Memory.alloc 1, effecting the function call Memory.alloc(2). The OS function alloc goes to work, finds an available RAM block of size 2, and pushes its base address onto the stack—the VM equivalent of returning a value. The next generated VM statement—pop pointer 0—sets THIS to the base address returned by alloc. From this point onward, the constructor's this segment will be aligned with the RAM block that was allocated for representing the newly constructed object.

Once the this segment is properly aligned, we can proceed to generate code easily. For example, when the compileLet routine is called to handle the statement let x = ax, it searches the symbol tables, resolving x to this 0 and ax to argument 0. Thus, compileLet generates the commands push argument 0, followed by pop this 0. The latter command rests on the assumption that the this segment is properly aligned with the base address of the new object, as indeed was done when we had set pointer 0 (actually, THIS) to the base address returned by alloc. This one-time initialization ensures that all the subsequent push / pop `this` *i* commands will end up hitting the right targets in the RAM (more accurately, in the *heap*). We hope that the intricate beauty of this contract is not lost on the reader.

According to the Jack language specification, every constructor must end with a `return this` statement. This convention forces the compiler to end the constructor's compiled version with `push pointer 0` and `return`. These commands push onto the stack the value of THIS, the base address of the constructed object. In some languages, like Java, constructors don't have to end with an explicit `return this` statement. Nonetheless, the compiled code of Java constructors performs exactly the same action at the VM level, since that's what constructors are expected to do: create an object and return its handle to the caller.

Recall that the elaborate low-level drama just described was unleashed by the caller-side statement `let` *varName* = *className* . *constructorName* (...). We now see that, by design, when the constructor terminates, *varName* ends up storing the base address of the new object. When we say "by design," we mean by the syntax of the high-level object construction idiom and by the hard work that the compiler, the operating system, the VM translator, and the assembler have to do in order to realize this abstraction. The net result is that high-level programmers are spared from all the gory details of object construction and are able to create objects easily and transparently.

11.1.5.2 Compiling Methods

As we did with constructors, we'll describe how to compile method calls and then how to compile the methods themselves.

Compiling method calls: Suppose we wish to compute the Euclidean distance between two points in a plane, `p1` and `p2`. In C-style procedural programming, this could have been implemented using a function call like `distance(p1,p2)`, where `p1` and `p2` represent composite data types. In object-oriented programming, though, `p1` and `p2` will be implemented as instances of some `Point` class, and the same computation will be done using a method call like `p1.distance(p2)`. Unlike functions, *methods* are subroutines that always operate on a given object, and it's the caller's responsibility to specify this object. (The fact that the `distance` method takes another `Point` object as an argument is a coincidence. In general, while a method is always designed to operate on an object, the method can have 0, 1, or more arguments, of any type).

Observe that `distance` can be described as a *procedure* for computing the distance from a given point to another, and `p1` can be described as the *data* on which the procedure operates. Also, note that both idioms `distance(p1,p2)` and `p1.distance(p2)` are designed to compute and return the same value. Yet while the C-style syntax puts the focus on `distance`, in the object-oriented syntax, the object comes first, literally speaking. That's why C-like languages are sometimes called *procedural*, and object-oriented languages are said to be *data-driven*. Among other things, the object-oriented programming style is based on the assumption that objects know how to take care of themselves. For example, a `Point` object knows how to compute the distance between it and another Point object. Said otherwise, the distance operation is *encapsulated* within the definition of being a Point.

The agent responsible for bringing all these fancy abstractions down to earth is, as usual, the hard-working compiler. Because the target VM language has no concept of objects or methods, the compiler handles object-oriented method calls like p1.distance(p2) as if they were procedural calls like distance(p1,p2). Specifically, it translates p1.distance(p2) into push p1, push p2, call distance. Let us generalize: Jack features two kinds of method calls:

// Applies a method to the object referred to by *varName*:
varName.*methodName*(exp_1, exp_2, ..., exp_n)

// Applies a method to the *current object*:
methodName(exp_1, exp_2, ..., exp_n)   // Same as this. *methodName*(exp_1, exp_2, ..., exp_n)

To compile the method call *varName*.*methodName*(exp_1, exp_2, ..., exp_n), we start by generating the command push *varName*, where *varName* is the symbol table mapping of *varName*. If the method call mentions no *varName*, we push the symbol table mapping of this. Next, we call compileExpressionList. This routine calls compileExpression n times, once for each expression in the parentheses. Finally, we generate the command call *className*.*methodName* $n + 1$, informing that $n + 1$ arguments were pushed onto the stack. The special case of calling an argument-less method is translated into call *className*.*methodName* 1. Note that *className* is the symbol table *type* of the *varName* identifier. See figure 11.9 for an example.

Compiling methods: So far we discussed the distance method abstractly, from the caller's perspective. Consider how this method could be implemented, say, in Java:

```
/** A Point class method: returns the distance between this Point and the other one. */
int distance(Point other) {
    int dx, dy;
    dx = x - other.x;
    dy = y - other.x;
    return Math.sqrt((dx*dx) + (dy*dy));
}
```

Like any method, distance is designed to operate on the *current object*, represented in Java (and in Jack) by the built-in identifier this. As the above example illustrates, though, one can write an entire method without ever mentioning this. That's because the friendly Java compiler handles statements like dx = x − other.x as if they were dx = this.x − other.x. This convention makes high-level code more readable and easier to write.

We note in passing, though, that in the Jack language, the idiom *object.field* is not supported. Therefore, fields of objects other than the current object can be manipulated only

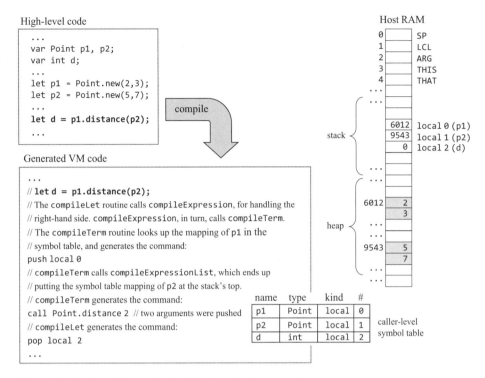

Figure 11.9   Compiling method calls: the caller's perspective.

using accessor and mutator methods. For example, expressions like x - other.x are implemented in Jack as x - other.getx(), where getx is an accessor method in the Point class.

So how does the Jack compiler handle expressions like x - other.getx()? Like the Java compiler, it looks up x in the symbol tables and finds that it represents the first field in the current object. But *which* object in the pool of so many objects out there does the *current object* represent? Well, according to the method call contract, it must be the first argument that was passed by the method's caller. Therefore, from the callee's perspective, the current object must be the object whose base address is the value of argument 0. This, in a nutshell, is the low-level compilation trick that makes the ubiquitous abstraction "apply a method to an object" possible in languages like Java, Python, and, of course, Jack. See figure 11.10 for the details.

The example starts at the top left of figure 11.10, where the caller's code makes the method call p1.distance(p2). Turning our attention to the compiled version of the callee, note that the code proper starts with push argument 0, followed by pop pointer 0. These commands set the method's THIS pointer to the value of argument 0, which, by virtue of the method calling contract, contains the base address of the object on which the method was called to operate. Thus, from this point onward, the method's this segment is properly aligned with the base address of the target object, making every push / pop this *i* command

High-level code

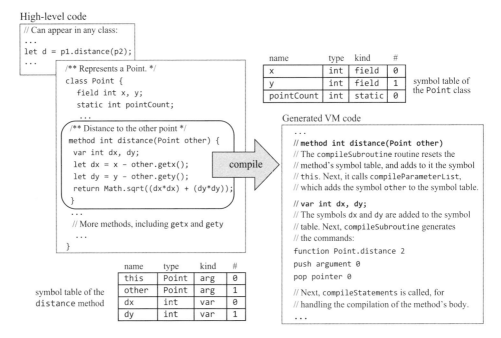

Figure 11.10 Compiling methods: the callee's perspective.

properly aligned as well. For example, the expression x − other.getx() will be compiled into push this 0, push argument 1, call Point.getx 1, sub. Since we started the compiled method code by setting THIS to the base address of the called object, we are guaranteed that this 0 (and any other reference this *i*) will hit the mark, targeting the right field of the right object.

11.1.6   Compiling Arrays

Arrays are similar to objects. In Jack, arrays are implemented as instances of an Array class, which is part of the operating system. Thus, arrays and objects are declared, implemented, and stored exactly the same way; in fact, arrays *are* objects, with the difference that the array abstraction allows accessing array elements using an index, for example, let arr[3] = 17. The agent that makes this useful abstraction concrete is the compiler, as we now turn to describe.

Using pointer notation, observe that arr[i] can be written as *(arr + i), that is, memory address arr + i. This insight holds the key for compiling statements like let x = arr[i]. To compute the physical address of arr[i], we execute push arr, push i, add, which results in pushing the target address onto the stack. Next, we execute pop pointer 1. According to the VM specification, this action stores the target address in the method's THAT pointer

(RAM[4]), which has the effect of aligning the base address of the virtual segment that with the target address. Thus we can now execute push that 0 and pop x, completing the low-level translation of let x = arr[i]. See figure 11.11 for the details.

This nice compilation strategy has only one problem: it doesn't work. More accurately, it works with statements like let a = b[j] but fails with statements in which the left-hand side of the assignment is indexed, as in let a[i]=b[j]. See figure 11.12.

The good news is that this flawed compilation strategy can be easily fixed to compile correctly any instance of let arr[*expression*1] = *expression*2. As before, we start by generating the command push arr, calling compileExpression, and generating the command add. This sequence puts the target address (arr + *expression*1) at the stack's top. Next, we call compileExpression, which will end up putting at the stack's top the value of *expression*2. At this point we save this value—we can do it using pop temp 0. This operation has the nice side effect of making (arr + *expression*1) the top stack element. Thus we can now pop pointer 1, push temp 0, and pop that 0. This little fix, along with the recursive nature of the compileExpression routine, makes this compilation strategy capable of handling let arr[*expression*1] = *expression*2 statements of any recursive complexity, such as, say, let a[b[i]+a[j+b[a[3]]]]=b[b[j]+2].

In closing, several things make the compilation of Jack arrays relatively simple. First, Jack arrays are not typed; rather, they are designed to store 16-bit values, with no restrictions. Second, all primitive data types in Jack are 16-bit wide, all addresses are 16-bit wide, and so is the RAM's word width. In strongly typed programming languages, and in

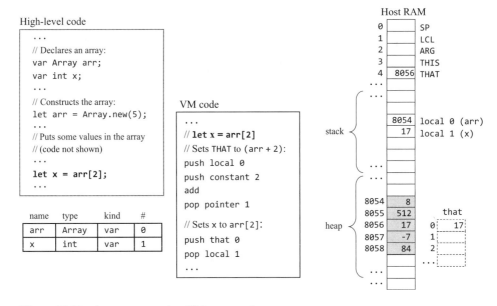

Figure 11.11 Array access using VM commands.

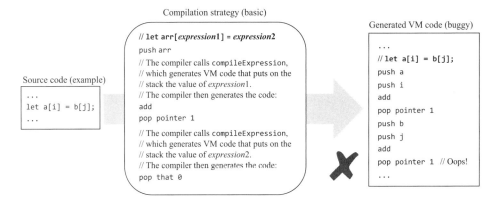

Figure 11.12   Basic compilation strategy for arrays, and an example of the bugs that it can generate. In this particular case, the value stored in `pointer 1` is overridden, and the address of `a[i]` is lost.

languages where this one-to-one correspondence cannot be guaranteed, the compilation of arrays requires more work.

11.2   Specification

The compilation challenges and solutions that we have described so far can be generalized to support the compilation of any object-based programming language. We now turn from the general to the specific: from here to the end of the chapter, we describe the *Jack compiler*. The Jack compiler is a program that gets a Jack program as input and generates executable VM code as output. The VM code realizes the program's semantics on the virtual machine specified in chapters 7–8.

Usage: The compiler accepts a single command-line argument, as follows,

```
prompt> JackCompiler source
```

where *source* is either a file name of the form *Xxx*.`jack` (the extension is mandatory) or the name of a folder (in which case there is no extension) containing one or more .`jack` files. The file/folder name may contain a file path. If no path is specified, the compiler operates on the current folder. For each *Xxx*.`jack` file, the compiler creates an output file *Xxx*.`vm` and writes the VM commands into it. The output file is created in the same folder as the input file. If there is a file by this name in the folder, it will be overwritten.

11.3   Implementation

We now turn to provide guidelines, implementation tips, and a proposed API for extending the syntax analyzer built in chapter 10 into a full-scale Jack compiler.

11.3.1   Standard Mapping over the Virtual Machine

Jack compilers can be developed for different target platforms. This section provides guidelines on how to map various constructs of the Jack language on one specific platform: the virtual machine specified in chapters 7–8.

Naming Files and Functions

- A Jack class file *Xxx*.jack is compiled into a VM class file named *Xxx*.vm
- A Jack subroutine *yyy* in file *Xxx*.jack is compiled into a VM function named *Xxx*.*yyy*

Mapping Variables

- The first, second, third,...*static* variable declared in a class declaration is mapped on the virtual segment entry static 0, static 1, static 2,...
- The first, second, third,...*field* variable declared in a class declaration is mapped on this 0, this 1, this 2,...
- The first, second, third,...*local* variable declared in the var statements of a subroutine is mapped on local 0, local 1, local 2,...
- The first, second, third, ... *argument* variable declared in the parameter list of a *function* or a *constructor* (but not a *method*) is mapped on argument 0, argument 1, argument 2,...
- The first, second, third, ... *argument* variable declared in the parameter list of a *method* is mapped on argument 1, argument 2, argument 3,...

Mapping Object Fields

To align the virtual segment this with the object passed by the caller of a *method*, use the VM commands push argument 0, pop pointer 0.

Mapping Array Elements

The high-level reference arr[*expression*] is compiled by setting pointer 1 to (arr + *expression*) and accessing that 0.

Mapping Constants

- References to the Jack constants `null` and `false` are compiled into `push constant 0`.
- References to the Jack constant `true` are compiled into `push constant 1, neg`. This sequence pushes the value −1 onto the stack.
- References to the Jack constant `this` are compiled into `push pointer 0`. This command pushes the base address of the current object onto the stack.

11.3.2   Implementation Guidelines

Throughout this chapter we have seen many conceptual compilation examples. We now give a concise and formal summary of all these compilation techniques.

Handling Identifiers

The identifiers used for naming variables can be handled using symbol tables. During the compilation of valid Jack code, any identifier not found in the symbol tables may be assumed to be either a subroutine name or a class name. Since the Jack syntax rules suffice for distinguishing between these two possibilities, and since the Jack compiler performs no "linking," there is no need to keep these identifiers in a symbol table.

Compiling Expressions

The `compileExpression` routine should process the input as the sequence *term op term op term ....* To do so, `compileExpression` should implement the `codeWrite` algorithm (figure 11.4), extended to handle all the possible *terms* specified in the Jack grammar (figure 11.5). Indeed, an inspection of the grammar rules reveals that most of the action in compiling *expressions* occurs in the compilation of their underlying *terms*. This is especially true following our recommendation that the compilation of subroutine calls be handled directly by the compilation of *terms* (implementation notes following the `CompilationEngine` API, section 10.3).

The *expression* grammar and thus the corresponding `compileExpression` routine are inherently recursive. For example, when `compileExpression` detects a left parenthesis, it should recursively call `compileExpression` to handle the inner expression. This recursive descent ensures that the inner expression will be evaluated first. Except for this priority rule, the Jack language supports *no operator priority*. Handling operator priority is of course possible, but in Nand to Tetris we consider it an optional compiler-specific extension, not a standard feature of the Jack language.

The expression x * y is compiled into `push x, push y, call Math.multiply 2`. The expression x / y is compiled into `push x, push y, call Math.divide 2`. The `Math` class is part of the OS, documented in appendix 6. This class will be developed in chapter 12.

Compiling Strings

Each string constant "*ccc...c*" is handled by (i) pushing the string length onto the stack and calling the `String.new` constructor, and (ii) pushing the character code of *c* on the stack and calling the `String` method `appendChar`, once for each character *c* in the string (the Jack character set is documented in appendix 5). As documented in the `String` class API in appendix 6, both the `new` constructor and the `appendChar` method return the string as the return value (i.e., they push the string object onto the stack). This simplifies compilation, avoiding the need to re-push the string each time `appendChar` is called.

Compiling Function Calls and Constructor Calls

The compiled version of calling a function or calling a constructor that has *n* arguments must (i) call `compileExpressionList`, which will call `compileExpression` *n* times, and (ii) make the call informing that *n* arguments were pushed onto the stack before the call.

Compiling Method Calls

The compiled version of calling a method that has *n* arguments must (i) push a reference to the object on which the method is called to operate, (ii) call `compileExpressionList`, which will call `compileExpression` *n* times, and (iii) make the call, informing that $n+1$ arguments were pushed onto the stack before the call.

Compiling do Statements

We recommend compiling do *subroutineCall* statements as if they were do *expression* statements, and then yanking the topmost stack value using `pop temp 0`.

Compiling Classes

When starting to compile a class, the compiler creates a class-level symbol table and adds to it all the *field* and *static* variables declared in the class declaration. The compiler also creates an empty subroutine-level symbol table. No code is generated.

Compiling Subroutines

- When starting to compile a subroutine (*constructor*, *function*, or *method*), the compiler initializes the subroutine's symbol table. If the subroutine is a *method*, the compiler adds to the symbol table the mapping <this, *className*, arg, 0>.
- Next, the compiler adds to the symbol table all the parameters, if any, declared in the subroutine's parameter list. Next, the compiler handles all the `var` declarations, if any, by adding to the symbol table all the subroutine's local variables.

- At this stage the compiler starts generating code, beginning with the command `function` *className.subroutineName nVars*, where *nVars* is the number of local variables in the subroutine.
- If the subroutine is a *method*, the compiler generates the code `push argument 0`, `pop pointer 0`. This sequence aligns the virtual memory segment `this` with the base address of the object on which the method was called.

Compiling Constructors

- First, the compiler performs all the actions described in the previous section, ending with the generation of the command `function` *className.constructorName nVars*.
- Next, the compiler generates the code `push constant` *nFields*, `call Memory.alloc 1`, `pop pointer 0`, where *nFields* is the number of fields in the compiled class. This results in allocating a memory block of *nFields* 16-bit words and aligning the virtual memory segment `this` with the base address of the newly allocated block.
- The compiled constructor must end with `push pointer 0`, `return`. This sequence returns to the caller the base address of the new object created by the constructor.

Compiling Void Methods and Void Functions

Every VM function is expected to push a value onto the stack before returning. When compiling a void Jack method or function, the convention is to end the generated code with `push constant 0`, `return`.

Compiling Arrays

Statements of the form `let arr[`*expression*1`] = `*expression*2 are compiled using the technique described at the end of section 11.1.6. *Implementation tip*: When handling arrays, there is never a need to use `that` entries whose index is greater than 0.

The Operating System

Consider the high-level expression `Math.sqrt((dx * dx)+(dy * dy))`. The compiler compiles it into the VM commands `push` *dx*, `push` *dx*, `call Math.multiply 2`, `push` *dy*, `push` *dy*, `call Math.multiply 2`, `add`, `call Math.sqrt 1`, where *dx* and *dy* are the symbol table mappings of dx and dy. This example illustrates the two ways in which operating system services come into play during compilation. First, some high-level abstractions, like the expression `x * y`, are compiled by generating code that calls OS subroutines like `Math.multiply`. Second, when a Jack expression includes a high-level call to an OS routine, for example, `Math.sqrt(x)`, the compiler generates VM code that makes exactly the same call using VM postfix syntax.

The OS features eight classes, documented in appendix 6. Nand to Tetris provides two different implementations of this OS—*native* and *emulated*.

Native OS Implementation

In project 12 you will develop the OS class library in Jack and compile it using a Jack compiler. The compilation will yield eight .vm files, comprising the native OS implementation. If you put these eight .vm files in the same folder that stores the .vm files resulting from the compilation of *any* Jack program, all the OS functions will become accessible to the compiled VM code since they belong to the same code base.

Emulated OS Implementation

The supplied VM emulator, which is a Java program, features a Java-based implementation of the Jack OS. Whenever the VM code loaded into the emulator calls an OS function, the emulator checks whether a VM function by that name exists in the loaded code base. If so, it executes the VM function. Otherwise, it calls the built-in implementation of this OS function. The bottom line is this: If you use the supplied VM emulator for executing the VM code generated by your compiler, as we do in project 11, you need not worry about the OS configuration; the emulator will service all the OS calls without further ado.

11.3.3   Software Architecture

The proposed compiler architecture builds upon the syntax analyzer described in chapter 10. Specifically, we propose to gradually evolve the syntax analyzer into a full-scale compiler, using the following modules:

- JackCompiler: main program, sets up and invokes the other modules
- JackTokenizer: tokenizer for the Jack language
- SymbolTable: keeps track of all the variables found in the Jack code
- VMWriter: writes VM code
- CompilationEngine: recursive top-down compilation engine

The JackCompiler

This module drives the compilation process. It operates on either a file name of the form *Xxx*.jack or on a folder name containing one or more such files. For each source *Xxx*.jack file, the program

1. creates a JackTokenizer from the *Xxx*.jack input file;
2. creates an output file named *Xxx*.vm; and

3. uses a `CompilationEngine`, a `SymbolTable`, and a `VMWriter` for parsing the input file and emitting the translated VM code into the output file.

We provide no API for this module, inviting you to implement it as you see fit. Remember that the first routine that must be called when compiling a `.jack` file is `compileClass`.

The JackTokenizer

This module is identical to the tokenizer built in project 10. See the API in section 10.3.

The SymbolTable

This module provides services for building, populating, and using symbol tables that keep track of the symbol properties *name*, *type*, *kind*, and a running *index* for each kind. See figure 11.2 for an example.

Routine	*Arguments*	*Returns*	*Function*
Constructor / initializer	—	—	Creates a new symbol table.
reset	—	—	Empties the symbol table, and resets the four indexes to 0. Should be called when starting to compile a subroutine declaration.
define	name (string) type (string) kind (STATIC, FIELD, ARG, or VAR)	—	Defines (adds to the table) a new variable of the given name, type, and kind. Assigns to it the index value of that kind, and adds 1 to the index.
varCount	kind (STATIC, FIELD, ARG, or VAR)	int	Returns the number of variables of the given kind already defined in the table.
kindOf	name (string)	(STATIC, FIELD, ARG, VAR, NONE)	Returns the kind of the named identifier. If the identifier is not found, returns NONE.
typeOf	name (string)	string	Returns the type of the named variable.
indexOf	name (string)	int	Returns the index of the named variable.

Implementation note: During the compilation of a Jack class file, the Jack compiler uses two instances of `SymbolTable`.

The VMWriter

This module features a set of simple routines for writing VM commands into the output file.

Routine	*Arguments*	*Returns*	*Function*
Constructor / initializer	Output file / stream	—	Creates a new output .vm file / stream, and prepares it for writing.
writePush	segment (CONSTANT, ARGUMENT, LOCAL, STATIC, THIS, THAT, POINTER, TEMP) index (int)	—	Writes a VM push command.
writePop	segment (ARGUMENT, LOCAL, STATIC, THIS, THAT, POINTER, TEMP) index (int)	—	Writes a VM pop command.
writeArithmetic	command (ADD, SUB, NEG, EQ, GT, LT, AND, OR, NOT)	—	Writes a VM arithmetic-logical command.
writeLabel	label (string)	—	Writes a VM label command.
writeGoto	label (string)	—	Writes a VM goto command.
writeIf	label (string)		Writes a VM if-goto command.
writeCall	name (string) nArgs (int)	—	Writes a VM call command.
writeFunction	name (string) nVars (int)	—	Writes a VM function command.
writeReturn	—	—	Writes a VM return command.
close	—	—	Closes the output file / stream.

The CompilationEngine

This module runs the compilation process. Although the CompilationEngine API is almost identical the API presented in chapter 10, we repeat it here for ease of reference.

The CompilationEngine gets its input from a JackTokenizer and uses a VMWriter for writing the VM code output (instead of the XML produced in project 10). The output is generated by a series of compile*xxx* routines, each designed to handle the compilation of a specific Jack language construct *xxx* (for example, compileWhile generates the VM code that realizes while statements). The contract between these routines is as follows: Each compile*xxx* routine gets from the input and handles all the tokens that make up *xxx*, advances the tokenizer exactly beyond these tokens, and emits to the output VM code effecting the semantics of *xxx*. If *xxx* is a part of an expression, and thus has a value, the emitted VM code should compute this value and leave it at the top of the stack. As a rule, each compile*xxx* routine is called only if the current token is *xxx*. Since the first token in a valid .jack file must be the keyword class, the compilation process starts by calling the routine compileClass.

Routine	Arguments	Returns	Function
Constructor / initializer	Input file / stream Output file / stream	–	Creates a new compilation engine with the given input and output. The next routine called must be compileClass.
compileClass	–	–	Compiles a complete class.
compileClassVarDec	–	–	Compiles a static variable declaration, or a field declaration.
compileSubroutine	–	–	Compiles a complete method, function, or constructor.
compileParameterList	–	–	Compiles a (possibly empty) parameter list. Does not handle the enclosing parenthesis tokens (and).
compileSubroutineBody	–	–	Compiles a subroutine's body.
compileVarDec	–	–	Compiles a var declaration.
compileStatements	–	–	Compiles a sequence of statements. Does not handle the enclosing curly bracket tokens {and }.
compileLet	–	–	Compiles a let statement.
compileIf	–	–	Compiles an if statement, possibly with a trailing else clause.
compileWhile	–	–	Compiles a while statement.
compileDo	–	–	Compiles a do statement.
compileReturn	–	–	Compiles a return statement.
compileExpression	–	–	Compiles an expression.
compileTerm	–	–	Compiles a *term*. If the current token is an *identifier*, the routine must resolve it into a *variable*, an *array element*, or a *subroutine call*. A single lookahead token, which may be [, (, or ., suffices to distinguish between the possibilities. Any other token is not part of this term and should not be advanced over.
compileExpressionList	–	int	Compiles a (possibly empty) comma-separated list of expressions. Returns the number of expressions in the list.

Note: The following Jack grammar rules have no corresponding compile xxx routines in the CompilationEngine: *type*, *className*, *subroutineName*, *varName*, *statement*, *subroutineCall*.

The parsing logic of these rules should be handled by the routines that implement the rules that refer to them. The Jack language grammar is presented in section 10.2.1.

Token lookahead: The need for token lookahead, and the proposed solution for handling it, are discussed in section 10.3, just after the `CompilationEngine` API.

11.4   Project

Objective: Extend the syntax analyzer built in chapter 10 into a full-scale Jack compiler. Apply your compiler to all the test programs described below. Execute each translated program, and make sure that it operates according to its given documentation.

This version of the compiler assumes that the source Jack code is error-free. Error checking, reporting, and handling can be added to later versions of the compiler but are not part of project 11.

Resources: The main tool that you need is the programming language in which you will implement the compiler. You will also need the supplied VM emulator for testing the VM code generated by your compiler. Since the compiler is implemented by extending the syntax analyzer built in project 10, you will also need the analyzer's source code.

Implementation Stages

We propose morphing the syntax analyzer built in project 10 into the final compiler. In particular, we propose to gradually replace the routines that generate passive XML output with routines that generate executable VM code. This can be done in two main development stages.

(Stage 0: Make a backup copy of the syntax analyzer code developed in project 10.)

Stage 1: Symbol table: Start by building the compiler's `SymbolTable` module, and use it for extending the syntax analyzer built in Project 10, as follows. Presently, whenever an identifier is encountered in the source code, say `foo`, the syntax analyzer outputs the XML line `<identifier> foo </identifier>`. Instead, extend your syntax analyzer to output the following information about each identifier:

- *name*
- *category* (`field`, `static`, `var`, `arg`, `class`, `subroutine`)
- *index*: if the identifier's category is `field`, `static`, `var`, or `arg`, the running index assigned to the identifier by the symbol table

• *usage*: whether the identifier is presently being *declared* (for example, the identifier appears in a static/field/var Jack variable declaration) or *used* (for example, the identifier appears in a Jack expression)

Have your syntax analyzer output this information as part of its XML output, using markup tags of your choice.

Test your new SymbolTable module and the new functionality just described by running your extended syntax analyzer on the test Jack programs supplied in project 10. If your extended syntax analyzer outputs the information described above correctly it means that you've developed a complete executable capability to understand the semantics of Jack programs. At this stage you can make the switch to developing the full-scale compiler and start generating VM code instead of XML output. This can be done gradually, as we now turn to describe.

(Stage 1.5: Make a backup copy of the extended syntax analyzer code).

Stage 2: Code generation: We provide six application programs, designed to gradually unit-test the code generation capabilities of your Jack compiler. We advise developing, and testing, your evolving compiler on the test programs in the given order. This way, you will be implicitly guided to build the compiler's code generation capabilities in sensible stages, according to the demands presented by each test program.

Normally, when one compiles a high-level program and runs into difficulties, one concludes that the program is screwed up. In this project the setting is exactly the opposite. All the supplied test programs are error-free. Therefore, if their compilation yields any errors, it's the compiler that you have to fix, not the programs. Specifically, for each test program, we recommend going through the following routine:

1. Compile the program folder using the compiler that you are developing. This action should generate one .vm file for each source .jack file in the given folder.

2. Inspect the generated VM files. If there are visible problems, fix your compiler and go to step 1. Remember: All the supplied test programs are error-free.

3. Load the program folder into the VM emulator, and run the loaded code. Note that each one of the six supplied test programs contains specific execution guidelines; test the compiled program (translated VM code) according to these guidelines.

4. If the program behaves unexpectedly, or if an error message is displayed by the VM emulator, fix your compiler and go to step 1.

Test Programs

Seven: Tests how the compiler handles a simple program containing an arithmetic expression with integer constants, a do statement, and a return statement. Specifically, the program computes the expression $1 + (2 * 3)$ and prints its value at the top left of the screen. To test whether your compiler has translated the program correctly, run the translated code in the VM emulator, and verify that it displays 7 correctly.

ConvertToBin: Tests how the compiler handles all the procedural elements of the Jack language: expressions (without arrays or method calls), functions, and the statements `if`, `while`, `do`, `let`, and `return`. The program does not test the handling of methods, constructors, arrays, strings, static variables, and field variables. Specifically, the program gets a 16-bit decimal value from `RAM[8000]`, converts it to binary, and stores the individual bits in `RAM[8001...8016]` (each location will contain 0 or 1). Before the conversion starts, the program initializes `RAM[8001...8016]` to −1. To test whether your compiler has translated the program correctly, load the translated code into the VM emulator, and proceed as follows:

- Put (interactively, using the emulator's GUI) some decimal value in `RAM[8000]`.
- Run the program for a few seconds, then stop its execution.
- Check (by visual inspection) that memory locations `RAM[8001...8016]` contain the correct bits and that none of them contains −1.

Square: Tests how the compiler handles the object-based features of the Jack language: constructors, methods, fields, and expressions that include method calls. Does not test the handling of static variables. Specifically, this multiclass program stages a simple interactive game that enables moving a black square around the screen using the keyboard's four arrow keys.

While moving, the size of the square can be increased and decreased by pressing the z and x keys, respectively. To quit the game, press the q key. To test whether your compiler has translated the program correctly, run the translated code in the VM emulator, and verify that the game works as expected.

Average: Tests how the compiler handles arrays and strings. This is done by computing the average of a user-supplied sequence of integers. To test whether your compiler has translated the program correctly, run the translated code in the VM emulator, and follow the instructions displayed on the screen.

Pong: A complete test of how the compiler handles an object-based application, including the handling of objects and static variables. In the classical Pong game, a ball is moving randomly, bouncing off the edges of the screen. The user tries to hit the ball with a small paddle that can be moved by pressing the keyboard's left and right arrow keys. Each time the paddle hits the ball, the user scores a point and the paddle shrinks a little, making the game increasingly more challenging. If the user misses and the ball hits the bottom the game is over. To test whether your compiler has translated this program correctly, run the translated code in the VM emulator and play the game. Make sure to score some points to test the part of the program that displays the score on the screen.

ComplexArrays: Tests how the compiler handles complex array references and expressions. To that end, the program performs five complex calculations using arrays. For each such calculation, the program prints on the screen the expected result along with the result computed by the compiled program. To test whether your compiler has translated the program correctly, run the translated code in the VM emulator, and make sure that the expected and actual results are identical.

A web-based version of project 11 is available at www.nand2tetris.org.

11.5   Perspective

Jack is a general-purpose, object-based programming language. By design, it was made to be a relatively simple language. This simplicity allowed us to sidestep several thorny compilation issues. For example, while Jack looks like a typed language, that is hardly the case: all of Jack's data types—int, char, and boolean—are 16 bits wide, allowing Jack compilers to ignore almost all type information. In particular, when compiling and evaluating expressions, Jack compilers need not determine their types. The only exception is the compilation of method calls of the form x.m(), which requires determining the class type of x. Another aspect of the Jack type simplicity is that array elements are not typed.

Unlike Jack, most programming languages feature rich type systems, which place additional demands on their compilers: different amounts of memory must be allocated for different types of variables; conversion from one type into another requires implicit and explicit casting operations; the compilation of a simple expression like x+y depends strongly on the types of x and y; and so on.

Another significant simplification is that the Jack language does not support *inheritance*. In languages that support inheritance, the handling of method calls like x.m() depends on the class membership of the object x, which can be determined only during run-time. Therefore, compilers of object-oriented languages that feature inheritance must treat all methods as virtual and resolve their class memberships according to the run-time type of the object on which the method is applied. Since Jack does not support inheritance, all method calls can be compiled statically during compile time.

Another common feature of object-oriented languages not supported by Jack is the distinction between private and public class members. In Jack, all static and field variables are private (recognized only within the class in which they are declared), and all subroutines are public (can be called from any class).

The lack of real typing, inheritance, and public fields allows a truly independent compilation of classes: a Jack class can be compiled without accessing the code of any other class. The fields of other classes are never referred to directly, and all linking to methods of other classes is "late" and done just by name.

Many other simplifications of the Jack language are not significant and can be relaxed with little effort. For example, one can easily extend the language with `for` and `switch` statements. Likewise, one can add the capability to assign character constants like `'c'` to `char` type variables, which is presently not supported by the language.

Finally, our code generation strategies paid no attention to optimization. Consider the high-level statement c++. A naïve compiler will translate it into the series of low-level VM operations `push c`, `push 1`, `add`, `pop c`. Next, the VM translator will translate each one of these VM commands further into several machine-level instructions, resulting in a considerable chunk of code. At the same time, an optimized compiler will notice that we are dealing with a simple increment and translate it into, say, the two machine instructions `@c` followed by `M=M+1`. Of course, this is only one example of the finesse expected from industrial-strength compilers. In general, compiler writers invest much effort and ingenuity to ensure that the generated code is time- and space-efficient.

In Nand to Tetris, efficiency is rarely an issue, with one major exception: the operating system. The Jack OS is based on efficient algorithms and optimized data structures, as we'll elaborate in the next chapter.

12 Operating System

Civilization progresses by extending the number of operations that we can perform without thinking about them.

—Alfred North Whitehead, *Introduction to Mathematics* (1911)

In chapters 1–6 we described and built a general-purpose hardware architecture. In chapters 7–11 we developed a software hierarchy that makes the hardware usable, culminating in the construction of a modern, object-based language. Other high-level programming languages can be specified and implemented on top of the hardware platform, each requiring its own compiler.

The last major piece missing in this puzzle is an *operating system*. The OS is designed to close gaps between the computer's hardware and software, making the computer system more accessible to programmers, compilers, and users. For example, to display the text Hello World on the screen, several hundred pixels must be drawn at specific screen locations. This can be done by consulting the hardware specification and writing code that turns bits on and off in selected RAM locations. Clearly, high-level programmers expect a better interface. They want to write print ("Hello World") and let someone else worry about the details. That's where the operating system enters the picture.

Throughout this chapter, the term *operating system* is used rather loosely. Our OS is minimal, aiming at (i) encapsulating low-level hardware-specific services in high-level programmer-friendly software services and (ii) extending high-level languages with commonly used functions and abstract data types. The dividing line between an *operating system* in this sense and a *standard class library* is not clear. Indeed, modern programming languages pack many standard operating system services like graphics, memory management, multitasking, and numerous other extensions into what is known as the language's *standard class library*. Following this model, the Jack OS is packaged as a collection of supporting classes, each providing a set of related services via Jack subroutine calls. The complete OS API is given in appendix 6.

High-level programmers expect the OS to deliver its services through well-designed interfaces that hide the gory hardware details from their application programs. To do so, the

OS code must operate close to the hardware, manipulating memory, input/output, and processing devices almost directly. Further, because the OS supports the execution of every program that runs on the computer, it must be highly efficient. For example, application programs create and dispose objects and arrays all the time. Therefore, we better do it quickly and economically. Any gain in the time- and space-efficiency of an enabling OS service can impact dramatically the performance of all the application programs that depend on it.

Operating systems are usually written in a high-level language and compiled into binary form. Our OS is no exception—it is written in Jack, just like Unix was written in C. Like the C language, Jack was designed with sufficient "lowness" in it, permitting an intimate closeness to the hardware when needed.

The chapter starts with a relatively long Background section that presents key algorithms normally used is OS implementations. These include mathematical operations, string manipulations, memory management, text and graphics output, and keyboard input. This algorithmic introduction is followed by a Specification section describing the Jack OS, and an Implementation section that offers guidance on how to build the OS using the algorithms presented. As usual, the Project section provides the necessary guidelines and materials for gradually constructing and unit-testing the entire OS.

The chapter embeds key lessons in system-oriented software engineering and in computer science. On the one hand, we describe programming techniques for developing low-level system services, as well as "programming at the large" techniques for integrating and streamlining the OS services. On the other hand, we present a set of elegant and highly efficient algorithms, each being a computer science gem.

12.1   Background

Computers are typically connected to a variety of input/output devices such as a keyboard, screen, mouse, mass storage, network interface card, microphone, speakers, and more. Each of these I/O devices has its own electromechanical idiosyncrasies; thus, reading and writing data on them involves many technical details. High-level languages abstract away these details by offering high-level abstractions like `let n = Keyboard.readInt("Enter a number:")`. Let's delve into what should be done in order to realize this seemingly simple data-entry operation.

First, we engage the user by displaying the prompt `Enter a number:`. This entails creating a `String` object and initializing it to the array of `char` values `'E'`, `'n'`, `'t'`, ..., and so on. Next, we have to render this string on the screen, one character at a time, while updating the *cursor* position for keeping track of where the next character should be physically displayed. After displaying the `Enter a number:` prompt, we have to stage a loop that waits until the user will oblige to press some keys on the keyboard—hopefully keys that represent digits. This requires knowing how to (i) capture a keystroke, (ii) get a single character input, (iii) append these characters to a string, and (iv) convert the string into an integer value.

If what has been elaborated so far sounds arduous, the reader should know that we were actually quite gentle, sweeping many gory details under the rug. For example, what exactly is meant by "creating a string object," "displaying a character on the screen," and "getting a multicharacter input"?

Let's start with "creating a string object." String objects don't pop out of thin air, fully formed. Each time we want to create an object, we must find available space for representing the object in the RAM, mark this space as used, and remember to free it when the object is no longer needed. Proceeding to the "display a character" abstraction, note that characters cannot be displayed. The only things that can be physically displayed are individual pixels. Thus, we have to figure out what is the character's *font*, compute where the bits that represent the font image can be found in the screen memory map, and then turn these bits on and off as needed. Finally, to "get a multicharacter input," we have to enter a loop that not only listens to the keyboard and accumulates characters as they come along but also allows the user to backspace, delete, and retype characters, not to mention the need to echo each of these actions on the screen for visual feedback.

The agent that takes care of this elaborate behind-the-scenes work is the operating system. The execution of the statement `let n = Keyboard.readInt("Enter a number:")` entails many OS function calls, dealing with diverse issues like memory allocation, input driving, output driving, and string processing. Compilers use the OS services abstractly by injecting OS function calls into the compiled code, as we saw in the previous chapter. In this chapter we explore *how these functions are actually realized*. Of course, what we have surveyed so far is just a small subset of the OS responsibilities. For example, we didn't mention mathematical operations, graphical output, and other commonly needed services. The good news is that a well-written OS can integrate these diverse and seemingly unrelated tasks in an elegant and efficient way, using cool algorithms and data structures. That's what this chapter is all about.

12.1.1 Mathematical Operations

The four arithmetic operations *addition*, *subtraction*, *multiplication*, and *division* lie at the core of almost every computer program. If a loop that executes a million times contains expressions that use some of these operations, they'd better be implemented efficiently.

Normally, addition is implemented in hardware, at the ALU level, and subtraction is gained freely, courtesy of the two's complement method. Other arithmetic operations can be handled either by hardware or by software, depending on cost/performance considerations. We now turn to present efficient algorithms for computing multiplication, division, and square roots. These algorithms lend themselves to both software and hardware implementations.

Efficiency First

Mathematical algorithms are made to operate on n-bit values, n typically being 16, 32, or 64 bits, depending on the operands' data types. As a rule, we seek algorithms whose running time is a polynomial function of this word size n. Algorithms whose running time depends on the *values* of n-bit numbers are unacceptable, since these values are exponential in n. For example, suppose we implement the multiplication operation $x \times y$ naïvely, using the repeated addition algorithm `for i = 1 ... y {sum = sum + x}`. If y is 64-bit wide, its value may well be greater than 9,000,000,000,000,000,000, implying that the loop may run for billions of years before terminating.

In sharp contrast, the running times of the multiplication, division, and square root algorithms that we present below depend not to the n-bit *values* on which they are called to operate, which may be as large as 2^n, but rather on n, the number of their bits. When it comes to efficiency of arithmetic operations, that's the best that we can possibly hope for.

We will use the *Big-O* notation, $O(n)$, to describe a running time which is "in the order of magnitude of n." The running time of all the arithmetic algorithms that we present in this chapter is $O(n)$, where n is the bit width of the inputs.

Multiplication

Consider the standard multiplication method taught in elementary school. To compute 356 times 73, we line up the two numbers one on top of the other, right-justified. Next, we multiply 356 by 3. Next, we shift 356 to the left one position, and multiply 3560 by 7 (which is the same as multiplying 356 by 70). Finally, we sum up the columns and obtain the result. This procedure is based on the insight that $356 \times 73 = 356 \times 70 + 356 \times 3$. The binary version of this procedure is illustrated in figure 12.1, using another example.

$x = 27 =$	... 0 0 0 0 **1 1 0 1 1**	
$y = 9 =$	... 0 0 0 0 0 **1 0 0 1**	i-th bit of y
	... 0 0 0 0 **1 1 0 1 1**	1
	... 0 0 0 **1 1 0 1 1** 0	0
	... 0 0 **1 1 0 1 1** 0 0	0
	... 0 **1 1 0 1 1** 0 0 0	1
$x * y = 243 =$	... 0 **1 1 1 1 0 0 1 1**	sum

```
// Returns x * y, where x, y ≥ 0.
multiply(x, y):
  sum = 0
  shiftedx = x
  for i = 0 ... n − 1 do
     if ((i-th bit of y) == 1)
        sum = sum + shiftedx
     shiftedx = 2 * shiftedx
  return sum
```

Figure 12.1 Multiplication algorithm.

Notation note: The algorithms presented in this chapter are written in a self-explanatory pseudocode syntax. We use indentation to mark blocks of code, obviating the need for curly brackets or begin/end keywords. For example, in figure 12.1, *sum = sum + shiftedx* belongs to the single-statement body of the `if` logic, and *shiftedx = 2 * shiftedx* ends the two-statement body of the `for` logic.

Let's inspect the multiplication procedure illustrated at the left of figure 12.1. For each i-th bit of y, we shift x i times to the left (same as multiplying x by 2^i). Next, we look at the i-th bit of y: If it is 1, we add the shifted x to an accumulator; otherwise, we do nothing. The algorithm shown on the right formalizes this procedure. Note that $2 * shiftedx$ can be computed efficiently either by left-shifting the bitwise representation of *shiftedx* or by adding *shiftedx* to itself. Either operation lends itself to primitive hardware operations.

Running time: The multiplication algorithm performs n iterations, where n is the bit width of the y input. In each iteration, the algorithm performs a few addition and comparison operations. It follows that the total running time of the algorithm is $a + b \cdot n$, where a is the time it takes to initialize a few variables, and b is the time it takes to perform a few addition and comparison operations. Formally, the algorithm's running time is $O(n)$, where n is the bit width of the inputs.

To reiterate, the running time of this $x \times y$ algorithm does not depend on the *values* of the x and y inputs; rather, it depends on the *bit width* of the inputs. In computers, the bit width is normally a small fixed constant like 16 (`short`), 32 (`int`), or 64 (`long`), depending on the data types of the inputs. In the Hack platform, the bit width of all data types is 16. If we assume that each iteration of the multiplication algorithm entails about ten Hack machine instructions, it follows that each multiplication operation will require at most 160 clock cycles, irrespective of the size of the inputs. In contrast, algorithms whose running time is proportional not to the bit width but rather to the values of the inputs will require $10 \cdot 2^{16} = 655,360$ clock cycles.

Division

The naïve way to compute the division of two n-bit numbers x/y is to count how many times y can be subtracted from x until the remainder becomes less than y. The running time of this algorithm is proportional to the value of the dividend x and thus is unacceptably exponential in the number of bits n.

To speed things up, we can try to subtract large chunks of y's from x in each iteration. For example, suppose we have to divide 175 by 3. We start by asking: What is the largest number, $x = (90, 80, 70, \ldots, 20, 10)$, so that $3 \cdot x \leq 175$? The answer is 50. In other words, we managed to subtract fifty 3's from 175, shaving fifty iterations from the naïve approach. This accelerated subtraction leaves a remainder of $175 - 3 \cdot 50 = 25$. Moving along, we now ask: What is the largest number, $x = (9, 8, 7, \ldots 2, 1)$, so that $3 \cdot x \leq 25$? The answer is 8, so we managed to make eight additional subtractions of 3, and the answer, so far, is $50 + 8 = 58$. The remainder is $25 - 3 \cdot 8 = 1$, which is less than 3, so we stop the process and announce that $175/3 = 58$ with a remainder of 1.

This technique is the rationale behind the dreaded school procedure known as *long division*. The binary version of this algorithm is identical, except that instead of accelerating the subtraction using powers of 10 we use powers of 2. The algorithm performs n iterations, n being the number of digits in the dividend, and each iteration entails a few multiplication (actually, shifting), comparison, and subtraction operations. Once again, we have an x/y algorithm whose running time does not depend on the values of x and y. Rather, the running time is $O(n)$, where n is the bit width of the inputs.

Writing down this algorithm as we have done for multiplication is an easy exercise. To make things interesting, figure 12.2 presents another division algorithm which is as efficient, but more elegant and easier to implement.

Suppose we have to divide 480 by 17. The algorithm shown in figure 12.2 is based on the insight $480/17 = 2 \cdot (240/17) = 2 \cdot (2 \cdot (120/17)) = 2 \cdot (2 \cdot (2 \cdot (60/17))) = \cdots$, and so on. The depth of this recursion is bounded by the number of times y can be multiplied by 2 before reaching x. This also happens to be, at most, the number of bits required to represent x. Thus, the running time of this algorithm is $O(n)$, where n is the bit width of the inputs.

One snag in this algorithm is that each multiplication operation also requires $O(n)$ operations. However, an inspection of the algorithm's logic reveals that the value of the expression $(2 * q * y)$ can be computed without multiplication. Instead, it can be obtained from its value in the previous recursion level, using addition.

Square Root

Square roots can be computed efficiently in a number of different ways, for example, using the Newton-Raphson method or a Taylor series expansion. For our purpose, though, a simpler algorithm will suffice. The square root function $y = \sqrt{x}$ has two attractive properties. First, it is monotonically increasing. Second, its inverse function, $y = x^2$, is a function

```
// Returns the integer division x / y,
// where x ≥ 0 and y > 0.
divide(x, y):
    if (y > x) return 0
    q = divide (x, 2 * y)
    if ((x − 2 * q * y) < y)
        return 2 * q
    else
        return 2 * q + 1
```

Figure 12.2   Division algorithm.

that we already know how to compute efficiently—multiplication. Taken together, these properties imply that we have all we need to compute square roots efficiently, using a form of *binary search*. Figure 12.3 gives the details.

Since the number of iterations in the binary search that the algorithm performs is bound by $n/2$ where n is the number of bits in x, the algorithm's running time is $O(n)$.

To sum up this section about mathematical operations, we presented algorithms for computing multiplication, division, and square root. The running time of each of the algorithms is $O(n)$, where n is the bit width of the inputs. We also observed that in computers, n is a small constant like 16, 32, or 64. Therefore, every addition, subtraction, multiplication, and division operation can be carried out swiftly, in a predictable time that is unaffected by the magnitude of the inputs.

12.1.2   Strings

In addition to primitive data types, most programming languages feature a *string* type designed to represent sequences of characters like `"Loading game..."` and `"QUIT"`. Typically, the string abstraction is supplied by a `String` class that is part of the standard class library that supports the language. This is also the approach taken by Jack.

All the string constants that appear in Jack programs are implemented as `String` objects. The `String` class, whose API is documented in appendix 6, features various string processing methods like appending a character to the string, deleting the last character, and so on. These services are not difficult to implement, as we'll describe later in the chapter. The more challenging `String` methods are those that convert integer values to strings and strings of digit characters to integer values. We now turn to discuss algorithms that carry out these operations.

String representation of numbers: Computers represent numbers internally using binary codes. Yet humans are used to dealing with numbers that are written in decimal notation. Thus, when humans have to read or input numbers, *and only then*, a conversion to or from

```
// Computes the integer part of y = √x
// Strategy: finds an integer y such that y² ≤ x < (y+1)²  (for 0 ≤ x < 2ⁿ)
// by performing binary search in the range 0 ... 2^(n/2) – 1
sqrt(x):
    y = 0
    for  j = (n/2 – 1) ... 0  do
        if (y+2^j)² ≤ x then y = y+2^j
    return y
```

Figure 12.3   Square root algorithm.

decimal notation must be performed. When such numbers are captured from an input device like a keyboard, or rendered on an output device like a screen, they are cast as strings of characters, each representing one of the digits 0 to 9. The subset of relevant characters is:

Character:	'0'	'1'	'2'	'3'	'4'	'5'	'6'	'7'	'8'	'9'
Character code:	48	49	50	51	52	53	54	55	56	57

(The complete Hack character set is given in appendix 5). We see that digit characters can be easily converted into the integers that they represent, and vice versa. The integer value of character c, where $48 \le c \le 57$, is $c - 48$. Conversely, the character code of the integer x, where $0 \le x \le 9$, is $x + 48$.

Once we know how to handle single-digit characters, we can develop algorithms for converting any integer into a string and any string of digit characters into the corresponding integer. These conversion algorithms can be based on either iterative or recursive logic, so figure 12.4 presents one of each.

It is easy to infer from figure 12.4 that the running times of the int2String and string2Int algorithms are $O(n)$, where n is the number of the digit-characters in the input.

12.1.3   Memory Management

Each time a program creates a new array or a new object, a memory block of a certain size must be allocated for representing the new array or object. And when the array or object is no longer needed, its RAM space may be recycled. These chores are done by two classical OS functions called alloc and deAlloc. These functions are used by compilers when generating low-level code for handling constructors and destructors, as well as by high-level programmers, as needed.

int to string:

```
// Returns the string representation of
// a nonnegative integer.
int2String(val):
    lastDigit = val % 10
    c = character representing lastDigit
    if (val < 10)
        return c (as a string)
    else
        return int2String(val / 10).appendChar(c)
```

string to int:

```
// Returns the integer value of a string
// of digit characters, assuming that str[0]
// represents the most significant digit.
string2Int(str):
    val = 0
    for (i = 0 ... str.length()) do
        d = integer value of str.charAt(i)
        val = val * 10 + d
    return val
```

Figure 12.4   String-integer conversions. (appendChar, length, and charAt are String class methods.)

The memory blocks for representing arrays and objects are carved from, and recycled back into, a designated RAM area called a *heap*. The agent responsible for managing this resource is the operating system. When the OS starts running, it initializes a pointer named `heapBase`, containing the heap's base address in the RAM (in Jack, the heap starts just after the stack's end, with `heapBase=2048`). We'll present two heap management algorithms: basic and improved.

Memory allocation algorithm (basic): The data structure that this algorithm manages is a single pointer, named `free`, which points to the beginning of the heap segment that was not yet allocated. See figure 12.5a for the details.

The basic heap management scheme is clearly wasteful, as it never reclaims any memory space. But, if your application programs use only a few small objects and arrays, and not too many strings, you may get away with it.

Memory allocation algorithm (improved): This algorithm manages a linked list of available memory segments, called `freeList` (see figure 12.5b). Each segment in the list begins with two housekeeping fields: the segment's *length* and a pointer to the *next* segment in the list.

When asked to allocate a memory block of a given size, the algorithm has to search the `freeList` for a suitable segment. There are two heuristics for doing this search. *Best-fit* finds the shortest segment that is long enough for representing the required size, while *first-fit* finds the first segment that is long enough. Once a suitable segment has been found, the required memory block is carved from it (the location just before the beginning of the returned block, `block[-1]`, is reserved to hold its length, to be used during deallocation).

Next, the *length* of this segment is updated in the `freeList`, reflecting the length of the part that remained after the allocation. If no memory was left in the segment, or if the remaining part is practically too small, the entire segment is eliminated from the `freeList`.

When asked to reclaim the memory block of an unused object, the algorithm appends the deallocated block to the end of the `freeList`.

```
init():
    free = heapBase

// Allocates a memory block of size words.
alloc(size):
    block = free
    free = free + size
    return block

// Frees the memory space of the given object.
deAlloc(object):
    do nothing
```

Figure 12.5a   Memory allocation algorithm (basic).

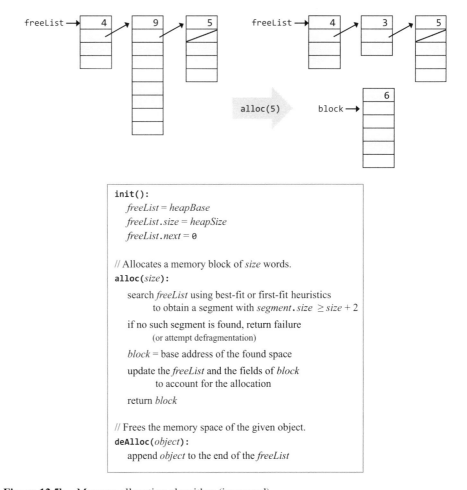

Figure 12.5b   Memory allocation algorithm (improved).

Dynamic memory allocation algorithms like the one shown in figure 12.5b may create block fragmentation problems. Hence, a *defragmentation* operation should be considered, that is, merging memory areas that are physically adjacent in memory but logically split into different segments in the freeList. The defragmentation can be done each time an object is deallocated, when alloc() fails to find a block of the requested size, or according to some other, periodical ad hoc condition.

Peek and poke: We end the discussion of memory management with two simple OS functions that have nothing to do with resource allocation. Memory.peek(*addr*) returns the value of the RAM at address *addr*, and Memory.poke(*addr, value*) sets the word in RAM address *addr* to *value*. These functions play a role in various OS services that manipulate the memory, including graphics routines, as we now turn to discuss.

12.1.4 Graphical Output

Modern computers render graphical output like animation and video on high-resolution color screens, using optimized graphics drivers and dedicated graphical processing units (GPUs). In Nand to Tetris we abstract away most of this complexity, focusing instead on fundamental graphics-drawing algorithms and techniques.

We assume that the computer is connected to a physical black-and-white screen arranged as a grid of rows and columns, and at the intersection of each lies a pixel. By convention, the columns are numbered from left to right and the rows are numbered from top to bottom. Thus pixel (0,0) is located at the screen's top-left corner.

We assume that the screen is connected to the computer system through a *memory map*—a dedicated RAM area in which each pixel is represented by one bit. The screen is refreshed from this memory map many times per second by a process that is external to the computer. Programs that simulate the computer's operations are expected to emulate this refresh process.

The most basic operation that can be performed on the screen is drawing an individual pixel specified by (x,y) coordinates. This is done by turning the corresponding bit in the memory map on or off. Other operations like drawing a line and drawing a circle are built on top of this basic operation. The graphics package maintains a *current color* that can be set to *black* or *white*. All the drawing operations use the current color.

Pixel drawing (`drawPixel`): Drawing a selected pixel in screen location (x,y) is achieved by locating the corresponding bit in the memory map and setting it to the current color. Since the RAM is an *n*-bit device, this operation requires reading and writing an *n*-bit value. See figure 12.6.

The memory map interface of the Hack screen is specified in section 5.2.4. This mapping should be used in order to realize the `drawPixel` algorithm.

```
// Sets pixel (x,y) to the current color.
drawPixel(x,y):
    Using x and y, compute the RAM address where
        the pixel is represented;
    Using Memory.peek, get the 16-bit value of
        this address;
    Using some bitwise operation, set (only) the bit
        that corresponds to the pixel to the current color;
    Using Memory.poke, write the modified 16-bit
        value "back" to the RAM address.
```

Figure 12.6 Drawing a pixel.

Line drawing (`drawLine`): When asked to render a continuous "line" between two "points" on a grid made of discrete pixels, the best that we can possibly do is approximate the line by drawing a series of pixels along the imaginary line connecting the two points. The "pen" that we use for drawing the line can move in four directions only: up, down, left, and right. Thus, the drawn line is bound to be jagged, and the only way to make it look good is to use a high-resolution screen with the tiniest possible pixels. Note, though, that the human eye, being yet another machine, also has a limited image-capturing capacity, determined by the number and type of receptor cells in the retina. Thus, high-resolution screens can fool the human brain to believe that the lines made of pixels are visibly smooth. In fact they are always jagged.

The procedure for drawing a line from $(x1,y1)$ to $(x2,y2)$ starts by drawing the $(x1,y1)$ pixel and then zigzagging in the direction of $(x2,y2)$ until that pixel is reached. See figure 12.7.

The use of two division operations in each loop iteration makes this algorithm neither efficient nor accurate. The first obvious improvement is replacing the $b \, / \, a > dy \, / \, dx$ condition with the equivalent $a \cdot dy < b \cdot dx$, which requires only integer multiplication. Careful inspection of the latter condition reveals that it may be checked without any multiplication.

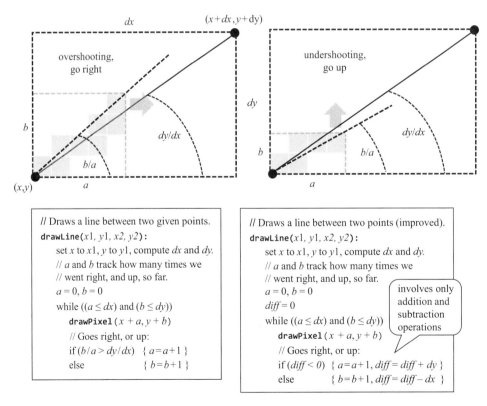

Figure 12.7 Line-drawing algorithm: basic version (bottom, left) and improved version (bottom, right).

As shown in the improved algorithm in figure 12.7, this may be done efficiently by maintaining a variable that updates the value of $(a \cdot dy - b \cdot dx)$ each time a or b is incremented.

The running time of this line-drawing algorithm is $O(n)$, where n is the number of pixels along the drawn line. The algorithm uses only addition and subtraction operations and can be implemented efficiently in either software or hardware.

Circle drawing (`drawCircle`): Figure 12.8 presents an algorithm that uses three routines that we've already implemented: multiplication, square root, and line drawing.

The algorithm is based on drawing a sequence of horizontal lines (like the typical line ab in the figure), one for each row in the range $y - r$ to $y + r$. Since r is specified in pixels, the algorithm ends up drawing a line in every row along the circle's north-south diameter, resulting in a completely filled circle. A simple tweak can cause this algorithm to draw only the circle's outline, if so desired.

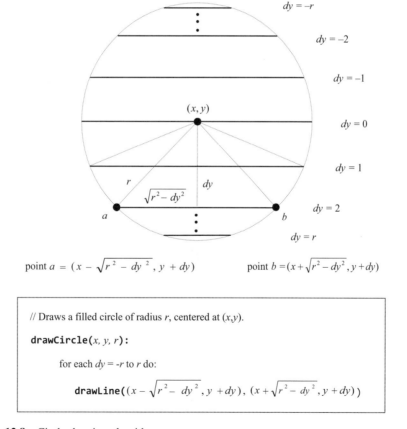

point $a = (x - \sqrt{r^2 - dy^2}, y + dy)$ point $b = (x + \sqrt{r^2 - dy^2}, y + dy)$

```
// Draws a filled circle of radius r, centered at (x,y).

drawCircle(x, y, r):

    for each dy = -r to r do:

        drawLine((x - √(r² - dy²), y + dy), (x + √(r² - dy²), y + dy))
```

Figure 12.8   Circle-drawing algorithm.

12.1.5   Character Output

To develop a capability for displaying characters, we first turn our physical, pixel-oriented screen into a logical, character-oriented screen suitable for rendering fixed, bitmapped images that represent characters. For example, consider a physical screen that features 256 rows of 512 pixels each. If we allocate a grid of 11 rows by 8 columns for drawing a single character, then our screen can display 23 lines of 64 characters each, with 3 extra rows of pixels left unused.

Fonts: The character sets that computers use are divided into *printable* and *non-printable* subsets. For each printable character in the Hack character set (see appendix 5), an 11-row-by-8-column bitmap image was designed, to the best of our limited artistic abilities. Taken together, these images are called a *font*. Figure 12.9 shows how our font renders the uppercase letter N. To handle character spacing, each character image includes at least a 1-pixel space before the next character in the row and at least a 1-pixel space between adjacent rows (the exact spacing varies with the size and squiggles of individual characters). The Hack font consists of ninety-five such bitmap images, one for each printable character in the Hack character set.

Font design is an ancient yet vibrant art. The oldest fonts are as old as the art of writing, and new ones are routinely introduced by type designers who wish to make an artistic statement or solve a technical or functional objective. In our case, the small physical screen, on the one hand, and the wish to display a reasonable number of characters in each row, on the

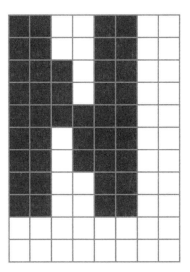

Figure 12.9   Example of a character bitmap.

other, led to the pragmatic choice of a frugal image area of 11×8 pixels. This economy forced us to design a crude font, which nonetheless serves its purpose well.

Cursor: Characters are usually displayed one after the other, from left to right, until the end of the line is reached. For example, consider a program in which the statement `print("a")` is followed (perhaps not immediately) by the statement `print ("b")`. This implies that the program wants to display `ab` on the screen. To effect this continuity, the character-writing package maintains a global *cursor* that keeps track of the screen location where the next character should be drawn. The cursor information consists of column and row counts, say, `cursor.col` and `cursor.row`. After a character has been displayed, we do `cursor.col++`. At the end of the row we do `cursor.row++` and `cursor.col = 0`. When the bottom of the screen is reached, there is a question of what to do next. Two possible actions are effecting a scrolling operation or clearing the screen and starting over by setting the cursor to `(0,0)`.

To recap, we described a scheme for writing individual characters on the screen. Writing other types of data follows naturally from this basic capability: strings are written character by character, and numbers are first converted to strings and then written as strings.

12.1.6   Keyboard Input

Capturing inputs that come from the keyboard is more intricate than meets the eye. For example, consider the statement `let name = Keyboard.readLine("enter your name:")`. By definition, the execution of the `readLine` function depends on the dexterity and collaboration of an unpredictable entity: a human user. The function will not terminate until the user has pressed some keys on the keyboard, ending with an `ENTER`. The problem is that humans press and release keyboard keys for variable and unpredictable durations of time, and often take a coffee break in the middle. Also, humans are fond of backspacing, deleting, and retyping characters. The implementation of the `readLine` function must handle all these irregularities.

This section describes how keyboard input is managed, in three levels of abstraction: (i) detecting which key is currently pressed on the keyboard, (ii) capturing a single-character input, and (iii) capturing a multicharacter input.

Detecting keyboard input (`keyPressed`): Detecting which key is presently pressed is a hardware-specific operation that depends on the keyboard interface. In the Hack computer, the keyboard continuously refreshes a 16-bit memory register whose address is kept in a pointer named `KBD`. The interaction contract is as follows: If a key is currently pressed on the keyboard, that address contains the key's character code (the Hack character set is given in appendix 5); otherwise, it contains 0. This contract is used for implementing the key-Pressed function shown in figure 12.10.

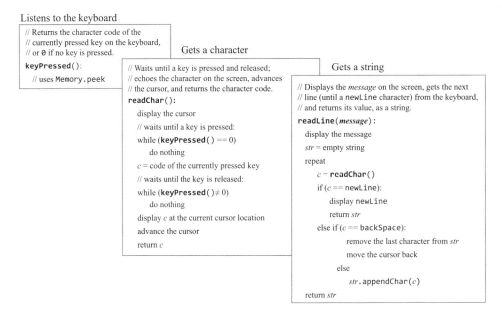

Listens to the keyboard

```
// Returns the character code of the
// currently pressed key on the keyboard,
// or 0 if no key is pressed.
keyPressed():
    // uses Memory.peek
```

Gets a character

```
// Waits until a key is pressed and released;
// echoes the character on the screen, advances
// the cursor, and returns the character code.
readChar():
    display the cursor
    // waits until a key is pressed:
    while (keyPressed() == 0)
        do nothing
    c = code of the currently pressed key
    // waits until the key is released:
    while (keyPressed() ≠ 0)
        do nothing
    display c at the current cursor location
    advance the cursor
    return c
```

Gets a string

```
// Displays the message on the screen, gets the next
// line (until a newLine character) from the keyboard,
// and returns its value, as a string.
readLine(message):
    display the message
    str = empty string
    repeat
        c = readChar()
        if (c == newLine):
            display newLine
            return str
        else if (c == backSpace):
            remove the last character from str
            move the cursor back
        else
            str.appendChar(c)
    return str
```

Figure 12.10 Handling input from the keyboard.

Reading a single character (readChar): The elapsed time between the *key pressed* and the subsequent *key released* events is unpredictable. Hence, we have to write code that neutralizes this uncertainty. Also, when users press keys on the keyboard, we want to give feedback as to which keys have been pressed (something that you have probably grown to take for granted). Typically, we want to display some graphical cursor at the screen location where the next input goes, and, after some key has been pressed, we want to echo the inputted character by displaying its bitmap on the screen at the cursor location. All these actions are implemented by the readChar function.

Reading a string (readLine): A multicharacter input typed by the user is considered final after the ENTER key has been pressed, yielding the newLine character. Until the ENTER key is pressed, the user should be allowed to backspace, delete, and retype previously typed characters. All these actions are accommodated by the readLine function.

As usual, our input-handling solutions are based on a cascading series of abstractions: The high-level program relies on the readLine abstraction, which relies on the readChar abstraction, which relies on the keyPressed abstraction, which relies on the Memory.peek abstraction, which relies on the hardware.

12.2 The Jack OS Specification

The previous section presented algorithms that address various classical operating system tasks. In this section we turn to formally specify one particular operating system—the Jack OS. The Jack operating system is organized in eight classes:

- Math: provides mathematical operations
- String: implements the String type
- Array: implements the Array type
- Memory: handles memory operations
- Screen: handles graphics output to the screen
- Output: handles character output to the screen
- Keyboard: handles input from the keyboard
- Sys: provides execution-related services

The complete OS API is given in appendix 6. This API can be viewed as the OS specification. The next section describes how this API can be implemented using the algorithms presented in the previous section.

12.3 Implementation

Each OS class is a collection of subroutines (constructors, functions, and methods). Most of the OS subroutines are simple to implement and are not discussed here. The remaining OS subroutines are based on the algorithms presented in section 12.2. The implementation of these subroutines can benefit from some tips and guidelines, which we now turn to present.

Init functions: Some OS classes use data structures that support the implementation of some of their subroutines. For each such *OSClass*, these data structures can be declared statically at the class level and initialized by a fucntion which, by convention, we call *OSClass*.init. The init functions are for internal purposes and are not documented in the OS API.

Math

multiply: In each iteration i of the *multiplication* algorithm (see figure 12.1), the i-th bit of the second multiplicand is extracted. We suggest encapsulating this operation in a helper function bit (x,i) that returns true if the i-th bit of the integer x is 1, and false otherwise. The bit(x,i) function can be easily implemented using shifting operations. Alas,

Jack does not support shifting. Instead, it may be convenient to define a fixed static array of length 16, say `twoToThe`, and set each element i to 2 raised to the power of i. The array can then be used to support the implementation of `bit (x,i)`. The `twoToThe` array can be built by the `Math.init` function.

divide: The *multiplication* and *division* algorithms presented in figures 12.1 and 12.2 are designed to operate on nonnegative integers. Signed numbers can be handled by applying the algorithms to absolute values and setting the sign of the return values appropriately. For the multiplication algorithm, this is not needed: since the multiplicands are given in two's complement, their product will be correct with no further ado.

In the *division* algorithm, y is multiplied by a factor of 2, until $y > x$. Thus y can overflow. The overflow can be detected by checking when y becomes negative.

sqrt: In the *square root* algorithm (figure 12.3), the calculation of $(y + 2^j)^2$ can overflow, resulting in an abnormally negative result. This problem can be addressed by changing efficiently the algorithm's if logic to: if $(y + 2^j)^2 \leq x$ and $(y + 2^j)^2 > 0$ then $y = y + 2^j$.

String

All the string constants that appear in a Jack program are realized as objects of the `String` class, whose API is documented in appendix 6. Specifically, each string is implemented as an object consisting of an array of `char` values, a `maxLength` property that holds the maximum length of the string, and a `length` property that holds the actual length of the string.

For example, consider the statement `let str="scooby"`. When the compiler handles this statement, it calls the `String` constructor, which creates a `char` array with `maxLength=6` and `Length=6`. If we later call the `String` method `str.eraseLastChar()`, the `length` of the array will become 5, and the string will effectively become `"scoob"`. In general, then, array elements beyond `length` are not considered part of the string.

What should happen when an attempt is made to add a character to a string whose `length` equals `maxLength`? This issue is not defined by the OS specification: the `String` class may act gracefully and resize the array—or not; this is left to the discretion of individual OS implementations.

intValue, setInt: These subroutines can be implemented using the algorithms presented in figure 12.4. Note that neither algorithm handles negative numbers—a detail that must be handled by the implementation.

newLine, backSpace, doubleQuote: As seen in appendix 5, the codes of these characters are 128, 129, and 34.

The remaining `String` methods can be implemented straightforwardly by operating on the `char` array and on the `length` field that characterizes each `String` object.

Array

new: In spite of its name, this subroutine is not a constructor but rather a function. Therefore, the implementation of this function must allocate memory space for the new array by explicitly calling the OS function `Memory.alloc`.

dispose: This void method is called by statements like do `arr.dispose()`. The `dispose` implementation deallocates the array by calling the OS function `Memory.deAlloc`.

Memory

peek, poke: These functions provide direct access to the host memory. How can this low-level access be accomplished using the Jack high-level language? As it turns out, the Jack language includes a trapdoor that enables gaining complete control of the host computer's memory. This trapdoor can be exploited for implementing `Memory.peek` and `Memory.poke` using plain Jack programming.

The trick is based on an anomalous use of a reference variable (pointer). Jack is a weakly typed language; among other quirks, it does not prevent the programmer from assigning a constant to a reference variable. This constant can then be treated as an absolute memory address. When the reference variable happens to be an array, this scheme provides indexed access to every word in the host RAM. See figure 12.11.

Following the first two lines of code, the base of the `memory` array points to the first address in the computer's RAM (address 0). To get or set the value of the RAM location whose physical address is i, all we have to do is manipulate the array element `memory[i]`. This will cause the compiler to manipulate the RAM location whose address is $0 + i$, which is what we want.

Jack arrays are not allocated space on the heap at compile-time but rather at run-time, if and when the array's new function is called. Note that if new were a constructor and not a function, the compiler and the OS would have allocated the new array to some obscure address in the

```
// Creates a Jack-level "proxy" of the RAM:
var Array memory;
let memory = 0;   // No problem . . .
...
// Gets the value of the RAM at address i:
let x = memory[i];
...
// Sets the value of the RAM at address i:
let memory[i] = 17;
...
```

Figure 12.11 A trapdoor enabling complete control of the host RAM from Jack.

RAM that we cannot control. Like many classical hacks, this trick works because we use the array variable without initializing it properly, as is normally done when using arrays.

The memory array can be declared at the class level and initialized by the Memory.init function. Once this hack is done, the implementation of Memory.peek and Memory.poke becomes trivial.

alloc, deAlloc: These functions can be implemented by either one of the algorithms shown in figures 12.5a and 12.5b. Either *best-fit* or *first-fit* can be used for implementing Memory.deAlloc.

The standard VM mapping on the Hack platform (see section 7.4.1) specifies that the *stack* be mapped on RAM addresses 256 to 2047. Thus the *heap* can start at address 2048.

In order to realize the freeList linked list, the Memory class can declare and maintain a static variable, freeList, as seen in figure 12.12. Although freeList is initialized to the value of heapBase (2048), it is possible that following several alloc and deAlloc operations freeList will become some other address in memory, as illustrated in the figure.

For efficiency's sake, it is recommended to write Jack code that manages the freeList linked list directly in the RAM, as seen in figure 12.12. The linked list can be initialized by the Memory.init function.

Screen

The Screen class maintains a *current color* that is used by all the drawing functions of the class. The current color can be represented by a static Boolean variable.

drawPixel: Drawing a pixel on the screen can be done using Memory.peek and Memory.poke. The screen memory map of the Hack platform specifies that the pixel at column *col* and row *row* ($0 \le col \le 511, 0 \le row \le 255$) is mapped to the $col \% 16$ bit of memory location $16384 + row \cdot 32 + col/16$. Drawing a single pixel requires changing a single bit in the accessed word (and that bit only).

drawLine: The basic algorithm in figure 12.7 can potentially lead to overflow. However, the algorithm's improved version eliminates the problem.

Some aspects of the algorithm should be generalized for drawing lines that extend to four possible directions. Be reminded that the screen origin (coordinates (0,0)) is at the top-left corner. Therefore, some of the directions and plus/minus operations specified in the algorithm should be modified by your drawLine implementation.

The special yet frequent cases of drawing straight lines, that is, when $dx = 0$ or $dy = 0$, should not be handled by this algorithm. Rather, they should benefit from a separate and optimized implementation.

drawCircle: The algorithm shown in figure 12.8 can potentially lead to overflow. Limiting circle radii to be at most 181 is a reasonable solution.

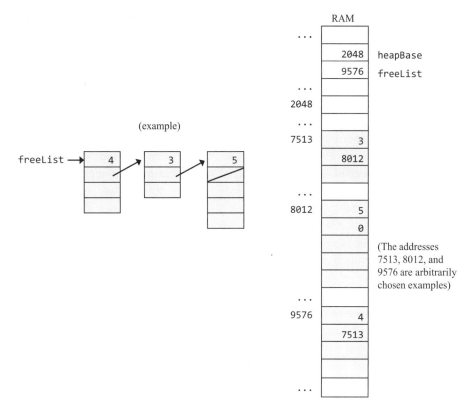

Figure 12.12 Logical view (left) and physical implementation (right) of a linked list that supports dynamic memory allocation.

Output

The Output class is a library of functions for displaying characters. The class assumes a character-oriented screen consisting of 23 rows (indexed $0 \ldots 22$, top to bottom) of 64 characters each (indexed $0 \ldots 63$, left to right). The top-left character location on the screen is indexed (0,0). A visible cursor, implemented as a small filled square, indicates where the next character will be displayed. Each character is displayed by rendering on the screen a rectangular image, 11 pixels high and 8 pixels wide (which includes margins for character spacing and line spacing). The collection of all the character images is called a *font*.

Font implementation: The design and implementation of a font for the Hack character set (appendix 5) is a drudgery, combining artistic judgment and rote implementation work. The resulting font is a collection of ninety-five rectangular bitmap images, each representing a printable character.

Fonts are normally stored in external files that are loaded and used by the character-drawing package, as needed. In Nand to Tetris, the font is embedded in the OS Output class. For each printable character, we define an array that holds the character's bitmap. The array consists of 11 elements, each corresponding to a row of 8 pixels. Specifically, we set the value of each array entry *j* to an integer value whose binary representation (bits) codes the 8 pixels appearing in the *j*-th row of the character's bitmap. We also define a static array of size 127, whose index values 32...126 correspond to the codes of the printable characters in the Hack character set (entries 0...31 are not used). We then set each array entry *i* of that array to the 11-entry array that represents the bitmap image of the character whose character code is *i* (did we mention drudgery?).

The project 12 materials include a skeletal Output class containing Jack code that carries out all the implementation work described above. The given code implements the ninety-five-character font, except for one character, whose design and implementation is left as an exercise. This code can be activated by the Output.init function, which can also initialize the cursor.

printChar: Displays the character at the cursor location and advances the cursor one column forward. To display a character at location (*row,col*), where $0 \leq row \leq 22$ and $0 \leq col \leq 63$, we write the character's bitmap onto the box of pixels ranging from $11 \cdot row$ to $11 \cdot row + 10$ and from $8 \cdot col$ to $8 \cdot col + 7$.

printString: Can be implemented using a sequence of printChar calls.

printInt: Can be implemented by converting the integer to a string and then printing the string.

Keyboard

The Hack computer memory organization (see section 5.2.6) specifies that the *keyboard memory map* is a single 16-bit memory register located at address 24576.

keyPressed: Can be implemented easily using Memory.peek().

readChar, readString: Can be implemented by following the algorithms in figure 12.10.

readInt: Can be implemented by reading a string and converting it into an int value using a String method.

Sys

wait: This function is supposed to wait a given number of milliseconds and return. It can be implemented by writing a loop that runs approximately duration milliseconds before terminating. You will have to time your specific computer to obtain a one millisecond wait, as this constant varies from one CPU to another. As a result, your `Sys.wait()` function will not be portable. The function can be made portable by running yet another configuration function that sets various constants reflecting the hardware specifications of the host platform, but for Nand to Tetris this is not needed.

halt: Can be implemented by entering an infinite loop.

init: According to the Jack language specification (see section 9.2.2), a Jack program is a set of one or more classes. One class must be named `Main`, and this class must include a function named `main`. To start running a program, the `Main.main` function should be called.

The operating system is also a collection of compiled Jack classes. When the computer boots up, we want to start running the operating system and have *it* start running the main program. This chain of command is implemented as follows. According to the Standard VM Mapping on the Hack Platform (section 8.5.2), the VM translator writes bootstrap code (in machine language) that calls the OS function `Sys.init`. This bootstrap code is stored in the ROM, starting at address 0. When we reset the computer, the program counter is set to 0, the bootstrap code starts running, and the `Sys.init` function is called.

With that in mind, `Sys.init` should do two things: call all the `init` functions of the other OS classes, and then call `Main.main`.

From this point onward the user is at the mercy of the application program, and the Nand to Tetris journey has come to an end. We hope that you enjoyed the ride!

12.4   Project

Objective: Implement the operating system described in the chapter.

Contract: Implement the operating system in Jack, and test it using the programs and testing scenarios described below. Each test program uses a subset of OS services. Each of the OS classes can be implemented and unit-tested in isolation, in any order.

Resources: The main required tool is Jack—the language in which you will develop the OS. You will also need the supplied Jack compiler for compiling your OS implementation, as well as the supplied test programs, also written in Jack. Finally, you'll need the supplied VM emulator, which is the platform on which the tests will be executed.

Your `projects/12` folder includes eight skeletal OS class files named `Math.jack`, `String.jack`, `Array.jack`, `Memory.jack`, `Screen.jack`, `Output.jack`, `Keyboard.jack`, and `Sys.jack`. Each file contains the signatures of all the class subroutines. Your task is completing the missing implementations.

The VM emulator: Operating system developers often face the following chicken-and-egg dilemma: How can we possibly test an OS class in isolation, if the class uses the services of other OS classes not yet developed? As it turns out, the VM emulator is perfectly positioned to support unit-testing the OS, one class at a time.

Specifically, the VM emulator features an executable version of the OS, written in Java. When a VM command `call foo` is found in the loaded VM code, the emulator proceeds as follows. If a VM function named `foo` exists in the loaded code base, the emulator executes its VM code. Otherwise, the emulator checks whether `foo` is one of the built-on OS functions. If so, it executes `foo`'s built-in implementation. This convention is ideally suited for supporting the testing strategy that we now turn to describe.

Testing Plan

Your `projects/12` folder includes eight test folders, named `MathTest`, `Memory-Test`, ..., for testing each one the eight OS classes `Math`, `Memory`, ... Each folder contains a Jack program, designed to test (by using) the services of the corresponding OS class. Some folders contain test scripts and compare files, and some contain only a `.jack` file or files. To test your implementation of the OS class *Xxx*`.jack`, you may proceed as follows:

- Inspect the supplied *Xxx*`Test/*.jack` code of the test program. Understand which OS services are tested and how they are tested.
- Put the OS class *Xxx*`.jack` that you developed in the *Xxx*`Test` folder.
- Compile the folder using the supplied Jack compiler. This will result in translating both your OS class file and the `.jack` file or files of the test program into corresponding `.vm` files, stored in the same folder.
- If the folder includes a `.tst` test script, load the script into the VM emulator; otherwise, load the folder into the VM emulator.
- Follow the specific testing guidelines given below for each OS class.

Memory, Array, Math: The three folders that test these classes include test scripts and compare files. Each test script begins with the command `load`. This command loads all the `.vm` files in the current folder into the VM emulator. The next two commands in each test script create an output file and load the supplied compare file. Next, the test script proceeds to execute several tests, comparing the test results to those listed in the compare file. Your job is making sure that these comparisons end successfully.

Note that the supplied test programs don't comprise a full test of `Memory.alloc` and `Memory.deAlloc`. A complete test of these memory management functions requires inspecting internal implementation details not visible in user-level testing. If you want to do so, you can test these functions by using step-by-step debugging and by inspecting the state of the host RAM.

String: Execution of the supplied test program should yield the following output:

```
new,appendChar: abcde
setInt: 12345
setInt: -32767
length: 5
charAt[2]: 99
setCharAt(2,'-'): ab-de
eraseLastChar: ab-d
intValue: 456
intValue: -32123
backSpace: 129
doubleQuote: 34
newLine: 128
```

Output: Execution of the supplied test program should yield the following output:

```
A                                                                              B
0123456789
ABCDEFGHIJKLMNOPQRSTUVWXYZ abcdefghijklmnopqrstuvwxyz
!#$%&'()*+,-./:;<=>?@[]^_`{|}~"
-12346789



C                                                                              D
```

Screen: Execution of the supplied test program should yield the following output:

Keyboard: This OS class is tested by a test program that effects user-program interaction. For each function in the Keyboard class (keyPressed, readChar, readLine, readInt) the program prompts the user to press some keys. If the OS function is implemented correctly and the requested keys are pressed, the program prints ok and proceeds to test the next OS function. Otherwise, the program repeats the request. If all requests end successfully, the program prints Test ended successfully. At this point the screen should show the following output:

```
keyPressed test:
Please press the 'Page Down' key
ok
readChar test:
(Verify that the pressed character is echoed to the screen)
Please press the number '3': 3
ok
readLine test:
(Verify echo and usage of 'backspace')
Please type 'JACK' and press enter: JACK
ok
readInt test:
(Verify echo and usage of 'backspace')
Please type '-32123' and press enter: -32123
ok

Test completed successfully
```

Sys

The supplied .jack file tests the Sys.wait function. The program requests the user to press a key (any key) and waits two seconds, using a call to Sys.wait. It then prints a message on the screen. Make sure that the time that elapses between your release of the key and the appearance of the printed message is about two seconds.

The Sys.init function is not tested explicitly. However, recall that it performs all the necessary OS initializations and then calls the Main.main function of each test program. Therefore, we can assume that nothing will work properly unless Sys.init is implemented correctly.

Complete Test

After testing successfully each OS class in isolation, test your entire OS implementation using the Pong game introduced earlier in the book. The source code of Pong is available in projects/11/Pong. Put your eight OS .jack files in the Pong folder, and compile the folder using the supplied Jack compiler. Next, load the Pong folder into the VM emulator, execute the game, and ensure that it works as expected.

12.5   Perspective

This chapter presented a subset of basic services that can be found in most operating systems. For example, managing memory, driving I/O devices, supplying mathematical operations not implemented in hardware, and implementing abstract data types like the string abstraction. We have chosen to call this standard software library an *operating system* to reflect its two main functions: encapsulating the gory hardware details, omissions, and idiosyncrasies in transparent software services, and enabling compilers and application programs to use these services via clean interfaces. However, the gap between what we have called an OS and industrial-strength operating systems remains wide.

For starters, our OS lacks some of the basic services most closely associated with operating systems. For example, our OS supports neither multi-threading nor multiprocessing; in contrast, the kernel of most operating systems is devoted to exactly that. Our OS supports no mass storage devices; in contrast, the main data store handled by operating systems is a file system abstraction. Our OS features neither a command-line interface (as in a Unix shell) nor a graphical interface consisting of windows and menus. In contrast, this is the operating system interface that users expect to see and interact with. Numerous other services commonly found in operating systems are not present in our OS, like security, communication, and more.

Another notable difference lies in the liberal way in which our OS operations are invoked. Some OS operations, for example, peek and poke, give the programmer complete access to the host computer resources. Clearly, inadvertent or malicious use of such functions can cause havoc. Therefore, many OS services are considered privileged, and accessing them requires a security mechanism that is more elaborate than a simple function call. In contrast, in the Hack platform, there is no difference between OS code and user code, and operating system services run in the same user mode as that of application programs.

In terms of efficiency, the algorithms that we presented for multiplication and division were standard. These algorithms, or variants thereof, are typically implemented in hardware rather than in software. The running time of these algorithms is $O(n)$ addition operations. Since adding two n-bit numbers requires $O(n)$ bit operations (gates in hardware), these algorithms end up requiring $O(n^2)$ bit operations. There exist multiplication and division algorithms whose running time is asymptotically significantly faster than $O(n^2)$, and for a large number of bits these algorithms are more efficient. In a similar fashion, optimized versions of the geometric operations that we presented, like line drawing and circle drawing, are often implemented in special graphics-acceleration hardware.

Like every hardware and software system developed in Nand to Tetris, our goal is not to provide a complete solution that addresses all wants and needs. Rather, we strive to build a working implementation and a solid understanding of the system's *foundation*, and then propose ways to extend it further. Some of these optional extension projects are mentioned in the next and final chapter in the book.

13   More Fun to Go

We shall not cease from exploration, and at the end we will arrive where we started, and know the place for the first time.

—T. S. Eliot (1888–1965)

Congratulations! We've finished the construction of a complete computing system, starting from first principles. We hope that you enjoyed this journey. Let us, the authors of this book, share a secret with you: We suspect that we enjoyed writing the book even more. After all, we got to design this computing system, and design is often the "funnest" part of every project. We are sure that some of you, adventurous learners, would like to get in on that design action. Maybe you would like to improve the architecture; maybe you have ideas for adding new features here and there; maybe you envision a wider system. And then, maybe, you want to be in the navigator's seat and decide where to go, not just how to get there.

Almost every aspect of the Jack/Hack system can be improved, optimized, or extended. For example, the assembly language, the Jack language, and the operating system can be modified and extended by rewriting portions of your respective assembler, compiler, and OS implementations. Other changes would likely require modifying the supplied software tools as well. For example, if you change the hardware specification or the VM specification, then you would likely want to modify the respective emulators. Or, if you want to add more input or output devices to the Hack computer, you would probably need to model them by writing new built-in chips.

In order to allow complete flexibility of modification and extension, we made the source code of all the supplied tools publicly available. All our code is 100 percent Java, except for some of the batch files used for starting the software on some platforms. The software and its documentation are available at www.nand2tetris.org. You are welcome to modify and extend all our tools as you deem desirable for your latest idea—and then share them with others, if you want. We hope that our code is written and documented well enough to make modifications a satisfying experience. In particular, we wish to mention that the supplied hardware simulator has a simple and well-documented interface for adding new built-in chips. This interface can be used for extending the simulated hardware platform with, say, mass storage or communications devices.

While we cannot even start to imagine what your design improvements may be, we can briefly sketch some of the ones we were thinking of.

Hardware Realizations

The hardware modules presented in the book were implemented either in HDL or as supplied executable software modules. This, in fact, is how hardware is actually designed. However, at some point, the HDL designs are typically committed to silicon, becoming "real" computers. Wouldn't it be nice to make Hack or Jack run on a real hardware platform made of atoms rather than bits?

Several different approaches may be taken toward this goal. On one extreme, you can attempt to implement the Hack platform on an FPGA board. This would require rewriting all the chip definitions using a mainstream Hardware Description Language and then dealing with implementation issues related to realizing the RAM, the ROM, and the I/O devices on the host board. One such step-by-step optional project, developed by Michael Schröder, is referred to in the www.nand2tetris.org website. Another extreme approach may be to attempt emulating Hack, the VM, or even the Jack platform on an existing hardware device like a cell phone. It seems that any such project would want to reduce the size of the Hack screen to keep the cost of the hardware resources reasonable.

Hardware Improvements

Although Hack is a *stored program* computer, the program that it runs must be prestored in its ROM device. In the present Hack architecture, there is no way of loading another program into the computer, except for simulating the replacement of the entire physical ROM chip.

Adding a *load program* capability in a balanced way would likely involve changes at several levels of the hierarchy. The Hack hardware should be modified to allow loaded programs to reside in the writable RAM rather than in the existing ROM. Some type of permanent storage, like a built-in mass storage chip, should probably be added to the hardware to allow storage of programs. The operating system should be extended to handle this permanent storage device, as well as new logic for loading and running programs. At this point an OS user interface *shell* would come in handy, providing file and program management commands.

High-Level Languages

Like all professionals, programmers have strong feelings about their tools—programming languages—and like to personalize them. And indeed, the Jack language, which leaves much to be desired, can be significantly improved. Some changes are simple, some are more involved, and some—like adding inheritance—would likely require modifying the VM specification as well.

Another option is realizing more high-level languages over the Hack platform. For example, how about implementing Scheme?

Optimization

Our Nand to Tetris journey has almost completely sidestepped optimization issues (except for the operating system, which introduced some efficiency measures). Optimization is a great playfield for hackers. You can start with local optimizations in the hardware, or in the compiler, but the best bang for the buck will come from optimizing the VM translator. For example, you may want to reduce the size of the generated assembly code, and make it more efficient. Ambitious optimizations on a more global scale will involve changing the specifications of the machine language or the VM language.

Communications

Wouldn't it be nice to connect the Hack computer to the Internet? This could be done by adding a built-in communication chip to the hardware and writing an OS class for dealing with it and for handling higher-level communication protocols. Some other programs would need to talk with the built-in communication chip, providing an interface to the Internet. For example, an HTTP-speaking web browser in Jack seems like a feasible and worthy project.

These are some of our design itches—what are yours?

Appendix 1: Boolean Function Synthesis

By logic we prove, by intuition we discover.

—Henri Poincaré (1854–1912)

In chapter 1 we made the following claims, without proof:

· Given a truth table representation of a Boolean function, we can synthesize from it a Boolean expression that realizes the function.

· Any Boolean function can be expressed using only And, Or, and Not operators.

· Any Boolean function can be expressed using only Nand operators.

This appendix provides proofs for these claims, and shows that they are interrelated. In addition, the appendix illustrates the process by which Boolean expressions can be simplified using Boolean algebra.

A1.1   Boolean Algebra

The Boolean operators And, Or, and Not have useful algebraic properties. We present some of these properties briefly, noting that their proofs can be easily derived from the relevant truth tables listed in figure 1.1 of chapter 1.

Commutative laws:	x And $y = y$ And x
	x Or $y = y$ Or x
Associative laws:	x And (y And z) = (x And y) And z
	x Or (y Or z) = (x Or y) Or z
Distributive laws:	x And (y Or z) = (x And y) Or (x And z)
	x Or (y And z) = (x Or y) And (x Or z)
De Morgan laws:	Not(x And y) = Not(x) Or Not(y)
	Not(x Or y) = Not(x) And Not(y)
Idempotent laws:	x And $x = x$
	x Or $x = x$

These algebraic laws can be used to simplify Boolean functions. For example, consider the function Not (Not (x) And Not (x Or y)). Can we reduce it to a simpler form? Let's try and see what we can come up with:

Not(Not(x) And Not(x Or y)) =	// by De Morgan law:
Not(Not(x) And (Not(x) And Not(y))) =	// by the associative law:
Not((Not(x) And Not(x)) And Not(y)) =	// by the idempotent law:
Not(Not(x) And Not(y)) =	// by De Morgan law:
Not(Not(x)) Or Not(Not(y)) =	// by double negation:
x Or y	

Boolean simplifications like the one just illustrated have significant practical implications. For example, the original Boolean expression Not (Not (x) And Not (x Or y)) can be implemented in hardware using five logic gates, whereas the simplified expression x Or y can be implemented using a single logic gate. Both expressions deliver the same functionality, but the latter is five times more efficient in terms of cost, energy, and speed of computation.

Reducing a Boolean expression into a simpler one is an art requiring experience and insight. Various reduction tools and techniques are available, but the problem remains challenging. In general, reducing a Boolean expression into its simplest form is an *NP-hard* problem.

A1.2   Synthesizing Boolean Functions

Given a truth table of a Boolean function, how can we construct, or synthesize, a Boolean expression that represents this function? And, come to think of it, are we *guaranteed* that every Boolean function represented by a truth table can also be represented by a Boolean expression?

These questions have very satisfying answers. First, yes: every Boolean function can be represented by a Boolean expression. Moreover, there is a constructive algorithm for doing just that. To illustrate, refer to figure A1.1, and focus on its leftmost four columns. These columns specify a truth table definition of some three-variable function $f(x,y,z)$. Our goal is to synthesize from these data a Boolean expression that represents this function.

We'll describe the synthesis algorithm by following its steps in this particular example. We start by focusing only on the truth table's rows in which the function's value is 1. In the function shown in figure A1.1, this happens in rows 3, 5, and 7. For each such row i, we define a Boolean function f_i that returns 0 for all the variable values except for the variable values in row i, for which the function returns 1. The truth table in figure A1.1 yields three such functions, whose truth table definitions are listed in the three rightmost columns in the table. Each of these functions f_i can be represented by a conjunction (And-

x	y	z	$f(x,y,z)$	$f_3(x,y,z)$	$f_5(x,y,z)$	$f_7(x,y,z)$
0	0	0	0	0	0	0
0	0	1	0	0	0	0
0	1	0	1	1	0	0
0	1	1	0	0	0	0
1	0	0	1	0	1	0
1	0	1	0	0	0	0
1	1	0	1	0	0	1
1	1	1	0	0	0	0

$$f_3(x,y,z) = \text{Not}(x) \text{ And } y \text{ And Not}(z)$$
$$f_5(x,y,z) = x \text{ And Not}(y) \text{ And Not}(z)$$
$$f_7(x,y,z) = x \text{ And } y \text{ And Not}(z)$$
$$f(x,y,z) = f_3(x,y,z) \text{ Or } f_5(x,y,z) \text{ Or } f_7(x,y,z)$$

Figure A1.1   Synthesizing a Boolean function from a truth table (example).

ing) of three terms, one term for each variable x, y, and z, each being either the variable or its negation, depending on whether the value of this variable is 1 or 0 in row i. This construction yields the three functions f_3, f_5, and f_7, listed at the bottom of the table. Since these functions describe the only cases in which the Boolean function f evaluates to 1, we conclude that f can be represented by the Boolean expression $f(x, y, z) = f_3(x, y, z)$ Or $f_5(x, y, z)$ Or $f_7(x, y, z)$. Spelling it out: $f(x, y, z) = (\text{Not}(x) \text{ And } y \text{ And Not}(z))$ Or $(x \text{ And Not}(y) \text{ And Not}(z))$ Or $(x \text{ And } y \text{ And Not}(z))$.

Avoiding tedious formality, this example suggests that any Boolean function can be systematically represented by a Boolean expression that has a very specific structure: it is the disjunction (Or-ing) of all the conjunctive (And-ing) functions f_i whose construction was just described. This expression, which is the Boolean version of a sum of products, is sometimes referred to as the function's *disjunctive normal form* (DNF).

Note that if the function has many variables, and thus the truth table has exponentially many rows, the resulting DNF may be long and cumbersome. At this point, Boolean algebra and various reduction techniques can help transform the expression into a more efficient and workable representation.

A1.3   The Expressive Power of Nand

As our *Nand to Tetris* title suggests, every computer can be built using nothing more than Nand gates. There are two ways to support this claim. One is to actually build a computer from Nand gates only, which is exactly what we do in part I of the book. Another way is to provide a formal proof, which is what we'll do next.

Lemma 1: Any Boolean function can be represented by a Boolean expression containing only And, Or, and Not operators.

Proof: Any Boolean function can be used to generate a corresponding truth table. And, as we've just shown, any truth table can be used for synthesizing a DNF, which is an Or-ing of And-ings of variables and their negations. It follows that any Boolean function can be represented by a Boolean expression containing only And, Or, and Not operators.

In order to appreciate the significance of this result, consider the infinite number of functions that can be defined over *integer numbers* (rather than binary numbers). It would have been nice if every such function could be represented by an algebraic expression involving only addition, multiplication, and negation. As it turns out, the vast majority of integer functions, for example, $f(x) = 2x$ for $x \neq 7$ and $f(7) = 312$, cannot be expressed using a close algebraic form. In the world of *binary numbers*, though, due to the finite number of values that each variable can assume (0 or 1), we do have this attractive property that every Boolean function *can* be expressed using nothing more than And, Or, and Not operators. The practical implication is immense: any computer can be built from nothing more than And, Or, and Not gates.

But, can we do better than this?

Lemma 2: Any Boolean function can be represented by a Boolean expression containing only Not and And operators.

Proof: According to De Morgan law, the Or operator can be expressed using the Not and And operators. Combining this result with Lemma 1, we get the proof.

Pushing our luck further, can we do better than this?

Theorem: Any Boolean function can be represented by a Boolean expression containing only Nand operators.

Proof: An inspection of the Nand truth table (the second-to-last row in figure 1.2 in chapter 1) reveals the following two properties:

· Not $(x) =$ Nand (x, x)

   In words: If you set both the x and y variables of the Nand function to the same value (0 or 1), the function evaluates to the negation of that value.

· And $(x, y) =$ Not (Nand (x, y))

   It is easy to show that the truth tables of both sides of the equation are identical. And, we've just shown that Not can be expressed using Nand.

Combining these two results with Lemma 2, we get that any Boolean function can be represented by a Boolean expression containing only Nand operators.

This remarkable result, which may well be called the fundamental theorem of logic design, stipulates that computers can be built from one atom only: a logic gate that realizes the Nand function. In other words, if we have as many Nand gates as we want, we can wire them in patterns of activation that implement any given Boolean function: all we have to do is figure out the right wiring.

Indeed, most computers today are based on hardware infrastructures consisting of billions of Nand gates (or Nor gates, which have similar generative properties). In practice, though, we don't have to limit ourselves to Nand gates only. If electrical engineers and physicists can come up with efficient and low-cost physical implementations of other elementary logic gates, we will happily use them directly as primitive building blocks. This pragmatic observation does not take away anything from the theorem's importance.

Appendix 2: Hardware Description Language

Intelligence is the faculty of making artificial objects, especially tools to make tools.
—Henry Bergson (1859–1941)

This appendix has two main parts. Sections A2.1–A2.5 describe the HDL language used in the book and in the projects. Section A2.6, named HDL Survival Guide, provides a set of essential tips for completing the hardware projects successfully.

A Hardware Description Language (HDL) is a formalism for defining *chips*: objects whose *interfaces* consist of input and output *pins* that carry binary signals, and whose *implementations* are connected arrangements of other, lower-level chips. This appendix describes the HDL that we use in Nand to Tetris. Chapter 1 (in particular, section 1.3) provides essential background that is a prerequisite to this appendix.

A2.1   HDL Basics

The HDL used in Nand to Tetris is a simple language, and the best way to learn it is to play with HDL programs using the supplied hardware simulator. We recommend starting to experiment as soon as you can, beginning with the following example.

Example: Suppose we have to check whether three 1-bit variables a, b, c have the same value. One way to check this three-way equality is to evaluate the Boolean function $\neg((a \neq b) \vee (b \neq c))$. Noting that the binary operator *not-equal* can be realized using a Xor gate, we can implement this function using the HDL program shown in figure A2.1.

The Eq3.hdl implementation uses four *chip-parts*: two Xor gates, one Or gate, and one Not gate. To realize the logic expressed by $\neg((a \neq b) \vee (b \neq c))$, the HDL programmer connects the chip-parts by creating, and naming, three *internal pins*: neq1, neq2, and outOr.

interface / implementation

```
/** If the three given bits are equal, sets out to 1; else sets out to 0. */
CHIP Eq3 {
   IN  a, b, c;
   OUT out;
   PARTS:
   Xor(a=a, b=b, out=neq1);          // Xor(a,b) → neq1
   Xor(a=b, b=c, out=neq2);          // Xor(b,c) → neq2
   Or (a=neq1, b=neq2, out=outOr);   // Or(neq1,neq2) → outOr
   Not(in=outOr, out=out);           // Not(outOr) → out
}
```

Figure A2.1 HDL program example.

Unlike internal pins, which can be created and named at will, the HDL programmer has no control over the names of the input and output pins. These are normally supplied by the chips' architects and documented in given APIs. For example, in Nand to Tetris, we provide *stub files* for all the chips that you have to implement. Each stub file contains the chip interface, with a missing implementation. The contract is as follows: You are allowed to do whatever you want *under* the `PARTS` statement; you are not allowed to change anything *above* the `PARTS` statement.

In the `Eq3` example, it so happens that the first two inputs of the `Eq3` chip and the two inputs of the `Xor` and `Or` chip-parts have the same names (`a` and `b`). Likewise, the output of the `Eq3` chip and that of the `Not` chip-part happen to have the same name (`out`). This leads to bindings like `a=a`, `b=b`, and `out=out`. Such bindings may look peculiar, but they occur frequently in HDL programs, and one gets used to them. Later in the appendix we'll give a simple rule that clarifies the meaning of these bindings.

Importantly, the programmer need not worry about how chip-parts are implemented. The chip-parts are used like black box abstractions, allowing the programmer to focus only on how to arrange them judiciously in order to realize the chip function. Thanks to this modularity, HDL programs can be kept short, readable, and amenable to unit testing.

HDL-based chips like `Eq3.hdl` can be tested by a computer program called *hardware simulator*. When we instruct the simulator to evaluate a given chip, the simulator evaluates all the chip-parts specified in its `PARTS` section. This, in turn, requires evaluating *their* lower-level chip-parts, and so on. This recursive descent can result in a huge hierarchy of downward-expanding chip-parts, all the way down to the terminal Nand gates from which all chips are made. This expensive drill-down can be averted using *built-in chips*, as we'll explain shortly.

HDL is a declarative language: HDL programs can be viewed as textual specifications of chip diagrams. For each chip *chipName* that appears in the diagram, the programmer writes a *chipName* `(...)` statement in the HDL program's `PARTS` section. Since the language is designed to describe *connections* rather than *processes*, the order of the PARTS statements is insignificant: as long as the chip-parts are connected correctly, the chip will function as stated. The fact that HDL statements can be reordered without affecting the chip's behavior may look odd to readers who are used to conventional programming. Remember: HDL is not a programming language; it's a specification language.

White space, comments, case conventions: HDL is case-sensitive: foo and Foo represent two different things. HDL keywords are written in uppercase letters. Space characters, newline characters, and comments are ignored. The following comment formats are supported:

```
//  Comment to end of line
/*  Comment until closing */
/** API documentation comment */
```

Pins: HDL programs feature three types of *pins*: input pins, output pins, and internal pins. The latter pins serve to connect outputs of chip-parts to inputs of other chip-parts. Pins are assumed by default to be single-bit, carrying 0 or 1 values. Multi-bit *bus* pins can also be declared and used, as described later in this appendix.

Names of chips and pins may be any sequence of letters and digits not starting with a digit (some hardware simulators disallow using hyphens). By convention, chip and pin names start with a capital letter and a lowercase letter, respectively. For readability, names can include uppercase letters, for example, xorResult. HDL programs are stored in .hdl files. The name of the chip declared in the HDL statement CHIP *Xxx* must be identical to the prefix of the file name *Xxx*.hdl.

Program structure: An HDL program consists of an *interface* and an *implementation*. The interface consists of the chip's API documentation, chip name, and names of its input and output pins. The implementation consists of the statements below the PARTS keyword. The overall program structure is as follows:

```
/** API documentation: what the chip does. */
CHIP ChipName {
    IN inputPin1, inputPin2, ... ;
    OUT outputPin1, outputPin2, ... ;
PARTS:
    // Here comes the implementation.
}
```

Parts: The chip implementation is an unordered sequence of chip-part statements, as follows:

```
PARTS:
  chipPart(connection, ... , connection);
  chipPart(connection, ... , connection);
  . . .
```

Each *connection* is specified using the binding *pin1* = *pin2*, where *pin1* and *pin2* are input, output, or internal pin names. These connections can be visualized as "wires" that the HDL programmer creates and names, as needed. For each "wire" connecting *chipPart1* and *chipPart2* there is an internal pin that appears twice in the HDL program: once as a *sink* in some *chipPart1* (...) statement, and once as a *source* in some other *chipPart2* (...) statement. For example, consider the following statements:

```
chipPart1(..., out = v,...);          // out of chipPart1 feeds the internal pin v

chipPart2(..., in = v, ...);          // in of chipPart2 is fed from v

chipPart3(..., in1 = v, ..., in2 = v,...);   // in1 and in2 of chipPart3 are also fed from v
```

Pins have fan-in 1 and unlimited fan-out. This means that a pin can be fed from a single source only, yet it can feed (through multiple connections) one or more pins in one or more chip-parts. In the above example, the internal pin v simultaneously feeds three inputs. This is the HDL equivalent of *forks* in chip diagrams.

The meaning of a = a: Many chips in the Hack platform use the same pin names. As shown in figure A2.1, this leads to statements like Xor (a=a, b=b, out=neq1). The first two connections feed the a and b inputs of the implemented chip (Eq3) into the a and b inputs of the Xor chip-part. The third connection feeds the out output of the Xor chip-part to the internal pin neq1. Here is a simple rule that helps sort things out: In every chip-part statement, the left side of each = binding always denotes an input or output pin *of the chip-part*, and the right side always denotes an input, output, or internal pin *of the implemented chip*.

A2.2   Multi-Bit Buses

Each input, output, or internal pin in an HDL program may be either a single-bit value, which is the default, or a multi-bit value, referred to as a *bus*.

Bit numbering and bus syntax: Bits are numbered from right to left, starting with 0. For example, sel=110, implies that sel[2]=1, sel[1]=1, and sel[0]=0.

Input and output bus pins: The bit widths of these pins are specified when they are declared in the chip's IN and OUT statements. The syntax is x[n], where x and n declare the pin's name and bit width, respectively.

Internal bus pins: The bit widths of internal pins are deduced implicitly from the bindings in which they are declared, as follows,

```
chipPart1(…, x[i] = u, …);
chipPart2(…, x[i..j] = v, …);
```

where x is an input or output pin of the chip-part. The first binding defines u to be a single-bit internal pin and sets its value to x[i]. The second binding defines v to be an internal bus-pin of width $j - i + 1$ bits and sets its value to the bits indexed i to j (inclusive) of bus-pin x.

Unlike input and output pins, internal pins (like u and v) may not be subscripted. For example, u[i] is not allowed.

True/false buses: The constants true (1) and false (0) may also be used to define buses. For example, suppose that x is an 8-bit bus-pin, and consider this statement:

```
chipPart(…, x[0..2] = true, …, x[6..7] = true, …);
```

This statement sets x to the value 11000111. Note that unaffected bits are set by default to false (0). Figure A2.2 gives another example.

A2.3   Built-In Chips

Chips can have either a *native* implementation, written in HDL, or a *built-in* implementation, supplied by an executable module written in a high-level programming language. Since

```
// Sets out = Not(in), bitwise
CHIP Not8 {
    IN  in[8];
    OUT out[8];
    ...
}
```

```
CHIP Foo {
    ...
    PARTS
    ...
    Not8(in[0..1]  = true,
         in[3..5]  = six,
         in[7]     = true,
         out[3..7] = out1,
         ...          );
    ...
}
```

Assumption: six is an internal pin, containing the value 110.

out1 is an internal pin, created by the Not8 chip-part statement.

Below: the resulting contents of the in input of Not8, and of out1.

7	6	5	4	3	2	1	0
1	0	1	1	0	0	1	1

in:

		4	3	2	1	0
out1:		0	1	0	0	1

Figure A2.2   Buses in action (example).

the Nand to Tetris hardware simulator was written in Java, it was convenient to realize the built-in chips as Java classes. Thus, before building, say, a Mux chip in HDL, the user can load a built-in Mux chip into the hardware simulator and experiment with it. The behavior of the built-in Mux chip is supplied by a Java class file named Mux.class, which is part of the simulator's software.

The Hack computer is made from about thirty generic chips, listed in appendix 4. Two of these chips, Nand and DFF, are considered *given*, or *primitive*, akin to axioms in logic. The hardware simulator realizes given chips by invoking their built-in implementations. Therefore, in Nand to Tetris, Nand and DFF can be used without building them in HDL.

Projects 1, 2, 3, and 5 evolve around building HDL implementations of the remaining chips listed in appendix 4. All these chips, except for the CPU and Computer chips, also have built-in implementations. This was done in order to facilitate behavioral simulation, as explained in chapter 1.

The built-in chips—a library of about thirty *chipName*.class files—are supplied in the nand2tetris/tools/builtInChips folder in your computer. Built-in chips have HDL interfaces identical to those of regular HDL chips. Therefore, each .class file is accompanied by a corresponding .hdl file that provides the built-in chip interface. Figure A2.3 shows a typical HDL definition of a built-in chip.

It's important to remember that the supplied hardware simulator is a general-purpose tool, whereas the Hack computer built in Nand to Tetris is a specific hardware platform. The hardware simulator can be used for building gates, chips, and platforms that have nothing to do with Hack. Therefore, when discussing the notion of built-in chips, it helps to broaden our perspective and describe their general utility for supporting any possible hardware construction project. In general, then, built-in chips provide the following services:

Foundation: Built-in chips can provide supplied implementations of chips that are considered *given*, or *primitive*. For example, in the Hack computer, Nand and DFF are given.

Efficiency: Some chips, like RAM units, consist of numerous lower-level chips. When we use such chips as chip-parts, the hardware simulator has to evaluate them. This is done by evaluating, recursively, all the lower-level chips from which they are made. This results in

```
/** 16-bit And gate, implemented as a built-in chip. */
CHIP And16 {
    IN   a[16], b[16];
    OUT out[16];
    BUILTIN And16;
}
```
Implemented by
tools/builtInChips/And16.class

Figure A2.3   Built-in chip definition example.

slow and inefficient simulation. The use of built-in chip-parts instead of regular, HDL-based chips speeds up the simulation considerably.

Unit testing: HDL programs use chip-parts abstractly, without paying attention to their implementation. Therefore, when building a new chip, it is always recommended to use built-in chip-parts. This practice improves efficiency and minimizes errors.

Visualization: If the designer wants to allow users to "see" how chips work, and perhaps change the internal state of the simulated chip interactively, he or she can supply a built-in chip implementation that features a graphical user interface. This GUI will be displayed whenever the built-in chip is loaded into the simulator or invoked as a chip-part. Except for these visual side effects, GUI-empowered chips behave, and can be used, just like any other chip. Section A2.5 provides more details about GUI-empowered chips.

Extension: If you wish to implement a new input/output device or create a new hardware platform altogether (other than Hack), you can support these constructions with built-in chips. For more information about developing additional or new functionality, see chapter 13.

A2.4   Sequential Chips

Chips can be either *combinational* or *sequential*. Combinational chips are time independent: they respond to changes in their inputs instantaneously. Sequential chips are time dependent, also called *clocked*: when a user or a test script changes the inputs of a sequential chip, the chip outputs may change only at the beginning of the next *time unit*, also called a *cycle*. The hardware simulator effects the progression of time using a simulated clock.

The clock: The simulator's two-phase clock emits an infinite sequence of values denoted 0, 0+, 1, 1+, 2, 2+, 3, 3+, and so on. The progression of this discrete time series is controlled by two simulator commands called `tick` and `tock`. A `tick` moves the clock value from t to $t+$, and a `tock` from $t+$ to $t+1$, bringing upon the next time unit. The *real time* that elapsed during this period is irrelevant for simulation purposes, since the simulated time is controlled by the user, or by a test script, as follows.

First, whenever a sequential chip is loaded into the simulator, the GUI enables a clock-shaped button (dimmed when simulating combinational chips). One click on this button (a `tick`) ends the first phase of the clock cycle, and a subsequent click (a `tock`) ends the second phase of the cycle, bringing on the first phase of the next cycle, and so on.

Alternatively, one can run the clock from a test script. For example, the sequence of scripting commands `repeat n {tick, tock, output}` instructs the simulator to advance the clock *n* time units and to print some values in the process. Appendix 3 documents the *Test Description Language* (TDL) that features these commands.

The two-phased time units generated by the clock regulate the operations of all the sequential chip-parts in the implemented chip. During the first phase of the time unit (`tick`), the inputs of each sequential chip-part affect the chip's internal state, according to the chip logic. During the second phase of the time unit (`tock`), the chip outputs are set to the new values. Hence, if we look at a sequential chip "from the outside," we see that its output pins stabilize to new values only at `tock`—at the point of transition between two consecutive time units.

We reiterate that combinational chips are completely oblivious to the clock. In Nand to Tetris, all the logic gates and chips built in chapters 1–2, up to and including the ALU, are combinational. All the registers and memory units built in chapter 3 are sequential. By default, chips are combinational; a chip can become *sequential* explicitly or implicitly, as follows.

Sequential, built-in chips: A *built-in chip* can declare its dependence on the clock explicitly, using the statement,

CLOCKED *pin, pin, ..., pin*;

where each *pin* is one of the chip's input or output pins. The inclusion of an input pin *x* in the CLOCKED list stipulates that changes to *x* should affect the chip's outputs only at the beginning of the next time unit. The inclusion of an output pin *x* in the CLOCKED list stipulates that changes in any of the chip's inputs should affect *x* only at the beginning of the next time unit. Figure A2.4 presents the definition of the most basic, built-in, sequential chip in the Hack platform—the DFF.

It is possible that only some of the input or output pins of a chip are declared as clocked. In that case, changes in the non-clocked input pins affect the non-clocked output pins instantaneously. That's how the `address` pins are implemented in RAM units: the addressing logic is combinational and independent of the clock.

```
/** D-Flip-Flop gate (DFF):
out[t]=in[t-1] where t is the current cycle, or time-unit. */
CHIP DFF {
    IN in;
    OUT out;                      Implemented by
    BUILTIN DFF;                  tools/builtInChips/DFF.class
    CLOCKED in;
}
              The in input is explicitly clocked
```

Figure A2.4   DFF definition.

It is also possible to declare the CLOCKED keyword with an empty list of pins. This statement stipulates that the chip may change its internal state depending on the clock, but its input-output behavior will be combinational, independent of the clock.

Sequential, composite chips: The CLOCKED property can be defined explicitly only in built-in chips. How, then, does the simulator know that a given chip-part is sequential? If the chip is not built-in, then it is said to be clocked when one or more of its chip-parts is clocked. The clocked property is checked recursively, all the way down the chip hierarchy, where a built-in chip may be explicitly clocked. If such a chip is found, it renders every chip that depends on it (up the hierarchy) "clocked." Therefore, in the Hack computer, all the chips that include one or more DFF chip-parts, either directly or indirectly, are clocked.

We see that if a chip is not built-in, there is no way to tell from its HDL code whether it is sequential or not. *Best-practice advice*: The chip architect should provide this information in the chip API documentation.

Feedback loops: If the input of a chip feeds from one of the chip's outputs, either directly or through a (possibly long) path of dependencies, we say that the chip contains a *feedback loop*. For example, consider the following two chip-part statements:

```
Not (in=loop1, out=loop1) // Invalid feedback loop
DFF (in=loop2, out=loop2) // Valid feedback loop
```

In both examples, an internal pin (loop1 or loop2) attempts to feed the chip's input from its output, creating a feedback loop. The difference between the two examples is that Not is a combinational chip, whereas DFF is sequential. In the Not example, loop1 creates an instantaneous and uncontrolled dependency between in and out, sometimes called a *data race*. In contrast, in the DFF case, the in-out dependency created by loop2 is delayed by the clock, since the in input of the DFF is declared clocked. Therefore, out(t) is not a function of in(t) but rather of in(t - 1).

When the simulator evaluates a chip, it checks recursively whether its various connections entail feedback loops. For each loop, the simulator checks whether the loop goes through a clocked pin somewhere along the way. If so, the loop is allowed. Otherwise, the simulator stops processing and issues an error message. This is done to prevent uncontrolled data races.

A2.5   Visualizing Chips

Built-in chips may be *GUI empowered*. These chips feature visual side effects designed to animate some of the chip operations. When the simulator evaluates a GUI-empowered chip-part, it displays a graphical image on the screen. Using this image, which may include interactive elements, the user can inspect the chip's current state or change it. The permissible

GUI-empowered actions are determined, and made possible, by the developer of the built-in chip implementation.

The present version of the hardware simulator features the following GUI-empowered, built-in chips:

ALU: Displays the Hack ALU's inputs, output, and the presently computed function.

Registers (ARegister, DRegister, PC): Displays the register's contents, which may be modified by the user.

RAM chips: Displays a scrollable, array-like image that shows the contents of all the memory locations, which may be modified by the user. If the contents of a memory location change during the simulation, the respective entry in the GUI changes as well.

ROM chip (ROM32K): Same array-like image as that of RAM chips, plus an icon that enables loading a machine language program from an external text file. (The ROM32K chip serves as the instruction memory of the Hack computer.)

Screen chip: Displays a 256-rows-by-512-columns window that simulates the physical screen. If, during a simulation, one or more bits in the RAM-resident *screen memory map* change, the respective pixels in the screen GUI change as well. This continuous refresh loop is embedded in the simulator implementation.

Keyboard chip: Displays a keyboard icon. Clicking this icon connects the real keyboard of your computer to the simulated chip. From this point on, every key pressed on the real keyboard is intercepted by the simulated chip, and its binary code appears in the RAM-resident *keyboard memory map*. If the user moves the mouse focus to another area in the simulator GUI, the control of the keyboard is restored to the real computer.

Figure A2.5 presents a chip that uses three GUI empowered chip-parts. Figure A2.6 shows how the simulator handles this chip. The GUIDemo chip logic feeds its in input into two destinations: register number address in the RAM16K chip-part, and register number address in the Screen chip-part. In addition, the chip logic feeds the out values of its three chip-parts to the "dead-end" internal pins a, b, and c. These meaningless connections are designed for one purpose only: illustrating how the simulator deals with built-in, GUI-empowered chip-parts.

Note how the changes effected by the user (step 3) impact the screen (step 4). The circled horizontal line shown on the screen is the visual side effect of storing –1 in memory location 5012. Since the 16-bit two's complement binary code of –1 is 1111111111111111, the computer draws 16 pixels starting at column 320 of row 156, which happen to be the screen coordinates associated with RAM address 5012. The mapping of memory *addresses* on (*row, column*) screen coordinates is specified in chapter 4 (section 4.2.5).

```
// Demo of GUI-empowered chips.
// The logic of this chip is meaningless, and is used merely to force
// the simulator to display the GUI effects of its built-in chip-parts.
CHIP GUIDemo {
    IN  in[16], load, address[15];
    OUT out[16];
    PARTS:
    RAM16K(in=in, load=load, address=address[0..13], out=a);
    Screen(in=in, load=load, address=address[0..12], out=b);
    Keyboard(out=c);
}
```

Figure A2.5   A chip that activates GUI-empowered chip-parts.

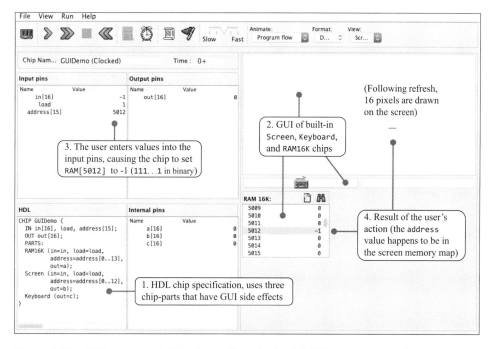

Figure A2.6   GUI-empowered chips demo. Since the loaded HDL program uses GUI-empowered chip-parts (step 1), the simulator renders their respective GUI images (step 2). When the user changes the values of the chip input pins (step 3), the simulator reflects these changes in the respective GUIs (step 4).

A2.6   HDL Survival Guide

This section provides practical tips about how to develop chips in HDL using the supplied hardware simulator. The tips are listed in no particular order. We recommend reading this section once, beginning to end, and then consulting it as needed.

Chip: Your `nand2tetris/projects` folder includes thirteen subfolders, named 01, 02, ..., 13 (corresponding to the relevant chapter numbers). The hardware project folders are 01, 02, 03, and 05. Each hardware project folder contains a set of supplied HDL *stub files*, one for each chip that you have to build. The supplied HDL files contain no implementations; building these implementations is what the project is all about. If you do not build these chips in the order in which they are described in the book, you may run into difficulties. For example, suppose that you start project 1 by building the Xor chip. If your `Xor.hdl` implementation includes, say, And and Or chip-parts, and you have not yet implemented `And.hdl` and `Or.hdl`, your `Xor.hdl` program will not work even if its implementation is perfectly correct.

Note, however, that if the project folder included no `And.hdl` and `Or.hdl` files, your `Xor.hdl` program will work properly. The hardware simulator, which is a Java program, features built-in implementations of all the chips necessary to build the Hack computer (with the exception of the `CPU` and `Computer` chips). When the simulator evaluates a chip-part, say And, it looks for an `And.hdl` file in the current folder. At this point there are three possibilities:

- No HDL file is found. In this case, the built-in implementation of the chip kicks in, covering for the missing HDL implementation.
- A stub HDL file is found. The simulator tries to execute it. Failing to find an implementation, the execution fails.
- An HDL file is found, with an HDL implementation. The simulator executes it, reporting errors, if any, to the best of its ability.

Best-practice advice: You can do one of two things. Try to implement the chips in the order presented in the book and in the project descriptions. Since the chips are discussed bottom-up, from basic chips to more complex ones, you will encounter no chip order implementation troubles—provided, of course, that you complete each chip implementation correctly before moving on to implement the next one.

A recommended alternative is to create a subfolder named, say, stubs, and move all the supplied `.hdl` stub files into it. You can then move each stub file that you want to work on into your working folder, one by one. When you are done implementing a chip successfully, move it into, say, a completed subfolder. This practice forces the simulator to always use built-in chips, since the working folder includes only the `.hdl` file that you are working on (as well as the supplied `.tst` and `.cmp` files).

HDL files and test scripts: The `.hdl` file that you are working on and its associated `.tst` test script file must be located in the same folder. Each supplied test script starts with a `load` command that loads the `.hdl` file that it is supposed to test. The simulator always looks for this file in the current folder.

In principle, the simulator's `File` menu allows the user to load, interactively, both an `.hdl` file and a `.tst` script file. This can create potential problems. For example, you can load the `.hdl` file that you are working on into the simulator, and then load a test script from another folder. When you execute the test script, it may well load a different version of the HDL program into the simulator (possibly, a stub file). When in doubt, inspect the pane named `HDL` in the simulator GUI to check which HDL code is presently loaded. *Best-practice advice*: Use the simulator's `File` menu to load either an `.hdl` file or a `.tst` file, but not both.

Testing chips in isolation: At some point you may become convinced that your chip is correct, even though it is still failing the test. Indeed, it is possible that the chip is perfectly implemented, but one of its chip-parts is not. Also, a chip that passed its test successfully may fail when used as a chip-part by another chip. One of the biggest inherent limitations of hardware design is that test scripts—especially those that test complex chips—cannot guarantee that the tested chip will operate perfectly in all circumstances.

The good news is that you can always diagnose which chip-part is causing the problem. Create a test subfolder and copy into it only the three `.hdl`, `.tst`, and `.out` files related to the chip that you are presently building. If your chip implementation passes its test in this subfolder as is (letting the simulator use the default built-in chip-parts), there must be a problem with one of your chip-part implementations, that is, with one of the chips that you built earlier in this project. Copy the other chips into this test folder, one by one, and repeat the test until you find the problematic chip.

HDL syntax errors: The hardware simulator displays errors on the bottom status bar. On computers with small screens, these messages are sometimes off the bottom of the screen, not visible. If you load an HDL program and nothing shows up in the `HDL` pane, but no error message is seen, this may be the problem. Your computer should have a way to move the window, using the keyboard. For example, on Windows use `Alt+Space`, `M`, and the arrow keys.

Unconnected pins: The hardware simulator does not consider unconnected pins to be errors. By default, it sets any unconnected input or output pin to `false` (binary value `0`). This can cause mysterious errors in your chip implementations.

If an output pin of your chip is always `0`, make sure that it is properly connected to another pin in your program. In particular, double-check the names of the internal pins ("wires") that feed this pin, either directly or indirectly. Typographic errors are particularly hazardous here, since the simulator doesn't throw errors on disconnected wires. For example, consider the statement `Foo(..., sum=sun)`, where the `sum` output of `Foo` is supposed to pipe its value to an internal pin. Indeed, the simulator will happily create an internal pin named sun. Now, if sum's value was supposed to feed the output pin of the implemented chip, or the input pin of another chip-part, this pin will in fact be 0, *always*, since nothing will be piped from Foo onward.

To recap, if an output pin is always 0, or if one of the chip-parts does not appear to be working correctly, check the spelling of all the relevant pin names, and verify that all the input pins of the chip-part are connected.

Customized testing: For every *chip*.hdl file that you have to complete your project folder also includes a supplied test script, named *chip*.tst, and a compare file, named *chip*.cmp. Once your chip starts generating outputs, your folder will also include an output file named *chip*.out. If your chip fails the test script, don't forget to consult the .out file. Inspect the listed output values, and seek clues to the failure. If for some reason you can't see the output file in the simulator GUI, you can always inspect it using a text editor.

If you want, you can run tests of your own. Copy the supplied test script to, say, *MyTest-Chip*.tst, and modify the script commands to gain more insight into your chip's behavior. Start by changing the name of the output file in the output-file line and deleting the compare-to line. This will cause the test to always run to completion (by default, the simulation stops when an output line disagrees with the corresponding line in the compare file). Consider modifying the output-list line to show the outputs of your internal pins.

Appendix 3 documents the Test Description Language (TDL) that features all these commands.

Sub-busing (indexing) internal pins: This is not permitted. The only bus-pins that can be indexed are the input and output pins of the implemented chip or the input and output pins of its chip-parts. However, there is a workaround for sub-busing internal bus-pins. To motivate the work-around, here is an example that doesn't work:

```
CHIP Foo {
    IN  in[16];
    OUT out;
    PARTS:
    Not16 (in=in, out=notIn);
    Or8Way (in=notIn[4..11], out=out);   // Error: internal bus cannot be indexed.
  }
```

Possible fix, using the work-around:

```
Not16 (in=in, out[4..11]=notIn);
Or8Way (in=notIn, out=out); // Works!
```

Multiple outputs: Sometimes you need to split the multi-bit value of a bus-pin into two buses. This can be done by using multiple out= bindings.

For example:

```
CHIP Foo {
    IN  in[16];
    OUT out[8];
    PARTS:
    Not16 (in=in, out[0..7]=low8, out[8..15]=high8);   // Splitting the out value
    Bar8Bit (a=low8, b=high8, out=out);
}
```

Sometimes you may want to output a value and also use it for further computations. This can be done as follows:

```
CHIP Foo {
    IN a, b, c;
    OUT out1, out2;
    PARTS:
    Bar (a=a, b=b, out=x, out=out1); // Bar's output feeds the out1 output of Foo
    Baz (a=x, b=c, out=out2);              // A copy of Bar's output also feeds Baz's a input
}
```

Chip-parts "auto complete" (sort of): The signatures of all the chips mentioned in this book are listed in appendix 4, which also has a web-based version (at www.nand2tetris.org). To use a chip-part in a chip implementation, copy-paste the chip signature from the online document into your HDL program, then fill in the missing bindings. This practice saves time and minimizes typing errors.

Appendix 3: Test Description Language

Mistakes are the portals of discovery.

—James Joyce (1882–1941)

Testing is a critically important element of systems development, and one that typically gets insufficient attention in computer science education. In Nand to Tetris we take testing very seriously. We believe that before one sets out to develop a new hardware or software module P, one must first develop a module T designed to test it. Further, T should be part of P's development's contract. Therefore, for every chip or software system specified in this book, we supply official test programs, written by us. Although you are welcome to test your work in any way you see fit, the contract is such that, ultimately, your implementation must pass *our* tests.

In order to streamline the definition and execution of the numerous tests scattered all over the book projects, we designed a uniform test description language. This language works almost the same across all the relevant tools supplied in Nand to Tetris: the *hardware simulator* used for simulating and testing chips written in HDL, the *CPU emulator* used for simulating and testing machine language programs, and the *VM emulator* used for simulating and testing programs written in the VM language, which are typically compiled Jack programs.

Every one of these simulators features a GUI that enables testing the loaded chip or program interactively, or batch-style, using a test script. A test script is a sequence of commands that load a hardware or software module into the relevant simulator and subject the module to a series of preplanned testing scenarios. In addition, the test scripts feature commands for printing the test results and comparing them to desired results, as defined in supplied compare files. In sum, a test script enables a systematic, replicable, and documented testing of the underlying code—an invaluable requirement in any hardware or software development project.

In Nand to Tetris, we don't expect learners to write test scripts. All the test scripts necessary to test all the hardware and software modules mentioned in the book are supplied with the project materials. Thus, the purpose of this appendix is not to teach you how to write test scripts but rather to help you understand the syntax and logic of the supplied test scripts. Of course, you are welcome to customize the supplied scripts and create new ones, as you please.

A3.1   General Guidelines

The following usage guidelines are applicable to all the software tools and test scripts.

File format and usage: The act of testing a hardware or software module involves four types of files. Although not required, we recommend that all four files have the same prefix (file name):

Xxx.yyy: where *Xxx* is the name of the tested module and *yyy* is either `hdl`, `hack`, `asm`, or `vm`, standing, respectively, for a chip definition written in HDL, a program written in the Hack machine language, a program written in the Hack assembly language, or a program written in the VM virtual machine language

Xxx.`tst`: a test script that walks the simulator through a series of steps designed to test the code stored in *Xxx*

Xxx.`out`: an optional output file to which the script commands can write current values of selected variables during the simulation

Xxx.`cmp`: an optional compare file containing the *desired* values of selected variables, that is, the values that the simulation *should* generate if the module is implemented correctly

All these files should be kept in the same folder, which can be conveniently named *Xxx*. In the documentation and descriptions of all the simulators, the term "current folder" refers to the folder from which the last file has been opened in the simulator environment.

White space: Space characters, newline characters, and comments in test scripts (*Xxx.*`tst` files) are ignored. The following comment formats can appear in test scripts:

```
//  Comment to end of line
/*  Comment until closing */
/** API documentation comment */
```

Test scripts are not case-sensitive, except for file and folder names.

Usage: For each hardware or software module *Xxx* in Nand to Tetris we supply a script file *Xxx.*`tst` and a compare file *Xxx.*`cmp`. These files are designed to test your implementation of *Xxx*. In some cases, we also supply a skeletal version of *Xxx*, for example, an HDL interface with a missing implementation. All the files in all the projects are plain text files that should be viewed and edited using plain text editors.

Typically, you will start a simulation session by loading the supplied *Xxx*.tst script file into the relevant simulator. The first command in the script typically loads the code stored in the tested module *Xxx*. Next, optionally, come commands that initialize an output file and specify a compare file. The remaining commands in the script run the actual tests.

Simulation controls: Each one of the supplied simulators features a set of menus and icons for controlling the simulation.

File menu: Allows loading into the simulator either a relevant program (.hdl file, .hack file, .asm file, .vm file, or a folder name) or a test script (.tst file). If the user does not load a test script, the simulator loads a default test script (described below).

Play icon: Instructs the simulator to execute the next simulation step, as specified in the currently loaded test script.

Pause icon: Instructs the simulator to pause the execution of the currently loaded test script. Useful for inspecting various elements of the simulated environment.

Fast-forward icon: Instructs the simulator to execute all the commands in the currently loaded test script.

Stop icon: Instructs the simulator to stop the execution of the currently loaded test script.

Rewind icon: Instructs the simulator to reset the execution of the currently loaded test script, that is, be ready to start executing the test script from its first command onward.

Note that the simulator's icons listed above don't "run the code." Rather, they run the test script, which runs the code.

A3.2   Testing Chips on the Hardware Simulator

The supplied hardware simulator is designed for testing and simulating chip definitions written in the Hardware Description Language (HDL) described in appendix 2. Chapter 1 provides essential background on chip development and testing; thus, we recommend reading it first.

Example: Figure A2.1 in appendix 2 presents an Eq3 chip, designed to check whether three 1-bit inputs are equal. Figure A3.1 presents Eq3.tst, a script designed to test the chip, and Eq3.cmp, a compare file containing the expected output of this test.

A test script normally starts with some setup commands, followed by a series of simulation steps, each ending with a semicolon. A simulation step typically instructs the simulator to bind the chip's input pins to test values, evaluate the chip logic, and write selected variable values into a designated output file.

```
/* Eq3.tst: Tests the Eq3.hdl program. The Eq3 chip sets out to 1 if its
three 1-bit inputs have the same values, or 0 otherwise. */

load Eq3.hdl,          // Loads the HDL program into the simulator.
output-file Eq3.out,   // Writes the script outputs to this file.
compare-to Eq3.cmp,    // Compares the script outputs to this file.
output-list a b c out; // Each subsequent output command will
                       // write the values of variables a, b, c and
                       // out to the output file.

set a 0, set b 0, set c 0, eval, output;
set a 1, set b 1, set c 1, eval, output;       | a | b | c |out|
set a 1, set b 0, set c 0, eval, output;       | 0 | 0 | 0 | 1 |
set a 0, set b 1, set c 0, eval, output;       | 1 | 1 | 1 | 1 |
set a 1, set b 0, set c 1, eval, output;       | 1 | 0 | 0 | 0 |
                                               | 0 | 1 | 0 | 0 |
                                               | 1 | 0 | 1 | 0 |
```

Eq3.cmp

Figure A3.1   Test script and compare file (example).

The Eq3 chip has three 1-bit inputs; thus, an exhaustive test would require eight testing scenarios. The size of an exhaustive test grows exponentially with the input size. Therefore, most test scripts test only a subset of representative input values, as shown in the figure.

Data types and variables: Test scripts support two data types: *integers* and *strings*. Integer constants can be expressed in decimal (%D prefix) format, which is the default, binary (%B prefix) format, or hexadecimal (%X prefix) format. These values are always translated into their equivalent two's complement binary values. For example, consider the following commands:

```
set a1 %B1111111111111111
set a2 %XFFFF
set a3 %D-1
set a4 -1
```

All four variables are set to the same value: 1111111111111111 in binary, which happens to be the binary, two's complement representation of −1 in decimal.

String values are specified using a %S prefix and must be enclosed by double quotation marks. Strings are used strictly for printing purposes and cannot be assigned to variables.

The hardware simulator's two-phase clock (used only in testing sequential chips) emits a series of values denoted 0, 0+, 1, 1+, 2, 2+, 3, 3+, and so on. The progression of these *clock cycles* (also called *time units*) can be controlled by two script commands named tick and tock. A tick moves the clock value from t to $t+$, and a tock from $t+$ to $t+1$, bringing upon the next time unit. The current time unit is stored in a system variable named time, which is read-only.

Script commands can access three types of variables: pins, variables of built-in chips, and the system variable `time`.

Pins: input, output, and internal pins of the simulated chip (for example, the command `set in 0` sets the value of the pin whose name is `in` to `0`)

Variables of built-in chips: exposed by the chip's external implementation (see figure A3.2.)

`time`: the number of time-units that elapsed since the simulation started (a read-only variable)

Script commands: A script is a sequence of commands. Each command is terminated by a comma, a semicolon, or an exclamation mark. These terminators have the following semantics:

Comma (`,`): Terminates a script command.

Semicolon (`;`): Terminates a script command and a simulation step. A *simulation step* consists of one or more script commands. When the user instructs the simulator to *single-step* using the simulator's menu or `play` icon, the simulator executes the script from the current command until a semicolon is reached, at which point the simulation is paused.

Exclamation mark (`!`): Terminates a script command and stops the script execution. The user can later resume the script execution from that point onward. Typically used for debugging purposes.

Below we group the script commands in two conceptual sections: *setup commands*, used for loading files and initializing settings, and *simulation commands*, used for walking the simulator through the actual tests.

Setup Commands

`load Xxx.hdl`: Loads the HDL program stored in *Xxx*.`hdl` into the simulator. The file name must include the `.hdl` extension and must not include a path specification. The simulator will try to load the file from the current folder and, failing that, from the `tools/builtInChips` folder.

`output-file Xxx.out`: Instructs the simulator to write the results of the `output` commands in the named file, which must include an `.out` extension. The output file will be created in the current folder.

`output-list v1, v2, ...`: Specifies what to write to the output file when the `output` command is encountered in the script (until the next `output-list` command, if any). Each value in the list is a variable name followed by a formatting specification. The command also produces a single header line, consisting of the variable names, which is written to the output file. Each item *v* in the `output-list` has the syntax *varName format padL.len.padR* (without any spaces). This directive instructs the simulator to write *padL* space characters, then the current value of the variable *varName*, using the specified *format* and *len* columns, then *padR* spaces, and finally the divider symbol |. The *format* can be either %B (binary), %X (hexa), %D (decimal), or %S (string). The default format is %B1.1.1.

For example, the `CPU.hdl` chip of the Hack platform has an input pin named `reset`, an output pin named `pc` (among others), and a chip-part named `DRegister` (among others). If we want to track the values of these entities during the simulation, we can use something like the following command:

```
Output-list time%S1.5.1      // The system variable time
            reset%B2.1.2     // One of the chip's input pins
            pc%D2.3.1        // One of the chip's output pins
            DRegister[]%X3.4.4  // The internal state of this chip-part
```

(State variables of built-in chips are explained below). This `output-list` command may end up producing the following output, after two subsequent `output` commands:

```
| time  |reset|   pc |DRegister[]|
|   20+ |  0  |   21 |   FFFF    |
|   21  |  0  |   22 |   FFFF    |
```

compare-to *Xxx*.cmp: Specifies that the output line generated by each subsequent `output` command should be compared to its corresponding line in the specified compare file (which must include the .cmp extension). If any two lines are not the same, the simulator displays an error message and halts the script execution. The compare file is assumed to be present in the current folder.

Simulation Commands

set *varName value*: Assigns the value to the variable. The variable is either a pin or an internal variable of the simulated chip or one of its chip-parts. The bit widths of the value and the variable must be compatible.

eval: Instructs the simulator to apply the chip logic to the current values of the input pins and compute the resulting output values.

output: Causes the simulator to go through the following logic:

1. Get the current values of all the variables listed in the last `output-list` command.

2. Create an output line using the format specified in the last `output-list` command.

3. Write the output line to the output file.

4. (If a compare file has been previously declared using a `compare-to` command): If the output line differs from the compare file's current line, display an error message and stop the script's execution.

5. Advance the line cursors of the output file and the compare file.

`tick`: Ends the first phase of the current time unit (clock cycle).

`tock`: Ends the second phase of the current time unit and embarks on the first phase of the next time unit.

`repeat` *n* *{commands}*: Instructs the simulator to repeat the commands enclosed in the curly brackets *n* times. If *n* is omitted, the simulator repeats the commands until the simulation has been stopped for some reason (for example, when the user clicks the `Stop` icon).

`while` *booleanCondition* *{commands}*: Instructs the simulator to repeat the commands enclosed in the curly brackets as long as the *booleanCondition* is true. The condition is of the form *x op y* where *x* and *y* are either constants or variable names and *op* is =, >, <, >=, <=, or < >. If *x* and *y* are strings, *op* can be either = or < >.

`echo` *text*: Displays the *text* in the simulator status line. The text must be enclosed in double quotation marks.

`clear-echo`: Clears the simulator's status line.

`breakpoint` *varName value*: Starts comparing the current value of the specified variable to the specified *value* following the execution of each subsequent script command. If the variable contains the specified *value*, the execution halts and a message is displayed. Otherwise, the execution continues normally. Useful for debugging purposes.

`clear-breakpoints`: Clears all the previously defined breakpoints.

builtInChipName method argument (s): Executes the specified method of the specified built-in chip-part using the supplied arguments. The designer of a built-in chip can provide methods that allow the user (or a test script) to manipulate the simulated chip. See figure A3.2.

Variables of built-in chips: Chips can be implemented either by HDL programs or by externally supplied executable modules. In the latter case, the chip is said to be *built-in*. built-in chips can facilitate access to the chip's state using the syntax *chipName[varName]*, where *varName* is an implementation-specific variable that should be documented in the chip API. See figure A3.2.

Chip name	Exposed variables	Data type / range	Methods
Register	Register[]	16-bit (-32768...32767)	
ARegister	ARegister[]	16-bit	
DRegister	DRegister[]	16-bit	
PC (prog. counter)	PC[]	15-bit (0...32767)	
RAM8	RAM8[0...7]	each entry is 16-bit	
RAM64	RAM64[0...63]	each entry is 16-bit	
RAM512	RAM512[0...511]	each entry is 16-bit	
RAM4K	RAM4K[0...4095]	each entry is 16-bit	
RAM16K	RAM16K[0...16383]	each entry is 16-bit	
ROM32K	ROM32K[0...32767]	each entry is 16-bit	load *Xxx*.hack / *Xxx*.asm
Screen	Screen[0...16383]	each entry is 16-bit	
Keyboard	Keyboard[]	16-bit, read-only	

Figure A3.2   Variables and methods of key built-in chips in Nand to Tetris.

For example, consider the script command set RAM16K[1017] 15. If RAM16K is the currently simulated chip, or a chip-part of the currently simulated chip, this command sets its memory location number 1017 to 15. And, since the built-in RAM16K chip happens to have GUI side effects, the new value will also be reflected in the chip's visual image.

If a built-in chip maintains a single-valued internal state, the current value of the state can be accessed through the notation *chipName*[]. If the internal state is a vector, the notation *chipName*[*i*] is used. For example, when simulating the built-in Register chip, one can write script commands like set Register[] 135. This command sets the internal state of the chip to 135; in the next time unit, the Register chip will commit to this value, and its output pin will start emitting it.

Methods of built-in chips: Built-in chips can also expose *methods* that can be used by scripting commands. For example, in the Hack computer, programs reside in an instruction memory unit implemented by the built-in chip ROM32K. Before running a machine language program on the Hack computer, the program must be loaded into this chip. To facilitate this service, the built-in implementation of ROM32K features a load method that enables loading a text file containing machine language instructions. This method can be accessed using a script command like ROM32K load *fileName*.hack.

Ending example: We end this section with a relatively complex test script designed to test the topmost Computer chip of the Hack computer.

One way to test the Computer chip is to load a machine language program into it and monitor selected values as the computer executes the program, one instruction at a time. For example, we wrote a machine language program that computes the maximum of RAM[0] and RAM[1] and writes the result in RAM[2]. The program is stored in a file named Max.hack.

Note that at the low level in which we are operating, if such a program does not run properly it may be either because the program is buggy or because the hardware is buggy (or, perhaps, the test script is buggy, or the hardware simulator is buggy). For simplicity, let us assume that everything is error-free, except for, possibly, the simulated Computer chip.

To test the Computer chip using the Max.hack program, we wrote a test script called ComputerMax.tst. This script loads Computer.hdl into the hardware simulator and then loads the Max.hack program into its ROM32K chip-part. A reasonable way to check whether the chip works properly is as follows: Put some values in RAM[0] and RAM[1], reset the computer, run the clock enough cycles, and inspect RAM[2]. This, in a nutshell, is what the script in figure A3.3 is designed to do.

How can we tell that fourteen clock cycles are sufficient for executing this program? This can be found by trial and error, by starting with a large value and watching the computer's outputs stabilizing after a while, or by analyzing the run-time behavior of the loaded program.

```
/* ComputerMax.tst script.
Uses a Max.hack program that sets
RAM[2] to max(RAM[0], RAM[1]). */

// Loads Computer and sets up for the simulation:
load Computer.hdl,
output-file ComputerMax.out,
compare-to ComputerMax.cmp,
output-list RAM16K[0] RAM16K[1] RAM16K[2];

// Loads Max.hack into the ROM32K chip-part:
ROM32K load Max.hack,

// Sets the first 2 cells of the RAM16K chip-part
// to test values:
set RAM16K[0] 3,
set RAM16K[1] 5,
output;

// Runs enough clock cycles to complete the
// program's execution:
repeat 14 {
    tick, tock,
    output;
}

// (Script continues on the right)
```

```
// Sets up for another test, using other values.

// Resets the Computer: Done by setting
// reset to 1, and running the clock
// in order to commit the Program Counter
// (PC, a sequential chip) to the new reset value:
set reset 1,
tick,
tock,
output;

// Sets reset to 0, loads new test values, and
// runs enough clock cycles to complete the
// program's execution:
set reset 0,
set RAM16K[0] 23456,
set RAM16K[1] 12345,
output;
repeat 14 {
    tick, tock,
    output;
}
```

Figure A3.3   Testing the topmost Computer chip.

Default test script: Each Nand to Tetris simulator features a default test script. If the user does not load a test script into the simulator, the default test script is used. The default test script of the hardware simulator is defined as follows:

```
// Default test script of the hardware simulator:
repeat {
    tick,
    tock;
}
```

A3.3   Testing Machine Language Programs on the CPU Emulator

Unlike the *hardware simulator*, which is a general-purpose program designed to support the construction of any hardware platform, the supplied *CPU emulator* is a single-purpose tool, designed to simulate the execution of machine language programs on a specific platform: the Hack computer. The programs can be written either in the symbolic or in the binary Hack machine language described in chapter 4.

As usual, the simulation involves four files: the tested program (*Xxx*.asm or *Xxx*.hack), a test script (*Xxx*.tst), an optional output file (*Xxx*.out), and an optional compare file (*Xxx*.cmp). All these files reside in the same folder, normally named *Xxx*.

Example: Consider the multiplication program Mult.hack, designed to effect RAM[2] = RAM[0] * RAM[1]. Suppose we want to test this program in the CPU emulator. A reasonable way to do it is to put some values in RAM[0] and RAM[1], run the program, and inspect RAM[2]. This logic is carried out by the test script shown in figure A3.4.

Variables: Scripting commands running on the CPU emulator can access the following elements of the Hack computer:

A:	Current value of the address register (unsigned 15-bit)
D:	Current value of the data register (16-bit)
PC:	Current value of the Program Counter (unsigned 15-bit)
RAM[i]:	Current value of RAM location i (16-bit)
time:	Number of *time units* (also called *clock cycles*, or *ticktocks*) that elapsed since the simulation started (a read-only system variable)

Commands: The CPU emulator supports all the commands described in section A3.2, except for the following changes:

load *progName*: Where *progName* is either *Xxx*.asm or *Xxx*.hack. This command loads a machine language program (to be tested) into the simulated instruction memory. If the program is written in assembly, the simulator translates it into binary, on the fly, as part of executing the load *programName* command.

eval: Not applicable in the CPU emulator.

builtInChipName method argument (*s*): Not applicable in the CPU emulator.

tickTock: This command is used instead of tick and tock. Each ticktock advances the clock one time unit (cycle).

Default Test Script

```
// Default test script of the CPU emulator:
repeat {
    ticktock;
}
```

```
// Loads the program and sets up for the simulation:
load Mult.hack,
output-file Mult.out,
compare-to Mult.cmp,
output-list RAM[2]%D2.6.2;

// Sets the first 2 RAM cells to test values:
set RAM[0] 2,
set RAM[1] 5;

// Runs enough clock cycles to complete the program's execution:
repeat 20 {
  ticktock;
}
output;

// Re-runs the program, with different test values:
set PC 0,
set RAM[0] 8,
set RAM[1] 7;

// Mult.hack is based on a naïve repetitive addition algorithm,
// so greater multiplicands require more clock cycles:
repeat 50 {
  ticktock;
}
output;
```

Figure A3.4   Testing a machine language program on the CPU emulator.

A3.4   Testing VM Programs on the VM Emulator

The supplied *VM emulator* is a Java implementation of the virtual machine specified in chapters 7–8. It can be used for simulating the execution of VM programs, visualizing their operations, and displaying the states of the effected virtual memory segments.

A VM program consists of one or more .vm files. Thus, the simulation of a VM program involves the tested program (a single *Xxx*.vm file or an *Xxx* folder containing one or more .vm files) and, optionally, a test script (*Xxx*.tst), a compare file (*Xxx*.cmp), and an output file (*Xxx*.out). All these files reside in the same folder, normally named *Xxx*.

Virtual memory segments: The VM commands push and pop are designed to manipulate *virtual memory segments* (argument, local, and so on). These segments must be allocated to the host RAM—a task that the VM emulator carries out as a side effect of simulating the execution of the VM commands call, function, and return.

Startup code: When the VM translator translates a VM program, it generates machine language code that sets the stack pointer to 256 and then calls the Sys.init function, which then initializes the OS classes and calls Main.main. In a similar fashion, when the VM emulator is instructed to execute a VM program (a collection of one or more VM functions), it is programmed to start running the function Sys.init. If such a function is not found in the loaded VM code, the emulator is programmed to start executing the first command in the loaded VM code.

The latter convention was added to the VM emulator to support unit testing of the VM translator, which spans two book chapters and projects. In project 7, we build a basic VM translator that handles only push, pop, and arithmetic commands without handling function calling commands. If we want to execute such programs, we must somehow anchor the virtual memory segments in the host RAM—at least those segments mentioned in the simulated VM code. Conveniently, this initialization can be accomplished by script commands that manipulate the pointers controlling the base RAM addresses of the virtual segments. Using these script commands, we can anchor the virtual segments anywhere we want in the host RAM.

Example: The FibonacciSeries.vm file contains a sequence of VM commands that compute the first *n* elements of the Fibonacci series. The code is designed to operate on two arguments: *n* and the starting memory address in which the computed elements should be stored. The test script listed in figure A3.5 tests this program using the arguments 6 and 4000.

Variables: Scripting commands running on the VM emulator can access the following elements of the virtual machine:

Contents of VM segments:

`local[`i`]`:	Value of the i-th element of the `local` segment
`argument[`i`]`:	Value of the i-th element of the `argument` segment
`this[`i`]`:	Value of the i-th element of the `this` segment
`that[`i`]`:	Value of the i-th element of the `that` segment
`temp[`i`]`:	Value of the i-th element of the `temp` segment

Pointers of VM segments:

`local`:	Base address of the `local` segment in the RAM
`argument`:	Base address of the `argument` segment in the RAM
`this`:	Base address of the `this` segment in the RAM
`that`:	Base address of the `that` segment in the RAM

```
/* The FibonacciSeries.vm program computes the first n Fibonacci numbers.
In this test n = 6, and the numbers will be written to RAM addresses 4000 to 4005. */

load FibonacciSeries.vm,
output-file FibonacciSeries.out,
compare-to FibonacciSeries.cmp,
output-list RAM[4000]%D1.6.2 RAM[4001]%D1.6.2 RAM[4002]%D1.6.2
            RAM[4003]%D1.6.2 RAM[4004]%D1.6.2 RAM[4005]%D1.6.2;

// The program's code contains no function/call/return commands.
// Therefore, the script initializes the stack, local and argument segments explicitly:

set SP 256,
set local 300,
set argument 400;

// Sets the first argument to n = 6, the second argument to the address where the series
// will be written, and runs enough VM steps for completing the program's execution:

set argument[0] 6,
set argument[1] 4000;
repeat 140 {
  vmstep;
}
output;
```

Figure A3.5 Testing a VM program on the VM emulator.

<u>Implementation-specific variables:</u>

`RAM[`*i*`]`:	Value of the *i*-th location of the host RAM
`SP`:	Value of the stack pointer
`currentFunction`:	Name of the currently executing function (read-only)
`line`:	Contains a string of the form

currentFunctionName.*lineIndexInFunction* (read-only).

For example, when execution reaches the third line of the function `Sys.init`, the `line` variable contains the value `Sys.init.3`. Can be used for setting breakpoints in selected locations in the loaded VM program.

Commands: The VM emulator supports all the commands described in Section A3.2, except for the following changes:

`load` *source*: Where the optional *source* parameter is either *Xxx*.`vm`, a file containing VM code, or *Xxx*, the name of a folder containing one or more .`vm` files (in which case all of them are loaded, one after the other). If the .`vm` files are located in the current folder, the source argument can be omitted.

`tick` / `tock`: Not applicable.

`vmstep`: Simulates the execution of a single VM command and advances to the next command in the code.

Default Script

```
// Default script of the VM emulator:
repeat {
    vmStep;
}
```

Appendix 4: The Hack Chip Set

The chips are sorted alphabetically by name. In the online version of this document, available in www.nand2tetris.org, this API format comes in handy: To use a chip-part, copy-paste the chip signature into your HDL program, then fill in the missing bindings (also called *connections*).

```
Add16(a= ,b= ,out= )  /* Adds up two 16-bit two's complement values */
ALU(x= ,y= ,zx= ,nx= ,zy= ,ny= ,f= ,no= ,out= ,zr= ,ng= )  /* Hack ALU */
And(a= ,b= ,out= )  /* And gate */
And16(a= ,b= ,out= )  /* 16-bit And */
ARegister(in= ,load= ,out= )  /* Address register (built-in) */
Bit(in= ,load= ,out= )  /* 1-bit register */
CPU(inM= ,instruction= ,reset= ,outM= ,writeM= ,addressM= ,pc= )  /* Hack CPU */
DFF(in= ,out= )  /* Data flip-flop gate (built-in) */
DMux(in= ,sel= ,a= ,b= )  /* Routes the input to one out of two outputs */
DMux4Way(in= ,sel= ,a= ,b= ,c= ,d= )  /* Routes the input to one out of four outputs */
DMux8Way(in= ,sel= ,a= ,b= ,c= ,d= ,e= ,f= ,g= ,h= )  /* Routes the input to one out of 8 outputs */
DRegister(in= ,load= ,out= )  /* Data register (built-in) */
HalfAdder(a= ,b= ,sum= , carry= )  /* Adds up two bits */
FullAdder(a= ,b= ,c= ,sum= ,carry= )  /* Adds up three bits */
Inc16(in= ,out= )  /* Sets out to in + 1 */
Keyboard(out= )  /* Keyboard memory map (built-in) */
Memory(in= ,load= ,address= ,out= )  /* Data memory of the Hack platform (RAM) */
Mux(a= ,b= ,sel= ,out= )  /* Selects between two inputs */
Mux16(a= ,b= ,sel= ,out= )  /* Selects between two 16-bit inputs */
Mux4Way16(a= ,b= ,c= ,d= ,sel= ,out= )  /* Selects between four 16-bit inputs */
Mux8Way16(a= ,b= ,c= ,d= ,e= ,f= ,g= ,h= ,sel= ,out= )  /* Selects between eight 16-bit inputs */
Nand(a= ,b= ,out= )  /* Nand gate (built-in) */
Not(in= ,out= )  /* Not gate */
Not16(in= ,out= )  /* 16-bit Not */
Or(a= ,b= ,out= )  /* Or gate */
Or16(a= ,b= ,out= )  /* 16-bit Or */
Or8Way(in= ,out= )  /* 8-way Or */
PC(in= ,load= ,inc= ,reset= ,out= )  /* Program Counter */
RAM8(in= ,load= ,address= ,out= )  /* 8-word RAM */
RAM64(in= ,load= ,address= ,out= )  /* 64-word RAM */
RAM512(in= ,load= ,address= ,out= )  /* 512-word RAM */
RAM4K(in= ,load= ,address= ,out= )  /* 4K RAM */
RAM16K(in= ,load= ,address= ,out= )  /* 16K RAM */
Register(in= ,load= ,out= )  /* 16-bit register */
ROM32K(address= ,out= )  /* Instruction memory of the Hack platform (ROM, built-in) */
Screen(in= ,load= ,address= ,out= )  /* Screen memory map (built-in) */
Xor(a= ,b= ,out= )  /* Xor gate */
```

Appendix 5: The Hack Character Set

32: space	56: 8	80: P	104: h	127: DEL
33: !	57: 9	81: Q	105: i	128: newLine
34: "	58: :	82: R	106: j	129: backSpace
35: #	59: ;	83: S	107: k	130: leftArrow
36: $	60: <	84: T	108: l	131: upArrow
37: %	61: =	85: U	109: m	132: rightArrow
38: &	62: >	86: V	110: n	133: downArrow
39: '	63: ?	87: W	111: o	134: home
40: (	64: @	88: X	112: p	135: end
41:)	65: A	89: Y	113: q	136: pageUp
42: *	66: B	90: Z	114: r	137: pageDown
43: +	67: C	91: [	115: s	138: insert
44: ,	68: D	92: /	116: t	139: delete
45: -	69: E	93:]	117: u	140: esc
46: .	70: F	94: ^	118: v	141: f1
47: /	71: G	95: _	119: w	142: f2
48: 0	72: H	96: `	120: x	143: f3
49: 1	73: I	97: a	121: y	144: f4
50: 2	74: J	98: b	122: z	145: f5
51: 3	75: K	99: c	123: {	146: f6
52: 4	76: L	100: d	124:		147: f7
53: 5	77: M	101: e	125: }	148: f8
54: 6	78: N	102: f	126: ~	149: f9
55: 7	79: O	103: g		150: f10
				151: f11
				152: f12

Appendix 6: The Jack OS API

The Jack language is supported by eight standard classes that provide basic OS services like memory allocation, mathematical functions, input capturing, and output rendering. This appendix documents the API of these classes.

Math

This class provides commonly needed mathematical functions.

`function int multiply(int x, int y)`: Returns the product of x and y. When a Jack compiler detects the multiplication operator * in the program's code, it handles it by invoking this function. Thus the Jack expressions x * y and the function call `Math.multiply(x,y)` return the same value.

`function int divide(int x, int y)`: Returns the integer part of x / y. When a Jack compiler detects the division operator / in the program's code, it handles it by invoking this function. Thus the Jack expressions x / y and the function call `Math.divide(x,y)` return the same value.

`function int min(int x, int y)`: Returns the minimum of x and y.

`function int max(int x, int y)`: Returns the maximum of x and y.

`function int sqrt(int x)`: Returns the integer part of the square root of x.

String

This class represents strings of `char` values and provides commonly needed string processing services.

`constructor String new(int maxLength)`: Constructs a new empty string with a maximum length of `maxLength` and initial length of 0.

method void dispose(): Disposes this string.

method int length(): Returns the number of characters in this string.

method char charAt(int i): Returns the character at the i-th location of this string.

method void setCharAt(int i, char c): Sets the character at the i-th location of this string to c.

method String appendChar(char c): Appends c to this string's end and returns this string.

method void eraseLastChar(): Erases the last character from this string.

method int intValue(): Returns the integer value of this string until a non-digit character is detected.

method void setInt(int val): Sets this string to hold a representation of the given value.

function char backSpace(): Returns the backspace character.

function char doubleQuote(): Returns the double quote character.

function char newLine(): Returns the newline character.

Array

In the Jack language, arrays are implemented as instances of the OS class Array. Once declared, the array elements can be accessed using the syntax arr[i]. Jack arrays are not typed: each array element can hold a primitive data type or an object type, and different elements in the same array can have different types.

function Array new(int size): Constructs a new array of the given size.

method void dispose(): Disposes this array.

Output

This class provides functions for displaying characters. It assumes a character-oriented screen consisting of 23 rows (indexed 0…22, top to bottom) of 64 characters each (indexed 0…63, left to right). The top-left character location on the screen is indexed (0,0). Each character is displayed by rendering on the screen a rectangular image 11 pixels high and 8 pixels wide (which includes margins for character spacing and line spacing). If needed, the bitmap images ("font") of all the characters can be found by inspecting the given code of the Output class. A visible cursor, implemented as a small filled square, indicates where the next character will be displayed.

`function void moveCursor(int i, int j)`: Moves the cursor to the j-th column of the i-th row and overrides the character displayed there.

`function void printChar(char c)`: Displays the character at the cursor location and advances the cursor one column forward.

`function void printString(String s)`: Displays the string starting at the cursor location and advances the cursor appropriately.

`function void printInt(int i)`: Displays the integer starting at the cursor location and advances the cursor appropriately.

`function void println()`: Advances the cursor to the beginning of the next line.

`function void backSpace()`: Moves the cursor one column back.

Screen

This class provides functions for displaying graphical shapes on the screen. The Hack physical screen consists of 256 rows (indexed 0…255, top to bottom) of 512 pixels each (indexed 0…511, left to right). The top-left pixel on the screen is indexed (0,0).

`function void clearScreen()`: Erases the entire screen.

`function void setColor(boolean b)`: Sets the current color. This color will be used in all the subsequent draw*Xxx* function calls. Black is represented by `true`, white by `false`.

`function void drawPixel(int x, int y)`: Draws the (x,y) pixel using the current color.

`function void drawLine(int x1, int y1, int x2, int y2)`: Draws a line from pixel (x1,y1) to pixel (x2,y2) using the current color.

`function void drawRectangle(int x1, int y1, int x2, int y2)`: Draws a filled rectangle whose top-left corner is (x1,y1) and bottom-right corner is (x2,y2) using the current color.

`function void drawCircle(int x, int y, int r)`: Draws a filled circle of radius $r \leq 181$ around (x,y) using the current color.

Keyboard

This class provides functions for reading inputs from a standard keyboard.

`function char keyPressed()`: Returns the character of the currently pressed key on the keyboard; if no key is currently pressed, returns 0. Recognizes all the values in the Hack character set (see appendix 5). These include the characters newLine (128, return value of String.newLine()), backSpace (129, return value of String.backSpace ()), leftArrow (130), upArrow (131), rightArrow (132), downArrow (133), home (134), end (135), pageUp (136), pageDown (137), insert (138), delete (139), esc (140), and f1–f12 (141–152).

function char readChar(): Waits until a keyboard key is pressed and released, then displays the corresponding character on the screen and returns the character.

function String readLine(String message): Displays the message, reads from the keyboard the entered string of characters until a newLine character is detected, displays the string, and returns the string. Also handles user backspaces.

function int readInt(String message): Displays the message, reads from the keyboard the entered string of characters until a newLine character is detected, displays the string on the screen, and returns its integer value until the first non-digit character in the entered string is detected. Also handles user backspaces.

Memory

This class provides memory management services. The Hack RAM consists of 32,768 words, each holding a 16-bit binary number.

function int peek(int address): Returns the value of RAM[address].

function void poke(int address, int value): Sets RAM[address] to the given value.

function Array alloc(int size): Finds an available RAM block of the given size and returns its base address.

function void deAlloc(Array o): Deallocates the given object, which is cast as an array. In other words, makes the RAM block that starts in this address available for future memory allocations.

Sys

This class provides basic program execution services.

function void halt(): Halts the program execution.

function void error(int errorCode): Displays the error code, using the format ERR<errorCode>, and halts the program's execution.

function void wait(int duration): Waits approximately duration milliseconds and returns.

Index